The L

ISBN 978-90-04-18682-8

Full text of the lecture published in June 2011 in the *Recueil des cours*, Vol. 344 (2009).

Cover illustration : *Key of the World*, an image created by Bruce Rolff, Clifton (NJ), United States.

HAGUE ACADEMY OF INTERNATIONAL LAW

*A collection of law lectures
in pocketbook form*

AIL-POCKET

2011

The Public
International Law Regime Governing
International Investment

The Public
International Law Regime Governing
International Investment

JOSÉ E. ALVAREZ

TABLE OF CONTENTS

Chapter I. The evolving international investment regime: an overview.   13

A. Introduction   13
B. Investment flows and globalization   16
C. The legalization of international investment . .   24
D. The contents of international investment treaties   30
E. Investor-State dispute settlement.   38

   (1) Party control   48
   (2) Remedies for past injury.   50
   (3) Impact on State sovereignty   54

F. Contemporary critiques of the investment regime   75

   (1) Vertical critiques   75
   (2) Horizontal critiques   84
   (3) Ideological   89
   (4) Rule of law critiques.   90

G. The regime and public international law   93

Chapter II. What are investment treaties for ?.   95

A. Guzman's account of the origins of the investment regime   119
B. Refuting Guzman   123
C. Explaining the contemporary investment regime   143
D. What is the most recent wave of US investment treaties trying to achieve ?.   162

Chapter III. Fair and equitable treatment : the heart of the investment regime   177

A. The limits of "treatification".   227
B. The "democratic" credentials of the investment regime   235
C. The entwined nature of treaty and non-treaty sources   237

   (1) Treatification does not equal precision . . .   240
   (2) The absence of precision in a treaty is not the last word   240
   (3) Fragmentation and its discontents   242

D. Globalization and its discontents   243

Chapter IV. Lessons from the Argentina crisis cases . 247

  A. Introduction 247
  B. The inconsistent Argentina cases 260

    (1) Inconsistent views of what is "necessary". . 266
    (2) Is there one defence or two? 268
    (3) Does the customary defence of necessity
        apply when a BIT is silent, that is, when the
        BIT does not have an essential security
        exception or measures not precluded clause? 272
    (4) Assuming that it is applicable, what does the
        customary defence of necessity require States
        (or claimants) to show? 273
    (5) Assuming that Article XI of the United
        States-Argentina treaty is a distinct defence
        from the excuse of necessity, what exactly
        does it require in order for it to be success-
        fully invoked? 278
    (6) What is the effect of a successful invocation
        of Article XI? 282

  C. Broader problems 284

    (1) The fragmentation of international investment
        law 284
    (2) The hazards of premature de-fragmentation. 299

Chapter V. The once and future investment regime. . 340

  A. The investment regime in transition. 340
  B. The Argentina cases and the regime's alleged
    legitimacy deficits 352

    (1) The problem of inconsistent arbitral awards 352
    (2) Is the investment regime a threat to sover-
        eignty? 367
    (3) Is the investment regime a threat to human
        rights? 370
    (4) Is the investment regime "biased" in favour
        of investors? 389

  C. Reform proposals 392
  D. Points of intersection between the investment
    regime and public international law 406

    (1) Treatification and other positivist sources . 407
    (2) Fragmentation. 407
    (3) Impact of non-State actors 410
    (4) Globalization and its discontents. 419

(5) The international law profession 427
(6) Judicialization. 429
(7) Hegemonic or imperial international law ?. 436
(8) Global administrative law ?. 440
(9) Constitutionalization ? 446
(10) Humanity's law ? 452

Bibliography 458

About the author 498

Biographical note 498
Principal publications 499

CHAPTER I

THE EVOLVING INTERNATIONAL INVESTMENT REGIME: AN OVERVIEW

A. *Introduction*

The idea that rules are needed to govern global capital flows when capital is used to establish a physical presence in a foreign nation, usually for profit, is an idea of relatively recent vintage. When the pharaohs of Egypt mined tin for forging bronze far from their shores or when the Phoenicians invested in ancient Israel there was no recognizable global law to govern these cross-border investments[1]. Nor were there clear global rules to govern Dutch investments undertaken by the East India Company when Grotius engaged in his well-known effort to enable that company (and his country) to have unimpeded passage on the high seas. Even much later, during the age of colonial expansion in the eighteenth and nineteenth centuries, the need for general rules of custom to govern or to protect foreign investment in colonial territories (that is the "periphery") was not self-evident, especially while colonial powers could rely on imperial treaties of capitulation for this purpose. Under those treaties, the colonial powers insisted that their traders be permitted to have recourse to special consular courts in lieu of the local courts of the host States[2]. And while customary law

---

[1] See R. D. Bishop *et al.*, *Foreign Investment Disputes: Cases, Materials, and Commentary* (The Hague, Kluwer Law International, 2005), p. 2.

[2] See, e.g., M. Sornarajah, *International Law on Foreign Investment* (Cambridge, Cambridge University Press, 2004), p. 19.

demanding compensation in cases relating to the seizure of an alien's property arguably extends as far back as the Declaration of the Rights of Man and the Citizen of 1789, only sporadic State practice and scholarly commentary suggested this ostensible rule until early in the twentieth century[3]. Before that time diplomatic espousals, the principal vehicle by which the law relating to the treatment of aliens and therefore the treatment of foreign investors develops, were relatively rare, as was State practice and *opinio juris* on point. Even as late as 1970, in the course of deciding the *Barcelona Traction* case, the International Court of Justice ("ICJ") found it "surprising" that despite the explosion in the international activities of corporations, "the evolution of the law [relating to diplomatic espousal] has not gone further and that no generally accepted rules in the matter have crystallized on the international plane"[4].

Forty years after *Barcelona Traction* much has changed. International lawyers have now managed to build a considerable body of law around the once threadbare principles governing State responsibility for injuries to aliens and their property. A rich body of arbitral case-law and scholarly commentary is now developing around rudimentary principles like the "international minimum standard" once used to guide the periphery's treatment of aliens.

This monograph concerns the legal rules that today govern a principal engine of economic globalization,

---

[3] See, e.g., A. F. Lowenfeld, *International Economic Law* (Oxford, Oxford University Press, 2002), pp. 391-395.

[4] S. Subedi, *International Investment Law : Reconciling Policy and Principle* (Portland, Hart Publishing, 2008), p. 1, n. 1 (citing *Barcelona Traction, Light and Power Co. Limited (Belgium* v. *Spain)*, Judgment, *ICJ Reports 1970*, paras. 46-47).

namely the transnational flow of capital made by one resident entity in one country with the purpose of establishing a "lasting interest" in an enterprise located in another country[5]. "Lasting interest" distinguishes foreign direct investment ("FDI") from transnational capital held only passively by investors, as when a person holds securities in a number of international enterprises in a stock portfolio (otherwise known as portfolio investment). FDI most commonly occurs through an outright merger with or an acquisition of an existing national firm, but it may also occur by establishing a wholly new enterprise (known as "greenfield" investment) or by acquiring a controlling share of a national firm's stock. The definition of a "controlling" share varies with the circumstances. For companies with widely dispersed publicly held shares, effective control can occur with very small percentage holdings. (Most countries, including the United States, define — for purposes of data collection under their national law — a stake of 10 per cent in the ordinary shares of an enterprise to constitute the minimum threshold for foreign "control".) However it occurs, the essence of FDI is the existence of a long-term relationship between a direct investor and its foreign affiliate, which usually means a significant degree of influence on the management of that affiliate[6].

---

[5] This is essentially the definition of "foreign investment" adopted by the OECD and the IMF. See L. Sachs and K. P. Sauvant (eds.), *The Effect of Treaties on Foreign Direct Investment: Bilateral Investment Treaties, Double Taxation Treaties, and Investment Flows* (Oxford, Oxford University Press, 2009), p. xxviii (quoting OECD and IMF documents).

[6] While this definition suffices for the general purposes of this monograph, readers should not assume that specific investment treaties will all define covered "investment" in the same way. The investment treaties that are the subject of this monograph as well as underlying treaties such as

B. Investment Flows and Globalization

Why are capital flows among nations intended to
secure the establishment of a business enterprise
widely considered the principal engine of economic
globalization? There are two reasons: quantitative and
qualitative. Although the World Trade Organization
("WTO") regime governing the sale of goods has
received the bulk of scholarly attention, the amount of
trade in goods associated with FDI flows now vastly
exceeds the amount of dollars involved in the transnational sale of goods (that is exports and imports) not
connected to FDI as such. Foreign investors around the
world sold some US$19 trillion of goods in 2005, as
compared to US$11 trillion in world exports that year[7].

---

the ICSID Convention contain definitions of what constitutes a covered "investment". Some of these treaties contain vague or circular definitions that are ample enough to
include portfolio (or passive) investment. Moreover, in
some cases, jurisdiction under a particular investment
treaty might be established through a shift in who controls
an enterprise, without any need to prove that a movement
of capital occurred at all. See, e.g., E. C. Schlemmmer,
"Investment, Investor, Nationality, and Shareholders", in
P. Muchlinski *et al.* (eds.), *The Oxford Handbook of International Investment Law* (Oxford, Oxford University
Press, 2008), pp. 49, 60-61. This monograph will not
address the increasing body of arbitral case-law dealing
with such questions as what constitutes "investment" for
purposes of establishing, for example, ICSID jurisdiction.
See *ibid.*, pp. 62-69 (noting that the ICSID Convention
does not define "investment" but that some arbitrators
have considered relevant whether the enterprise has made
a "substantial" contribution to the host country's economy,
the duration of a project or enterprise, whether the investor
has engaged in any risk, or the significance of the enterprise or project to the host State's economic development).
[7] K. P. Sauvant, "A Backlash against Foreign Investment?", in *World Investment Prospects to 2010: Boom or
Backlash?* (London, Economist Intelligence Unit, 2006),

The amount of capital associated with FDI exceeds that encompassed by the WTO regime for trade in goods, whether we focus on FDI inflows (that is the sheer amount of equity, loans, or reinvestment earnings provided by investors to their foreign affiliates) or FDI stock (that is the total value of foreign owned assets held at a given time). Further, the impact of FDI on global economic transactions has been growing. FDI inflows have expanded from US$40 billion at the beginning of the 1980s to US$200 billion in 1990 to some US$1.8 trillion in 2008, an 18-fold increase that is far larger than the increase in trade in goods over this period[8]. Although these inflows are slowing dramatically in the midst of the economic crisis that began in late 2008[9], the dire effects of that slowdown demonstrate just how crucial FDI flows have become to continued economic growth and prosperity around the world. The current global economic crisis stems from, in substantial part, and is measured by, the decrease in the flows of capital that enable national economies (including those of superpowers such as the United States) to function. Even those who question the extent to which particular enterprises contribute to a host State's economic development do not deny that incoming FDI flows remain the principal vehicle for generating growth in less developed countries or that the activity of the roughly 80,000 transnational corporations ("TNC")[10] that control assets abroad is crucial to

---

available at <http://www.vcc.columbia.edu/pubs/documents/WIP_to_2010_Backlash_KPS.pdf >, p. 7.

[8] See, e.g., Sachs and Sauvant, *supra* footnote 5, p. xxviii.

[9] K. P. Sauvant, "The FDI Recession Has Begun", *Columbia FDI Perspectives*, No. 1 (2008), available at <http://www.vcc.columbia.edu/pubs/documents/KPS Perspective-FDIrecessionhasbegun_001.pdf>.

[10] See K. P. Sauvant, "The Rise of International Investment, Investment Agreements and Investment Disputes",

the extraction of natural resources, the construction of infrastructure, and the production of goods and services — in short, the factors that make most economies thrive.

FDI defines the current age of globalization for a more significant qualitative reason. It is not just the sheer amount of capital crossing borders that matters. It is what investment capital does when it arrives in a host State. The impact of trade in goods is not the same as the impact of FDI. As compared to the import of one more foreign produced good, the permanent presence of a foreign controlled enterprise produces far more sociological, economic, and cultural consequences for the home State of the enterprise and particularly for the host State in which that foreign enterprise is located. These effects can be positive or negative or in all like-lihood both, but they are hard to ignore. This reality is reflected in the colloquial usage of the term "economic globalization". What most of us associate with this term is the physical presence of identical commercial establishments globally (such as the global presence of Wal-Mart), or the fact that public utilities or sectors associated with the national patrimony (such as oil or mining), are, once privatized, often held by enormous (and enormously powerful) TNCs. Economic globali-zation is also associated with the fact that through globally integrated manufacturing processes — namely TNCs that use the ore from country A to manufacture products in country B for sale in countries A through Z — most countries are drawn into a web of economic interdependence and resulting cycles of boom and bust from which few can escape[11]. Simply put: in the usual

---

in K. P. Sauvant (ed.), *Appeals Mechanism in International Investment Disputes* (New York, Oxford University Press, 2008), pp. 3-4 (estimating the number of TNCs).

[11] See, e.g., P. Muchlinski, "Policy Issues", in *Oxford Handbook of International Investment Law*, *supra* foot-note 6, pp. 11-12.

case, FDI affects, positively or negatively, people and their communities far more directly than does the import of foreign produced goods.

FDI is an especially potent driver of globalization in least developed countries (LDCs). These States receive more than one-third of all investment flows[12]. The political impact of FDI is clear if one asks the typical Mexican national, for example, what her reactions are, pro or con, with respect to the North American Free Trade Agreement ("NAFTA") or about the thousands of maquiladoras attributed to that Agreement that are now located in Northern Mexico and which produce goods for export across the border[13]. Public opinion surveys in Mexico and elsewhere suggest that many people, north and south, east and west, are passionate about the subject of FDI. Indeed, in Mexico and elsewhere public attitudes towards FDI are often a solid predictor of political party affiliation or perceptions of foreign affairs[14].

Even in places with a tradition of strong support for liberal capital flows — where people ostensibly support the proliferation of Wal-Marts — such as the United States and Europe, the extent of foreign controlled enterprises within one's borders, or within particular "sensitive" sectors, prompts considerable public

---

[12] See, e.g., T. R. Braun, "Globalization: The Driving Force in International Investment Law", in A. Kaushal *et al.* (eds.), *The Backlash against Investment Arbitration* (The Netherlands, Kluwer Law International, 2010), p. 491.

[13] J. E. Alvarez, "The NAFTA's Investment Chapter and Mexico", in R. Dolzer *et al.* (eds.), *Foreign Investment: Its Significance in Relation to the Fight against Poverty, Economic Growth and Legal Culture* (Singapore, Konrad-Adenauer-Siftung, 2006).

[14] For one survey of studies of the impact of the North American Free Trade Agreement's ("NAFTA's") investment chapter, see *ibid.*, p. 253.

attention[15]. Even citizens of wealthy nations consider that decisions on whether to welcome foreign enterprises and on how to treat such "guests" after they arrive are, like decisions to permit or treat any individual alien seeking to enter the country, matters that each nation should have the right to decide on its own[16]. Most Governments, including those of Europe and the United States, believe that it is a fundamental right of sovereigns to decide who may enter their borders and why — and that this basic right of statehood does not change merely because some of those seeking entry offer the prospect of considerable capital. Thus, when United States-based TNCs appeared to be threatening European companies in the 1960s, books like Servan-Schreiber's *The American Challenge* led clarion calls of alarm[17] — just as succeeding waves of FDI from the Middle East and later from Japan led to similar concerns and proposed protectionist legislation in the United States[18]. In some countries, reactions to FDI

[15] See, e.g., K. P. Sauvant, "Driving and Countervailing Forces: A Rebalancing of National FDI Policies", in K. P. Sauvant (ed.), *Yearbook on International Investment Law & Policy 2008-2009* (New York, Oxford University Press, 2009), pp. 259-260.

[16] See, e.g., S. Clarkson, "Hijacking the Canadian Constitution: NAFTA's Investor-State Dispute Arbitration", in A. S. Alexandroff (ed.), *Investor Protection in the NAFTA and Beyond: Private Interest and Public Purpose* (Toronto, Ontario, C. D. Howe Institute, 2006), p. 85.

[17] J. J. Servan-Schreiber, *The American Challenge* (New York, Atheneum, 1968).

[18] See, e.g., Organization for International Investment, "Summary of Bills Affecting Foreign Investment in the United States" (1993) (copy on file with author). Among the many books addressing challenges to the United States presented by "foreign takeovers", see, e.g., M. Tolchin and S. J. Tolchin, *Selling Our Security: The Erosion of America's Assets* (New York, Knopf, 1992); P. Choate, *Agents of Influence* (New York, Knopf, 1990); N. J. Glickman and

and to ethnic or religious minorities that seem to unduly benefit from engaging in it, have helped to define domestic politics for decades if not centuries[19].

Flows of FDI, and perceived threats to "sovereignty" prompted by them, have inspired a number of critical theoretical frameworks for understanding the phenomenon, and several of these continue to have an impact on the perceived legitimacy of the relevant international rules. Critical frameworks focused on or involving FDI include theories of *"dependencia"* touted by some Latin American scholars in the 1970s[20], Raymond Vernon's view of the TNC as a competitor or rival to the power of national sovereigns[21], and Third World Approaches to International Law ("TWAIL")[22]. While, as will be addressed in Chapter II, most Governments now accept in principle that they need foreign capital to thrive, they continue to have a love-hate relationship with it. FDI has prompted strikingly similar concerns in a wide range of contexts, irrespective of whether the host of FDI is a developed economy, a poor developing country, or a State that finds itself somewhere in between. While today the backlash against FDI by certain left-leaning Latin American regimes has received considerable atten-

---

D. P. Woodward, *The New Competitors* (New York, Basic Books, 1989).

[19] See, e.g., A. Chua, "The Privatization-Nationalization Cycle: The Link between Markets and Ethnicity in Developing Countries", 95 *Columbia Law Review* 223 (1995).

[20] See, e.g., O. Sunkel, "Big Business and 'Dependencia'", 50 *Foreign Affairs* 517 (1972).

[21] R. Vernon, "The Multilateral Enterprise: Power versus Sovereignty", 49 *Foreign Affairs* 736 (1971).

[22] See, e.g., B. S. Chimni, "The Past, Present and Future of International Law: A Critical Third World Approach", 8 *Michigan Journal of International Law* 499 (2007).

tion[23], we should not lose sight of the fact that adverse reactions to some forms of FDI have emerged everywhere. The level of hostility towards it may only be a matter of degree and is not limited to certain forms of government. Today, incoming FDI emerging from the BRICs (Brazil, Russia, India or China), for example, appears to be prompting adverse reaction, including new protectionist measures, in some rich capitalist host nations[24].

The most frequently cited concerns prompted by FDI relate to economics, politics, and national security.

Among the economic concerns are fears that foreign enterprises will employ fewer nationals or ship jobs overseas, buy up valuable assets or real estate at "fire sale" prices, put local enterprises out of business, monopolize certain sectors, import more foreign produced inputs (and thereby increase a host State's trade deficit), or shift valued national technology to their overseas affiliates.

Political concerns include fears that foreign enterprises will unduly influence (or corrupt) politicians or meddle in national affairs, violate local laws or cultural norms, fail to respect the environment, or undermine certain domestic constituencies (such as the power of labour unions). United States-based non-governmental organizations ("NGOs"), such as the Center for International Environmental Law ("CIEL"), express concerns that granting "special" rights to foreign investors

---

[23] Sachs and Sauvant, *supra* footnote 5.
[24] See, e.g., J. Elliott, "Riding the Elephant", *Fortune* (17 December 2007), available at <http://ridingtheelephant.wordpress.com/2007/12/17/tata-hits-image-problems-in-the-us/>; A. Giridharadas, "Lobbying in US, Indian Firms Present an American Face", *New York Times* (4 September 2007), available at <http://www.nytimes.com/2007/09/04/business/worldbusiness/04outsource.html>.

through international treaties will undermine host States' right to regulate in the public interest, for example[25].

National security worries include fears that foreign firms will control and compromise access to technology needed for national defence or that foreign enterprises, especially when owned or controlled by foreign Governments or by sovereign wealth funds[26], will constitute a disloyal or subversive "fifth column" within a country's social fabric, that is, act in ways that advance the goals of their parent States and not merely the dictates of the market[27].

For these reasons, even today when most national economies have been open to most forms of FDI for decades and are mutually dependent on the continuation of such flows, FDI is often the first target of reform-minded new Governments.

At the same time, despite the relatively recent development of the international investment regime that is this subject of this monograph, it has long been the case that the protection accorded to foreign enterprises by host States has not been simply left to the unfettered discretion of Governments subject only to

---

[25] See, e.g., D. Magraw and R. H. Karpatkin, "Separate Comments on the United States-Morocco Free Trade Agreement" (Center for International Environmental Law, 2004), available at <http://www.ciel.org/Publications/TEPAC_Comments_Morocco.pdf> (hereinafter "CIEL Letter"), p. 3 (questioning the need for the investor rights provided under the recently concluded United States-Morocco Free Trade Agreement).

[26] C. Kovacs, "Sovereign Wealth Funds: Much Ado about Some Money", *Columbia FDI Perspectives*, No. 14 (2009), available at <http://www.vcc.columbiaedu/content/sovereign-wealth-funds-much-ado-about-some-money>.

[27] For one set of responses to these concerns by defenders of FDI, see, e.g., E. M. Graham and P. R. Krugman, *Foreign Direct Investment in the United States* (Washington, DC, Institute for International Economics, 1995).

national law and policy. At least during the colonial era, wealthy nations such as the United States threatened the use of military force to defend the rights of their alien investors. Those who ordered US gunships to be stationed off certain Latin American coastlines to encourage those countries to pay their debts to foreign nationals believed that international law, specifically the doctrine of State responsibility to aliens, limited the actions that nations could take with respect to foreign investors within their borders. Although, in the view of capital exporting States like the United States, customary international law did not require that a particular foreign enterprise be admitted into a country, it required that once admitted, alien investors had the right to be treated in accordance with the "international minimum standard"[28]. As the next section indicates, today, as much else that bears on world politics, international investment flows have been subjected to a considerable degree of legalization at the supranational level.

C. The Legalization of International Investment

Like many other international regimes, this "move to law" has proceeded along three dimensions: increasing levels of obligation, precision, and delegation[29]. More than ever before, FDI is subject to a broad number of obligatory legal rules consisting of national laws and administrative practices, customary international law ("CIL"), treaties, general principles of law, and institutionally generated law or forms of regulation.

---

[28] See, e.g., Sornarajah, *supra* footnote 2, p. 140.
[29] See J. Goldstein *et al.*, "Introduction: Legalization and World Politics", 54 *International Organization* 385 (2000).

While, as will be addressed in a later chapter, these rules are not necessarily coherent or consistent, they are becoming increasingly precise over time, not only as a result of ever more detailed provisions in treaty and national law, but also thanks to the ever more elaborate interpretations of relevant law rendered by international arbitrators sitting in investor-State disputes. As this last suggests, the investment regime is among the few international regimes in which States have implicitly delegated some of their former regulatory authority to third parties who are not within their exclusive control. These third parties include formal international institutions, such as the International Monetary Fund ("IMF") whose operations generally support the protections accorded to investors under investment treaties, but, most importantly, also include the private investors who are now given the power to bring their complaints of ill treatment before arbitrators. The third parties also include, of course, these arbitrators who are charged with the interpretation of investors' rights under treaties designed for investor protection or under contracts between investors and host States that provide for international arbitration in case of dispute.

The international investment legal regime has other defining characteristics[30]. Unlike the regime governing

---

[30] Like many commentators on international investment (see, e.g., D. Schneiderman, *Constitutionalizing Economic Globalization* (Cambridge, Cambridge University Press, 2007), p. 26), I am using the term "regime" here in the sense deployed by many political scientists. See, e.g., R. Keohane, *After Hegemony: Cooperation and Discord in the World Political Economy* (Princeton, Princeton University Press, 1984), p. 57 (defining international regimes as "sets of implicit or explicit principles, norms, rules and decision-making procedures around which actors' expectations converge in a given area of international relations"). As will be addressed in the final

trade in goods, it lacks a single definitive multilateral treaty text or a single over-arching institution. There is no equivalent to the General Agreement on Tariffs and Trade ("GATT") for investment, or a single over-arching institution (comparable to the WTO) charged with the governance of FDI flows. This is not for lack of trying. The international community has tried to negotiate binding multilateral rules for FDI at least since 1948, when the effort to create an international trade organization that would embrace both trade and investment through the Havana Charter floundered and left only the GATT in its wake. Since that time, a number of other multilateral attempts to negotiate an investment treaty have failed. These included a 1961 effort by Professors Louis Sohn and Richard Baxter of Harvard Law School to draft a Convention on the International Responsibility of States for Injuries to Aliens, attempts in 1963 and 1967 by the Organisation for Economic Co-operation and Development ("OECD") to draft a Convention on the Protection of Foreign Property, and that organization's later effort to secure a Multilateral Agreement on Investment (which ended in failure in 1998)[31]. At the same time, soft law efforts at global regulation have included a number of

---

chapter, the term "regime" does not have the normative implications of more loaded descriptions, from "system" at one end to "framework" at the other. See C. H. Brower II, "Legitimacy and Inconsistency: Is Investment Treaty Arbitration Broken?", Third Annual Investment Treaty Arbitration Conference: Interpretation in Investment Arbitration, Washington, DC (30 April 2009) (copy on file with author) (noting that "system" appears to anticipate a more organized set of consistent norms than the description "framework").

[31] For a concise history of prior efforts to "multilateralize" the investment regime, see S. W. Schill, *The Multilateralization of International Investment Law* (New York, Cambridge University Press, 2009), pp. 23-64.

famous resolutions by the UN General Assembly, particularly its 1962 and 1973 resolutions on Permanent Sovereignty over Natural Resources and its 1974 Charter of the Economic Rights and Duties of States ("CERDS"). These efforts, along with the OECD's voluntary Guidelines for Multinational Enterprises or the United Nations Conference on Trade and Development's ("UNCTAD") attempt, never completed, to promulgate a UN Code of Conduct on Transnational Corporations, have had some impact on the law[32].

The international investment regime broadly understood includes: Bilateral Investment Treaties ("BITs"); Free Trade Agreements ("FTAs" such as NAFTA's Chapter 11)[33]; the Energy Charter Treaty[34]; the WTO's Trade-Related Investment Measures ("TRIMs"), Services Agreement ("GATS"), and Trade-Related Aspects of Intellectual Property ("TRIPS")[35]; a number of rele-

---

[32] For an account of some of these soft law efforts, see, e.g., Lowenfeld, *supra* footnote 3, pp. 407-445; United Nations ECOSOC, "Draft Code of Conduct on Transnational Corporations", in S. Zamora and R. A. Brand, 1 *Basic Documents of International Economic Law* (Chicago, Commerce Clearing House International, 1990), p. 533.

[33] North American Free Trade Agreement, 32 *International Legal Materials* 612, signed on 17 December 1992, entered into force on 1 January 1994 (hereinafter "NAFTA"), Chap. 11.

[34] Energy Charter Treaty, 2080 *United Nations Treaty Series* 95, signed on 17 December 1994, entered into force on 16 April 1998, available at <http://www.encharter.org/fileadmin/user_upload/document/EN.pdf>.

[35] Agreement on Trade Related Investment Measures, signed on 15 April 1994, entered into force on 1 January 1995 (hereinafter "TRIMs Agreement"); General Agreement on Trade in Services, 1869 *United Nations Treaty Series* 183, signed on 15 April 1994, entered into force on 1 January 1995 (hereinafter "GATS Agreement"); Agreement on Trade-Related Aspects of Intellectual Property

vant General Assembly resolutions and other soft law efforts (e.g., OECD's Guidelines for Multinational Enterprises)[36]; the OECD's Code of Capital Movements[37]; the World Bank's International Centre for the Settlement of Investment Disputes ("ICSID") (and other arbitral mechanisms, such as UNCITRAL)[38]; and the Multilateral Investment Guarantee Agency ("MIGA")[39] (and other mechanisms for political risk insurance such as the United States' Overseas Private Investment Corporation ("OPIC"))[40].

Rights, 1869 *United Nations Treaty Series* 299, signed on 15 April 1994, entered into force on 1 January 1995 (hereinafter "TRIPS Agreement").

[36] Organisation for Economic Co-operation and Development ("OECD"), Directorate for Financial and Enterprise Affairs, *OECD Guidelines for Multinational Enterprises* (OECD, 2008), available at <http://www.oecd.org/dataoecd/56/36/1922428.pdf>.

[37] OECD, Directorate for Financial and Enterprise Affairs, *OECD Code of Liberalization of Capital Movements* (OECD, 2010), available at <http://www.oecd.org/dataoecd/10/62/39664826.pdf>.

[38] Convention on the Settlement of Investment Disputes between States and Nationals of Other States, 575 *United Nations Treaty Series* 259, signed on 18 March 1965, entered into force on 14 October 1966, available at <http://icsid.worldbank.org/ICSID/StaticFiles/basicdoc/CRR_English-final.pdf> (hereinafter "ICSID Convention"); *UNCITRAL Model Law on International Commercial Arbitration*, UN Sales No. E.08.V.4 (Vienna, United Nations, 2008), available at <http://www.uncitral.org/pdf/english/texts/arbitration/ml-arb/07-86998_Ebook.pdf> (adopted by UN General Assembly resolution A/RES/61/33 on 18 December 2006).

[39] Convention Establishing the Multilateral Investment Guarantee Agency, 1508 *United Nations Treaty Series* 100, signed on 10 November 1985, entered into force on 12 April 1988 (hereinafter "MIGA Convention").

[40] See the Overseas Private Investment Corporation's ("OPIC") legislative charter, 22 *United States Code Annotated* §§ 2191-2200b (2010).

That regime is most closely identified however with some 2,600 BITs and an additional 300 or so regional FTAs that include, along with trade provisions, investment chapters that often resemble BITs[41]. The latter include treaties such as the NAFTA of 1994, whose Chapter 11, devoted to investment, includes its own separate form of international dispute settlement, or the comparable investment provisions in the more recent FTA between the United States and Morocco[42].

Despite the formally bilateral nature of this regime, the reach of international investment protections is arguably as universal as that of the WTO[43]. Indeed, more countries — 180 — were, by the end of 2008, parties to one or more treaties for investment protection than belonged to the WTO[44]. Even as early as 2002-2003, when fewer investment treaties had been concluded than is the case today, approximately 60 per cent of the total FDI stock invested by OECD countries in non-OECD countries were covered by BITs or

---

[41] See, e.g., United Nations Conference on Trade and Development ("UNCTAD"), "The Entry into Force of Bilateral Investment Treaties (BITs)", *International Investment Agreements Monitor*, No. 3, UNCTAD Doc. No. UNCTAD/WEB/ITE/IIA/2006/9 (2006).

[42] United States-Morocco Free Trade Agreement, signed on 15 June 2004, entered into force 1 Januay 2006, available at <http://www.moroccousafta.com/ftafulltext.htm> (hereinafter "United-States-Morocco FTA"), Chap. 10 (containing protections and restrictions regarding investment).

[43] For a forceful contention that the investment regime is effectively multilateral despite the formally bilateral form of most investment treaties, see Schill, *supra* footnote 31.

[44] Braun, *supra* footnote 12 , pp. 3-4 (citing UNCTAD figures for 2008). See also K. J. Vandevelde, "A Brief History of International Investment Agreements", in Sachs and Sauvant (eds.), *supra* footnote 5, pp. 3, 28 (citing UNCTAD's figures).

FTAs[45]. Binding commitments for the protection of foreign investors are also contained in a handful of multilateral agreements designed for specific purposes (such as the Energy Charter Treaty) or exist within international organizations principally designed for other purposes (such as the WTO's TRIMs, GATS, and TRIPS Agreements) or the OECD's Code of Capital Movements. Other multilateral agreements, such as the World Bank's ICSID Convention — which is intended to facilitate the international arbitration of disputes between foreign investors and host States — or the World Bank's Convention Establishing the Multilateral Investment Guarantee Agency — which complements the political risk insurance programmes offered to foreign investors by some countries, such as the United States' OPIC — facilitate the cross-border movement of capital[46].

D. *The Contents of International Investment Treaties*

This monograph will focus on typical BITs and FTAs containing investment chapters. Although these treaties vary in terms of the specific rights provided, they usually include the following guarantees on behalf of foreign investors: national and most-favoured-nation treatment ("NT" and "MFN"); other guarantees against "arbitrary" and/or "discriminatory" treatment; provisions assuring "fair and equitable treatment" ("FET"), "full protection and security", prompt, adequate and effective compensation upon expropriation; and rights to transfer profits abroad. Note that while

---

[45] OECD Secretariat, *Novel Features in OECD Countries' Recent Investment Agreements: An Overview* (Paris, OEDC, 2005), available at <http://www.oecd.org/dataoecd/42/9/35823420.pdf>, p. 2.

[46] See generally Lowenfeld, *supra* footnote 3, pp. 94-97, 102-107, 115-130, 456-461.

some of these guarantees provide relative rights against discrimination, some investor protections anticipate absolute minimum guarantees, namely rights to "fair and equitable treatment", "full protection and security", compensation upon expropriation, and the unimpeded right to repatriate profits stemming from the operation of their enterprise[47].

Some investment agreements, such as the US Model BIT of 1987 and the Energy Charter Treaty (but not post-2004 US investment treaties such as the United States-Morocco FTA) include another absolute treaty guarantee, known as the "umbrella clause" whereby the States parties agree to "observe any obligations" they have entered into with an investor.

The relevant text (in context) from the US Model BIT of 1987 states as follows:

> "1. Each Party shall permit and treat investment, and activities associated therewith, on a basis *no less favorable than that accorded in like situations* to investment or associated activities of its own nationals or companies, or of nationals or companies of any third country, whichever is the most favorable, subject to the right of each Party to make or maintain exceptions falling within one of the sectors or matters listed in the Annex to this Treaty . . .
>
> 2. Investment shall at all times be accorded *fair and equitable treatment*, shall enjoy *full protection* and security and shall in no case be accorded treatment less than that required by *international law*.

---

[47] For a detailed description of these rights, citing specific texts from different investment treaties as well as arbitral decisions on point, see R. D. Bishop *et al.*, *supra* footnote 1, pp. 1007-1169. For a concrete example of these rights, see United States-Morocco FTA, *supra* footnote 42, Arts. 10.3 (NT), 10.4 (MFN), 10.5 (FET and full protection and security), 10.6 (expropriation), 10.7 (transfers).

Neither Party shall in any way impair by *arbitrary* and *discriminatory* measures the management, operation, maintenance, use, enjoyment, acquisition, expansion, or disposal of investments. Each Party shall *observe any obligation* it may have entered into with regard to investments."[48]

The comparable provision from the 1994 Energy Charter Treaty states:

> "*Article 10 — Promotion, Protection and Treatment of Investments*
>
> 1. Each Contracting Party shall, in accordance with the provisions of this Treaty, encourage and create stable, equitable, favourable and transparent conditions for investors of other Contracting Parties to make Investments in its Area. Such conditions shall include a commitment to accord at all times to Investments of Investors of other Contracting Parties *fair and equitable treatment*. Such Investments shall also enjoy the *most constant protection and security* and no Contracting Party shall in any way impair by unreasonable or *discriminatory measures* their management, maintenance, use, enjoyment or disposal. In no case shall such Investments be accorded treatment less favourable than that required by *international law*, including treaty obligations. Each Contracting Party shall *observe any obligations* it has entered into with an Investor or an Investment of an Investor of any other Contracting Party.

. . . .

---

[48] For the text of the United States Model BIT of 1987, see K. J. Vandevelde, *United States Investment Treaties: Policy and Practice* (Boston, Kluwer Law and Taxation, 1992), Appendix A-4 (hereinafter "1987 US Model BIT"), Art. II (emphasis added).

7. Each Contracting Party shall accord to Investments in its Area of Investors of other Contracting Parties, and their related activities including management, maintenance, use, enjoyment or disposal, *treatment no less favourable* than that which it accords to its Investments of its own Investors or of the Investors of any other Contracting Party or any third State and their related activities including management, maintenance, use, enjoyment or disposal, whichever is the most favourable."[49]

Taken at face value, both of these provisions elevate a breach of contract between a host State and an investor to a treaty breach. These clauses permit investors to bring an international arbitral claim based on that breach, even if their original contract with the host State contained no such dispute settlement clause. Notice that the broad wording of the umbrella clause in these treaties would seem to include any other "obligation" that a host State has offered to an investor, even one not contained in a contract, such as a guarantee in a Government-issued licence to operate. Whether these umbrella clauses or comparable provisions in other investment treaties go so far has led to conflicting decisions in the course of investor-State arbitrations[50].

As these texts indicate, the Energy Charter Treaty which has now been ratified by 51 nations (including the whole of Europe) and the US Model BIT of 1987, which inspired a generation of strongly protective investment treaties by a number of countries, include a

---

[49] Energy Charter Treaty, *supra* footnote 34, Art. 10 (emphasis added).

[50] See, e.g., R. Dolzer and C. Schreuer, *Principles of International Investment Law* (Oxford, Oxford University Press, 2008), pp. 153-162.

number of comparable treaty guarantees. These treatment standards are not unique to the United States but are now pervasive throughout many of the nearly 3,000 BITs and FTAs currently in existence. At the same time, the precise ways in which these similar obligations are stated vary from one investment treaty to another, as is clear even from the two examples cited above.

The requirement to provide "full protection and security" in the US Model of 1987 becomes a requirement to extend "constant protection and security" in the Energy Charter, for example. It is typically up to the arbitrators charged with settling disputes under these respective treaties to tell us if these differences in terminology are significant given particular facts. As is addressed in a later chapter, arbitrators face a conflict between deciding the case before them in accordance with the precise terms used in the treaty before them (as is required by the ordinary rules of treaty interpretation that stress the singular importance of "plain meaning")[51] and their desire to render the consistent or harmonious interpretations of "international investment law" that many assume are needed to best protect the stable and settled expectations of both investors and host States.

Another interpretative issue that is now emerging in the course of investor-State arbitrations would be familiar to students of "fragmentation": to what extent can law from other international regimes, including the WTO, be relevant to the interpretation of investment treaties? As we consider the texts from the Energy Charter and the US Model BIT noted above, the most

---

[51] Vienna Convention on the Law of Treaties, 1155 *United Nations Treaty Series* 331, signed on 23 May 1969, entered into force on 27 January 1980 (hereinafter "VCLT"), Art. 31 (1) *(a)*.

obvious area of potential overlap between the trade and investment regimes would seem to be their mutual guarantees of non-discrimination. The intent behind the non-discrimination assurances given in the US Model BIT of 1987 and the Energy Charter Treaty would appear to be comparable to that motivating the NT/MFN guarantees contained in the GATT for the protection of traders in goods. In all three cases, it would seem that States are barred from discriminating against either foreign goods or foreign investment. And yet, the three treaties differ somewhat even with respect to this guarantee. The phrase "in like situations" contained in the US Model BIT does not, for example, appear in the Energy Charter Treaty. Nor does that phrase appear in the relevant provisions of the GATT (which address "like products")[52]. This and other textual differences may lead an objective dispute settler to different results — not only between the trade and investment regimes but perhaps even as between different investment treaties. Close reading of the Energy Charter and US Model BIT texts cited also suggest other, more subtle, differences. Does the US Model's protection against impairment by "arbitrary and discriminatory measures" in Article II (1) really mean the same thing as the Energy Charter's reference to "unreasonable or discriminatory" mea-

---

[52] See General Agreement on Tariffs and Trade, 55 *United Nations Treaty Series* 187, signed on 30 October 1947, entered into force 1 January 1948, Art. III (4) (incorporated into the General Agreement on Tariffs and Trade, signed on 15 April 1994, entered into force on 1 January 1995) (hereinafter "GATT"). ("The products of the territory of any contracting party imported into the territory of any other contracting party shall be accorded treatment no less favourable than that accorded to like products of national origin in respect of all laws, regulations and requirements affecting their internal sale, offering for sale, purchase, transportation, distribution or use.")

sures[53]? Should either of these provisions elicit the
same analysis that WTO panellists apply under the
chapeau clause to the GATT, Article XX, which bars
"arbitrary or unjustifiable discrimination between
countries where the same conditions prevail or a disguised restriction on international trade"[54]? Although
in a general sense all of these treaties appear to share a
common purpose, precluding government measures
that have no legitimate purpose and are forms of trade
or investment protectionism, even arbitrators concurring on that purpose may disagree on how to give it
effect. Textual differences among these treaties may
only facilitate differing outcomes. These textual differences also help to explain the persistence of scholarly
debates about whether the concept of discriminatory
treatment as applied in the GATT (as well as other
trade law) can be transferred in its entirety to the
investment regime[55].

There are other reasons to exercise caution in drawing from increasingly sophisticated and developed

---

[53] See, e.g., Dolzer and Schreuer, *supra* footnote 50,
pp. 173-178 (discussing possible differences and areas of
interpretative overlap among BIT or FTA guarantees barring "arbitrary" or "discriminatory" measures and assurances of fair and equitable treatment).

[54] For a comparison of GATT and investment law on
this and other issues, see J. Alvarez and T. Brink, "Revisiting the Necessity Defense in the Argentina Cases", *Yearbook on International Law & Policy 2010-2011* (2011), also
available on Investment Claims Database (Oxford), see
<http://wwww.investmentclaims.com/subscriber_article?
script=yes&id=/ic/Journal%20Articles/law-iic-journal052
&recno=20&searchType=browse>.

[55] See, e.g., Dolzer and Schreuer, *supra* footnote 50,
pp. 178-186. There are even differences among US investment treaties over time in terms of how the national treatment obligation is defined; in some treaties the relevant
comparator is "in like circumstances" and not "in like
situations". See *ibid.*

trade law principles for the purpose of interpreting BITs and FTAs. The trade and investment regimes obviously do not overlap when it comes to other substantive rights typically provided to foreign investors that have no analogue in the context of trade in goods. The GATT covered agreements do not mention "fair and equitable treatment" or "full" or "constant" protection and security, for example. There is also no equivalent to an umbrella clause in the GATT (as contained in both the Energy Charter and US Model BIT noted above). Nor is there anything in the GATT comparable to the absolute property protections reflected in the typical BIT guarantee recognizing the need for prompt, adequate and effective compensation upon expropriation[56]. Furthermore, there is no mention in the GATT of the typical BIT guarantee indicating that investors are to be treated "no less than is required by international law" (as contained in both the US Model BIT and the Energy Charter texts noted above). Notably, these rights apply even when investors are not otherwise treated any differently than a host State's citizens or its most favoured trading partner. These protections

---

[56] Compare GATT, *supra* footnote 52, with 1987 US Model BIT, *supra* footnote 48, Art. III ("1. Investments shall not be *expropriated or nationalized either directly or indirectly through measures tantamount to expropriation or nationalization* ('expropriation') except for a public purpose; in a non-discriminatory manner; *upon payment of prompt, adequate and effective compensation; and in accordance with due process of law and the general principles of treatment provided for in Article II (2)*. Compensation shall be equivalent to the *fair market value* of the expropriated investment immediately before the expropriatory action was taken or became known; be paid without delay, include interest at a commercially reasonable rate from the date of expropriation; be fully realizable; and be freely transferable at the prevailing market rate of exchange on the date of expropriation.") (Emphasis added.)

do not necessarily have anything to do with discriminatory intent; violations of these guarantees may not be
caused by trade protectionism. To this extent the
investment regime appears to protect discrete property
rights to a much greater degree than in the GATT, a
regime which focuses on measures that have an impermissible intent or purpose. For these reasons, among
others that will be addressed in subsequent chapters,
WTO or GATT law may offer only limited assistance
to those interpreting investment treaties.

E. *Investor-State Dispute Settlement*

Investor-State arbitrators charged with applying
BITs and FTAs also need to be aware of another set of
distinctions from trade law: the procedural remedies
provided in case of breach of these investment treaties
are totally different from those that apply in the WTO.
The trade regime contains its own dispute settlement
mechanism under which the GATT contracting parties
can bring complaints against one another. These inter-
state complaints are considered by GATT panels and, if
appealed, by the WTO Appellate Body, a kind of permanent international trade court. These complaints, if
successful, are intended to secure the removal of
GATT-inconsistent measures[57]. If a State withdraws an
offending measure or discontinues a practice that has

---

[57] But consider the dispute between Jackson and Bello.
Compare J. H. Bello, "The WTO Dispute Settlement
Understanding: Less Is More", 90 *American Journal of
International Law* 416 (1996), p. 417 (arguing that compliance with WTO dispute settlement rulings is voluntary),
with J. H. Jackson, "The WTO Dispute Settlement Understanding — Misunderstandings on the Nature of Legal
Obligations", 91 *American Journal of International Law*
60 (1997) (refuting Bello's point and arguing that a dispute
settlement ruling creates an international legal obligation
on the party concerned).

been found to violate the GATT, the complaint is considered to be over and no further remedy is authorized under the WTO's dispute settlement system. Under that system only if a State refuses to remove its GATT-illegal measure does the regime proceed to the next step: namely an order from the WTO permitting the claimant State to raise the level of its bound duties vis-à-vis the author of the illegal act. In that instance, the WTO dispute settlers determine what goods can be retaliated against as well as what constitutes the appropriate level of retaliation; they authorize only such retaliation as would be proportionate to the breach and that would approximate the extent of injury should the offending measure continue in effect. As this indicates, even when the WTO dispute settlement system orders the ultimate trade retaliation remedy available, that regime is not designed to provide recompense to the actual traders who have been victimized by a State's illegal action.

The WTO's remedial scheme is *prospective* in nature. It is most comparable to countermeasures permitted in response to prior treaty breach under the Articles of State Responsibility[58]. Like a countermeasure, GATT-authorized trade retaliation is a transitional means to induce compliance and prevent future violations of the GATT. The intent of the WTO's dispute settlement system is not to provide the equivalent of damages to particular injured traders but to restore the status quo between the GATT Contracting Parties as

---

[58] See International Law Commission, "Draft Articles on Responsibility of States for Internationally Wrongful Acts", 2:2 *Yearbook of the International Law Commission* 1 (2001), available at <http://untreaty.un.org/ilc/texts/instruments/english/commentaries/9_6_2001.pdf> (hereinafter "Draft Articles"), Arts. 49-53. See also VCLT, *supra* footnote 51, Art. 60 (authorizing responses to material breaches of a multilateral treaty).

soon as possible[59]. Accordingly, the WTO dispute settlement scheme is appropriately delimited to disputes between States since States are both its intended targets and its intended beneficiaries. This also explains why authorizations to engage in trade retaliation (that is, authorizations to "suspend concessions") are in the WTO quite rare[60]. When a State is authorized to retaliate, that State is in effect being authorized to raise tariffs to an extent that would otherwise not be legal under the GATT. Such remedies might be said to defeat the purpose of the trade regime, which, after all, seeks to lower tariffs globally — to the benefit of consumers worldwide. Indeed, an injured WTO member may regard its hard-won authority to impose higher tariffs as a mixed blessing subject to a cost/benefit analysis since its suspension of concessions imposes costs on its own consumers who will pay more for the targeted imports.

For these reasons, an authorization to impose punishing tariffs on a WTO member is, in that system, a regrettable concession to realpolitik. It is a tool to secure compliance that should hardly ever prove necessary and if deployed should be over and done with as soon as possible so that unimpeded trade in goods can resume without artificially high tariffs or other non-tariff barriers.

The purposes of investor-State remedies as well as the actual remedies provided under the investment regime could not be more different.

---

[59] For one attempt to compare countermeasures to GATT remedies, see P. C. Mavroidis, "Remedies in the WTO Legal System: Between a Rock and a Hard Place", 11:4 *European Journal of International Law* 763 (2000).

[60] As of December 2005, there were only 15 cases where countermeasures have been imposed in the WTO. See J. Dunoff *et al.*, *International Law: Norms, Actors, Process* (New York, Aspen Publishers, 2006), p. 846.

The typical investment agreement includes a clause that permits the States parties to a treaty to complain to an arbitral body[61]. This State-to-State dispute settlement system is, to some extent, comparable to that of the WTO. But as in the case of State-to-State complaint mechanisms in other treaties, this is rarely used[62]. With exceptions, such as WTO complaints, States don't like to file complaints against one another — since these are likely to come back to haunt them. Indeed, even under the WTO, there is some evidence that once State A complains about State B's conduct, it is very likely that State B will retaliate by bringing some complaint against State A.

More important for our purposes and the real world of disputes is the existence in investment agreements of clauses like Article VI of the US Model BIT of 1987.

That clause provides:

"1. . . . an investment dispute is defined as a dispute involving (a) the interpretation or application of an investment agreement between a Party and a national or company of the other Party; (b) the interpretation or application of any investment authorization granted by a Party's foreign investment authority to such national or company; or (c) an alleged breach of any right conferred or created by this Treaty with respect to an investment.

2. . . . if the dispute cannot be resolved through consultation and negotiation, the dispute shall be submitted for settlement in accordance with pre-

---

[61] See, e.g., 1987 US Model BIT, *supra* footnote 48, Art. VII.

[62] See, e.g., International Covenant on Civil and Political Rights, 999 *United Nations Treaty Series* 171, signed on 16 December 1966, entered into force on 23 March 1976 (hereinafter "ICCPR"), Art. 41.

viously agreed, applicable dispute-settlement procedures . . .

[Subject to paragraph 3 below]

3. (a) The national or company concerned may choose to consent in writing to the submission of the dispute to the International Centre for the Settlement of Investment Disputes ("Centre") or to ad hoc arbitration applying the rules of the Centre, for the settlement by conciliation or binding arbitration, at any time after six months from the date upon which the dispute arose. Once the national or company concerned has so consented, either party to the dispute may institute such proceedings provided:

(i) the dispute has not been submitted by the national or company for resolution in accordance with any applicable previously agreed dispute settlement procedures; and

(ii) the national or company concerned has not brought the dispute before the courts of justice or administrative tribunals or agencies of competent jurisdiction of the Party that is a party to the dispute . . .

(b) *Each Party hereby consents* to the submission of an investment dispute to the Centre for settlement by conciliation or binding arbitration, or, in the event the Centre is not available, to the submission of the dispute to ad hoc arbitration applying the rules of the Centre." (Emphasis added.)

Notice that under Article VI, known as an investor-State dispute settlement clause, in the event that an "investment dispute" arises, the private investor can itself bring the dispute to international arbitration, namely to ICSID under the auspices of the World Bank, or if the State has not ratified the ICSID Convention, to arbitration under the Additional Facility of ICSID[63]. Parties to the ICSID Convention agree in advance to permit investment disputes to be brought against them, provided the particular dispute is the subject of a separate agreement whereby the parties have consented to submit the dispute to ICSID[64]. At the time the ICSID Convention was concluded in 1966, it was assumed that consent to arbitration would occur through an *ad hoc* submission to arbitration contained in an agreement between the host State and the investor after a particular dispute between them had arisen or because of a clause providing advance consent to arbitration contained in an investment contract between an investor and a host State. The rise of BITs and FTAs containing advance consent to investor-State arbitration for disputes arising under them, including BIT and FTA clauses specifically accepting the jurisdiction of ICSID for this purpose, has vastly expanded the universe of potential investor-State claims.

The ICSID Convention contained an important feature designed to entice States that were leery of international arbitration, such as those Governments who agreed with the Argentine jurist Carlos Calvo's assertion that investors are only entitled to national treatment and should only have access to national courts just like host State nationals[65]. Such Governments

---

[63] See ICSID Administrative Council, *Rules Governing the Additional Facility for the Administration of Proceedings by the Secretariat of the International Centre for Settlement of Investment Disputes* (Washington, DC, ICSID, 2006), available at <http://icsid.worldbank.org/ICSID/ICSID/AdditionalFacilityRules.jsp>.

[64] See ICSID Convention, *supra* footnote 38, Art. 25.

[65] M. Sornarajah, *The International Law on Foreign Investment* (Cambridge, Cambridge University Press, 3rd ed., 2010), p. 21, n. 65 (citing C. Calvo, 6 *Le droit international théorique et pratique* (Paris, ed. A. Rousseau, 5th ed., 1896) ("Aliens who established themselves in a country are certainly entitled to the same rights of pro-

were enticed to become parties to the ICSID Convention by its assurance that once ISCID jurisdiction was triggered, contracting States would be precluded from resorting to diplomatic espousal[66]. ISCID parties would no longer bear the brunt of angry and politically powerful TNC's home State's demands. ICSID arbitration promised the end of gunboat diplomacy intended to enforce the rights of aliens.

ICSID arbitral tribunals consist of three persons: one selected by each party to the dispute (investor and host State) and one presiding arbitrator selected either by the parties, or, if they cannot agree, by the Chairman of ICSID who is ex officio the President of the World Bank[67]. This resembles the pattern followed in commercial arbitration except that under ICSID's rules the majority of the arbitrators must be nationals of States other than the host State or the home State of the investor[68]. ICSID Contracting States agree to recognize as binding any ICSID arbitral award issued and promise to "enforce the pecuniary obligations imposed by that award within its territories as if it were a final judgment of a court in that State"[69]. ICSID arbitral awards are not subject to appeal but can be the subject of a request for annulment. If such a request is made, an Annulment Committee, consisting of another *ad hoc* committee of three arbitrators distinct from those who heard the original dispute, considers whether the original tribunal was not properly constituted, whether it "manifestly exceeded" its powers, engaged in corruption, seriously departed from a "fundamental rule of procedure", or failed to state the reasons for its

---

tection as nationals, but they cannot claim any greater measure of protection").
[66] See ICSID Convention, *supra* footnote 38, Art. 27.
[67] See *ibid*., Arts. 37-38.
[68] See Lowenfeld, *supra* footnote 3, pp. 457-458.
[69] ICSID Convention, *supra* footnote 38, Art. 54 (1).

award[70]. This limited form of review falls well short of the kind of appeal typically applied in national courts, international criminal courts or tribunals, or even in the WTO (whose Appellate Body can fully review the law applied by the original panel).

Although Article VI of the US Model BIT of 1987 only anticipates arbitration under ICSID, many investment agreements provide investors with a menu of other arbitral options, including resort to arbitration under the rules of the United Nations Commission on International Trade Law ("UNCITRAL") or before other arbitration bodies such as those the regularly decide commercial disputes between private parties (such as the Arbitration Institute of the Stockholm Chamber of Commerce, which is provided as one option under the Energy Charter Treaty)[71].

As is evident from the text of Article VI (1) of the US Model BIT of 1987, that treaty defines the jurisdiction of an investor-State arbitration quite broadly to include disputes arising under a government contract or authorization as well as any dispute arising from violation of the treaty itself. Further, under Article VI (2) an investor has the option of bringing his or her complaint to any other forum, such as the host State's local courts, but is not required to do so. There is no requirement (as is usual under the customary international law of espousal) of exhaustion of local remedies. On the contrary, even when an investor has previously agreed to go to local courts through a provision in her investment contract, Article VI (2) of this Model BIT permits the investor to forego such prior commitments and go directly to international arbitration. Under a clause such as Article VI, the investor thus faces a

---

[70] ICSID Convention, *supra* footnote 38, Art. 52 (1).
[71] See Energy Charter Treaty, *supra* footnote 34, Art. 26 (4).

choice about whether to bring a complaint to local courts in the host State or to international arbitration and cannot go back to arbitration once this choice is made[72]. This is known as a "fork in the road" dispute settlement provision. Other BITs or FTAs may not contain such a clause but may impose other pre-conditions to investor-State arbitration, such as a delay for a specified period to permit the parties to negotiate; some investment treaties may even anticipate the continued application of the traditional rule requiring exhaustion of local remedies.

Under a clause like Article VI (1), neither the investor's home State nor the host State can prevent a claim from being filed against the State that has violated the BIT by a private investor. In the typical instance, the States parties to a BIT know whether or not they have each already adhered to the ICSID Convention. If they have, the BIT itself may provide the necessary additional consent to ICSID's hearing the dispute (as does Article VI (3) *(b)* of the US Model BIT of 1987). Under such a perfected arbitration clause, each State party to the BIT has consented in advance to any potential investment claim under the treaty and it is only the investor, once a dispute has arisen, who gets to choose between arbitration, local courts, or some other option to address the dispute (see Article VI (3) *(a)*). For this reason, some suggest that arbitration under such treaties occurs "without privity"[73]. This descriptive phase describes the situation where, pursuant to a clause like that in the US Model BIT, an investor has the right to go to arbitration even when she does not have a pre-existing contract with the

---

[72] See 1987 US Model BIT, *supra* footnote 48, Art. VI (3) (i)-(ii).

[73] J. Paulsson, "Arbitration without Privity", 10 *ICSID Review* 232 (1995).

host State permitting this. (Others have suggested that this characterization is misleading since the State merely has given its advance consent to arbitration in the BIT itself and can be said to have anticipated any subsequent investor-State claims.) In any case, no one disputes that the basis for investor-State arbitration under treaties such as the US Model of 1987 is an inter-state compact whereby both States agree in advance to settle prospective treaty disputes that may arise[74]. In such cases, the investors might be regarded as third party beneficiaries who simply take advantage of the States parties' advance consent whenever a dispute arises[75].

Investor-State dispute settlement accordingly differs from interstate dispute settlement as in the WTO (or for that matter the ICJ) in the following ways.

---

[74] None of the elements of investor-State dispute settlement are in of themselves novel and all have historical precedents. As Barton Legum has pointed out, what is novel is the *combination* of direct non-State claims, comprehensive investment protection, prospective application, *ad hoc* tribunals, and at least some prospect that claims will be brought against rich Western States to the extent a BIT or FTA involves parties with substantial two-way exchanges of capital, such as Canada and the United States under the NAFTA. B. Legum, "The Innovation of Investor-State Arbitration under NAFTA", 43 *Harvard International Law Journal* 531 (2002).

[75] This characterization does not, however, resolve an important ambiguity that is only now starting to be raised in the literature and in some arbitrations: namely whether investors, as third party beneficiaries, ought to be treated as bearers of their own independent rights, analogous to other "subjects" of international law that are entitled to pursue their own claims at the international level, or whether they are merely agents of their home countries delegated with the authority to pursue their home countries' claims of espousal. Chapters II and V address the potential consequences of these differing conceptions of investor rights.

(1) Party control

Under the investment regime, unlike interstate mechanisms like the WTO, States no longer control which claims are brought or, equally significantly, how such claims are litigated. States are no longer in control of the legal issues that are given to arbitrators to decide. In the WTO, States may decide, for example, not to press controversial claims — such as whether the United States' long-standing trade sanctions under its Helms-Burton law directed at Cuba are really justified by the United States' "essential security" interests[76]. Under such systems States have protected themselves to some extent from having supranational arbitrators telling them, for example, what their "essential" or "national security" interests actually are. In the absence of special clauses removing particular questions from investor-State dispute settlement or seeking to limit the arbitrators' discretion with respect to some issues, States parties to BITs and FTAs cannot prevent private investors from raising such controversial issues — and indeed, as is further addressed in Chapter IV, the Argentine Government's assertions of security have been challenged repeatedly (and often successfully) by private investors under the United States-Argentina BIT of 1991 (which is modelled after the US Model BIT of 1987)[77]. Who is entitled to bring claims also matters a great deal with respect to the intensity with

---

[76] Such a WTO complaint was once contemplated. See J. H. Jackson and A. F. Lowenfeld, "Helms-Burton, the US, and the WTO", *American Society of International Law Insights* (March 1997), available at <http://www.asil.org/insight7.cfm>.

[77] For a review of some of these cases, see J. E. Alvarez and K. Khamsi, "The Argentine Crisis and Foreign Investors", in *Yearbook on International Investment Law & Policy 2008-2009*, *supra* footnote 15, p. 379.

which issues may be pursued, the prospect of annulment or enforcement challenges or for settlement, and
the likelihood that litigants will raise "political" or
other extraneous issues in the course of adjudication.
On all these questions, it has been suggested that
investor-State arbitrations more closely resemble the
hard-fought, scorched-earth approaches common to
United States "adversarial" litigation[78]. It is therefore
no surprise that some investor-State arbitrations are no
longer the speedy alternative to national court litigation
that they were once touted to be. The *Vivendi* case
against Argentina, involving two annulment proceedings, lasted 11 years[79]; more recently, the *CMS* v.
Argentina case, addressed later in this monograph, took
six years to resolve and has yet to result in payment to
the successful claimants[80].

Nor is it the case that States retain unfettered control
over the procedures that govern investor-State arbitration. Once an investor exercises his or her option in an
investment agreement to make a claim under a particular venue (such as ICSID), established rules to govern
such arbitrations need to be followed. Under such
rules, States parties defending investor claims may find
it difficult to preclude procedural rulings that, for
example, permit *amicus* briefs, even from groups hostile to the State's interests or that compel the State to
disclose certain information. As has been particularly
apparent in the course of NAFTA arbitrations, both
investors and States may face considerable pressures to

---

[78] See generally L. Reed and J. Sutcliffe, "The 'Americanization' of International Arbitration?", 16:4 *Mealey's
International Arbitration Reporter* 11 (2001).

[79] See, e.g., N. Antonovics, "Vivendi Wins Decade-
Long Argentina Legal Battle", *Reuters* (21 August 2007),
available at <http://www.reuters.com/article/idUSL2181
989720070821>.

[80] See Alvarez and Khamsi, *supra* footnote 77.

make the investor-State process more transparent in a number of respects, including with respect to oral proceedings[81]. Absent an agreement between investor and defendant State, it may prove difficult to keep arbitral awards or even the briefs filed from being made public. While no one knows the numbers of investor-State awards that are not made public, what is clear is that an increasing number of such awards, as well as underlying briefs, are now widely available, including on government websites — and that forms of accountability are now widely expected[82].

(2) Remedies for past injury

The WTO and the investor-State dispute settlement regimes are similar insofar as under both States have agreed to submit themselves to an unknown number of prospective and unpredictable claims. This is a sharp difference from, for example, prior claims commissions charged with adjudicating a defined set of outstanding claims, such as the Iran-United States

---

[81] See, e.g., "Notes of Interpretation of Certain Chapter 11 Provisions", *NAFTA Free Trade Commission* (31 July 2001), available at <http://www.international.gc. ca/trade-agreements-accords-commerciaux/disp-diff/nafta-interpr.aspx?lang=en>, § 1 (b) (whereby NAFTA parties agree to make available to the public all documents submitted to Chapter 11 tribunals subject to certain narrow exceptions).

[82] For a forceful defence of the need for accountability mechanisms for investor-State arbitrations on the basis that these are a form of "global administrative law", see B. Kingsbury and S. Schill, "Investor-State Arbitration as Governance: Fair and Equitable Treatment, Proportionality and the Emerging Global Administrative Law", in *El nuevo derecho administrativo global en América Latina : desafíos para las inversiones extranjeras, la regulación nacional y el financiamiento para el desarrollo* (Buenos Aires, Ediciones RAP S.A., 2009), p. 221.

Claims Tribunal. The trade and investment regimes are also comparable insofar as neither generally requires exhaustion of local remedies prior to resort to international adjudication. As noted, many BITs and FTAs, like the US Model BIT noted above, forgo this requirement and the WTO system anticipates, for example, that States avoid implementing legal remedies of their own for an alleged violation of the law of the GATT without first seeking a WTO decision determining that such a violation has indeed occurred[83]. Moreover, both dispute settlement systems are, as compared to other international adjudicative schemes, relatively effective in terms of securing State compliance. After the reforms of the 1994 Uruguay Round, GATT contracting parties are obligated to abide by the decisions issued by the WTO's dispute settlers unless all members, including the State that has won a decision in its favour, agrees not to do so. Investor-State arbitrators can take advantage of the relatively efficacious system for enforcement of arbitral awards, established under the ICSID or New York Conventions, through which arbitral awards can be enforced in virtually every country's national courts[84]. This is not to suggest, however, that either the trade or investment regime achieves perfect compliance. As is suggested by the strenuous efforts to secure Europe's compliance with WTO rulings relating to bananas[85] or investors' struggle to

---

[83] GATT, *supra* footnote 52, Art. 23.

[84] ICSID Convention, *supra* footnote 38, Arts. 53, 54; United Nations Convention on the Recognition and Enforcement of Foreign Arbitral Awards, 330 *United Nations Treaty Series* 38, signed on 10 June 1958, entered into force on 7 June 1959 (hereinafter "New York Convention").

[85] For an overview of the "Banana War" at the WTO, see, e.g., T. B. Simi and A. Kaushik, "The Banana War at the GATT/WTO", 2008:1 *Trade Law Brief: Making Trade Law Simple* (2008), available at <http://www.cuts-citee.org/pdf/TLB08-01.pdf>.

secure payment of Argentina's numerous investor-State liability awards[86], both dispute settlement systems have yet to overcome international law's systemic difficulties in securing compliance by States.

But WTO and investor-State remedies differ in other respects. Unlike the WTO regime, which, as noted, is designed to get States accused of violations to correct their mistakes, the point of investor-State dispute settlement is to secure a compensatory remedy for past harms done to a private party stemming from a violation of an investment treaty. What that compensation might be is suggested by Article III (1) of the US Model BIT of 1987 which provides that

"1. Investments shall not be *expropriated or nationalized either directly or indirectly through measures tantamount to expropriation or nationalization* ("expropriation") except for a public purpose; in a non-discriminatory manner; *upon payment of prompt, adequate and effective compensation; and in accordance with due process of law and the general principles of treatment provided for in Article II (2)*. Compensation shall be equivalent to the *fair market value* of the expropriated investment immediately before the expropriatory action was taken or became known; be paid without delay; include interest at a commercially reasonable rate from the date of expropriation; be fully realizable; and be freely transferable at the prevailing market rate of exchange on the date of expropriation." (Emphasis added.)

Under this provision, an investor whose property has been taken is entitled to the "fair market value of

---

[86] See, e.g., *Sempra Energy International* v. *Argentina*, Decision on the Argentine Republic's Request for a Continued Stay of Enforcement of the Award, ICSID Case No. ARB/02/16 (5 March 2009).

the expropriated investment" plus interest. The clause responds to old North/South debates in the UN General Assembly by affirming the North's preferred outcome — as opposed to that provided in, for example, the 1974 Charter of Economic Rights and Duties of States which left the matter of "appropriate compensation" up to local law[87]. The clause provides investors with the "prompt, adequate and effective compensation" that the US Government had long argued is due under customary international law when Governments expropriate alien property[88]. While most investment treaties do not say what kind of compensation is owed for other violations of such treaties apart from expropriation, investor-State arbitrators have tended to find that, in principle, other breaches of a BIT or FTA entitle injured investors to recompense for the full value of whatever they lost as a result of violation of the treaty, irrespective of whether this occurred because of a violation of the provision for fair and equitable treatment, NT or MFN, or because the host State violated its obligations under the "umbrella clause"[89].

The typical remedy for a violation of an investment treaty involves an award of damages to a private party, not to a State. Accordingly investor-State arbitrators (unlike WTO adjudicators) need to assess *whether and to what extent* a private investor has suffered prior harm as a result of State action. This assessment often

---

[87] Charter of Economic Rights and Duties of States, General Assembly res. 3281 (XXIX), 29 *General Assembly Official Records*, Supp. No. 31, p. 50, UN doc. A/9631 (1974).

[88] Lowenfeld, *supra* footnote 3, pp. 395-403 (describing the diplomatic exchanges between the United States and Mexico leading to the enunciation of the "Hull Rule").

[89] See generally T. W. Wälde and B. Sabahi, "Compensation, Damages, and Valuation", in *The Oxford Handbook of International Investment Law*, *supra* footnote 6, p. 1049.

involves expert testimony to measure the extent of that injury and to determine the proper monetary recompense. Investor-State damages are not calculated on the basis of whether the anticipated remedy will entice a State to withdraw an offending measure (as under the WTO) and accordingly they do not involve a proportionality calculus (at least for this purpose). Once investor-State arbitrators determine that an investment treaty has indeed been violated, they are charged with determining what monetary amount will fully reimburse the private, non-State claimant for her prior or on-going loss. Remedies in investor-State dispute settlement are not like counter-measures but are more like tort damages awarded by national courts where the point is to make claimants whole for their losses. The arbitral enquiry is not prospective (as in the WTO) but retrospective — to identify precisely what damage the investor suffered to her propriety interests. Depending on the treaty breach, this may sometimes require, however, determinations of an investors' expected stream of profits[90].

(3) Impact on State sovereignty

Because of (1) and (2) above, investor-State dispute settlement is likely to be perceived as a threat to "sovereignty". Consider just three ways in which sovereign concerns may be more affected in the course of investor-State dispute settlement than under the WTO: (1) because investor-State remedies are more comprehensive; (2) because the resulting law may be more intrusive; and (3) because the regime as a whole produces more "global governance".

---

[90] As in instances where the arbitrators find the existence of a compensable taking or expropriation, See *ibid.*, pp. 1065-1067.

Unlike WTO-authorized tariff retaliation, which, as noted, is relatively rare and considered something of a defeat for a regime that seeks to achieve lower trade barriers, the sometimes considerable damage awards rendered in the course of investor-State arbitration are not seen as a regrettable defeat for the system but as its vindication. The whole point of the investment regime is precisely to enable States to provide credible commitments to foreign investors that they will not be hurt, and if hurt, that they will be compensated[91]. BITs and FTAs protect investors by providing them with not only substantive rights that either reflect or exceed those in customary international law, but they go beyond customary law by offering a real forum that, unlike biased local courts, can be counted on to provide investors with recompense when their rights are violated. Interestingly, investment treaties do not say, as the relevant WTO commitments do, that States are supposed to remove offending measures. Nonetheless, a host State that is obligated under an investor-State arbitral award to pay millions of dollars to an investor is bound to get the same message just as quickly if not more so than under the WTO. Of course, the sheer extent of such remedies also matters for those worried about "sovereignty". The fact that at this writing the State involved in the greatest number of disputes (Argentina) faces claims approaching US$40 billion surely raises "sovereignty" concerns in and of itself.

The vast number of investor-State claims also raise concerns. As tends to happen whenever access to international dispute settlement is provided to non-States parties, such "transnational" forms of dispute settle-

---

[91] See, e.g., A. T. Guzman, "Why LDCs Sign Treaties That Hurt Them: Explaining the Popularity of Bilateral Investment Treaties", 38 *Virginia Journal of International Law* 639 (1998).

ment (as in regional human rights courts or the European Court of Justice applying European Community law) tend to produce many more claims — and much more "case-law" — than purely "interstate" dispute settlement systems (such as in the WTO's or the ICJ's contentious jurisdiction). As of March 2008, ICSID — which, as noted, is only one prominent forum for the bringing of investor-State claims — had arbitrated 136 cases, with another 123 pending. While no one knows the actual numbers since some claims remain confidential, it is estimated that there are over 200 known investor-State claims being heard around the world — a number that easily exceeds the number of claims heard each year by the WTO's Appellate Body and the ICJ combined[92]. Of course, the more claims that are brought to international dispute settlers, the more these adjudicators have opportunities to interpret and make law[93]. The intrusive nature of many of these claims — involving challenges to environmental regulations, to the way States conduct administrative proceedings at all levels of government, or to national measures taken to handle a financial crisis — is exacerbated by the unpredictability of the resulting awards. And the prospect of more arbitral legal precedents seem all the more troubling when these involve the application of vague standards such as fair and equitable treatment by *ad hoc* panels of three that only come together to resolve one dispute at a time with no prospect of an appeal to a single appellate court that is capable of har-

---

[92] Between 1948 and 1994, by comparison, there were only 91 panel reports issued under Article XXIII of the GATT and only another 161 panels were established by the WTO's Dispute Settlement Body between 1995 and 24 November 2008, with only 118 of these resulting in panel reports (as opposed to settlements or withdrawals). See Sauvant, *supra* footnote 15, pp. 259-260.

[93] See Keohane, *supra* footnote 30.

monizing diverse results. The perceived threat to "sovereignty" is also heightened to the extent that investor-State cases appear to be relying upon, and therefore affecting, general rules of international law, including customary law.

But if investor-State dispute settlement does not resemble that in the WTO, is it more like other international forms of adjudication, such as those under regional human rights treaties?

Is the purpose or the effect of investor-State dispute settlement comparable to the purpose or the effect of decisions by the European Court of Human Rights, for example?

The answer is not obvious. Structurally BITs and FTAs resemble regional instruments like the European Convention for the Protection of Human Rights and Fundamental Freedoms ("ECHR") insofar as both are interstate pacts which assign rights to third parties. In both instances these non-State treaty beneficiaries are recognized as at least partial subjects (and not mere objects) of international law[94]. In addition, as in regional systems of protection such as the ECHR, investor-State dispute settlement hands over the power to enforce interstate pacts to "private attorney generals". (One difference though is that while the ECHR's third party beneficiaries are primarily the States parties' own nationals and only rarely include foreign cor-

---

[94] See generally Z. Douglas, "The Hybrid Foundations of Investment Treaty Arbitration", 74 *British Year Book of International Law* 151 (2003), pp. 181-184; T. R. Braun, "Globalization-Fueled Innovation: The Investor as Subject of International Law" (copy on file with author); but see J. E. Alvarez, "Are Corporations 'Subjects' of International Law", *Santa Clara Journal of International Law* (forthcoming 2010) (questioning whether it is useful to derive substantive conclusions from the idea that investors in the investment regime are "subjects" of international law).

porate entities as claimants[95], under BITs and FTAs the opposite is the case: those who benefit from investment treaties are usually, and intentionally, foreign individuals or companies.) While at first glance the European human rights system appears to be more inclusive in terms of potential claimants, since there are *millions* of potential individual claimants living in Europe, it is important to remember that potential claimants in the investment regime include not only the over 80,000 TNCs in the world but the many thousands of foreign subsidiaries that may also be entitled to bring claims under BITs and FTAs. In addition, many investment treaties (such as the US Model BIT discussed above) extend at least some of their protections to those who own shares in a company and not only foreign companies. Thus, the definition of "investment" in that BIT includes "shares of stock or other interests in a company or interests in the assets thereof"[96]. To the extent that such investment treaties enable individual shareholders and not merely companies to bring claims, there are millions of potential claimants under BITs and FTAs as well.

There are other similarities between the two regimes. Regional human rights conventions as well as investment treaties entail comparable renunciations of "sovereignty", insofar as both delegate to impartial third party adjudicators the ability to render decisions. All of these regimes anticipate the possibility that such adjudication may include an award of damages for past harm and in both States accept such potential liability

---

[95] See M. Emberland, *The Human Rights of Companies* (Oxford, Oxford University Press, 2006), p. 12 (noting that insofar as companies file claims before the European Court of Human Rights, most are small or medium sized enterprises organized under the laws of the State whose laws it is challenging and not large TNCs).

[96] 1987 US Model BIT, *supra* footnote 48, Art. I (1) (ii).

over an unpredictable set of prospective claims. Both the ECHR and investment treaties establish a relatively efficacious way to render legally binding decisions against entities that normally enjoy sovereign immunity; indeed both anticipate (and usually secure) the co-operative assistance of local courts (if needed) to secure enforcement. In both systems, the disputes that are assigned to supranational adjudicators would otherwise have been made exclusively by national entities, especially national courts. To a certain extent these regimes even share comparable goals: both attempt to use international law and international adjudicative mechanisms — a permanent court or *ad hoc* international arbitration respectively — as a way to juridify, proceduralize, and hopefully depoliticize certain disputes[97]. Both regimes impose an additional layer of supranational scrutiny on national decisions. Both share an assumption that in the instances encompassed by these treaties, national processes, including but not limited to national courts, cannot be wholly trusted to adhere to the rule of law and may be improperly influenced by, for example, political concerns[98].

---

[97] See Braun, *supra* footnote 12, p. 10. For a more critical description of the "depoliticization" brought about by the investment regime, see Schneiderman, *supra* footnote 30; see also *infra* Chap. V.

[98] For these reasons, among others, proponents of both regimes emphasize that they are seeking to establish or deepen the rule of law. For an account of the rise and deepening of the European human rights regime consistent with such goals, see, e.g., A. Moravcsik, "Explaining International Human Rights Regimes: Liberal Theory and Western Europe", 1 *European Journal of International Relations* 157 (1995); but see T. Ginsburg, "International Substitutes for Domestic Institutions: Bilateral Investment Treaties and Governance", 25 *International Review of Law and Economics* 107 (2005) (critiquing the assumption that investment treaties contribute to the promotion or establishment of the national rule of law).

Finally, many of the substantive rights accorded under these respective regimes are similar. As is true of individuals under the ECHR, covered investors under BITs and FTAs are typically entitled to due process, a fair opportunity to be heard, and non-discriminatory treatment. As will be addressed in later chapters, these regimes may share certain understandings of the kinds of rights that are embraced by the underlying treaties' mutual reliance on international law, "full" or "constant" protection and security, or guarantees against "arbitrary" or "discriminatory" treatment. In addition, both the ECHR and investment treaties recognize the need to protect the right to property, consistent with general principles of international law[99].

---

[99]   Article I, Protocol One, of the ECHR provides:

"Every natural or legal person is entitled to the peaceful enjoyment of his possessions. *No one shall be deprived of his possessions except in the public interest and subject to the conditions provided for by law and by the general principles of international law.* The preceding provisions shall not, however, in any way *impair the right of a State to enforce such laws as it deems necessary to control the use of property in accordance with the general interest* or to secure the payment of taxes or other contributions or penalties." European Convention on Human Rights, 213 *United Nations Treaty Series* 222, signed on 4 November 1950, entered into force on 3 September 1953 (hereinafter "ECHR") (emphasis added).

Article 21 (1) of the American Convention on Human Rights provides a comparable provision: "Everyone has the right to the use and employment of his property. The law may subordinate such use and enjoyment in the interest of society." But that provision continues "No one shall be deprived of his property except upon payment of just compensation, for reasons of public utility or social interest, and in the cases and according to the forms established by law." American Convention on Human Rights, 1144 *United Nations Treaty Series* 123, signed on 22 November

Some might be offended by the notion that the rights accorded to foreign investors — which may be rich TNCs and their shareholders — are somehow comparable to the human rights accorded to abused and often marginalized individuals. Respect for human rights is, after all, a deontological goal that is worthy of respect simply because human beings and their dignity are worth protecting at all costs. The granting of rights to foreign investors, on the other hand, is usually justified as merely a convenient stratagem for achieving other important social goals, especially the economic development of States that are hosts to foreign investors[100]. Few attempt to make the case that moral-

---

1969, entered into force on 18 July 1978, Art. 21 (2). Note that Article 17 of the Universal Declaration of Human Rights also provides protection from the "arbitrary" deprivation of property, while Article 15 of the International Covenant on Economic, Social, and Cultural Rights recognizes everyone's protection of the "moral and materials interests resulting from any scientific, literary or artistic production of which he is the author". Universal Declaration on Human Rights, General Assembly res. 217A (III), UN doc. A/777 (1948), Art. 17; International Covenant on Economic, Social, and Cultural Rights, 999 *United Nations Treaty Series* 3, signed on 16 December 1966, entered into force on 3 January 1976, reprinted in 6 *International Legal Materials* 360, Art. 15. The right to property, and more specifically the entitlement to procedural safeguards before it can be interfered with, has also been recognized by the European Court of Justice. See, e.g., *Kadi* v. *Council and Commission*, Judgment, Grand Chamber of the European Court of Justice, Case No. C-402/05 (2008), paras. 354-371 (finding restrictions on appellants' property interests under European legislation implementing Security Council counter-terrorism sanctions to be illegal).

[100] See, e.g., M. Orellana, "Science, Risk, and Uncertainty: Public Health Measures and Investment Disciplines", in P. Kahn and T. Wälde (eds.), *New Aspects of International Investment Law* (Leiden, Martinus Nijhoff, 2007), p. 720 (arguing that human rights and investment

ity or natural law demands that the "dignity" of corporate entities be accorded protection, especially when those companies are owned or controlled by persons who are not part of the polity of the State from which they are demanding protection and are therefore alien to the national social contract[101].

Investment treaties are generally seen as different from human rights conventions insofar as they are just a means to an end rather than is the case for human rights — which most see as an end in themselves. At the same time, however, the social goal of those who conclude investment treaties — securing sustainable economic development — is itself important precisely because it enables human beings to flourish. Indeed, at least States parties to the International Covenant on Economic, Social and Cultural Rights appear to have accepted the proposition that economic development, as well as the rights to shelter, food, or health that this enables, is itself a human right. Moreover, at least some might contend that respect for the right of private property, along with *pacta sunt servanda* (respect for sovereign promises made not only among nations but between a nation and an individual investor), are no less morally worthy rights than are other rights included in human rights treaties. Some might contend that investors (including those shareholders who are sometimes eligible claimants under BITs and FTAs) are no less "persons" worthy of protection. And those who adhere to the core elements of the so-called Washington Consensus model of development might add that encouraging respect for the rights of both for-

---

protections operate on "different planes" and are not amenable to balancing).

[101] See, e.g., *ibid*., p. 720 (noting that certain human rights bodies have found that corporations lack *locus standi*).

eign investors as well as a country's own nationals ought to be the goal of any society that seeks to uphold the rule of law as well as flourish economically [102].

But even if we put aside such fundamentally political questions, we need to recall that historically human rights and many of the rights contained in investment treaties have common roots. Some of the rights in BITs and FTAs — such as those requiring fair and equitable treatment, full protection and security and in any case treatment no less than that required by international law — stem from the ancient doctrine of denial of justice (recognized as far back as ancient Greece and embraced as part of the law of nations by Hugo Grotius and Emerich de Vattel) and the international minimum standard of treatment articulated early in the twentieth century in arbitral decisions such as *United States (L.F. Neer)* v. *United Mexican States* [103].

The *Neer* case is a good reminder that, at its outset, the investment regime began by recognizing rights owed to individuals and that the doctrines of State responsibility which remain at its core are the precursors to what became, after World War II, "human

---

[102] See generally B. Simmons *et al.*, "Introduction: The International Diffusion of Liberalism", 60 *International Organization* 781 (2006) (discussing the interdependence of liberal policies); M. O'Grady, "Free Markets, Free People", *Wall Street Journal* (9 January 2004) (reporting on an index of "Economic Freedom" purporting to rank 153 countries). For a more critical view of the "Washington Consensus" and of its recommendations for "good governance", see, e.g., D. Rodrik, "Growth Strategies", in P. Aghion and S. N. Durlauf (eds.), *Handbook of Economic Growth* (Amsterdam, Elsevier, 2005), available at <http://econ2.econ.iastate.edu/classes/econ502/tesfatsion/Growth Strategies.DRodrik.GrowthHB2005.pdf>, p. 968.

[103] *United States (L.F. Neer)* v. *United Mexican States*, General Claims Commission, 4 *Reports of International Arbitral Awards* 60 (15 October 1926).

rights". Neer was a US national who was murdered
in Mexico. His wife filed a claim arguing that the
Mexican Government had shown a lack of diligence in
investigating and prosecuting his murder. The United
States-Mexican Claims Commissioners rejected the
claim because in their view the facts did not demonstrate a violation of the international minimum standard of treatment to which aliens are entitled to under
customary international law. In their most famous passage, the Commissioners stated that

> "[t]he treatment of an alien, in order to constitute
> an international delinquency, should amount to an
> outrage, to bad faith, to willful neglect of duty, or to
> an insufficiency of governmental action so far short
> of international standards that every reasonable and
> impartial man would readily recognize its insuffi-
> ciency. Whether this insufficiency proceeds from
> deficient execution of an intelligent law or from the
> fact that the laws of the country do not empower the
> authorities to measure up to international standards
> is immaterial."[104]

For students of contemporary human rights law, the
facts in *Neer* evoke comparisons with the famous
Velásquez-Rodriguez decision rendered by the Inter-
American Court of Human Rights, which also concerned a Government's alleged lack of due diligence in
investigating murders committed in its territory[105].

---

[104] *Op. cit., supra* footnote 103.

[105] *Velásquez Rodríguez* v. *Honduras*, Inter-American
Court of Human Rights (Ser. C) No. 4 (29 July 1988).
Velásquez, a student who was last seen in the custody of
the Honduras police, disappeared and was presumed dead.
The Court found the Honduran Government responsible in
part because under Article 1 (1) of the Inter-American
Convention on Human Rights, Governments undertake
not only to "respect" but to "ensure" the rights of their

The "duty to protect" that Governments owe individuals subject to their jurisdiction under human rights treaties such as the International Covenant on Civil and Political Rights or the American Convention on Human Rights is accompanied by specific procedural rights that such treaties also recognize and which also appear in, for example, Article 6 of the ECHR[106]. In the modern age, the rights of aliens that were only weakly recognized in *Neer* have now expanded in depth and scope. These rights to fair process now extend to a State's nationals, under customary law as well as regional and global human rights conventions. Indeed, many scholars now subsume the old doctrine of State responsibility to aliens under the rubric of human (and not merely alien) rights. Even if one believes that contemporary human rights regimes and the investment regime should not be put on the same plane, the lawyers who are bringing investor-State claims are drawing parallels between the rights accorded in these respective regimes that are increasingly difficult to ignore. The drawing of connections between the rights recognized in human rights and investment treaties is rendered more likely by the rise of "forum" or "treaty" shopping among litigants. Some investor claimants have discovered that they can sometimes mount complaints before both the European Court of Human Rights and investor-State arbitral tribunals, for example[107].

---

nationals and Honduras had not prevented, investigated or punished those responsible.

[106] Article 6 (1) of the European Convention on Human Rights, *supra* footnote 99, provides, *inter alia*, that "[i]n the determination of his civil rights and obligations or of any criminal charge against him, everyone is entitled to a fair and public hearing within a reasonable time by an independent and impartial tribunal established by law".

[107] See, e.g., *Limited Liability Company AMTO* v. *Ukraine*, Award, Stockholm Chamber of Commerce

Indeed, the potential as well as actual trans-judicial communications across investor-State and human rights tribunals suggest to some observers the dawning of a new kind of "humanity's law"; that is, a common law among international adjudicators that is attentive to human rights concerns [108].

Of course, there remain considerable differences between regional systems for protecting human rights and the investment regime. Treaties such as the ECHR contain a far more comprehensive set of protections than those accorded under a typical BIT or FTA. Moreover, regional human rights regimes differ from the investment regime insofar as they extend their protections to all individuals subject to a State's jurisdiction and not merely to entrepreneurial aliens armed with capital. There are also differences between the remedies provided to individuals in regional human rights courts and those provided investors under BITs and FTAs. Table 1 suggests some of the relevant differences in procedures or remedies.

As Table 1 indicates, human rights courts are presided over by full-time judges, not arbitrators chosen by the parties for the purpose of hearing a single dispute as in investor-State arbitration. The hearings at the European

---

Arb. No. 080/2005 (26 March 2008), available at <http://ita.law.uvic.ca/documents/AmtoAward.pdf> (noting the parallel proceeding against the Ukraine in the European Court of Human Rights and finding that it did not necessitate a suspension of the arbitration). For a critical view of forum-shopping, see, e.g., A. Bjorklund, "Private Rights and Public International Law: Why Competition among International Courts Is Not Working", 59 *Hastings Law Journal* 241 (2007).

[108] R. Teitel and R. Howse, "Cross-Judging: Tribunalization in a Fragmented but Interconnected Global Order", 41 *New York University Journal of International Law and Politics* 959 (2009). This contention is revisited in Chapter V.

TABLE 1. COMPARING HUMAN RIGHTS
AND INVESTOR ADJUDICATION

Regional Human Rights Tribunals	*Investor State Arbitration*
— Full time judges	— *Ad hoc* arbitrators
— Hearings open to public	— Hearings normally not open to public
— Claims and decisions available to the public	— Claims and decisions not always available to public
— Exhaustion of local remedies required	— Exhaustion of local remedies typically not required
— Emphasis on preventing repeated violation	— Emphasis on remedial damages
— "Balanced" property right	— Property right not typically subject to explicit balancing

Court of Human Rights and the Inter-American Court are open to the public and the claims and decisions are likewise public. By contrast, the degree of transparency of investor-State arbitrations varies with the chosen forum. The rules by which such tribunals are governed usually determines the extent to which proceedings, claims, and awards are publicly available. Under some arbitral rules, such decisions are left solely for the parties to decide. While ICSID proceedings are sometimes public, those conducted under the UNCITRAL's rules or conducted under the auspices of Stockholm or the International Chamber of Commerce may not be. In some arbitral settings very little may be public. Moreover, it is believed that many investor-State disputes are, like many trade disputes under the WTO, settled quietly among the respective parties. As in such trade disputes, little is publically known about the terms of such settlements or whether these actually respect the terms of BITs and FTAs or merely consist of concessions extracted by the party with the greatest bargaining leverage in a particular case.

As Table 1 also indicates, unlike investors under many investment treaties, claimants before the European Court of Human Rights (as well as those before global bodies such as the Human Rights Committee) need to first exhaust local remedies[109]. This requirement accords with the original conception of the customary international minimum standard which only came into play if it could be shown that national remedies were either futile or exhausted[110]. Underlying rationales for the exhaustion requirement include the propositions that foreign nationals owe a duty to their host State to attempt to redress wrongs through domestic means, that local courts (and co-equal sovereigns) ought not to be presumed incapable of rendering justice, that attempts at local justice help ensure that the wrongful act (especially when committed by a private party) was a deliberate governmental act, and that the host State accused of an international wrong needs to be given a fair opportunity to correct its mistake[111]. As is evident from the "fork in the road" provision in the US Model BIT of 1987 previously discussed, these rationales were not regarded as determinative in the case of many BITs and FTAs. Fork in the road provisions are the very opposite of an exhaustion requirement. They encourage an investor to first seek international arbitration, rather than run the risk of biased local courts. Such jurisdictional provisions in invest-

---

[109] ECHR, *supra* footnote 99, Art. 35 (1).

[110] See, e.g., M. Shaw, *International Law* (Cambridge, Cambridge University Press, 2003), p. 730.

[111] See, e.g., G. Van Harten and M. Loughlin, "Investment Treaty Arbitration as a Species of Global Administrative Law", 17 *European Journal of International Law* 121 (2006), p. 130.

ment treaties, like provisions anticipating jurisdiction by consular courts run by investors' home countries in colonial era capitulation agreements, reflect the deep suspicion — often justified — of local courts that runs through the history of international law's treatment of foreign investment.

As Table 1 also indicates, the remedies accorded successful claimants in these two types of regimes may differ considerably, at least in practice. Even a successful claimant before the European Court of Human Rights or the Inter-American Court of Human Rights is not likely to be awarded the kinds of monetary damages that a successful investor is likely to get from an investor-State arbitral tribunal. As Gus Van Harten and Martin Loughlin have pointed out, while regional human rights courts have sometimes accorded damages, these awards have been limited by cautious doctrines that constrain the "just satisfaction" that claimants may receive[112]. Human rights courts sometimes decide that non-pecuniary relief may be adequate; they may even decide to limit such relief on the basis of a State's ability to pay[113]. Such rulings would be extremely rare in the investor-State context. The self-imposed limits on monetary damages that human rights bodies recognize

---

[112] Harten and Loughlin, *supra* footnote 111, p. 132.

[113] *Ibid*. These authors also indicate limits to monetary damages awarded under the *Francovich* doctrine in European Community law. *Ibid*., pp. 132-133. As Tomuschat indicates, Strasbourg's judges have not given the calculation of damages much attention, have tended to award amounts far less than that necessary to cover the actual loss suffered, and have even suggested that they grant compensation in "equity", based on rough estimates. C. Tomuschat, "The European Court of Human Rights and Investment Protection", in C. Binder *et al*. (eds.), *International Investment Law for the 21st Century : Essays in Honor of Christoph Schreuer* (New York, Oxford University Press, 2009), p. 654.

appear to stem from the residual idea that these regimes should emphasize the need to get a State to remove any measures that offend human rights and that mobilizing shame to secure this goal may be more important — and be more valuable to greater numbers of people who would be spared continual human rights violations — than securing full compensation for a single injured plaintiff[114]. The emphasis on mobilizing shame as opposed to monetary compensation is, of course, self-evident with respect to individual complaints mechanisms contained in UN human rights conventions, none of which anticipate the issuance of legally binding monetary awards[115]. International human rights efforts' emphasis on preventing future abuses by the State suggests that these regimes may have, at least to this extent, more in common with the WTO regime — which also focuses on preventing protectionist legislation and not on providing recompense to those harmed by past protectionism[116]. Investor-State dispute settle-

---

[114] For a scholarly attempt to change these conceptions and apply tort liability in the context of human rights injuries at least under the Alien Tort Claims Act as applied by US courts, see G. P. Fletcher, *Tort Liability for Human Rights Abuses* (Portland, Oregon, Hart Publishing, 2008).

[115] See generally H. J. Steiner and P. Alston, *International Human Rights in Context : Law, Politics, Morals* (Oxford, Oxford University Press, 2nd ed., 2000), pp. 592-704 (canvassing UN human rights mechanisms).

[116] This is one reason why venues like the European Court of Human Rights are not seen as promising alternatives to investor-State arbitration under BITs. See, e.g., Tomuschat, *supra* footnote 113, p. 636. Other reasons include the fact that some human rights mechanisms are not available to corporate bodies, require the exhaustion of local remedies, or may fail to include comparable substantive guarantees as those under investment treaties. It is also the case that even the judgments of the European Court of Human Rights are not directly enforceable and

ment, by contrast, is all about compensating the investor for past harm.

Finally, as Table 1 suggests, investors may be able to succeed before investor-State tribunals where individuals cannot in human rights courts due to underlying differences in the ways that some of the relevant substantive rights are cast under the respective treaties. Put more bluntly: some of the rights accorded investors in some investment treaties are broader or subject to fewer exceptions or caveats than are some human rights recognized in regional human rights treaties. Consider once again, for example, Article 1 from Protocol 1 of the ECHR quoted above.

The ECHR's right to property is limited since it cannot

> "impair the right of a State to enforce such laws as it deems necessary to control the use of property in accordance with the general interest or to secure the payment of taxes or other contributions or penalties" [117].

Article III of the US Model BIT cited above, which provides investors with an assurance of prompt, adequate and effective compensation, contains no comparable limitation. Indeed, as the text of Article III makes clear, the fact that a State has a "public purpose" for taking property does not excuse payment of prompt, adequate and effective compensation [118]. Moreover,

---

may be subject to considerable delays in execution. Tomuschat, *supra* footnote 113, p. 655.

[117] ECHR, *supra* footnote 99, Art. 1.

[118] Indeed, as has been found by some arbitral tribunals, the absence of such a public purpose or the fact that the expropriation of an alien was discriminatory may be a reason to impose greater liability on a host State. It also may be a factor in justifying an award for lost profits. See generally P. M. Norton, "A Law of the Future or a

the only general exception contained in that BIT, in
Article X [119], appears to be a great deal more limited in
scope that the general licence to regulate in the "general interest" suggested by Article 1, Protocol 1 of the
EHCR. Whether investment treaties with limited
exceptions of this kind contain an implicit limit on the
residual power of States to regulate in the public interest remains a contested question among investor-State
arbitrators and scholars [120]. Irrespective of whether that
is the case, what is clear is that the most clearly articulated right to property contained in investment treaties
— namely the rights to compensation upon expropriation — recognizes a right to full compensation without
the limits suggested by the ECHR, at least with respect
to direct takings of property [121]. The vast majority of
BITs, which apparently do not contain even the limited
exceptions reflected in Article X of the US Model of

Law of the Past? Modern Tribunals and the International
Law of Expropriation", 85 *American Journal of Interna-
tional Law* 474 (1991) (discussing cases from the Iran-
United States Claims Tribunal).

[119] The US Model BIT of 1987 provides:

"1. This Treaty shall not preclude the application by
either Party of measures *necessary for the maintenance
of public order*, the fulfillment of its obligations with
respect to the maintenance or restoration of international peace or security, *or the protection of its own
essential security interests.*" 1987 US Model BIT, *supra*
footnote 48, Art. X (emphasis added).

[120] For further discussion of this question see *infra*,
Chaps. IV, V.

[121] But see US Department of State and US Trade
Representative, "2004 US Model BIT", available at
<http://www.state.gov/documents/organization/117601.
pdf>, Annex B, para. 4 *(b)* (adopting a balancing test for
determining whether an "indirect" taking or expropriation
has occurred, as when a State does not take title to alien
property but engages in a regulatory taking).

1987[122], may limit States' regulatory discretion and provide them with fewer defences from liability[123].

What this means is that while the ECHR anticipates, with respect to property as well as most of the other rights in that treaty, a proportionality analysis that seeks to "balance" the individual rights protected with the rights of sovereigns to regulate in the general public interest[124], no such general balancing is evident on the face of the US Model BIT that we have been examining — or in most BITs and FTAs. Investment treaties typically do not explicitly "balance" the substantive rights accorded foreign investors in the way that Article 1 of Protocol 1 does[125]. (Nor do most investment treaties currently in existence contain a residual list of exceptions designed to protect States' regulatory

---

[122] According to one survey, perhaps as many as nine out of ten BITs lack a "measures not precluded" clause comparable to Article X of the US Model of 1987. W. W. Burke-White and A. von Staden, "Investment Protection in Extraordinary Times: The Interpretation and Application of Non-Precluded Measures Provisions in Bilateral Investment Treaties", 48 *Virginia Journal of International Law* 307 (2008), p. 313 (noting that of 2000 BITs surveyed, only 200 had measures not precluded clauses).

[123] For a general critique of investment treaties on the grounds that they unduly interfere with the sovereign power to regulate, see, e.g., Schneiderman, *supra* footnote 30. For a case suggesting that investment treaties that do not contain explicit derogation clauses (such as Article X of the 2004 US Model) may restrict States' ability to rely on even customary defences such as necessity, see *BG Group PLC* v. *Argentina*, Award, UNCITRAL Arbitration Rules (24 December 2007), para. 409 (considering but not deciding that proposition).

[124] ECHR, *supra* footnote 99, Protocol 1, Art. 1; see also T. Allen, "Compensation for Property under the European Convention on Human Rights", 28 *Michigan Journal of International Law* 287 (2007), p. 288.

[125] Compare ECHR, *supra* footnote 99, Protocol 1, Art. 1, with 1987 US Model BIT, *supra* footnote 48.

discretion comparable to Article XX of the GATT[126].)
The European Court of Human Rights' attempts to balance the competing rights of individuals, sovereigns
and, where applicable, the competing rights of other individuals, are most readily seen in that court's application of a so-called "margin of appreciation"[127]. While
traces of proportionality balancing may now be emerging in certain arbitral interpretations of some investment treaties, it is not at all clear that the right to property under the ECHR and under investment treaties that
have wording comparable to that in the US Model of
1987 will be subject to comparable interpretations[128].

As this suggests, despite their common roots, the
rights contained in investment and human rights
regimes may diverge over time. While the former are
fewer in number, the property rights reflected in investment treaties may receive the most reliable international protection. To put it more forcefully and controversially : investors' rights to legitimate expectations in
their property may be the most effectively protected
"human" right that there is, at least at the global level[129].

---

[126] For an exception, see Foreign Affairs and International Trade Canada, "Foreign Investment Promotion
and Protection Agreement Model" (2003), available at
<http://ita.law.uvic.ca/documents/Canadian2004-FIPA-
model-en.pdf> (hereinafter "Canada Model BIT"), Art. 10.

[127] For a classic description of the "margin of apprecia-
tion" and its origins, see, e.g., R. St. J. Macdonald, "The
Margin of Appreciation", in R. St. J. Macdonald (ed.), *The
European System for the Protection of Human Rights* (The
Netherlands, Kluwer, 1993), p. 83.

[128] But see A. Stone Sweet, "Investor-State Arbitration :
Proportionality's New Frontier", 4 *Law & Ethics of Human
Rights* 47 (2010) (suggesting such comparisons).

[129] See also Braun, *supra* footnote 12, p. 5 (noting that
since no comparable individualized remedy is anticipated
under consular law, investors under BITs enjoy a benefit
that is "likely even to exceed current human rights law and
consular law").

Not surprisingly, the international investment regime has prompted considerable scholarly controversy and growing political backlash[130].

F. Contemporary Critiques of the Investment Regime

Contemporary critiques of the investment regime parallel those faced by other international legal regimes or international organizations. Like other institutionalized processes designed to implement the international rule of law, the investment regime's legitimacy deficits can be characterized as vertical, horizontal, ideological and legal[131].

(1) Vertical critiques

As have those of the WTO and international financial institutions such as the IMF, the investment regime's "democratic" credentials have come under fire[132]. The charge is that this regime, like a number of others, constitutes an illegitimate top-down form of regulation on States; that there is, in short, a vertical

---

[130] See generally M. Waibel *et al.* (eds.), *The Backlash against Investment Arbitration: Perceptions and Reality* (The Netherlands, Kluwer Law International, 2010).

[131] See, e.g., J. E. Alvarez, *International Organizations as Law-Makers* (New York, Oxford University Press, 2005), pp. 630-645 (discussing "horizontal", "vertical", and "ideological" critiques of international organizations). See also W. Grieder, *One World, Ready or Not* (New York, Touchstone, 1997); L. Gruber, *Ruling the World* (Princeton, Princeton University Press, 2000); S. Marks, "Big Brother is Bleeping Us — With the Message that Ideology Doesn't Matter", 12 *European Journal of International Law* 109 (2001).

[132] See, e.g., Clarkson, *supra* footnote 16, p. 86. For consideration of general "democratic" critiques of international law and a response, see A. Chander, "Globalization and Distrust", 114 *Yale Law Journal* 1193 (2005).

disconnect between the supranational law that it produces and that created by a country's elected representatives or enforced by local court. Alleged "vertical" deficits of the investment regime are also driven by perceptions that in this instance, more than is the case with other forms of international governance, a considerable part of delegated international "law-making" is occurring in the course of deciding investor-State disputes and the establishment of arbitral "case-law" that other investor-State arbitrations attempt to follow. While comparable critiques have been levied against other international adjudicators, especially those in the WTO, the high profile public issues with which many investor-State arbitrators contend as well as the fact that such disputes are brought by private parties, lend this critique considerable salience. Investor-State arbitral decisions are more prone to criticism than most[133]. Critics argue that it is not democratically legitimate to assign cases that "second-guess" politically sensitive actions taken by sovereigns — that contest the Argentine government's decisions to respond to a serious economic or political crisis, for example — to three arbitrators, only one of which is appointed by the host State whose actions are challenged[134]. Others are offended precisely by the fact that unique rights to internationalize a claim and impose supranational

---

[133] See generally B. Choudhury, "Recapturing Public Power: Is Investment Arbitration's Engagement of the Public Interest Contributing to the Democratic Deficit?", 41 *Vanderbilt Journal of Transnational Law* 775 (2008); C. N. Brower, "NAFTA's Investment Chapter: Dynamic Laboratory, Failed Experiments, and Lessons for the FTAA", 97 *Proceedings of the Annual Meeting of the American Society of International Law* 251 (2003) (surveying concerns raised by investor-State arbitration).

[134] See, e.g., G. Van Harten, *Investment Treaty Arbitration and Public Law* (Oxford, Oxford University Press, 2007).

scrutiny on State laws are accorded to those who are not even entitled to be considered part of the democratic polity of that State[135]. "Vertical" concerns are exacerbated to the extent particular BITs and FTAs forgo the favoured tool for according local deference, namely the requirement to exhaust local remedies.

The substantive decisions issued by investor-State arbitrations, and not merely their procedures, sometimes draw fire for being insufficiently deferential to legitimate (and vitally necessary) forms of public regulation in a democracy[136] or for intruding on fundamental questions of "sovereignty" or ostensibly sacrosanct matters relating to "domestic jurisdiction"[137]. The perceived democracy deficits are aggravated to the extent many investment treaties are not terminable at will or

---

[135] See, e.g., Alvarez and Khamsi, *supra* footnote 77 (discussing certain cases against Argentina).

[136] Recent investor-State cases have involved claims arising from States' actions in the field of public health and have involved challenges to waste management, land regulation, urban sprawl, air pollution, transboundary movement of hazardous waste, and hazardous waste sites. See, e.g., Orellana, *supra* footnote 100, p. 672.

[137] Indeed, it is probable that some state judges in the United States, who have expressed surprise that their rulings can now be questioned in the course of NAFTA investor-State dispute settlement, would sympathize with the positions taken by the Argentine Government in these cases, and especially its contention that only Argentine courts ought to consider such critical questions of public policy. See, e.g., H. P. Monaghan, "Article III and Supranational Judicial Review", 107 *Columbia Law Review* 833 (2007), p. 833 (citing the "surprise" of the Chief Justice of the Massachusetts Supreme Court that its judgments were subject to "review" under NAFTA investor-State dispute settlement). The controversy over the Argentina cases has even played a role in debates over the wisdom of free trade agreements on the Presidential campaign trail in the United States. See, e.g., A. Beattie, "Concern Grows over Global Trade Regulation", *Financial Times* (12 March 2008).

upon 12 months' notice but instead provide, as does the
US Model addressed here, that States parties cannot
terminate their treaty for 10 years and that even if this
is done, existing investors remain protected for an
additional period of 10 years thereafter[138].

For some the "democratic" problem originates not
with the arbitrators but with the treaties themselves.
There is a widespread perception that some of the
guarantees contained in BITs and FTAs — from the
right to fair and equitable treatment to umbrella clauses
— operate as a new kind of stabilization clause at the
international level that, like those controversial provisions endemic to imbalanced investment contracts, dis-
empower Governments from modifying their laws,
even in reaction to new threats to the public welfare[139].
Of course, the investment regime has always anticipated the potential for conflict between BITs and
national law. But the perception of a "vertical" disconnect between the requirements of investment treaties
and those imposed by national law is heightened when
investment rules challenge the highest ranking national
rules, namely those in a national constitution. Such
clashes elevate the "public" nature of investor-State
disputes. Thus, NGOs from the United States to the
Philippines have brought constitutional challenges in
national courts challenging some of the rights accorded
to foreign investors in BITs or at least demanding disclosure of relevant negotiating documents[140]. Even

---

[138] See, e.g., 1987 US Model BIT, *supra* footnote 48,
Art. XIII.
[139] See, e.g., H. Mann, *International Investment
Agreements, Business and Human Rights : Key Issues and
Opportunities* (International Institute for Sustainable
Development, 2008), available at <http://www.iisd.org/
pdf/2008/iia_business_human_rights.pdf>, pp. 17-18.
[140] See, e.g., D. Vis-Dunbar, "NGOs Claim the Philippine-Japan Free Trade Agreement Is Unconstitutional",

more controversial is the proposition, advanced by both defenders and critics of the investment regime, that its rules are intended to be a competing source of "constitutional" or higher level norms. Thus, David Schneiderman, a Canadian scholar, contends that the investment regime

> "freezes existing distributions of wealth and privileges 'status quo neutrality'. It does not merely commit citizens to predetermined institutions and rules through which political objectives are realized but also institutionalizes a legal incapacity to act in a variety of economic matters. It is not an enabling precommitment strategy; rather, it is largely a disenabling one. At bottom, the investment rules regime represents a form of constitutional precommitment binding across generations that unreasonably constrains the capacity for self-government."[141]

Beyond perceived "vertical" disconnects between what States are required to do for foreign investors under BITs and FTAs and what democratic polities expect by way of regulation from their legislatures, administrative agencies, and national courts, lie tensions between the different kinds of international obligations owed by States. Some arbitral disputes suggest the potential for conflicts between the rights accorded to foreign investors under investment treaties and those given to all of a nation's citizens under instruments

---

Investment Treaty News (June 2009); Schneiderman, *supra* footnote 30, pp. 135-157 (describing conflicts between the rights protected by BITs and property rights and the black empowerment policies pursued by South Africa as permitted under its constitution), pp. 164-191 (describing likely conflicts between the privatization rules in Colombia's constitution and some BITs).

[141] Schneiderman, *supra* footnote 30, p. 37. See also *infra*, Chap. V.

such as the Covenant on Economic, Social and Cultural Rights. Host States facing claims by privatized public utilities, for example, have tried to justify their actions by arguing that they intended to protect their citizens' right to water[142]. Human rights and environmental NGOs and some academics argue that investment treaty obligations raise serious public policy questions that were not addressed or scarcely mentioned during the ratification processes for those treaties, perhaps because the actual constraints imposed by investment treaties have only become clear over time, as investors have filed their claims. Some suggest that what these treaties are coming to require of Governments may even prove destabilizing for fragile democracies insofar as they further empower already powerful multinational corporations while undermining these Governments' underfunded efforts to respond to the legitimate demands of their polities.

The backlash in some quarters against investment treaties or investor-State arbitration is such that there is now considerable sympathy, including among many members of the US Congress, for the Calvo-inspired notion that foreign investors should get no more favourable treatment than that accorded to national enterprises or that if "special rights" are accorded to foreign TNCs, comparable international remedies should also be available to others who may be injured by the TNCs' operations[143]. The range of concerns,

---

[142] See, e.g., U. Kriebaum, "Privatizing Human Rights — The Interface between International Investment Protection and Human Rights", 3 *Transnational Dispute Management* 165 (2006).

[143] See, e.g., Mann, *supra* footnote 139; Van Harten, *supra* footnote 134, p. 142; see generally J. E. Alvarez, "Critical Theory and the North American Free Trade Agreement's Chapter Eleven", 28 *University of Miami Inter-American Law Review* 303 (1997); J. E. Alvarez,

even within the context of a developed country that has a relatively small portion of its economy controlled by foreign investors, is suggested by the testimony of a prominent academic testifying before the US Congress in May of 2009. According to Robert Stumberg, US policy-makers ought to be worried about:

1. Forum shopping by foreign investors. Stumberg points out the United States has a BIT with Panama and that Panama is seeking to become the legal domicile of companies because it is a tax haven. He suggests that companies may use their Panamanian operations to challenge domestic regulations in the United States [144].

2. Being sued by foreign investors. Stumberg points out that the United States is now a prominent capital

---

"Foreword: The Ripples of NAFTA", in T. Weiler (ed.), *NAFTA Investment Law and Arbitration: Past Issues, Current Practice, Future Prospects* (Ardsley Park, Transnational Publishers, 2004), p. xxi. For a recent example of such concerns, see "Statement of Thea M. Lee, Policy Director and Chief International Economist, AFL-CIO", in US House of Representatives, Committee on Ways and Means, Subcommittee on Trade, "Hearing on Investment Protections in US Trade and Investment Agreements", Serial No. 111-20 (14 May 2009), available at <http://www.gpo.gov/fdsys/pkg/CHRG-111hhrg11153473/pdf/CHRG-111 hhrg11153473.pdf> (hereinafter "Investment Protections Hearing"), p. 7 (noting that investment agreements are "imbalanced" insofar as they (1) "significantly enhance the rights of investors vis-à-vis governments, but they fail to establish commensurate responsibilities for investors . . ." and (2) because the substantive rights and procedural advantages given to foreign investors "raises the possibility that investment tribunals can be used to circumvent the democratic process and to achieve deregulatory outcomes in a secretive and inaccessible forum").

[144] "Statement of Robert K. Stumberg, Professor of Law and Director of the Harrison Institute for Public Law, Georgetown University Law Center", in Investment Protections Hearing, *supra* footnote 143, p. 37.

importer and needs to worry about its defensive posture in investor-State disputes. Specifically, Stumberg notes that China's current ownership of US investments grew by 62 per cent over the five years preceding the current recession and that it could be looking for a stake in companies like Wal-Mart, Target or Sears. He asks "is it wise to provide investor arbitration to Chinese-owned firms that are significant actors in the U.S. economy"?[145]

3. Threats by foreign investors to local autonomy, including efforts by States to protect the rights of indigenous peoples. Stumberg highlights the example of a current NAFTA case, *Glamis Gold*, involving a challenge by a Canadian company to California legislation blocking Glamis's plans to engage in open-pit mining next to areas where the Quechen Indians practise their religion and venerate their ancestors[146].

4. Threats that the investment regime poses to the US Government's effort to deal with the current global economic crisis. Stumberg suggests that the US commitments to foreign investors may threaten its purchases of troubled assets and the bailouts of some troubled industries, since such US Government efforts tend to be restricted to US banks and firms and may there-

---

[145] Stumberg, *supra* footnote 144, p. 37.

[146] *Ibid.*, pp. 37-38. But note that the United States won the *Glamis* claim. *Glamis Gold Ltd.* v. *United States*, Award, UNCITRAL Arbitration Rules (8 June 2009), available at <http://www.state.gov/documents/organization/125798.pdf>. For related concerns regarding potential conflicts between South Africa's BITs and its Black Economic Empowerment (BEE) policies, see L. E. Peterson, "South Africa's Bilateral Investment Treaties: Implications for Development and Human Rights", Dialogue on Globalization, Occasional Papers Series, No. 26 (2006), available at <http://library.fes.de/pdf-files/iez/global/04137-20080708.pdf>.

fore be contested as violations of FET or national treatment.[147]

Stumberg's specific concerns appear to be driven by a more general one: namely that investor-State arbitration constitutes an undemocratic delegation of authority to "unaccountable" bodies and trumps the freedom of action of national law-making authorities[148]. For such critics, BITs and FTAs essentially "outsource" the application and interpretation of State constitutional law[149]. Certain investor-State arbitral outcomes are perceived as "affronts to sovereignty" that may even threaten the right of States to self-preservation[150]. For the regime's critics, investment treaties threaten Governments' continuing ability to protect their own citizens' rights to equality, life, liberty and security of the person[151]; they undermine, and do not promote, the rule of

---

[147] Stumberg, *supra* footnote 144, p. 39 (citing *Saluka Investment BV* v. *Czech Republic*, Partial Award, UNCITRAL Arbitration Rules (17 March 2006)). See also A. van Aaken and J. Kurtz, "The Global Financial Crisis: Will State Emergency Measures Trigger International Investment Disputes?", *Columbia FDI Perspectives*, No. 3 (2009), available at <http://www.vcc.columbia.edu/content/global-financial-crisis-will-state-emergency-measures-trigger-international-investment-dispu>.

[148] See, e.g., M. Bottari and L. Wallach, *NAFTA's Threat to Sovereignty and Democracy: The Record of NAFTA Chapter 11 Investor-State Cases 1994-2005* (Public Citizen, 2005), available at <http://www.citizen.org/documents/Chapter%2011%20Report%20Final.pdf>; see also J. Atik, "Repenser NAFTA Chapter 11: A Catalogue of Legitimacy Critiques", 3 *Asper Review of International Business and Trade Law* 215 (2003), pp. 218-220.

[149] See, e.g., Stumberg, *supra* footnote 144, p. 37.

[150] G. Bottini, "Protection of Essential Interests in the BIT Era", in T. J. Grierson Weiler (ed.), *Investment Treaty Arbitration and Public Law* (Huntington, New York, Juris Publishing, 2008), p. 145.

[151] See, e.g., C. Forcese, "Does the Sky Fall? NAFTA Chapter 11 Dispute Settlement and Democratic Account-

law and democratic governance because they create
legal enclaves that *discourage* generalized rule of law
reforms in developing countries and "retard the development of certain regulatory initiatives" that are the
hallmarks of the democratic social welfare state [152].

(2) Horizontal critiques

Investment treaties are seen by some critics, particularly those based in developing countries, as asymmetrical bargains struck along sadly familiar and predictable North/South lines [153]. The investment regime,

---

ability", 14 *Michigan State Journal of International Law*
315 (2006), pp. 321-322 (citing applicants in *Council of
Canadians* v. *Canada*, Ontario Superior Court of Justice,
Court File No. 01-CV-208141 (8 July 2005), para. 1); see
also Office of the High Commissioner of Human Rights,
Human Rights, Trade and Investment, UN doc. E/CN.4/
Sub.2/2003/9 (2003), p. 17 (making statements to the same
effect).

[152] A. Newcombe, "Sustainable Development and
Investment Treaty Law", 8 *Journal of World Investment &
Trade* 357 (2007), p. 394; see also T. Ginsburg, "Inter-
national Substitutes for Domestic Institutions: Bilateral
Investment Treaties and Governance", 25 *International
Review of Law and Economics* 107 (2005) (arguing that
the spread of investment agreements permitting powerful
players to bypass national courts may help to explain the
intractability of LDCs' efforts to improve such courts);
S. Krislov, "Do Free Markets Create Free Societies?", 33
*Syracuse Journal of International Law and Comparative
Politics* 155 (2005) (expressing scepticism about the
alleged connection between markets and freedom). For a
response, see S. D. Franck, "Foreign Direct Investment,
Investment Treaty Arbitration, and the Rule of Law", 19
*Pacific McGeorge Global Business and Development Law
Journal* 337 (2007), pp. 366-372 (contending that treaty
arbitration and national courts enjoy a positive symbiotic
relationship).

[153] Even before the onslaught of investor claims a number of commentators had suggested that less wealthy coun-

on this view, violates the principle of sovereign equality. Although the regime was premised on putting all States on a "level playing field" — at least as compared to the bad old days of gunboat diplomacy — it falls well short of that goal.

The critique along "horizontal" lines borrows a page from old UN debates over the New International Economic Order ("NIEO"). It is no accident, on this view, that BITs originated with capital exporters such as Germany. For some, investment agreements have not overcome their biased origins and they continue to reward principally the capital exporting States whose investors are the beneficiaries. Capital importing States, typically in the Global South, on the other hand, are promised untenable economic rewards in the future and effectively have had no choice but to yield to the power and wealth disparities that such treaties reflect and perpetuate. According to a leading account of how BITs proliferated, developing countries concluded BITs because they were caught in a prisoner's dilemma from which they could not individually defect; they concluded treaties that "hurt them" because they were individually pressured to do so, in some cases because they were effectively under the barrel of an IMF gun to

---

tries needful of foreign capital had been forced, *individually*, to consent to treaties that harm or impoverish them as a group or that make it more difficult for them to fulfil other international commitments (as under the International Covenant on Economic, Social and Cultural Rights). See, e.g., Guzman, *supra* footnote 91. More radical critics have suggested that these agreements are merely a more diplomatic version of colonial-era capitulation treaties in which the metropole forced non-Western countries to "civilize" along Western models. See generally D. P. Fidler, "The Return of the Standard of Civilization", 2 *Chicago Journal of International Law* 137 (2001); W. Greider, *One World, Ready or Not: The Manic Logic of Global Capitalism* (New York, Simon and Schuster, 1997).

demonstrate their commitment to the free market principles that such institutions demanded in exchange for
their financial assistance. The most provocative critiques assert that investment treaties are merely contemporary versions of the capitulation agreements once
imposed by colonial rulers against the periphery. Like
those products of imperialism BITs also seek to impose
rules of "civilization" on the ostensibly "uncivilized".
Like capitulation agreements they displace host States'
"uncivilized" courts. Instead of relying on adjudication
of aliens' rights by imperial consular officers, modern
investment treaties rely on the modern equivalent:
commercial arbitrators doing the bidding of empire
under the auspices of the World Bank's ICSID[154]. On
this view, investor-State arbitration has merely replaced
gunboat diplomacy with "gunboat-arbitration"[155]. Accordingly, some deride investor-State arbitral tribunals as
"businessmen's' courts"[156] that apply "privilege law for
foreigners"[157]. Only slightly less provocative are those

---

[154] See, e.g., H. Mann, "International Investment
Agreements: Building the New Colonialism?", 97 *Proceed-
ings of the Annual Meeting of the American Society of
International Law* 247 (2003). For a description of colo-
nial era capitulations, see W. E. Grigsby, "The Mixed
Courts of Egypt", 12 *Law Quarterly Review* 252 (1896);
A. M. Latter, "The Government of the Foreigners in
China", 19 *Law Quarterly Review* 316 (1903).

[155] See, e.g., S. Montt, "What International Investment
Law and Latin America Can and Should Demand from
Each Other: Updating the Bello/Calvo Doctrine in the BIT
Generation", 3 *Res Publica Argentina* 75 (2007), available
at <http://www.iilj.org/GAL/documents/SantiagoMontt.GAL.
pdf>, p. 80.

[156] Van Harten, *supra* footnote 134, p. 153 (title of his
Chapter 7).

[157] Montt, *supra* footnote 155, p. 80; see also M. Sornarajah, "The Neo-Liberal Agenda in Investment", in
W. Shah *et al.* (eds.), *Redefining Sovereignty in International Economic Law* (Portland, Oregon, Hart Publish-

who imply that BITs are essentially contracts of adhesion that ought to be interpreted, where possible, against the interests of their rich country drafters[158].

Others worry not only that investor-State arbitrations are skewed in favour of claimants but that they may be skewed in favour of more powerful Governments. Such suspicions fuel speculations about why the United States, the third leading investor-State defendant in investor-State disputes, has, to date, managed not to lose a single claim against it[159]. Debates about

---

ing, 2008), p. 203 (arguing that investor-State arbitrations enable arbitrators to "outdo each other in their ability to recognize new expansionary doctrines favouring neoliberal trends"); *ibid.*, pp. 205, 219 (arguing that some arbitrations are motivated to rule in favour of investors to sustain the business of investor-State arbitration); *ibid.*, p. 208 (suggesting that investor-State arbitrations have a "hidden agenda" to advance the cause of one of the parties); *ibid.*, p. 214 (contending that investor-State tribunals "clearly evinced a desire to ensure that the regulatory space for the host state was curtailed as much as possible"). For responses to many of these critiques, see generally T. W. Wälde, "The Specific Nature of Investment Arbitration", in *New Aspects of International Investment Law*, *supra* footnote 100.

[158] For one response to this suggestion, see Alvarez and Khamsi, *supra* footnote 77, pp. 83-86.

[159] The most prominent source of speculation is the *Loewen* case. In that instance, the US Government's appointed arbitrator, Abner Mikva, reported that some US officials noted that if the United States were to lose that case, "we could lose the NAFTA". Mikva remarked that if that had been intended to put pressure on him, "then that does it". Stumberg, *supra* footnote 144, p. 40 (quoting remarks of Judge Mikva at a Pace University School of Law Symposium on 7 December 2004). Others contend that investor-State arbitrators are predisposed in favour of developed States. Consider the contention by a leading investment scholar, expert witness and arbitrator, Thomas Wälde that "[t]he higher the credibility of a domestic court system, the greater the readiness to accept its determina-

whether win/loss records in investor-State arbitrations
fall along North/South lines underlie concerns over
whether investor-State arbitration has truly managed to
"level the playing field" between States or instead
subtly violates the "equality of arms" principle that is
foundational to any legitimate scheme of international
adjudication. Those who express such concerns may
support reforms that are further addressed in Chapter V, including establishment of an advisory facility
that would assist poorer respondent States in defending investor-State claims[160].

Other allegations of alleged "horizontal" inequities
among States are far more finely grained. Thus, some

---

tion on municipal law". T. W. Wälde, "Denial of Justice: A
Review Comment on Jan Paulsson, Denial of Justice in
International Law", 21 *ICSID Review* 449 (2006), p. 460.
While this may be an innocuous comment, consider the
implications of such a deferential burden of proof when, as
is sometimes the case, the result in an investor-State dispute turns precisely on whether the investor has been
treated in accord with preexisting local law.

[160] See, e.g., UNCTAD Work Programme on International Investment Agreements, Policies and Capacity-
building Branch, Division on Investment and Enterprise,
"Consultations Report on the Feasibility of an Advisory
Facility on International Investment Law and Investor-
State Disputes for Latin American Countries", non-paper
(2009) (copy on file with author). Susan Franck's empirical work analysing the results of known investor-State
cases casts doubt on the idea that LDCs are systematically
disadvantaged. S. D. Franck, "Empirically Evaluating
Claims about Investment Treaty Arbitration", 86 *North
Carolina Law Review* 1 (2008), pp. 26-44. However, her
own work also provides some examples of the types of
disadvantages some LDCs face in responding effectively
to investor claims. See, e.g., S. D. Franck, "The Nature
and Enforcement of Investor Rights under Investment
Treaties: Do Investment Treaties Have a Bright Future?",
12 *University of California Davis Journal of International
Law & Policy* 52 (2005), p. 92.

complain that the application of substantive investor protections such as national treatment may subtly disadvantage developing countries, as where a requirement demanding that host States justify an arguably discriminatory measure anticipates a level of scientific documentation and expertise that can only be fairly expected of richer States having a concentration of scientific centres and sufficient funding[161].

(3) Ideological

Closely allied with the above critiques but conceptually distinct are ideological critiques of the investment regime that resemble those directed at other international institutions, and especially at the WTO or the IMF. On this view, the investment regime — both its substance and its procedures for interpretation and enforcement — are structurally biased in favour of the ideology of the free market and privatization, namely many of the elements associated with the "Washington Consensus". Like other adherents to that Consensus, the investment regime empowers private non-State actors to pursue an ideologically driven agenda that is blind to other views of what is in the public interest[162]. As another manifestation of the flawed "Washington Consensus model" of governance[163], BITs and FTAs appear to some as legalized manifestations of the "Golden Straitjacket" that Thomas Friedman, apparently without irony, has endorsed[164]. Although many

---

[161] See, e.g., Orellana, *supra* footnote 100, p. 684 (citing GATT cases for the concern).

[162] See, e.g., Schneiderman, *supra* footnote 30.

[163] See generally D. Kalderimis, "IMF Conditionality as Investment Regulation: A Theoretical Analysis", 13 *Social & Legal Studies* 104 (2004).

[164] See T. Friedman, *The Lexus and the Olive Tree* (New York, Anchor Publishing, 1st ed., 2000), Chap. 6.

associate ideological concerns with traditional North/
South divides, the CIEL Letter noted above — from a
northern based NGO — suggests that such ideological
concerns also extend to elements of civil society located
within developed countries. Thus, CIEL has com-
plained, for example, that the United States-Morocco
FTA protects investors at the expense of environmental
concerns, without imposing "minimum standards of
corporate conduct on investors acting abroad"[165].

(4) Rule of law critiques

As might be expected, lawyers emphasize the
alleged flaws of the investment regime from a rule of
law perspective. For academics like Gus Van Harten,
international arbitration, long used to resolve purely
private commercial disputes (that is breaches of contract between two private parties), is a fundamentally
inapposite mechanism for deciding weighty issues of
public policy[166]. Contested and political loaded issues,
such as whether an environmental regulation constitutes a compensable taking of property, need to be
resolved, in his view, before constitutionally accountable national courts and cannot be settled legitimately
through unpredictable, haphazard and potentially
inconsistent decisions issued by transnational and *ad
hoc* arbitrators drawn only from limited specialties
within international law. Moreover, as Van Harten
points out, such adjudicators are given the limited
jurisdiction of examining such claims only on the basis
of whether these violate treaties designed to protect

---

[165] CIEL Letter, *supra* footnote 25.
[166] See, e.g., Van Harten, *supra* footnote 134, *passim*;
see generally S. Sassen, "De-Nationalized State Agendas
and Privatized Norm-Making", in K. Ladeur (ed.), *Public
Governance in the Age of Globalization* (Burlington,
Vermont, Ashgate Publishing, 2004).

alien investors' property interests. Such questions ought to be decided, he argues, by national judges capable of examining a wider spectrum of concerns, or at least a permanent body of international judges whose tenure in office, as well as independence from the litigants is more likely to produce a politically acceptable result[167].

Another rule of law concern focuses on the potential for forum-shopping by foreign investors, whose options may include shopping around for the best available investment treaty (as is possible by incorporating elsewhere) or for the best available treatment (as is possible by resorting to MFN guarantees in investment treaties). In addition, the proliferation of specialized international dispute settlers, as well as national courts, may enable foreign investors to have multiple bites at the apple, to the detriment of harassed and overworked government lawyers. For critics, the potential for forum and BIT shopping encourages strategic behaviour by TNCs without producing any of the anticipated benefits to host States[168]. Instead, investor-State dispute settlement might be (mis)used to address trade issues that States assumed would be handled by the WTO's inter-state dispute settlement mechanism,

---

[167] See, e.g., Van Harten, *supra* footnote 134, pp. 175-184.

[168] See, e.g., A. J. Bjorklund, *supra* footnote 107. Bjorklund addresses, for example, the *Lauder* cases arising from the same set of facts but brought by different claimants against the Czech Republic and other respondents in three different arbitral tribunals (under two different BITs and in the International Chamber of Commerce), along with proceedings in municipal court in the Czech Republic. *Ibid.*, pp. 286-290. According to Bjorklund, the different results in these cases "offer an example of a duplication trifecta — the perception of unfairness, potential duplicate relief, and inconsistent decisions." *Ibid.*, p. 286.

for example [169]. There is also concern that some arbitrators are giving unanticipated scope to MFN clauses of investment treaties and have, for instance, permitted investors to insist on better procedural protections found in other BITs. Such interpretations are seen as undermining particular States' attempts to insist on the exhaustion of local remedies or other preconditions to international arbitration [170].

As the CIEL Letter suggests, worries about recourse to investor-State arbitration are not limited to scholarly circles. In the United States and Canada in particular there has been tremendous concern expressed by some NGOs over the prospect that policy issues are now being relegated, under the NAFTA's investor-State mechanism, to "unaccountable" supranational tribunals operating in secret and closed to other stakeholders [171]. Although, as is addressed in a later chapter, such concerns have led to changes to the NAFTA to enhance its transparency, not all forms of investor-State dispute resolution are similarly open to public scrutiny or to the participation of *amicus* briefs by, for example, interested NGOs. Nor is all criticism silenced by the turn to greater transparency that has occurred within ICSID and especially within the NAFTA. The CIEL

---

[169] See generally Bjorklund, *supra* footnote 107.

[170] *Emilio Agustin Maffezini* v. *Kingdom of Spain*, Decision on Jurisdiction, ICSID Case No. ARB/97/7 (25 January 2000), para. 63.

[171] See "Bill Moyers Reports: Trading Democracy", *NOW* (1 February 2002), available at <http://www.pbs.org/now/transcript/transcript_tdfull.html>; J. J. Coe, "Transparency in the Resolution of Investor-State Disputes — Adoption, Adaptation, and NAFTA Leadership", 54 *University of Kansas Law Review* 1339 (2006); see also Montt, *supra* footnote 155 (describing "BIT law" as a tool to undermine the *domaine reservé* of States and as a form of "global constitutional law" and "global administrative law").

Letter indicates, for instance, that in the absence of any specific concerns about how US investors have been treated in Morocco, the FTA's provision for investor-State arbitration is unnecessary since US investors should be content with taking their disputes to Morocco's courts [172].

A final rule of law concern, addressed in a later chapter, relates to a perceived threat to public international law more generally: namely that investor-State arbitrators are failing to produce decisions that are either *consistent* with other investment treaties or with other international law regimes, including those dealing with human rights. The concern is that the investment regime is failing on its own terms to the extent it fails to produce the stable and predictable rules of the road to which investors are entitled and is, in addition, contributing to the overall fragmentation of international law that will ultimately undermine its efficacy [173].

G. *The Regime and Public International Law*

This introduction to the investment regime highlights why this author has chosen to address this topic as part of the Hague Academy's courses on "public international law". There was some resistance to this idea within the Academy. Some maintain that the investment regime should continue to be framed in terms of private international law. To be sure, if one focuses only on certain features of the investment regime, particularly the procedural rules that it shares

---

[172] CIEL Letter, *supra* footnote 25, p. 2.
[173] See generally A. Bjorklund, "Investment Treaty Arbitral Decisions as Jurisprudence Constante", in C. Picker *et al.* (eds.), *International Economic Law: The State and Future of the Discipline* (Portland, Oregon, Hart Publishing, 2008), p. 265.

with international commercial arbitration, or even some of its substantive legal rules that overlap with private international law concerns (such as the rules governing investment contracts), such a description of the investment regime remains plausible. But this monograph does not focus on such concerns — or many other issues that arise in the course of investor-State disputes such as choice of law. The emphasis here will be on examining the structural dimensions of the regime — and how it relates to general public international law. Accordingly the substantive investment protections accorded in investment treaties will only be addressed in passing — as necessary to understand these structural dimensions.

The investment regime should be of interest to public international lawyers. It is a creature of treaty and, as will be addressed in subsequent chapters, is deeply intertwined with other traditional sources of international law, particularly custom. The regime was nurtured and established during and partly as a reaction to the process of decolonization that has structured so much of contemporary public international law and its institutions, including those of the UN system. Its substantive guarantees react to well-worn North/South debates that every public international law student is familiar with — especially those surrounding the attempt to establish the New International Economic Order — and which, as we all know, continue to challenge us today in various new forms. Further, the regime's procedures for enforcement are inspired by, but go a step beyond, those in prototypical international courts, including the European Court of Human Rights. Accordingly this monograph is an attempt to understand the evolving ideological, political and legal natures of the international investment regime — and what lessons it may hold for other treaty regimes and their dispute settlers.

CHAPTER II

WHAT ARE INVESTMENT TREATIES FOR?

This chapter explores the object and purpose of investment treaties and explanations for why States, developing, developed, and others in between, conclude them. The US BIT programme will be used as the starting point to explore these questions. One would think that the best place to start would be the treaties themselves. To return to the example used in Chapter I, the title of the US Model BIT of 1987 itself suggests that it concerns "the reciprocal encouragement and protection of investment". That treaty's brief preamble states:

> "The United States of America and —, desiring to promote greater economic cooperation between them, with respect to investment by nationals and companies of one Party in the territory of the other Party; and
>
> Recognizing that agreement upon the treatment to be accorded such investment will stimulate the flow of private capital and the economic development of the Parties,
>
> Agreeing that *fair and equitable treatment of investment is desirable in order to maintain a stable framework for investment and maximum effective utilization of economic resources*, and
>
> Having resolved to conclude a Treaty concerning the encouragement and reciprocal protection of investment,
>
> Have agreed as follows . . ." (Emphasis added.)

As is well known, the preambles of treaties are frequently used to develop the "object and purpose" of a treaty in light of the familiar injunction in the Vienna Convention on the Law of Treaties that treaties be given their plain meaning in light of their object and purpose[174]. What is the object and purpose of this treaty?

The United States concluded treaties with this language with Haiti, Morocco, Panama, Senegal, Turkey, Zaire, Argentina, Cameroon, Egypt, Bangladesh and Grenada. Capital flows between these nations and the United States can hardly be said to be truly *reciprocal*. In each of these cases, it is clear that the United States is, relatively speaking, the capital exporter and its BIT partner is the potential recipient of US capital. If these treaties were truly intended to rectify this situation — to secure more reciprocal capital flows — we would expect provisions imposing distinct treaty obligations on the United States to "encourage" the flow of capital to, for example, Grenada. Yet, no such obligation appears in the text of the US Model BIT or in the concluded agreement between the United States and Grenada[175]. Consistent with the US Model text, none of these treaties impose any specific obligation on the United States directed at promoting greater economic co-operation, stimulating the flow of private capital, encouraging economic development, or maximizing

---

[174] See, e.g., O. K. Fauchald, "The Legal Reasoning of ICSID Tribunals — An Empirical Analysis", 19 *European Journal of International Law* 301 (2008), p. 322 (noting that 48 out of the 98 arbitral decisions surveyed relied on "object and purpose" as an interpretative argument and the most frequent way to find object and purpose was to look at the treaty's preamble).

[175] Treaty between the United States of America and Grenada concerning the Reciprocal Encouragement and Protection of Investment, signed on 2 May 1986, entered into force on 3 March 1989, <http://www.state.gov/documents/organization/43562.pdf>. The text of that agreement is virtually identical to the US model text used at that time.

the effective utilization of economic resources. These treaties do not have provisions requiring, for example, that trade fairs be organized under government auspices to promote the virtues of investing in these countries. They do not, for example, require the US Government as a BIT party to give subsidies or tax incentives to investors to entice them to go to Egypt or Grenada. They do not anticipate that the capital exporting Government will do anything to incentivize its investors, even though such provisions were sometimes requested by the United States' prospective BIT partners.

As US BIT negotiators from that period confirm, this omission was not inadvertent: the US Government resisted investment promotion provisions as a matter of policy [176]. Also, the texts of these treaties do not have a single obligation directly relating to the economic development goal that is briefly mentioned in their preambles. There is nothing in the US Model BIT text of 1987 suggesting that, for example, the US Government will encourage greater aid flows or will vote in favour of World Bank loans with respect to BIT partners. These are treaties that, as we will see, trust that once freed of artificial government restrictions, private entrepreneurs will assist the host State in reaching those worthy development goals [177].

---

[176] K. J. Vandevelde, "Of Politics and Markets: The Shifting Ideology of the BITs", 11 *International Tax & Business Lawyer* 159 (1993), p. 162.

[177] As David Schneiderman indicates, the preambles of such BITs suggest the "embedded preferences" of their drafters, namely their assumption that investment protections and the subsequent inflows of FDI will stimulate business initiative, increase prosperity, and bring technology, managerial skills and marketing know-now as attendant spill-over effects. D. Schneiderman, *Constitutionalizing Economic Globalization* (Cambridge, Cambridge University Press, 2007), pp. 26, 30.

This market orientation is subtly suggested in the text and preamble of the US Model BIT. Note that the title of the US Model mentions the "encouragement" of investment, not its "promotion". One can "encourage" or, in the words of the preamble, "stimulate" capital flows by doing what the US Model actually does: focusing only on the protection of foreign capital. In addition, all the aspirational goals mentioned in the preamble, such as economic co-operation and economic development, are stated as merely desirable outcomes flowing from the real object and purpose of this treaty, which, as the preamble states, is to promote the "fair and equitable treatment of investment".

This reading of the model treaty's sparse preamble was repeatedly confirmed by the contemporaneous public statements of US BIT negotiators to prospective BIT partners during the early years of the US BIT programme and to the US Senate in seeking its approval for ratification [178]. It is also affirmed in scholarship and, for the most part, by investor-State arbitral tribunals charged with interpreting US BITs based on the 1987 Model. Indeed, Kenneth Vandevelde, one of the principal US BIT negotiators from this period, has stated that at the outset of its BIT programme the United States had three principal goals: (1) to build a treaty network adopting the principle that the expropriation of foreign investment was unlawful unless accompanied by prompt, adequate and effective compensation; (2) to protect existing stocks of US foreign direct investment by establishing certain other minimum standards of protection, including national and MFN treatment and

---

[178] See, e.g., US State Department Letter of Submittal to US Senate, for Treaty with Argentina concerning the Reciprocal Encouragement and Protection of Investment, 19 January, 103rd Congress, 1st Sess., Treaty Doc. 103-2 (1993).

transparent host State laws on point; and (3) to extricate the US Government from involvement in private investment disputes by enabling investors to pursue their own claims against host States through a binding dispute settlement procedure[179]. As Vandevelde indicates, while prospective BIT partners tended to assume that the goal of concluding a BIT was to encourage future capital flows and therefore sometimes resisted extending BIT protections to foreign investors already present in their country, the United States insisted that existing investments be covered, no less than it resisted the inclusion of investment promotion obligations. The US stance stemmed from political and ideological concerns. The Administration of President Jimmy Carter, which was solicitous of the US labour movement, sought to avoid any impression that BITs were designed to encourage the "outsourcing" of US jobs by encouraging outward capital flows. Later on similar conclusions were reached, during the Reagan Administration, on somewhat different grounds: because BITs were market facilitative devices, not tools to encourage government interference in the market[180].

The first and probably most important goal of the US Model BIT of 1987 is therefore to protect the foreign investor who operates within the territory of a BIT signatory. As the provisions of that treaty demonstrate, the goal is to provide substantive guarantees of treatment — such as "fair and equitable treatment" — within a "stable framework" on the premise that in doing so, other desirable goals not required or indeed covered by anything in the treaty (such as greater FDI flows and presumptive economic development) will

---

[179] K. J. Vandevelde, "The BIT Program: A Fifteen-Year Appraisal", 86 *ASIL Proceedings* 532 (1992), pp. 534-535.

[180] *Ibid.*, p. 535.

hopefully follow. At the same time, this foremost market facilitative device unmistakably sought to *regulate* the FDI host State. It sought to establish a regulatory framework for FDI that would be relatively transparent, stable, predictable and secure, and sought to enforce that framework at the international level at the option of the investor. As one commentator has suggested, perhaps in overly candid terms, the intent of such a treaty is

> "to restrain host country action against the interests of investors — in other words, to enable the form of legal commitments made to investor[s] to resist the forces of change often demanded by the political and economic life in host countries"[181].

Secondly, US BITs of this era sought to protect the existing and future stocks of US investment in BIT partners, and to set an example to be heeded around the world, while getting the US Government out of the business of taking its own protective measures on their behalf. The US Government concluded BITs in order to avoid recourse to formal diplomatic espousal of the claims of US investors and to avoid the internal and external political pressures suggested by blunt instruments such as the Hickenlooper Amendment, a US law permitting the President of the United States to impose economic sanctions on countries that expropriated the investments of US nationals[182]. As Vandevelde indi-

---

[181] J. W. Salacuse, "The Treatification of International Investment Law: A Victory of Form over Life? A Crossroads Crossed?", 3 *Transnational Dispute Management Issue* 3 (2006).

[182] Hickenlooper Amendment to the Foreign Assistance Act of 1964, 22 USC § 2370 (e) (2), as amended, 79 Stat. 658-659 (6 September 1965) (authorizing the US Government to deny foreign assistance to States that expropriate US nationals).

cates, the BITs' alternative to such actions — investor-State dispute settlement — was intended to "depoliticize" investment disputes [183].

The third goal of the US Model BIT of 1987 is to *facilitate* market arrangements, that is, to enable private parties and host States to enter into and enforce their contracts with minimal interference. Accordingly, the 1987 Model BIT includes a number of provisions to defend the sanctity of investor-State contracts:

> *Article II (2):*
>
> "Each Party shall observe any obligation it may have entered into with regard to investments."
>
> *Article IV (1):*
>
> "Each Party shall permit all transfers related to an investment to be made freely and without delay into and out of its territory. Such transfers include: . . . (d) payments made under a contract . . ."
>
> *Article VI (1):*
>
> "For the purposes of this Article, an investment dispute is defined as a dispute involving *(a)* the

---

[183] See, e.g., Vandevelde, *supra* footnote 176, pp. 160-161. Investor-State dispute settlement mechanisms contained in BITs are accordingly intended to correct the structural shortcomings of the older system of investor protection, namely diplomatic espousal by the investor's home State. Diplomatic espousal is unsatisfactory from the perspective of the investor because it remains the prerogative of the home State (which may find it impolitic to press the claim), leaves the matter (and any remedy) in the hands of the home State (which has no obligation to provide the injured investor with any damages received), and remains subject to exhaustion of local remedies. See, e.g., S. Schill, "Enabling Private Ordering — Function, Scope and Effect of Umbrella Clauses in International Investment Treaties", IILJ Working Paper, 2008/9, available at <http://www.iilj.org/publications/documents/2008-9.Schill.pdf>, pp. 17-18 (hereinafter "Enabling Private Ordering").

interpretation or application of an *investment agreement* between a Party and a national or company of
the other Party; *(b)* the interpretation or application
of any *investment authorization* granted by a Party's
foreign investment authority to such national or
company; or *(c)* an *alleged breach* of any right conferred or created by this *Treaty* with respect to an
investment."

Article VI (2):

"any *dispute-settlement procedures* including those
relating to expropriation and specified in the *investment agreement* shall remain binding and shall be
enforceable in accordance with the terms of the
investment agreement, relevant provisions of
domestic laws, and applicable international agreements regarding enforcement of arbitral awards".

Article IX:

"This Treaty shall not derogate from:
(a) laws and regulations, administrative practices
     or procedures, or administrative or adjudica-
     tory decisions of either party;
(b) international legal obligations; or
(c) obligations assumed by either Party, includ-
     ing those contained in an *investment agree-
     ment or an investment authorization*,

that entitle investments or associated activities to
treatment more favorable than that accorded by this
Treaty in like situations." (Emphasis added.)

As the cited provisions indicate, the US Model BIT
requires States to "observe any obligation" they have
entered into (presumably including investment contracts)
(the "umbrella clause" in Article II (2)); requires States
to permit transfers of funds out of the country including payment made under contract (Art. IV (1)); enables

investors to bring questions of interpretation and application of such investment contracts to international arbitration by defining such issues as "investment disputes" (Art. VI (1) *(a)*); specifies that such contracts remain binding and enforceable even in cases of expropriation (Art. VI (2)); and "does not derogate" from any better investor protections contained in that investor's contract (Art. IX). At the same time, the 1987 Model permits investors to violate their existing contracts with the host State to the extent that such contracts would require resolving disputes within local courts or would enable the State to accord the investor treatment that was less favourable than that required by international law (that is, the international minimum standard)[184]. In that instance, the facilitative goal of the US BIT gives way to its regulatory aim. As Stephan Schill has suggested, the point of these contractual protections in BITs is to (1) enhance the capacity of host States to make credible and enforceable commitments by making available treaty-based arbitration; (2) allow investors and host States to achieve more cost-efficient bargains since both are reassured that their contracts will be effective; and (3) mitigate the perceived inequalities between foreign investors and host States stemming from the fact that once the investment is made it would otherwise be subject to a sovereign's prerogatives[185]. It was assumed that entering into a

---

[184] See Articles IX and VI (2), US Model BIT of 1987, reproduced in K. J. Vandevelde, *United States Investment Treaties: Policy and Practice* (Boston, Kluwer Law and Taxation, 1992), Appendix A-4 (hereinafter "1987 US Model BIT").

[185] Schill, "Enabling Private Ordering", *supra* footnote 183. See also A. Schwartz and R. E. Scott, "Contract Theory and the Limits of Contract Law", 113 *Yale Law Journal* 541 (2003), p. 561 (describing the consequences of unenforceable contracts). Treaty-based investment pro-

solemn international commitment was the most effective way to prevent opportunistic host State behaviour that had been resistant to comparable guarantees made under a host State's own laws or had been subject to enforcement by its own courts.

As noted, through the early years of the negotiation of BITs (that is through much of the 1990s) most BITs were concluded along these lines as is suggested by the early US BITs. In most cases rich capital exporters negotiated BITs based on their own model texts with poorer capital importers — and the latter often concluded such treaties with the equivalent of an IMF gun pointed at their heads. Despite the formal equality suggested by their texts, the political realities of such treaties were starkly different. The vast bulk of BITs — certainly in the early years — contemplate (despite their formally reciprocal terms) a largely one-way flow of FDI from one relatively more developed State towards a LDC partner. In practice, the regulatory burdens imposed under these treaties fell almost entirely on LDC host States, and not the drafters of influential BIT texts such as Germany or the United States. The Grenadas and the Bangladeshes of the world had to reform their laws and practices to be sure that they could satisfy BIT standards. The United States and other capital exporting BIT signatories did not need to worry very much about adapting their laws or practices, not only because these countries were drafting the texts on which these negotiations were conducted and could be sure not to include in them anything that

---

tection is particularly important for smaller foreign investors who are at an even greater disadvantage when bargaining with a host State. *Ibid.*, p. 21. As Schill acknowledges however, not all arbitrators have recognized these three rationales and there is a great deal of disagreement about the interpretation and scope of umbrella clauses in BITs. *Ibid.*

was not already consistent with their laws, but also because, given the one-way flow of capital, it was extremely unlikely that capital exporting States would face investor claimants from countries such as Grenada or Bangladesh. Countries like the United States and Germany could afford to assume that their laws and practices were already consistent with the minimal standards contained in their BITs and could be reasonably certain that their assumptions were not likely to be tested given the BIT partners with whom they were then dealing. Thus, while US BIT partners, as well as the partners of other Western States concluding BITs during this period, often needed to reform their laws and practices either prior to concluding such agreements or immediately thereafter, the United States, like other capital exporters, scarcely had to do anything to its law in response to concluding BITs — except perhaps to make sure that US courts were available to enforce any arbitration awards brought by their own nationals in response to the actions of LDC BIT partners [186].

US BITs, as well as those of leading European States with comparable BIT programmes, were in these early years highly asymmetrical agreements. These asymmetries were intentional. The United States, like its European allies that had established BIT programmes decades before, sought BITs with LDCs and not developed countries because these were the States that had caused the most problems to their investors for decades. As Vandevelde suggests was true for the United States, developed States also sought to conclude such treaties in order to affirm traditional rules of

---

[186] See generally J. Alvarez, "Critical Theory and the North America Free Trade Agreement's Chapter Eleven", 28 *University of Miami Inter-American Law Review* 303 (1997), pp. 309-310.

customary international law that protected aliens from ill treatment.

Today's norms for the protection of international investment as affirmed in BITs stem from customary rules of State responsibility towards aliens formulated during the colonial era, such as the "international minimum standard" that was viewed as reflecting the rule of law among "civilized" nations [187]. Conflicts over the legitimacy and content of the standards that should govern the conduct of States in relation to foreign investors emerged at least by the late nineteenth and early twentieth centuries. Between 1829 and 1910 the United States alone entered into some 40 arbitrations with Latin American countries resulting from diplomatic "espousal" efforts on behalf of US investors [188]. These efforts generated predictable resistance from the periphery vis-à-vis the metropole, most famously in the form of the Calvo and Drago Doctrines espoused by Latin American jurists [189]. The response by the United States — that it was permissible to use force to

---

[187] For an account of the historical development of international investment law, see A. Newcombe and L. Paradell, *Law and Practice of Investment Treaties* (The Hague, Kluwer Law International, 2009), pp. 1-73; K. Vandevelde, "A Brief History of International Investment Agreements", 12 *UC Davis Journal of International Law & Policy* 157 (2005).

[188] Vandevelde, "A Brief History", *supra* footnote 187, p. 6, n. 24.

[189] Under the Calvo Doctrine, first articulated by an Argentine jurist, foreign investors would be treated no differently than nationals and would only have access to the same avenues for redress as nationals (namely national courts). The Drago Doctrine, also articulated by an Argentine jurist, barred the use of force by States when intended to seek redress for debts owed to its foreign investors. Newcombe and Paradell, *supra* footnote 187, pp. 8-10. The Roosevelt Corollary was the United States' response to the Drago Doctrine.

collect its nationals' debts in the Western Hemisphere[190] — suggests the vehemence of positions on both sides.

North/South disputes over the applicable legal rules only grew in intensity as decolonization progressed after World War II, when many newly independent States re-examined the merits of investment contracts concluded under prior regimes, while others opted for socialist models for development that eschewed the market altogether, encouraged massive expropriations of the private sector, or sought to close their economies to foreign influences. Some developing States came to adhere to import substitution models that often proved to be nearly as hostile to the entry of foreign investors[191]. This was the "larger context of world social events and processes" that culminated in the actions of the UN General Assembly in 1973, where over 100 nations proclaimed that all States have "full permanent sovereignty" over their natural resources and economic activities, including the right to nationalize or transfer ownership of assets to their nationals, without mention of an international legal obligation to pay compensation[192]; and led to the adoption, with the support of 120 nations, in 1974, of a Charter of Economic Rights

---

[190] Vandevelde, *supra* footnote 187, p. 6 (discussing the Roosevelt Corollary to the Monroe Doctrine).

[191] Newcombe and Paradell, *supra* footnote 187, pp. 26-33; Vandevelde, "A Brief History", *supra* footnote 187, p. 11. As Vandevelde indicates, key moments in this history were the seizure of petroleum assets in Iran in 1951, in Libya in 1955, Castro's expropriations starting in 1959, and a wave of expropria-tions in the 1970s. Vandevelde cites one study identifying 875 expropriations occurring in 62 countries between 1960 and 1974. *Ibid.*, n. 52.

[192] Declaration of Permanent Sovereignty over Natural Resources, General Assembly rs. 3171 (XXVIII), 28 *General Assembly Official Records*, Supp. No. 30, p. 52, UN doc. A/9030 (1973).

and Duties of States[193]. The latter acknowledged only that "appropriate compensation" as provided under national law would be payable in such cases[194].

The United States, which was a relative latecomer to signing BITs, developed its BIT model in reaction to the challenge at the United Nations to traditional norms of State responsibility to aliens. The US Model BIT of 1987, and particularly its reliance on investor-State arbitration for the resolution of disputes, was a direct response to Western investors' distrust of the national courts of many of the States in which they established their operations, particularly when those host States were suggesting, at least in forums such as the United Nations, that they owed no responsibilities to investors apart from those they imposed on themselves through national law. The United States decided to target for BIT negotiations precisely those States, namely LDCs, that as a group had supported the new international economic order ("NIEO") but which, as of the 1980s when the United States began its BIT programme, appeared to be becoming more amenable to free market policies. The United States modelled its BIT on existing investment protection agreements concluded by prominent European States like Germany. At the same time, the US BIT was also a successor to its own treaties of Friendship, Commerce and Navigation ("FCNs") which it had concluded over the course of the early twentieth century with its major trading partners. The US Model BIT could afford to focus on investment and ignore those provisions of FCNs dealing with trade in goods because, at least by the early

---

[193] Charter of Economic Rights and Duties of States, General Assembly res. 3281 (XXIX), 29 *General Assembly Official Records*, Supp. No. 30, p. 50, UN doc. A/9631 (1974), adopted with 120 votes for, 6 against, and 10 abstentions. Text reprinted in 14 *ILM* 251 (1975).

[194] *Ibid.*, Article 2 (2) *(c)*.

1980s, the GATT could be relied upon to protect cross-border traders of goods. At the same time, the United States decided that it would not waste its time attempting to replace its old FCNs with BITs and therefore that it would not attempt to negotiate BITs with European States with which the United States had concluded FCNs. Although those FCNs did not contain the detailed investment protections contained in a modern BIT and only provided for inter-State resolution of treaty disputes, typically in the ICJ, and not investor-State arbitration, the United States decided that it was not worth the trouble of going to FCN partner States like Germany or Japan since those Western allies had not, for the most part, posed enormous problems for US investors and a treaty to ensure that such investors could avoid those countries' courts through arbitration was not vital. (Indeed, it would not be until 1994, when the United States concluded the North American Free Trade Agreement (NAFTA) with Mexico and Canada that the United States would enter into an investment treaty with an advanced economy whose investors had a serious stake in the US economy and could be expected to make claims directly on the US Government pursuant to investor-State arbitration. As we will discuss in a later chapter, the NAFTA made the United States Government aware of what "reciprocal" investment protections really meant. Thanks to the NAFTA, the United States would eventually learn that even its legal system could be challenged by the standards it had blithely sought to impose on others for so many years.)

But in the early days of the US BIT programme the United States approached BIT negotiations with prospective partners like Bangladesh as if it were engaged in a training session on political economy. As would be later summarized by Vandevelde, US BIT negotiators adopted a highly ideological and relatively inflexible bargaining position[195]. They sold the US BIT as an essential (but minimal) building block for nations that were intent on building free market economies based on the rule of law[196]. The United States argued that signing a US BIT would send a signal that a country had accepted the basic premises of liberal economic theory, namely that free markets, consistent with the insights of David Ricardo, would yield the most efficient use of resources and the greatest productivity[197]. Concluding a BIT, US negotiators argued, would be consistent with, but would not itself ensure the establishment of, a particular model of the State vis-à-vis the market[198]. The kind of Government that the US Model BIT anticipated was one that established and protected private rights of property and contract and that adhered to a basic rule of law framework protecting the bargains struck by private parties against infringement by public or private actors. The US Model BIT assumed and sought to preserve a State that would otherwise defer to the market's allocation of resources and would not, for example, chose winners and losers or pre-determine which sectors would be subject to market forces[199]. At the same time, the US BIT anticipated a State that, like the United States, could otherwise intervene as necessary to correct market failures such as to supply public goods (e.g., build public infrastructure), to counteract inefficiencies

---

[195] K. Vandevelde, *United States Investment Treaties: Policy and Practice* (Boston, Kluwer Law and Taxation, 1992), pp. 1-43.

[196] See, e.g., K. Vandevelde, "Investment Liberalization and Economic Development: The Role of Bilateral Investment Treaties", 36 *Columbia Journal of Transnational Law* 501 (1998).

[197] *Ibid.*, pp. 504-506.

[198] *Ibid.*, pp. 515-519.

[199] *Ibid.*, pp. 504-506.

caused by externalities (e.g., to control pollution), or to restore market access threatened by anti-competitive conduct (e.g., to enact laws against monopolies)[200].

US BIT negotiators contended that concluding a BIT was a "bare first step" in establishing a liberal investment regime along these lines but one which would not in and of itself guarantee an increase in FDI flows, even from the United States[201]. Concluding a BIT, after all, did not ensure that a country would be otherwise attractive to a foreign investor seeking particular natural resources, a labour pool with certain skills, or a huge new consumer market for its goods. Nor did the conclusion of a BIT ensure that the domestic rule of law was fully in place. The United States saw its new treaty as a limited tool for liberalization that would not require that all foreign investors be admitted, would not guarantee that investors could rely on independent courts to resolve their private disputes, and would provide only limited guarantees with respect to private interference with investors' rights (such as protection of intellectual property). Further, its treaty would ensure access to international arbitration only with respect to certain treaty disputes between foreign investors and host States, and would not prevent a huge range of government actions (from those designed to protect infant industries to tax incentives to particular investors) — any of which may admittedly be ineffective, costly, or counterproductive. For these reasons US negotiators saw their BIT as imposing only a few, non-onerous, and uncontroversial constraints on government action – a treaty that, in short, was scarcely necessary for those investing in the United States. They perceived it however as a vital first step for those Governments whose prior actions suggested a

---

[200] Vandevelde, *supra* footnote 196, pp. 504-506.
[201] *Ibid.*, pp. 522-525.

hostility to the market and which needed to send a signal to convince investors that they were ready to
adhere to free market principles for the long-term and
were ready to so indicate by tying themselves to the
mast[202].

In hindsight, it is easy to see the initiation of the US
BIT programme in the mid-1980s and the explosion in
the ratifications of BITs after 1989 as a perfect storm
inspired by the victory of the capitalist West over what
was then its only rival, namely planned economies
under socialist and communist regimes. What US
negotiators saw as a "minimal commitment" to liberal,
free market principles was, in retrospect, a politically
loaded treaty obligation that reflected the then reigning
"Washington Consensus" among US Government
departments, aid agencies, and the international financial institutions[203]. According to mainstream development thinkers of the time, all societies, rich or poor,
needed to maximize their economic performance by
enabling market actors to transact with each other,
nationally and internationally[204]. Economies were seen
as markets and governmental policies not narrowly
tailored to support the market were perceived as
"problems" that needed correcting. Under the Washington Consensus, governmental failures of the past — subsidies, price controls, tariffs, licensing arrangements,

---

[202] See, e.g, Vandevelde, *US Investment Treaties*, *supra*
footnote 195.

[203] See generally D. Rodrik, "Growth Strategies", in
P. Aghion and D. Steven (eds.), *Handbook of Economic
Growth* (Amsterdam, Elsevier, 2004), available at <http://
econ2.econ.iastate.edu/classes/econ502/tesfatsion/Growth
Strategies.DRodrik.GrowthHB2005.pdf>.

[204] See, e.g., D. Kennedy, "The 'Rule of Law' Political
Choices, and Development Common Sense", in D. M. Trubek
and A. Santos (eds.), *The New Law and Economic Development* (New York, Cambridge University Press, 2006),
p. 129.

exchange controls, preferences for infant industries, State-owned sectors, and so on — needed to be dismantled to avoid distorting the operation of the market and to enable the national market to be penetrated by global forces that were more competitive and efficient. This ideological concept of what "good governance" meant lay behind the US Model BIT of the period.

The US BIT of the 1980s, and of those nations that came to emulate it, was a prominent element of what Thomas Friedman dubbed the "Golden Straightjacket" — a necessary element in a package of reforms directing nations to acquire fiscal discipline, reorient public expenditures, engage in tax reform, liberalize their interest rates, adopt unified and competitive exchange rates, open their economies to trade and foreign direct investment ("FDI"), privatize government-owned sectors, engage in deregulation, and make every effort to secure property rights[205]. Although these goals were in fact politically intrusive — and would prove to be so even for countries such as the United States — the Model BIT sought to make openness to FDI appear to be above politics. "The function of the BIT", Vandevelde argues, "was to insulate private investment from politically driven foreign or domestic public policy — in effect, to depoliticize investment matters by placing the protection of private investment under an apolitical legal regime."[206] The goal was to separate "the market" from "politics" by establishing a stable legal regime that would avoid leaving investors at the mercy of the political branches of the host Government, while at the same time avoiding the disruptions (and possible distortions) to US foreign policy that had been caused by prior US Government interventions in foreign investment disputes. The BIT's investor-State

---

[205] See, e.g., Rodrik, *supra* footnote 203, p. 974, table 2.
[206] Vandevelde, *supra* footnote 176, pp. 160-161.

dispute settlement was intended to erect a "wall of separation" that would "insulate politics from business as much as business from politics" [207].

The United States' view that the BIT's requirements were but minimal intrusions on a Government's ability to regulate in the public interest was also based on the belief that much of what the US BIT provided was already contained in the traditional principles of international law regarding the treatment of aliens, drawn from principles of State responsibility. These included the rule proclaimed by US Secretary of State Cordell Hull against Mexico on behalf of prompt, adequate, and effective compensation upon expropriation (the "Hull Rule"), the international minimum standard of treatment, and the requirement to ensure "full protection and security" to aliens and avoid "denials of justice". US BITs entrenched these customary rights by providing an arbitral forum for their enforcement, thereby also entrenching the underlying private law regimes necessary to support market transactions [208]. As this suggests, the US BIT uses international law to dismantle public law regulations inimical to the market.

The US Model BIT of 1987 explicitly or implicitly relies on general international law in a number of provisions. Thus, the US Model provides in Article II (2) that "[i]nvestment shall at all times be accorded fair and equitable treatment, shall enjoy full protection and

---

[207] Vandevelde, *supra* footnote 176, p. 161.

[208] The United States was not the only country to use BITs to affirm traditional customary rights while adding enhanced treaty protections for the benefit of investors (such as national treatment and most-favoured-nation treatment). See, e.g., E. Denza and S. Brooks, "Investment Protection Treaties: United Kingdom Experience", 36 *International & Comparative Law Quarterly* 908 (1987), p. 912 (noting that UK BITs sought to affirm customary protections while adding NT and MFN).

security and shall in no case be accorded treatment less than that required by international law". Secondly, it provides that in cases of expropriation, investors have the right to be treated "in accordance with due process of law and the general principles of treatment provided for in Article II (2)"[209]. Thirdly, it states that investors subject to expropriation have the right to prompt review by the appropriate judicial or administrative authorities of the host State which, among other things, shall ensure that any compensation "conforms to the provisions of this Treaty and the principles of international law"[210]. Finally, it asserts that the treaty does not derogate from any better treatment accorded under, among other things, "international legal obligations"[211]. (Other provisions of that BIT, such as a clause according investors "effective means of asserting claims" in local fora (Art. II (6)) or directing States to make "public" all relevant laws (Art. II (7)), are open-ended invitations to deploy relevant customary international law ("CIL") or general principles of law, given, for example, emerging principles to promote due process, transparency, or accountability across a number of regimes, including those involving human rights.)[212]

As these clauses demonstrate, the US Model BIT of 1987, like many other BITs, is, at least in part, an

---

[209] Article III, US Model BIT of 1987, *supra* footnote 184.

[210] *Ibid*., Article III (2).

[211] *Ibid*., Article IX.

[212] These provisions do not exhaust the ways that BITs may rely on customary international law or general principles of law. According to one view of the intent of an "umbrella clause", for example, such clauses may also be "a declaratory codification of customary international law that clarifies that rights of an investor under an investor-State contract can form the object of an expropriation and accordingly require compensation in case they are taken". Schill, "Enabling Private Ordering", *supra* footnote 183, p. 3.

explicit effort to provide investors with the traditional protections of customary law, including the international minimum standard and protections against denials of justice and assurances of full protection and security. Clauses such as those enumerated above are not efforts to *exclude* these ordinarily applicable general legal rules, as does *lex specialis, but on the contrary to affirm them*[213]. This is certainly what US BIT negotiators have confirmed was their intent[214]. Of

---

[213] It may therefore be misleading to state, as a leading casebook does, that BITs "[a]s *lex specialis* between the parties . . . supersede any inconsistent customary international law and may embrace or exclude any incipient norms", R. D. Bishop *et al.*, *Foreign Investment Disputes: Cases, Materials, and Commentary* (The Hague, Kluwer Law International, 2005), p. 1007. The language of most BITs welcomes or even requires the residual application of customary international law ("CIL"); it is much harder to point to concrete instances where such treaties explicitly exclude it. For consideration of the consequences of this in connection with some cases against Argentina raising the applicability of the CIL norm governing necessity, see Chapter V of this monograph and also J. E. Alvarez and K. Khamsi, "The Argentine Crisis and Foreign Investors", in K. P. Sauvant (ed.), *Yearbook on International Investment Law & Policy 2008-2009* (New York, Oxford University Press, 2009).

[214] Thus, one of the early negotiators of US BITs and the leading scholar on the US BIT programme has stated:

"One of the most important of the absolute standards requires that covered investment enjoy treatment no less favourable than that required by international law. This provision incorporates customary international law into the BIT, so that any violation of customary international law also would violate the BIT. The practical implication is that the BIT dispute mechanisms, which apply to treaty violations, can be used to remedy violations of customary international law." Vandevelde, "The BIT Program", *supra* footnote 179, p. 537.

Vandevelde also attributes the United States' resistance to making concessions regarding the BIT's treatment pro-

course, as noted, the incorporation of customary legal protections into BITs was not a useless or superfluous act. By including these clauses in a BIT and making these the basis of an investor-State claim — alongside other BIT rights that are not customary but based only on the treaty, such as the right to national treatment and most favourable treatment — rights that would otherwise depend, for enforcement, on the political intercession of Governments (and once led to gunboat diplomacy) would now also be subject to ostensibly "apolitical" dispute settlement. To this end, these treaties defined "investment disputes" that could be brought to international arbitration as including breaches of any right *"conferred"* by the treaty (that is where merely the forum is supplied by the treaty but that forum is applying pre-existing rights under CIL or an investment contract) and not merely those "created" by the treaty[215].

All of this provides background for understanding what some see as a puzzle: why is it that States have constructed a treaty regime that elevates the rights of one particular group — private foreign investors — while saying scarcely one word about those investors' possible duties to Governments, any possible duties by the home Governments of the investors, or the corre-

---

visions to the felt need to use these treaties to "bolster" and not undermine CIL. *Ibid.*, p. 536. He indicates that, by contrast, since the NT and MFN provisions were not grounded in CIL, the United States was more ready to make concessions on those provisions (as with respect to derogations from MFN when BIT partners were members of customs unions). *Ibid.*, p. 537.

[215] See, e.g., Article VII (1) of the Treaty between the United States of America and the Argentine Republic concerning the Reciprocal Encouragement and Protection of Investment, signed on 14 November 1991, entered into force on 20 October 1994, available at <http://www.unctad.org/sections/dite/iia/docs/bits/argentina_us.pdf>.

sponding rights of the host State in which investors find themselves? Why do States conclude strikingly asymmetrical treaties that anticipate obligations almost entirely on the part of host States and that enable private investors to sue those Governments that fail to uphold these obligations?

As this account of the rise of BITs suggests, BITs were designed to deal with a particular perceived problem: the salient fact that a private investor has maximum leverage with respect to a host State only when deciding whether to invest but that once he or she does so, the investment becomes subject to an "obsolescing bargain"[216]. Once an investor sinks his capital into the host State, the host State gains enormous leverage over the investment, which is now subject to the host State's regulatory or even expropriatory measures, and there is frequently little that an investor can do about it. The asymmetries of the typical BIT respond to perceived asymmetries that bedevil private investors who are, but for a BIT, at the mercy of the State that serves as their host. BITs were designed to compensate for the fact that foreign investors are totally exposed to national law and courts and for the most part remain so, even under BITs, which after all provide only a limited exception from host country jurisdiction. A BIT is accordingly "an instrument of control over abusive changes of national law by the host State"[217]. As Thomas Wälde put it, BITs seek

"to balance this pre-existing and inherent structural

---

[216] See R. Vernon, *Sovereignty at Bay: The Multinational Spread of US Enterprises* (New York, Basic Books, 1971), p. 46.

[217] T. W. Wälde, "The Specific Nature of Investment Arbitration", in P. Kahn and T. Wälde (eds.), *New Aspects of International Investment Law* (Leiden, Martinus Nijhoff, 2007), p. 55.

asymmetry in which foreign investors find them-selves: to compensate them for exposure to the host State as contract party, regulator, sovereign and judge by having a forum for disputes that is not con-trolled by the host State. The apparent asymmetry of investment treaties is thus nothing but the reverse mirror image of investor exposure to host State adjudication."[218]

This gives us a sense of what rich Western Govern-ments who established BIT programmes were trying to accomplish. But why did LDCs agree to them? Why would countries that have few TNCs with the size and clout to invest abroad conclude treaties whose effect is to restrain their own freedom of action against power-ful, foreign TNCs in their own territories? Why do LDCs "constrain their sovereignty" in this fashion[219]?

A. Guzman's Account of the Origins of the Investment Regime

Andrew Guzman attempted to answer this question in a 1998 article[220]. To this day, his answer, which its author has updated for publication in 2009[221], is the most frequently cited explanation for the rise and spread of investment treaties. Although told in the dry jargon of law and economics, Guzman's response is that the investment regime is the product of a game played by the West on the rest. Guzman addresses the puzzle of LDCs' actions by addressing another appar-

---

[218] Wälde, *supra* footnote 217, p. 55.

[219] See, e.g., Salacuse, *supra* footnote 181, p. 6.

[220] A. T. Guzman, "Why LDCs Sign Treaties that Hurt Them: Explaining the Popularity of Bilateral Investment Treaties", 38 *Virginia Journal of International Law* 639 (1998).

[221] *Ibid.*, p. 73.

ent paradox: why did developing States oppose the
Hull Rule and embrace the NIEO at the United Nations
as a group while simultaneously flocking to bilateral
treaties that contradicted their collective efforts?
To Guzman the answer lies in a simple prisoner's
dilemma. As a group, developing States had a common
interest in toppling the Hull Rule and other rules of
customary international law that sought to protect alien
investors. They successfully did so through their
General Assembly efforts but they were unable to sustain a united front; instead, as individual prisoners they
defected from the NIEO and concluded BITs with
wealthier nations for purely economic reasons, that is,
to try to get a leg up on their neighbours by attracting
foreign investors to their own shores first.

BITs address what Guzman calls a "dynamic inconsistency problem", that is, "a situation when a preferred course of action, once undertaken, cannot be
adhered to without the establishment of some commitment mechanism"[222]. "The central problem", Guzman
explains, "is that a sovereign country is not able,
absent a BIT, to credibly bind itself to a particular set
of legal rules when it negotiates with a potential
investor."[223] Guzman explains that individual LDCs
conclude BITs out of economic self-interest, intent on
striking particular tit-for-tat remedies for the dynamic
inconsistency problem with particular capital exporting
nations but without any intention of restoring the former (pre-NIEO) general rules of investment protection.
Individual LDCs conclude BITs, then, in an ultimately
fruitless and self-defeating competitive effort to secure
an economic advantage vis-à-vis other LDCs, with predictably sub-optimal results: their acts as BIT signatories generate a race to the bottom whereby all LDCs

---

[222] Guzman, *supra* footnote 220, p. 78.
[223] *Ibid.*

are ultimately worse off than if they had stuck together, adhered to the NIEO and gotten the most out of foreign investors stuck in obsolescing bargains[224].

Guzman's recourse to game theory also offers an ostensible legal pay-off. Guzman contends that since LDCs adhered to BITs for "economic reasons", they did not have the *opinio juris* to affect or change the underlying customary international legal protections that had been destroyed by the NIEO[225]. Accordingly, he argues that today's network of investment agreements constitute *lex specialis* between their particular parties and should not be considered to codify or provide evidence of, let alone affect, general customary international law[226].

Guzman's game theoretic account has a singular appeal to the many commentators who see bilateral and regional investment treaties through a North/South lens or even as law imposed by "Anglo-American" empire[227].

---

[224] Guzman, *supra* footnote 220, pp. 85-88, 90-91.

[225] *Ibid*., pp. 93-96.

[226] Indeed, Guzman contends that BITs are more plausibly described as "permissible derogations from the existing rules of customary law". *Ibid*., p. 95.

[227] See generally M. Sornarajah, *International Law on Foreign Investment* (Cambridge, Cambridge University Press, 2004). For more general articulations of the "imperial" character of contemporary international law, see, e.g., U. Mattei, "A Theory of Imperial Law: A Study on US Hegemony and the Latin Resistance", 10 *Indiana Journal of Global Legal Studies* 383 (2003); B. S. Chimni, "International Institutions Today: An Imperial Global State in the Making", 15 *European Journal of International Law* 1 (2004); W. R. Mead, *God and Gold: Britain, America, and the Making of the Modern World* (New York, Vintage Books, 2007). For a response, see J. Alvarez, "Contemporary Foreign Investment Law: An 'Empire of Law' or the 'Law of Empire'?" 60 *Alabama Law Review* 943 (2009). For an authoritative account of how the colonial encounter has shaped modern conceptions of international

Guzman's story of imperial overreach achieved through
the deployment of bilateral leverage and of LDCs'
unwilling collaboration in their own impoverishment is
particularly entrancing to those who see BITs as modern day versions of the nineteenth-century capitulation
agreements that Western empires once extracted from
the periphery. Guzman affirms that BITs are indeed
neo-colonial, one-sided agreements which only seek to
protect the capital of the West in the Global South[228].
Guzman's account is also appealing to those who see
BITs as analogous to "contracts of adhesion" imposed
on the unwilling poor by the rich[229], to critics of BITs
and FTAs who see these as part and parcel of a much

law, see A. Anghie, *Imperialism, Sovereignty, and the
Making of International Law* (Cambridge, Cambridge
University Press, 2005).

[228] Under those imperial products, colonial powers
expanded their extraterritorial jurisdiction by exempting
Western merchants and investors from the local laws of the
countries in which they operated. Capitulation agreements
imposed the "standard of civilization" on the "uncivilized"
by granting jurisdiction over Western nationals and their
property to consular officials of Western states in lieu of
local courts. Imperial powers justified these treaties on the
premise that some States were incapable of satisfying the
standard of justice granted by civilized nations. Today's
BITs, like the old capitulation agreements, generally
exempt foreign investors from having to go to local courts
but they substitute international arbitral mechanisms
for the former recourse to consular officials. See, e.g.,
D. P. Fidler, "A Kinder, Gentler System of Capitulations?
International Law, Structural Adjustment Policies, and the
Standard of Liberal, Globalization Civilization", 35 *Texas
International Law Journal* 387 (2000) (comparing capitulation agreements and structural adjustment programmes).
But see Alvarez, "Contemporary Foreign Investment",
supra footnote 227 (critiquing analogies between BITs and
capitulation agreements).

[229] For a critique of this contention as a matter of positive law, see Alvarez and Khamsi, *supra* footnote 213,
pp. 407-460.

broader ideological effort to impose a one-size-fits-all "Washington Consensus" model of "good governance" on the world[230], and to those who suggest that "gunboat arbitration" has merely replaced the gunboat diplomacy of Calvo's day with "biased" investor-State arbitrators who continue to apply "privilege law for foreigners"[231].

Guzman's account is broadly consistent with the story of how the US BIT programme developed and early negotiations under that programme. His story plays into the North/South dynamics which are so pervasive in the history of all prior efforts to regulate international investment. It suggests that BITs are merely another front in the West's long lost war against the NIEO.

B. *Refuting Guzman*

Despite its surface appeal, however, Guzman's explanation of why LDCs individually "sign treaties that hurt them" runs into serious difficulties. To begin, the facts do not bear out the existence of the alleged "paradox" that begins Guzman's enquiry. It is probably not true that LDCs were "simultaneously" engaged in contradictory actions, that they had successfully toppled the Hull Rule or other relevant customary legal norms prior to entering into BITs, that they had

---

[230] For popular accounts both in favour and against, see, e.g., T. Friedman, *The Lexus and the Olive Tree* (New York, Anchor, 1st ed., 2000) (praising LDC's turn to the "golden straight-jacket"); J. E. Stiglitz, *Globalization and Its Discontents* (New York, W. W. Norton and Company, 2002) (criticizing the promulgation of the "Washington Consensus").

[231] S. Montt, "What International Investment Law and Latin America Can and Should Demand from Each Other, Updating the Bello Doctrine in the BIT Generation", 3 *Revista Argentina Del Régimen de la Administración Pública* (2007), p. 80.

no other option except to enter into BITs to surmount a dynamic inconsistency problem, that they entered into BITs solely to surmount the dynamic inconsistency problem, or that, for all of these reasons, the spread of BITs has not affected customary international law.

The investment regime was probably not built on the failure of collective action. Guzman's timeline is wrong. The vast majority of LDCs were not, in 1973-1974, doing one thing at the UN General Assembly, while simultaneously engaged in undermining those efforts through the individual negotiation of BITs. The highpoint of the NIEO effort, never to be duplicated, came in 1974. Yet, even when the Cold War ended many years later, in 1989, there were only 385 investment agreements in place (as opposed to nearly 3,000 today)[232]. Guzman is correct to point out that at least some LDCs had concluded some bilateral investment treaties by 1974, but he is wrong to suggest that such BITs responded to either the alleged "toppling" of the customary international laws or to his crucial "dynamic inconsistency" problem. What Guzman ignores is that nearly all BITs of that early period were extremely weak devices for the protection of investment rights and most lacked the perfected investor-State arbitration clause that is in the US Model BIT of 1987 — and which makes that treaty a credible commitment device (at least over investment contracts that are enforceable only through recourse to host State courts). Of the few BITs concluded by 1974 only an even smaller number contained effective investor-State dispute settlement clauses[233].

---

[232] Vandevelde, *supra* footnote 187, p. 16.
[233] J. W. Yackee, "Bilateral Investment Treaties, Credible Commitment, and the Rule of (International) Law: Do BITs Promote Foreign Direct Investment?", 42 *Law & Society Review* 805 (2008), p. 815, fig. 1.

What this means is that at the time that LDCs were, as a group, resisting the traditional international legal protections for investors and the recourse to international arbitration at the General Assembly, they had not yet acted any differently in their bilateral relations. While the NIEO was in fashion, BITs were not. At the time the General Assembly was promoting the NIEO, few BITs had been concluded and most of these did not yet provide that foreign investors could unilaterally initiate binding arbitration to enforce their treaty rights. This is scarcely surprising insofar as the possibility that BITs could become a vehicle for States giving their advance consent to international arbitration did not emerge until 1965, with the conclusion of the ICSID Convention, and for all practical purposes not until much later, when it became clear that ICSID could become a general vehicle for *treaty-based* arbitration "without privity" (as opposed to a device to implement distinct arbitral commitments contained in investment contracts between investors and States)[234]. As one survey of BITs indicates, the majority of BITs did not contain States parties' pre-commitment to international arbitration for investor-State disputes until well into the 1990s[235]. Most policymakers were probably not even aware that this was a possibility as the first award affirming that consent to arbitration could be provided through a State's advance offer provided via a treaty came only in 1990[236]. The few BITs in existence in 1974 were more like the Canada-Poland BIT of 1990 — a typical treaty for its time that com-

---

[234] J. Paulsson, "Arbitration without Privity", 10 *ICSID Review* 232 (1995).

[235] Yackee, *supra* footnote 233, p. 815.

[236] T. Wälde, "Introduction: International Investment Law Emerging from the Dynamics of Direct Investor-State Arbitration", in Kahn and Wälde, *supra* footnote 217, p. 58.

bines relatively weak investment protections with a comparably ineffectual investor-State dispute settlement clause[237].

Investment treaties of this kind do not provide investors with the assurances that their rights will be credibly protected. They do little, in short, to correct the conditions of "dynamic inconsistency" which Guzman claims motivated LDCs to defect from the NIEO.

The modern BIT era began then not with the first weak BITs concluded by Germany in the late 1950s or with the tiny trickle of investment treaties concluded by 1974, but with the development of much more investor-protective later agreements, generally following the decision by the United States to develop its own BIT programme in the early 1980s. At the same time, it should not be forgotten that the United States concluded very few BITs in the early 1980s and that BITs began to be concluded in large numbers only after 1989, long after the NIEO efforts in the General Assembly had come to an end[238]. BIT ratifications generally, and particularly ratifications of "strong" BITs with effective investor-State dispute settlement clauses as in the 1987 US Model, began to accumulate in significant numbers only after the fall of the Berlin Wall.

Moreover, Guzman's explanation for why LDCs turned to BITs is inadequate not only because of dis-

---

[237] See, e.g., Article IX of the Agreement between the Government of Canada and the Republic of Poland for the Promotion and Reciprocal Protection of Investments, signed 6 April 1990, entered into force 14 November 1991, available at <http://www.unctad.org/sections/dite/iia/docs/bits/canada_poland.pdf> (failing to provide the States' advance consent to arbitration within the treaty).

[238] For a history of the US BIT Programme, see Vandevelde, *supra* footnote 195, pp. 29-43.

crepancies of timing. Guzman is wrong to contend that BITs were the *only* mechanism LDCs had to overcome what he calls the dynamic inconsistency problem, that in the absence of BITs individual LDCs could not defect from the NIEO, or that only reputational constraints affected the behaviour of LDCs prior to the advent of BITs. Even without BITs, LDCs had at least two other methods to alleviate the fears of skittish investors: political risk insurance and express commitments through contract[239]. Depending on the circumstances, neither of these would impose only "reputational" constraints on host States' subsequent actions towards investors. Both also offered plausible alternative courses of action for those States seeking to "defect" from Guzman's alleged prisoners' dilemma.

Political risk insurance is one method by which investors can secure a credible commitment that may encourage them to make an investment. (For this reason, the United States, for example, insisted even at the outset of its BIT programme that LDCs conclude an agreement with its Overseas Private Investment Corporation (OPIC) prior to concluding a BIT and, of course, some countries have entered into only such agreements but have not concluded a BIT with the United States.[240]) Guzman is also wrong, or at best mis-leading, when he writes that international law "does not provide a way for a host country to make credible and binding commitments to an investor" through an investor-State contract since the "precise status of such contracts is the subject of ongoing debate in the field of public international law and is far from being settled"[241]. Jason Webb

---

[239] Of course, all countries have at least one other option: to establish credible and independent national courts that foreign investors can trust to affirm host States' commitments to them.

[240] Vandevelde, *supra* footnote 195.

[241] Guzman, *supra* footnote 220, p. 569.

Yackee has persuasively rebutted Guzman's contentions on this point by showing that many international tribunals have consistently held that State contractual promises to investors, particularly when these are governed by international law, including agreements to arbitrate these promises, are presumptively enforceable and entitle the investor to meaningful compensation in the event of breach[242].

Guzman is correct to the extent that what he means to say is that BITs may be a necessary complement to political risk insurance. Political risk insurance does not eliminate the need for a BIT. Such insurance may

---

[242] J. Webb Yackee, "Pacta Sunt Servanda and State Promises to Foreign Investors before Bilateral Investment Treaties: Myth and Reality", 32 *Fordham International Law Journal* 1550 (2009). Note, however, that arbitrators have disagreed as to why States need to respect their contracts with investors. Some have suggested that this is the case because *pacta sunt servanda* is a residual principle of natural law reflected in international law that remains applicable as "an overarching standard against which all aspects of national law, procedural as well as substantive, are to be judged". O. Spiermann, "Applicable Law", in P. Muchlinski *et al.* (eds.), *The Oxford Handbook of International Investment Law* (Oxford, Oxford University Press, 2008). Others have suggested that *pacta sunt servanda* is a "general principle of law" or part of "mandatory rules" or "*ordre public*", directly applicable as part of the proper law of such contracts. *Ibid.*, p. 97. Yet others have included *pacta sunt servanda* as among the applicable international law principles for the protection of aliens. *Ibid.*, p. 98. See also R. B. von Mehren and P. N. Kourides, "International Arbitration between States and Foreign Private Parties: The Libyan Nationalization Cases", 75 *American Journal of International Law* 476 (1981). But arbitrators do not all agree on whether *pacta sunt servanda* requires the enforcement of contractual stabilization clauses that would preempt a State from changing its law. See, e.g., R. Dolzer and C. Schreuer, *Principles of International Investment Law* (New York, Oxford University Press, 2008), pp. 75-77.

not always be available, either in the context of particular regions or States, or with respect to some of the kinds of risks covered by modern BITs[243]. Further, the subrogation remedy provided under a political risk insurance programme such as OPIC's — whereby the home Government of the investor stands in the shoes of the injured investor — may politicize a dispute far more than providing a remedy directly to the investor (as under BITs). Subrogation forces home Governments to resume a role reminiscent of those in the days when espousal and gunboat diplomacy were the only remedies for capital exporters. As noted, BITs (as well as the ICSID Convention), no less than, for example, the United States' Foreign Sovereign Immunities Act, were seen as mechanisms to get foreign ministries out of the business of needing to respond to perennial complaints by investors seeking their intervention.

The possibility that a State may agree to protect an investor's rights via contract does not make BITs unnecessary either. What Guzman should have argued is that BITs complement both political risk insurance and investor-State contracts to provide additional ways for States to surmount the dynamic inconsistency problem[244]. In the absence of a credible treaty commitment to submit to international arbitration, such as a country's ratifications of the ICSID and New York Conventions and a clause in a BIT whereby a State provides its advance consent to any such arbitration, an arbitral clause in an investment contract may prove unenforce-

---

[243] See generally L. S. Poulsen, "The Importance of BITs for Foreign Direct Investment and Political Risk Insurance: Revisiting the Evidence", in K. Sauvant (ed.), *Yearbook on International Investment Law & Policy 2009-2010* (Oxford, Oxford University Press, forthcoming 2010).

[244] See Yackee, "Pacta Sunt Servanda", *supra* footnote 242.

able. In addition, despite the judgments of most arbitral bodies affirming the enforceability of investment contracts as a matter of public international law, a commitment by an LDC in a discrete investment contract to an investor may prove easier to breach or to renegotiate under threat than a solemn commitment made in a BIT to the investor's State. Investors have not found it easy to rely on, for example, stabilization clauses contained in their investment contracts concluded with prior LDC Governments[245].

In any case, it is unrealistic to believe that every foreign investor can rely on the prospect of an investment contract with a host Government. The vast majority of investment flows do not involve a contract between an investor and a State. In all but the most rigid State-run economies, such arrangements are most common with respect to those enterprises that require host Government intervention, such as long-term mineral or oil contracts involving concessions on government land. In the world of free market States envisioned by BITs, where Governments and State enterprises are not dominant actors in the market, there is no need to seek the Government's intervention in entering or establishing an investment. A merger, an acquisition or a greenfield investment involving a foreigner simply takes place, as if these involved local investors. To require an investment contract with a Government is, from this standpoint, a defeat for the world of liberal investment flows that many States, including LDCs, sought to establish, particularly after the fall of the Soviet bloc. Strict reliance on investment contracts alone would also tend

---

[245] See, e.g., Dolzer and Schreuer, *supra* footnote 242, pp. 75-77; P. Kuruk, "Renegotiating Transnational Investment Agreements: Lessons for Developing Countries from the Ghana-Valco Experience", 13 *Michigan Journal of International Law* 43 (1991).

to privilege those large TNCs in certain sectors capable of exerting their leverage vis-à-vis host States anxious to draw them in through specific contractual guarantees. And even with respect to such investors, to the extent the underlying deal reflects the dynamics of an obsolescing bargain, exclusive reliance on contractual guarantees and the precise remedies negotiated by the two parties to a deal poses predictable risks for investors who will face, at the time of any subsequent breach by the host State, the problems of sunk costs and few credible exit options[246]. The relevant question then is not whether BITs are the "sole" way to overcome the dynamic inconsistency problem but whether they are relatively better or worse than the alternatives.

BITs were a *marginal* improvement over political risk insurance and investment contracts as credible commitment devices but, as we will see[247], it would be a mistake to assume that BITs provide a foolproof method of forcing compliance on a reluctant State[248].

---

[246] See generally Kuruk, *supra* footnote 245.

[247] For an attempt by an ICSID tribunal to deal with the enforcement "gap" in investor-State arbitration, see *Sempra Energy International* v. *Argentina*, Decision on the Argentine Republic's Request for a Continued Stay of Enforcement of the Award, ICSID Case No. ARB/02/16 (5 March 2009) (directing Argentina to put US$75 million into an escrow account if it wishes to stay an award against it pending pursuit of annulment).

[248] BITs are more reliable "commitment devices" than investment contracts, at least insofar as the latter do not include enforceable arbitration clauses; in addition, BITs promise investors protection in the myriad instances in which they have no contracts with a host State or where their injuries result from harms that are not cognizable in contractual terms. As noted, BITs extend protection to risks not usually covered by political risk insurance (even when this is available) and enable the investor itself to bring a claim against the host State. This last enables investors to control the kinds of issues that would be pre-

Accordingly, despite Guzman's efforts, the puzzle
remains. Why would States take the trouble to negotiate BITs that constrain their authority given that these
treaties only contribute to but do not wholly resolve the
dynamic inconsistency problem?

Contrary to what Guzman contends, there are many
explanations for the popularity of BITs with LDCs, not
just one. The most prevalent, and the one most consistent with global events coinciding with the explosion
of BITs after the end of the Cold War, is that LDCs
turned to BITs roughly at the same time (and for the
same reasons) that they turned towards liberalized
capital flows and market approaches to running their
economies: because they believed this was the best
way to promote economic development. A global turn
to economic liberalization in the 1990s, not a tit-for-tat
defection from the NIEO in the 1970s, coincides with
the turn to modern strong BITs and provides a powerful rationale for their proliferation. On this view, LDCs
accepted treaties like the US Model BIT of 1987 because
they sincerely believed in that treaty's grand bargain:
the promise of capital flows in exchange for a promise
to protect foreign capital now and in the future[249].
They adopted at least this much of the Washington
Consensus because their prior efforts to build their
economies on State-led planning, government enter-

---

sented to arbitrators for their decision and at least in theory
assists in depoliticizing disputes in a way that is not possible under the subrogation schemes of political risk insurance mechanisms where the home State of the investor
(and issuer of the insurance) assumes the investor's claim.
These are all relative improvements over possible alternatives but none are foolproof. As Argentina's resistance to
paying arbitral awards suggests, none of these — BITs,
investment contracts, or political risk insurance — *ensure*
that States' commitments to private parties will be
respected.

[249] See Salacuse, *supra* footnote 181, p. 7.

prises, heavy regulation, and/or restricted trade and FDI flows appeared not to have worked[250]. BITs were concluded precisely for the reasons suggested by the preamble to the US Model BIT of 1987: as one more step towards market liberalization.

Guzman ignores the salient facts that strongly suggest why, particularly after the end of the Cold War, LDCs were likely to be in support of the traditional customary protections for investors. The explosion in the number of investment agreements — what Vandevelde calls the "global era" of such agreements — is rooted in a global (if perhaps short-lived) victory for market ideology[251]. As is further addressed above, the proliferation of BITs has been accompanied by pervasive changes in how both foreign and national investors are treated under national laws. This turn to liberal capital flows and respect for property rights has also been encouraged by the "good governance" efforts of the World Bank, the IMF, and other market participants. The vast bulk of BITs came at the same time as multilateral organizations — from the World Bank to the IMF to UNCTAD — were also changing their perspective on free capital flows and their impact on development. Guzman ignores these multilateral dimensions of the investment regime as well as the impact of other significant global events, such as the establishment of the WTO in 1994, along with its complementary rules for reducing States' reliance on trade-related investment measures ("TRIMs"), for protecting trade in services ("GATS"), and for protecting intellectual property rights ("TRIPS"). The TRIMs Agreement has helped to encourage the inclusion of comparable restrictions on trade distorting performance requirements within investment agreements and there is sig-

---

[250] See, e.g., Salacuse, *supra* footnote 181, p. 8.
[251] Vandevelde, *supra* footnote 187, p. 21.

nificant overlap with the goals sought to be achieved through the TRIPS and GATS agreements as well[252].

Guzman's alleged "prisoner's dilemma" exists in a rarified vacuum unconnected to how the financial constraints faced by LDCs are likely to have affected the motivations of their government officials as well as other internal actors. Quite apart from the odd premise that capital flows constitute a zero sum game[253], his "prisoner's dilemma" ignores the consequences brought on by the disintegration of the Soviet bloc or by the debt crisis of the 1980s. It does not take full account of the wider ripples of decline in private lending during this period which, as Vandevelde points out, by 1980, had accounted for half of all capital flows to developing countries[254]. It ignores the likely attitudinal effects brought on by the massive federal deficits of the Reagan era, which prompted extensive borrowing by the United States and put further pressure on private markets for credit or the impact of reductions in development assistance at the behest of that same administration. Guzman ignores, in short, the possibility that LDCs, *both as a group and as individual States,* had more than sufficient reasons to abandon any lingering hostilities to traditional customary protections for foreign investment and more than enough reasons to adopt (or to resume) policies, including concluding investment agreements with investors and investment treaties with States, intended to create a generally favourable environment for capital flows (and not merely for investors from specific BIT parties). Indeed, it would have been extraordinary if, given all of these

---

[252] For discussion of the impact of these developments, see Vandevelde, *supra* footnote 187, pp. 19-28.

[253] For one critique of such "mercantilistic" zero-sum thinking as applied to the investment regime, see, e.g., Wälde, *supra* footnote 236, pp. 72-73.

[254] Vandevelde, *supra* footnote 187, p. 21.

events, rational LDCs had continued to voice support for the NIEO[255].

There is no need to adopt any single explanation for why LDCs opted for BITs. There are probably as many explanations for entering into BITs as there are LDCs. If BITs are like other treaties, there are in all likelihood multiple (perhaps even inconsistent) rationales on offer, depending on which governmental actor one asks. It is quite probable that distinct government elites

---

[255] Guzman argues that if LDCs were intending to affirm customary norms, they would have signed multilateral treaties rather than bilateral ones, see A. T. Guzman, "Explaining the Popularity of Bilateral Investment Treaties", in L. Sachs and K. P. Sauvant (eds.), *The Effect of Treaties on Foreign Direct Investment* (New York, Oxford University Press, 2009), p. 73. This is a *non sequitur*. Although BITs vary in their terms, they do not generally undermine customary international law and in any case such derogation would need to be explicit. The fact that States may opt to preserve some differences in how they treat investors from different nations and, subject to MFN, extend certain preferences to only some treaty partners, says little about their attitudes toward the basic customary rights protected by most BITs. The absence of a multilateral agreement among LDCs or between LDCs and developed States says no more about investment agreements' impact on customary norms than does the failure of OECD members to conclude the MAI. There is no question that OECD members share among themselves relatively compatible views about the applicable customary norms and the MAI's failure does not undermine that consensus. As Vandevelde suggests, the failure of the MAI

"may have been in part the result of that very consensus: that is, because these states already provide a favourable environment for investment as a matter of national policy, most of the participants had little to gain from the agreement and thus, once negotiations were underway, the focus shifted to that which they would be conceding". Vandevelde, *supra* footnote 187, p. 33.

are motivated to enter into BITs and FTAs for political as well as economic reasons. Given the evident fact that in some cases a country that enters into an investment agreement with the United States cannot realistically expect increases in US capital flows as a result[256], an LDC with a checkered history of investor-State relations, including experiments with socialism, might adhere to the exceptionally investor-protective US Model BIT circa 1984-1987 in order to send a forceful general signal that it is ready to change its ways and protect all foreign investors irrespective of country of origin. The intent to send this general message is especially likely if, as in most cases, it would be politically untenable to extend the guarantees contained in such a treaty to US investors and no one else[257].

There may also be powerful internal forces at work leading a country to conclude a BIT. If, as Robert Putnam argues, treaties are often part of "two level" games intended to respond to both domestic political pressures as well as international ones[258], some BITs might have been encouraged by national elites or

---

[256] Indeed, as veteran US BIT negotiators have repeatedly pointed out, US negotiators routinely alerted prospective BIT partners not to expect that BITs would necessarily increase such flows from US investors and US investors frequently resisted attempts by prospective BIT partners to include investment promotion devices within such treaties. See, e.g., Vandevelde, *supra* footnote 195, p. 32; Vandevelde, *supra* footnote 196.

[257] For consideration of the evidence that BITs may increase a party's general appeal to all foreign investors and not merely to investors from the particular signatory country, see, e.g., T. Büthe and H. V. Milner, "Bilateral Investment Treaties and Foreign Direct Investment: A Political Analysis", in Sachs and Sauvant, *supra* footnote 255.

[258] R. Putnam, "Diplomacy and Domestic Politics: The Logic of Two-Level Games", 42 *International Organization* 427 (1988).

domestic entrepreneurs seeking reassurance of their Government's long-term commitments to private capital or, as is implied by the US Model BIT's preamble, to a "stable" legal framework based on the national rule of law [259]. Some BITs might have been concluded, in short, to signal a Government's commitment to protecting its own entrepreneurs and not merely foreigners.

As this suggests, it is important to understand the domestic constituencies within an LDC that may be pressing for or against BIT ratification. Even some internal elites within an LDC may favour concluding a strong investor-protective BIT with the United States if they believe that such a treaty could make more stable or predictable the national rule of law as it applies to them [260]. This would suggest comparisons between concluding BITs and the deepening treaty commitments of European States, after World War II, within the European human rights regime [261].

---

[259] See, e.g., Salacuse, *supra* footnote 181, p. 10; Schneiderman, *supra* footnote 177, pp. 3-6 (arguing that investment treaties impose "constitution-like" constraints to bind States into the future despite changes in political regime).

[260] As Thomas Wälde has suggested, this would follow from the application of Putnam's analysis of the two-level games often undertaken through the conclusion of international legal commitments. See, e.g., Wälde, *supra* footnote 236, p. 91. See also A. Moravcsik, "The Origins of Human Rights Regimes: Democratic Delegation in Postwar Europe", 54 *International Organization* 253 (2000) (explaining how fragile government elites in Europe turned to human rights treaties after World War II to buttress their States' commitment to democracy).

[261] See Moravcsik, *supra* footnote 260. Salacuse quotes a private conversation with the Minister of Uruguay who explained his ratification of a US BIT in these terms: "We are not signing this treaty for them [i.e., the United States], we are signing it for us", Salacuse, *supra* footnote 181, p. 11.

Alternatively, an LDC may have entered into such a treaty as part of what some scholars have called "relationship building", that is, to strengthen its relationship with a particular BIT partner "such as to obtain other benefits and favours", and therefore to encourage more aid from the US Congress or strengthen export markets [262]. Or it may conclude a strong BIT with the United States to align itself with the United States and its Western allies, that is, to express solidarity with those states vis-à-vis other issues — or even to signal that it would now vote with the United States should NIEO-type resolutions be proposed in the General Assembly. Or, perhaps a BIT ratification is intended to send messages to other actors, such as to demonstrate to the IMF a country's seriousness with respect to complying with that organization's structural adjustment demands.

All of these are credible rationales for adhering to BITs. Unlike the single (inadequate) rationale offered by Guzman, none of them is inconsistent with the text of many of these treaties, which affirm the continued validity of relevant customary norms, from the Hull Rule to "full protection and security" [263].

These alternative explanations for why LDCs adhere to BITs render Guzman's conclusions about the disconnect between BITs and customary law dubious.

---

[262] See, e.g., Salacuse, *supra* footnote 181, p. 8.

[263] In addition to the language affirming the Hull Rule, customary international law "minimum" standards of treatment such as "fair and equitable treatment" and "full protection and security", the typical US BIT also reaffirms that investors have a right, under the treaty, to treatment no less than that provided under international law. See Article II (2), 1987 US Model BIT, *supra* footnote 184. But see Guzman, *supra* footnote 220, p. 95 (stating that BITs do not contain language affirming customary international law).

Guzman contends that if LDCs had intended to resurrect customary international law investment protections apart from their entry into BITs they would have undertaken collective efforts to undo the effects of their earlier NIEO efforts within the General Assembly. This contention ignores some troublesome facts, apart from the timing issues noted above.

First, contrary to what Guzman argues, there is little concrete evidence that the NIEO efforts in the General Assembly had successfully toppled — as opposed to merely threatened — the Hull Rule or other relevant customary norms encompassed by the doctrine of State responsibility to aliens. As noted above, the United States turned to BITs and to the inclusion of various provisions in that treaty that explicitly relied on customary international law in order to buttress customary law[264]. US BIT negotiators would hardly have sought to conclude treaties explicitly relying on customary law and indicating that US investors needed to be treated in accord with it had they thought that those traditional norms no longer existed. And these negotiators had good reason to continue to put their trust in such norms since, whenever the viability of such rules had been questioned before reasonably neutral bodies, relevant arbitral tribunals continued to conclude even after 1974 that neither the General Assembly resolution on Permanent Sovereignty nor its Charter of Economic Rights and Duties of States had changed the underlying customary norms[265]. Guzman makes no mention of

---

[264] See, e.g., Vandevelde, *supra* footnote 195, pp. 7-22.

[265] See, e.g., Interlocutory Award in case concerning *SEDCO, Inc. v. National Iranian Oil Company and the Islamic Republic of Iran*, Iran-United States Claims Tribunal, 10 *Iran-US Cl. Rep.* 180 (1986); Award on the Merits in Dispute between Texaco Overseas Petroleum Company/California Asiatic Oil Company and the Government of the Libyan Arab Republic, 17 *ILM* 1 (1978). See

famous decisions such as those emerging from the
Libyan oil expropriations, or of the many well-known
scholarly debates over whether General Assembly resolutions that had drawn the opposition of "specially
affected" States could nonetheless displace traditional
law, whether General Assembly resolutions in general
can be seen as a form of "State practice" or *"opinio
juris"*, or whether it is easier for the General Assembly
to *displace* existing custom than to replace it[266]. Given
arbitral decisions on point and the absence of a scholarly consensus otherwise, it is strange to suggest that
there was a self-evident need to "revoke" the NIEO to
restore the standing of customary rules.

Moreover, even if some Governments believed that
the General Assembly's efforts had indeed successfully
toppled the customary rules governing the treatment of
aliens, it would have been extraordinary for the
General Assembly to attempt to "revoke" a prior
General Assembly resolution even if the vast majority
of States no longer agreed with their prior proclama-
tions[267]. When a General Assembly effort is no longer
viable, it is far more common for the relevant resolution simply to disappear from the General Assembly's
agenda. This is, of course, what eventually occurred
with respect to the NIEO. It is equally plausible to
assume that as former supporters of the NIEO changed
their minds about the wisdom of those efforts, they
merely failed to re-introduce affirmations of the Charter
in subsequent sessions of the General Assembly.

---

also A. F. Lowenfeld, *International Economic Law*
(Oxford, Oxford University Press, 2002), pp. 16-31.

[266] See, e.g., Lowenfeld, *supra* footnote 265.

[267] The closest example, which suggests its exceptional
nature, is the Assembly's effort to renounce its prior
Assembly equating Zionism with racism. See General
Assembly res. 46/86, 46 *General Assembly Official
Records*, p. 39, UN doc. A/Res/46/86 (1991).

Subsequent inaction by the General Assembly on the NIEO, coupled with other General Assembly actions, such as its passage of a resolution in praise of "entrepreneurship" in 1993, could be taken as evidence that LDCs as a group *and* as BIT parties no longer supported the NIEO[268].

Of course, as traditional positivist international lawyers would be quick to point out, the content of customary norms is determined by actual State practice and *opinio juris*. It is wrong to focus only on the possible impact of either a network of investment treaties or a series of General Assembly resolutions. If the question is what is the state of relevant customary law at a particular moment in time, there is no substitute for looking at what States were doing and not merely their rhetoric. Guzman ignores the fact that the proliferation of BITs did not occur in a vacuum.

As suggested above, BITs were often concluded only after an LDC had demonstrated its commitment to free market principles through changes in local law. This may help to explain why the wave of investment treaty ratifications in the 1990s was generally accompanied or preceded by a wave of reforms of relevant national laws and practices[269]. According to UNCTAD,

---

[268] Compare General Assembly res. 48/180, 48 *General Assembly Official Records*, p. 159, UN doc. A/Res/48/180 (1993) (entitled "Entrepreneurship and Privatization for Economic Growth and Sustainable Development"). Knowledgable Assembly watchers know that when a majority of States continue to support action in the Assembly, this is inevitably accompanied by Assembly resolutions *seriatim*. The sheer absence of subsequent Assembly affirmations of the Charter of Economic Rights and Duties of States in the 1980s and beyond suggests how the NIEO effort effectively died from lack of affirmative support.

[269] Indeed, as noted, changes to local law and even constitutions in order to harmonize these with BIT or FTA obligations leads some to describe the investment regime

of 2,394 changes in national FDI laws from 1991 to 2005, 92 per cent of the changes were in the direction of making the investment climate more welcoming to FDI[270]. These changes in law, and not merely the practice of concluding BITs, are part of the "State practice" that needs to be examined with respect to relevant customary law[271].

---

as "constitution-like" in its effects. See, e.g., Schneiderman, *supra* footnote 177, pp. 114-120 (describing the domestic legal reforms triggered by the NAFTA, particularly in Mexico).

[270] Sachs and Sauvant, "BITs, DTTs, and FDI Flows: An Overview", in Sachs and Sauvant, *supra* footnote 255, p. xlix and table 3.

[271] The fact that States are entering into such commitments under laws (both national and international) would certainly support using these developments as evidence of *opinio juris*. Indeed, the relevant changes to national law in the direction of a liberal investment regime could also support an argument on the basis of general principles of law, see J. E. Alvarez, "A BIT on Custom", 42 *New York University Journal of International Law and Politics* 17 (2009). Nor is there clear evidence, as would be implied by Guzman's "economic" rationale for LDCs' conclusion of BITs, that market-oriented changes to national laws were intended to benefit only select investors from specific BIT partners. The evidence that we have suggests that most of these national laws sought to benefit investors generally. This makes sense as particularized benefits to only certain foreign investors, even if attempted, would likely prove to be short-lived given the MFN protections accorded under most BITs, while domestic legal reforms suggesting that foreign investors would receive greater rights than local investors could prove politically controversial. For a specific example of the use of BITs as a device to improve conditions for all investors, national or foreign, see, e.g., S. W. Schill, "Tearing Down the Great Wall: The New Generation Investment Treaties of the People's Republic of China", 15 *Cardozo Journal of International and Comparative Law* 73 (2007), pp. 92-93 (discussing Chinese efforts to use its BITs to redress local rule of law shortcomings).

Even assuming that Guzman is correct that LDCs' turn to BITs was principally driven by "economic" concerns, this economic rationale for concluding a BIT does not necessarily undercut the potential for BITs to affirm or otherwise affect customary international law. Even if, contrary to the many rationales we have canvassed, LDCs entered into such agreements only to secure scarce capital, this is not inconsistent with using a BIT to express support for the customary norms on which that treaty relies. Economic self-interest is one reason States may express support for a rule of custom. Indeed, most rules of custom (and treaties) exist because relevant States see these as in their political, economic, or other interests. These rationales do not undercut the existence of *opinio juris*.

C. Explaining the Contemporary Investment Regime

But even if Guzman were correct about why LDCs originally concluded BITs, his explanation for the spread of BITs is surely inadequate to account for the contemporary investment regime, which is now composed of some 180 countries as signatories to at least one BIT and includes, among the countries with the greatest number of BITs, States such as China (which had signed by the end of 2008, 124 BITs, making it second only to Germany as the country with the greatest number of BITs) or Cuba (which has as many concluded BITs as does the United States).

Circumstances have changed considerably from the days when US BIT negotiators could approach such negotiations as training lessons for others having no impact on the United States. Guzman's North/South perspective on BITs is an awkward fit for a regime that at least today includes a significant number of BITs between LDCs themselves (some 27 per cent of all BITs). A North/South perspective does not do justice to the world of investor-State arbitrations, which as of 2005, included 61 Governments as respondent States in known disputes (37 LDCs, 14 developed countries, and 10 from Southeast Europe and the Commonwealth of Independent States)[272].

Indeed, a system of dispute settlement in which the United States is the third most frequently sued defendant State is difficult to caricature as a product of neo-imperialist empire[273].

Today's flows of investment are not merely uni-directional. In most years after World War II, the United States has been the largest recipient of FDI as well as the leading capital exporter[274]. The United States shares this duality with others, such as the so-called BRICs, Brazil, Russia, India and China — all leading recipients and exporters of capital. Indeed, of the net stock of outward foreign direct investment capital, one fifth (or about US$300 billion in 2007) comes from TNCs from emerging markets[275]. Emerging market TNCs are now important players in the investment

---

[272] UNCTAD, Latest Developments in Investor-State Dispute Settlement, IIA Monitor No. 4 (2005), WEB/ITE/IIT/2005/2, available at <http://www.unctad.org/en/docs/webiteiit20051_en.pdf>, p. 3.

[273] *Ibid.* (noting that only Argentina and Mexico were then ahead of the United States in the number of investor-State claims).

[274] See, e.g., C. Congyan, "China-US BIT Negotiations and the Future of Investment Treaty Regime: A Grand Bilateral Bargain with Multilateral Implications", 12 *J. International Economic Law* 457 (2009), p. 462 (noting that in 2006, FDI flows into the United States amounted to US$217 billion while outflows reached US$175 billion). Of course, the United States' stake in existing FDI stock around the world, given its leading position as capital exporter, is substantial. Congyan indicates that US outward FDI stock amounted to US$2.4 trillion in 2006. *Ibid.*

[275] Sachs and Sauvant, *supra* footnote 270, pp. xxxii-xxiii.

regime and among the most dynamic TNCs are those from the Chinese mainland[276]. Indeed, during the current global financial crisis, while global FDI fell by about 20 per cent, China's outward FDI actually accelerated at least through the first quarter of 2009; this would confirm a trend since China's outward FDI has nearly doubled over the past couple of years, going from US$26.5 billion in 2007 to US$52.2 billion in 2008[277].

It is also no longer accurate to contend that rich countries do not regulate investment flows as between themselves. While the United States resisted concluding BITs with its old FCN partners in Europe and Japan, it has since entered NAFTA, as well as investment protection agreements with medium sized economies such as Singapore and Chile, thereby exposing itself to a significant threat of investor-State claims. It is also engaged in serious BIT negotiations with China. Moreover, the Energy Charter Treaty is an investment

---

[276] It is estimated that more than one third of capital inflows into LDCs originated in other developing economies. See D. Aykut and D. Ratha, "South-South FDI Flows: How Big Are They?", 13 *Transnational Corparations* 149 (2003), p. 149. For one account of the massive increases in Chinese outflows of foreign investment from 1992 to the present, see, e.g., Vale Columbia Center on Sustainable International Investment, "Chinese Multinationals Make Steady Progress", Press Release, 22 October 2008, available at <http://www.vcc.columbia.edu/files/vale/documents/RankingofChineseMultinationals-Final_2008.pdf>. For an assessment of the involvement of TNCs from the BRICs in integrating global production processes, see K. P. Sauvant, "New Sources of FDI: The BRICs. Outward FDI from Brazil, Russia, India, and China", Paper presented at Conference on Global Players from Emerging Markets, 30 May 2005.

[277] K. Davies, "While Global FDI Falls, China's Outward FDI Doubles", *Columbia FDI Perspectives*, No. 5 (2009).

protection treaty among over 50 developed nations, while OECD members have entered into among themselves at least some investment-related international obligations through their conclusion of FCNs (which remain in effect), their participation in the OECD Code of Capital Movements, as well as under the investment obligations of the WTO.

The evolution of China's BIT programme is also suggestive of why the North/South paradigm that grounds the "horizontal" critique of the investment regime identified in Chapter I may be a misleading description of the contemporary BIT scene. Stephan W. Schill has explored what China's status as both capital exporter and capital importer has meant for the Chinese BIT programme[278]. Schill traces the evolution of Chinese BITs and finds a significant change occurring in the late 1990s when that country broke with its long-standing reservations concerning national treatment and comprehensive investor-State dispute settlement. Schill points out that while, until 1979, the Government of the People's Republic of China ("PRC") associated itself with other LDCs in support of the NIEO, it changed its mind in order to attract foreign investment. He shows that, particularly as the PRC evolved into becoming both a capital importer and capital exporter, that country's reservations to the international legal guarantees contained in Western BITs crumbled. Consistent with the rival story to Guzman's that is suggested here, Schill describes how Chinese BITs evolved from the relatively weak treaty concluded with Sweden in 1982 (which did not contain investor-State dispute settlement at all and was therefore similar to the Canada-Poland BIT mentioned earlier), through treaties predating the PRC's (1990) signature to the ICSID convention (which offered

---

[278] Schill, *supra* footnote 271.

investors an arbitral remedy only with respect to the narrow question of the amount of compensation due in case of expropriation), to a "new generation" of Chinese BITs in the late 1990s and early 2000s (which finally combined broad guarantees of national treatment, clearer compensation standards, an umbrella clause, and capital transfer provisions with a comprehensive and effective investor-State arbitration clause)[279]. These later Chinese BITs are more like the US Model BIT of 1987. Schill notes that what he calls the "new generation" of Chinese BITs is not limited to treaties concluded with LDCs (where Chinese investors would be expected to be the principal beneficiaries) but also include recent treaties with capital exporting European States, including the Netherlands (2001) and Germany (2003)[280].

Schill explains changing Chinese attitudes toward the international investment regime in terms that are strikingly different from Guzman's "prisoner's dilemma". He writes that the PRC's new generation of BITs was "brought about by the continuous exposure to the needs and requirements of the global economy and China's increasing engagement with the international community"[281]. Whereas once the PRC sought to uphold the structures of a socialist economy and resisted making commitments on national treatment that would put its State-owned enterprises on the same plane as foreign investors, Schill contends that "China's interest in protecting its own investment ventures abroad" led to its acceptance of an ever stronger BIT, as would be expected of any State that needs to balance its dual position as both capital exporter and capital importer[282].

---

[279] Schill, *supra* footnote 271, pp. 89-113.
[280] *Ibid.*, pp. 93-94.
[281] *Ibid.*, p. 81.
[282] *Ibid.*, p. 99.

At a time when the investment regime is approaching universal participation and with a considerable portion of capital flows going into wealthy Western States and some emerging nations coming into their own as capital exporters, the proliferation of investment treaties cannot be explained simply as variations of the one-sided capitulation agreements once concluded between colonial powers and the periphery[283]. If that is what is meant by those who contend that the investment regime constitutes a form of "imperial" or "hegemonic" international law, this is an overly crude description of reality. Cuba's BITs, to cite another example from outside the "Anglo-American empire", are not very different from the highly investor protective US Model BIT of 1987. The Cuba-Cambodia BIT of 2001, for example, includes a very expansive definition of protected investment. It protects all forms of property, stocks, any claims to money or performance under contract, and intellectual property rights[284]. It protects investors as well as their returns, and accords fair and equitable treatment, full protection and security, and most favoured nation treatment[285]. Those familiar with

---

[283] This is not to deny that some bilateral relationships concerning capital flows or some BITs may indeed be forms of neo-colonialism. See, e.g., J. Thuo Gathii, "Foreign and Other Economic Rights upon Conquest and under Occupation: Iraq in Comparative and Historical Context", 25 *University of Pennsylvania Journal of International Economic Law* 491 (2004) (critiquing the massive privatizations and other actions during the US occupation of Iraq).

[284] Article I (1) of the Agreement between the Government of the Kingdom of Cambodia and the Government of the Republic of Cuba concerning the Promotion and Protection of Investments, signed on 28 May 2001, available at <http://www.unctad.org/sections/dite/iia/docs/bits/cuba_cambodia.pdf> (definition of "investment").

[285] *Ibid.*, Articles II, III, and VI.

Cuba's prominent role in resisting the Hull Rule will be amused to discover that the Cuba-Cambodia BIT even includes a provision on expropriation that affirms, as does the US BIT of 1984, the need to extend prompt, adequate, and effective compensation[286].

As the Cuba-Cambodia BIT suggests, the United States' affection for David Ricardo is now widely shared — and even includes Governments that do not identify themselves as capitalist. It is difficult to see such countries — or other leading BIT signatories such as Egypt — as tools of "empire" as that term is traditionally defined. Most countries no longer need training lessons in liberal economics to understand the merits of the theory of comparative advantage. Virtually all nations now regard mutual flows of transnational

---

[286] *Op. cit., supra* footnote 284, Article IV:

"Each Contracting Party shall not take measures of expropriation, nationalization, or otherwise subjected *[sic]* to any other measures having legal nature similar to nationalization or expropriation ('expropriation') against the investments of an investor of the other Contracting Party except under the following conditions: a. the measures are taken for a lawful purpose, for public interest and under due process of law; b. the measures are non discriminatory basis *[sic]*; c. the measures are accompanied by provisions for the payment of prompt, adequate and effective compensation. Such compensation shall amount to the fair market value of the investments affected immediately before the measures of expropriation became a *[sic]* public knowledge. Such market value shall be determined in accordance with internationally acknowledged practices and methods or, where such fair market value cannot be determined, it shall be such reasonable amount as may be mutually agreed between the Contracting Parties hereto, and it shall be freely transferable in the freely convertible currency in which the investment was made or in any other currency agreed upon by both Contracting Parties."

capital as indispensable for economic growth. Virtually all of them have taken to heart one of the lessons of the twentieth century, namely that reducing the risk of nationalist protectionist policies also reduces the risk of global and national depressions that inspire political extremism. Many States, not just those involved in establishing the Washington Consensus, may believe that liberal capital flows help prevent the rise of dictators and ensuing threats to the peace[287]. Whatever they once were, investment agreements are no longer one-sided tools for the imposition of Western power. Leading players who are signing such agreements to protect their foreign investors – countries such as Cuba, China or Egypt — are not credibly characterized as dupes of Western capital[288].

None of this is to suggest that there has been a worldwide (much less permanent) consensus in favour of the Washington Consensus or that, even if this was the case when BIT ratifications exploded in the 1990s, that remains the case today[289]. The world of BITs and FTAs has always been too complex to reduce to any

---

[287] See, e.g., T. W. Wälde, "The Present State of Research Carried Out by the English-Speaking Section of the Centre for Studies and Research", in Kahn and Wälde (eds.), *supra* footnote 217, p. 95. Of course, the WTO regime has also been justified as a mechanism to reduce asymmetries of power among nations and to protect international peace.

[288] For a more general argument that international regimes, including the investment regime, should not be reduced to simplified descriptions of territorially defined "empire", see J. Alvarez, "Contemporary International Law: An 'Empire of Law' or the 'Law of Empire'?", 24 *American University International Law Review* 811 (2009); J. Alvarez, *supra* footnote 227; see also S. Marks, "Empire's Law", 10 *Indiana Journal Global Studies* 449 (2003).

[289] Compare F. Fukuyama's notorious conclusion to the contrary in *The End of History and the Last Man* (New York, Free Press, 1992).

one story and the investment regime — to the extent a single regime exists — continues to evolve, as will be clear from other chapters. Despite the surface similarity among investment treaties, it would be a mistake to view the investment regime only through the lens of the US Model BIT of 1987 or that treaty's ideology.

This is especially the case because the US Model BIT itself has not stood still. Today, the United States negotiates off a very different model agreement, released in 2004 but heavily influenced by the United States' NAFTA experience. This model text has now formed the basis for concluded agreements with Chile, Morocco, Singapore, and Uruguay. There is no greater evidence of the changing dynamics and shifting ideologies of some investment treaties over time than the changes that have been made to the US Model BIT. While, as discussed, the Chinese BIT programme appears to be evolving towards greater acceptance of what Schill considers the prevailing "international standards" toward the treatment of foreign investors[290], over roughly the same period the US BIT programme has been going in the opposite direction. But the Chinese BIT programme is also a moving target. If the most recent Chinese treaties concluded between the PRC and Mexico, India, and New Zealand (over the past two years) are any indication, it would appear that the United States and the Chinese BIT programmes are meeting somewhere in the middle. These countries' respective model texts contain some strikingly similar provisions[291].

If we were to compare the texts of the US Model

---

[290] Schill, *supra* footnote 271, pp. 113-115.

[291] Congyan, *supra* footnote 274, pp. 461-462 (tracing the evolution of the Chinese BIT through three periods, when the PRC adhered to a "conservative", "liberal" or a "balanced" paradigm in their model BITs).

BIT of 2004 with its 1984-1987 predecessors, we
would find that the United States has, in the course of
20 years, developed a more cautious attitude when it
comes to protecting foreign investment. It is no longer
accurate to portray today's US Model BIT as a single-
minded quest to protect the interests of US investors
overseas. Its content – and its ideology – has shifted.
Comparing the texts suggests the extent to which the
United States' experience, particularly as a defendant
under the NAFTA's investment chapter over the past
decade, has made it considerably more cautious about
extending treaty based protections to foreigners[292].
The United States is no longer as sanguine about proposing open-ended relative or absolute guarantees to
foreign investors or about its own ability to comply
with these[293].

---

[292] For a detailed discussion of how the United States'
experiences as a NAFTA respondent has shaped changes to
the dispute settlement provisions in its 2004 Model BIT,
see B. Legum, "Lessons Learned from the NAFTA: The
New Generation of US Investment Treaty Arbitration
Provisions", 19 *ICSID Review* 344 (2004). Although at
this writing, the United States has yet to lose a single
investor-State claim, by the end of 2007 it had been forced
to defend its actions in 12 such cases and was the fourth
largest respondent host State in the world according to
UNCTAD (UNCTAD, Latest Developments in Investor-
State Dispute Settlement, IIA Monitor No. 1, UNCTAD/
WEB/ITE/IIA/2008/3 (2008) available at <http://www.
unctad.org/en/docs/iteiia20083_en.pdf>, p. 14.

[293] For a more thorough comparison of the 2004 and
earlier US Models, see K. J. Vandevelde, "A Comparison
of the 2004 and 1994 US Model BITs: Rebalancing
Investor and Host Country Interests", in K. P. Sauvant
(ed.), *supra* footnote 213. For a critical view of the new
US model, contending that it is a significant retreat from
its more investor protective earlier text, see S. M. Schwebel,
"The United States 2004 Model Bilateral Investment Treaty:
An Exercise in the Regressive Development of International
Law", 3:2 *Transnat'l Dispute Management* (2006).

The US Model BIT of 2004, as well as most US investment protection treaties concluded since 2004 (as compared to the US Model BIT of 1987):

(1) Narrow the definition of covered investments. The 2004 US Model narrows the definition of investments protected by the treaty by, for example, excluding some claims to payment such as debts for sale of goods or services or authorizations/instruments "that do not create any rights protected under domestic law"[294].

(2) Narrow the scope of NT and MFN. Recent US investment treaties permit greater exceptions to both NT and MFN and indicate that MFN rights do not extend to grant treaty parties the benefits of prior, more expansive US BITs[295].

(3) Eliminate the umbrella clause. The umbrella clause that was part of the US Model BIT of 1987 is now gone, as was true of the NAFTA[296]. The 2004 Model also restricts the scope of arbitral investment disputes brought on the basis of an investment contract to claims arising from violations of other BIT guarantees[297].

---

[294] See Article 1, notes 1 and 2, US Department of State and US Trade Representative, US Model BIT 2004 available at <http://www.state.gov/documents/organization/117601.pdf> (hereinafter "2004 US Model BIT"); see also Article 10.27, n. 9, n. 10 of the United States-Morocco Free Trade Agreement, signed 15 June 2004, entered into force 1 January 2006, available at <http://www.ustr.gov/trade-agreements/free-trade-agreements/morocco-fta/final-text>.

[295] See, e.g., the non-conforming measures provision, Article 10.12 of United States-Morocco Free Trade Agreement, *supra* footnote 294.

[296] Compare Article II (2), 1987 US Model BIT, *supra* footnote 184.

[297] This seems to be the effect of Article 24 (1) *(b)*, 2004 US Model BIT, *supra* footnote 121 (stating that any claims brought for breach of an investment agreement

(4) Eliminate the guarantee barring "arbitrary and discriminatory" treatment[298].

(5) Narrow the scope of FET and full protection and security. The 2004 text restricts the meaning of these guarantees to the protection provided to aliens under customary international law[299]. The new language reflects the "Note of Interpretation" of the NAFTA issued by the parties to that treaty in 31 July 2001[300].

(6) Reduce investors' rights to due process. The 2004 Model eliminates the clause from the 1987 Model that guaranteed investors' rights to local remedies[301]. It also eliminates from the scope of investor-State arbitration claims for violation of investors' rights to participate in domestic administrative proceedings; indeed, the United States-Morocco FTA appears to omit any right to transparent local regulations or to a remedy in local courts[302].

---

must "directly relate to the covered investment that was established or acquired, or sought to be established or acquired, in reliance on the relevant investment agreement").

[298] Compare Article II (2), 1987 US Model BIT, *supra* footnote 184.

[299] See Article 5 and Annex A, 2004 US Model BIT, *supra* footnote 294; see also Annex 10-A which is intended to be read along with Article 10.5 of United States-Morocco Free Trade Agreement, *supra* footnote 294.

[300] "Notes of Interpretation of Certain Chapter 11 Provisions", *NAFTA Free Trade Commission* (31 July 2001), available at <http://www.international.gc.ca/trade-agreements-accords-commerciaux/disp-diff/nafta-interpr.aspx?lang=en> (hereinafter "NAFTA Interpretation"). This Note of Interpretation is addressed in detail in Chapter III. See also Annex 10-A of United States-Morocco Free Trade Agreement, *supra* footnote 299.

[301] Compare Article II (6), 1987 US Model BIT, *supra* footnote 184.

[302] Thus, Article 24 of the 2004 US Model BIT, *supra* footnote 294, does not extend the right to bring an investor-State claim for violation of its Article 11 (the transparency provision).

(7) Reduce the scope of indirect expropriation. The 2004 Model eliminates the "tantamount to expropriation" language originally contained in the 1987 Model's expropriation provision and subjects claims of indirect takings to a three-factor balancing test (requiring consideration of the economic impact of the Government's action, the extent to which it interferes with distinct, reasonable investment-backed expectations, and the character of the government action) that is drawn from US Supreme Court precedents[303]. The new language governing claims for indirect takings also states that, except in rare circumstances, such takings cannot result from non-discriminatory regulations to protect "public welfare objectives" such as public health, safety and the environment[304].

(8) Limit claims based on violations of intellectual property rights. The 2004 Model exempts revocation or limitation of intellectual property rights from the expropriation clause when such actions are in accord with the TRIPS Agreement of the GATT[305].

---

[303] Compare Article III, 1987 US Model BIT, *supra* footnote 184, to Article 6 and Annexes A and B, 2004 US Model BIT, *supra* footnote 294 (attempting to conform the expropriation guarantees in BITs to those contained in the US Constitution as interpreted by US courts in cases such as *Penn Central* v. *City of New York*, 438 US 104 (1978)). This provision appears intended to make sure that newer US BITs do not provide foreign investors with greater rights than those accorded nationals.

[304] Annex B, 4 *(b)*, 2004 US Model BIT, *supra* footnote 294. See also Article 10.6 governing expropriation in the United States-Morocco Free Trade Agreement, *supra* footnote 294, along with the parties' shared understanding at Annex 10-B of what it means. The three-factor balancing test adopted from *Penn Central* (see *supra* footnote 303), along with the exception for legitimate regulatory measures, appears in that annex.

[305] Article 6 (5), 2004 US Model BIT, *supra* footnote 294; see also Article 10.6, para. 5, of the United

(9) Limit expropriation claims based on tax measures. The 2004 Model requires that expropriation claims based on tax measures can be presented to investor-State arbitration only if these are first presented to the competent tax authorities of both parties and if within 180 days of referral these authorities fail to agree that the taxation measure is not an expropriation[306].

(10) Include explicit recognition of States' rights to regulate to protect health, safety, and the environment. Post-2004 US investment treaties typically include preamblar language, as well as specific provisions that recognize States' rights to take action to protect labour rights and the environment[307].

(11) Impose new restrictions on investor-State dispute settlement. The 2004 US Model imposes a new 90-day advance notice requirement on investors' claims where such notice indicates the basis of such claims[308]. Its much revised dispute settlement procedures also permit the consolidation of claims, incorporate a three-year statute of limitation on claims, permit the filing of *amicus* briefs by third parties, authorize an expedited preliminary procedure to dismiss frivolous claims, anticipate that the disputing parties will be able to make comments on the arbitrator's proposed award before it is finalized, and require that documents

---

States-Morocco Free Trade Agreement, *supra* footnote 294.

[306] Article 21 (2), 2004 US Model BIT, *supra* footnote 294; see also Article 21.3, para. 6, of United States-Morocco Free Trade Agreement, *supra* footnote 294.

[307] Preamble and Articles 12 and 13, 2004 US Model BIT, *supra* footnote 294; see also preamble to United States-Morocco Free Trade Agreement, *supra* footnote 294 and its Article 10.10 concerning environmental laws.

[308] Article 24 (2), 2004 US Model BIT, *supra* footnote 294; see also Article 10.15 of United States-Morocco Free Trade Agreement, *supra* footnote 294.

produced in the course of investor-State arbitrations be made publically available[309].

(12) Make the "essential security" portion of the non-precluded clauses self-judging. Post-2004 US investment treaties indicate that measures not precluded are those which a State "considers" to be in its essential security; indeed in some recent US treaties, the provision indicates that when a State invokes this exception that exception "shall" apply[310].

(13) Authorize States parties to issue interpretations of the treaty. Beginning with the NAFTA, US investment treaties now routinely authorize the States parties to such agreements to issue, from time to time and only if all the States parties agree, interpretations of their agreement that are binding on investor-State arbitrations[311]. As there is no apparent restriction on when

---

[309] Article 33 (consolidation of claims); Article 26 (3-year limit), 28 (2) (*amicus* briefs); Article 5 (preliminary procedure), Article 28 (9) *(a)* (authorizing written comments on proposed award), and Article 29 (transparency), 2004 US Model BIT, *supra* footnote 294.

[310] Article 18 (2), 2004 US Model BIT, *supra* footnote 294; Article 21.2 of the United States-Morocco Free Trade Agreement, *supra* footnote 294 (both containing the "which it considers" language on essential security). See also Peru-United States Free Trade Agreement, signed 12 April 2006, entered into force 1 February 2009, which states, as a footnote to its essential security clause at Article 22.2: "[f]or greater certainty, if a Party invokes [the measures not precluded clause] in an arbitral proceeding . . . the tribunal or panel hearing the matter shall find that the exception applies". For the text of the Peru-United States Free Trade Agreement, see <http://www.ustr. gov/trade-agreements/free-trade-agreements/peru-tpa/final-text>. The essential security issue is further addressed in Chapter IV.

[311] Article 30 (3), 2004 US Model BIT, *supra* footnote 294; Article 10.21, para. 3, of the United States-Morocco Free Trade Agreement, *supra* footnote 294.

such interpretations can be issued or on their subject matter, presumably States parties threatened by a pending claim can issue interpretations specifically intended to preclude the success of that claim[312].

The provisions of the 2004 US Model suggest some of the latest trends in recently concluded investment treaties, as other countries are now emulating the United States and introducing, for example, explicit public interest safeguards[313]. The latest US Model has influenced China in particular. While no single Chinese BIT yet incorporates all the innovative provisions evident in the US 2004 Model, it is striking that the China-Mexico BIT of 2008, for example, adopts a hedged definition of "fair and equitable" and the minimum standard of treatment that approximates that contained in the NAFTA's July 2001 Note of Interpretation and which is now standard in post-2004 US investment agreements[314]. Other examples include the China-India

---

[312] The possibility that such interpretations may undermine investors' settled expectations and that they may serve as a disguised form of amending such treaties has provoked controversy in some arbitrations and among some scholars. See, e.g., C. Brower, "Investor-State Disputes under NAFTA: The Empire Strikes Back", 40 *Columbia Journal of Transnational Law* 41, pp. 56-57, n. 71 (2001) (discussing, among other cases, *Pope & Talbot* v. *Canada*).

[313] OECD, "Novel Features in OECD Countries' Recent Investment Agreements: An Overview", 12 December 2005, available at <http://www.oecd.org/dataoecd/42/9/35823420.pdf>, p. 4.

[314] See Bilateral Investment Treaty, Mexico-People's Republic of China, Article 5, reportedly signed in Beijing on 11 July 2008 (on file with Transnational Dispute Management) (stating that the concepts of fair and equitable treatment and full protection and security "do not require treatment in addition to or beyond that which is required by the international law minimum standard of treatment of aliens as evidence of State practice and *opinio*

BIT of 2006, which largely reproduces the United States' new limits on "indirect takings"[315], or the New Zealand-China FTA of 2008, which includes innovations to investor-State dispute settlement presumably inspired by the NAFTA and the 2004 US Model, including requirements of transparency and advance notice for claims, along with provisions permitting the consolidation of claims and authorizing binding joint interpretations by the States parties[316]. Perhaps more surprising is the New Zealand-China FTA, which, like the 2004 US Model, evinces comparable concerns with respect to labour and the environment[317].

The new generation of US BITs, like the new generation of Canadian investment agreements which they

---

juris" and that " a determination that there has been a breach of another provision of this Agreement, or of a separate international agreement, does not establish that there has been a breach of this Article"). Compare NAFTA Interpretation, *supra* footnote 300. Given their own interpretation of comparable guarantees in the NAFTA, the Mexican negotiators may have insisted on such a provision.

[315] See Protocol, China-India BIT (qualifying the meaning of "takings" for purposes of Article 5), as quoted in Congyan, *supra* footnote 274, p. 478, n. 120.

[316] See Free Trade Agreement between the Government of New Zealand and the People's Republic of China, signed 7 April 2008, entered into force 1 October 2008, available at <http://www.chinafta.govt.nz/1-The-agreement/2-Text-of-the-agreement/0-downloads/NZ-ChinaFTA-Agreement-text.pdf> (hereinafter New Zealand-China Free Trade Agreement), Articles 153-154, 156-157.

[317] See *ibid.*, Memorandum of Understanding on Labor Cooperation and Environment Cooperation Agreement, available at <http://www.chinafta.govt.nz/1-The-agreement/1-Key-outcomes/0-downloads/MOU-NZ.pdf> and <http://www.chinafta.govt.nz/1-The-agreement/1-Key-outcomes/0-downloads/ECA-NZ.pdf> (respectively), both of which are integral parts of the New Zealand-China Free Trade Agreement, *supra* footnote 316.

closely resemble[318], are more than twice as long as the 1984 Model. In this instance, however, a longer treaty means far more hedged investment guarantees for investors. The new generation of US BITs has become longer to better protect the rights of host States as sovereigns. While the new US Model does not protect host States as much as the NIEO — which avoided imposing any international legal obligations on States vis-à-vis foreign investors altogether — it is not far-fetched to suggest that the new text evinces a new-found respect for many of the "sovereign rights" that the United States ridiculed at the General Assembly during the 1970s. The 2004 US Model, like the current Canadian model investment agreement, reflects a Government that has faced the brunt of claims under the NAFTA challenging California's rights to protect its ground water as a violation of the overly broad guarantees of fair and equitable treatment or asserting that a Mississippi jury award of punitive damages against a Canadian investor constituted an illegal taking of property[319]. The newly hedged essential security clause also reflects awareness of ICSID decisions that have found Argentina liable for harms inflicted on foreign investors as a result of general measures that it took in response to a serious economic and political

---

[318] For the text of Canada's latest model treaty for investment promotion and protection, see <http://www.international.gc.ca/trade-agreements-accords-commerciaux/assets/pdfs/2004-FIPA-model-en.pdf>. See also J. McIlroy, "Canada's New foreign Investment Protection and Promotion Agreement Two Steps Forward, One Step Back ?", 5 *Journal of World Investment & Trade* 621 (2004).

[319] See, e.g., *Methanex Corp.* v. *US (Can.* v. *US)*, 44 *ILM* 1345 (NAFTA Chap. 11 Arb. Trib. 2005), available at <http://naftaclaims.com/Disputes/USA/Methanex/Methanex_Final_Award.pdf>; *The Loewen Group, Inc. et al.* v. *US*, ICSID Case No. ARB(AF)/98/3, 42 *ILM* 811 (2003).

crisis (which will be addressed in Chapter IV)[320]. The changes to the United States' model treaties also reflect a decade of pressure by numerous NGOs, some of which were involved in the successful effort to unravel the negotiations for the OECD's Multilateral Agreement on Investment (MAI) and who remain convinced, rightly or wrongly, that the network of BITs and other investment agreements threaten the rights of federal, state, or provincial governments to regulate in the public interest[321].

It is possible to justify some of the changes to the 2004 US Model as merely "clarifying" matters to better reflect what US negotiators always intended[322]. And some changes are obviously intended to bring post-2004 US BITs in line with changes originally introduced in the NAFTA's Chapter 11[323]. Some changes also demonstrate a point suggested in Chapter I — namely that the network of BITs and FTAs are also affected by complementary efforts pursued elsewhere, including in the WTO. This explains, for example,

---

[320] For a more detailed discussion of some of these cases, see Alvarez and Khamsi, *supra* footnote 213.

[321] See, e.g., S. Anderson and S. Grusky, "Challenging Corporate Investor Rule", Institute for Policy Studies and Food and Water Watch (2007), available at <http://www.ips-dc.org/getfile.php?id=146>. For a particular manifestation of these concerns, see, for example, the Center for International Environmental Law's (CIEL) comments on the report filed by the US Government's Trade and Environment Policy Advisory Committee ("TEPAC") on the United States-Morocco Free Trade Agreement, 6 April 2004, available at <http://ustraderep.gov/assets/Trade_Agreements/Bilateral/Morocco_FTA/Reports/asset_upload_file892_3119.pdf>. These comments suggest that this environmental NGO is not yet satisfied by the changes made to the 2004 US Model BIT, *supra* footnote 294, and believes that a further narrowing of investor rights is needed.

[322] See, e.g., Vandevelde, *supra* footnote 293.

[323] *Ibid.*

changes to the US model, as well as changes to recent Chinese BITs, that seek to avoid conflicts with GATT law[324]. Nonetheless, the changes in recent US BITs and FTAs go beyond mere concerns for harmonization. The cumulative impact of these changes has given the new US Model a different purpose. That treaty now reflects a somewhat different ideology.

D. What is the Most Recent Wave of US Investment Treaties Trying to Achieve?

If the US Model BIT circa 1984-1987 represented the triumph of the Washington Consensus, US post-2004 investment treaties reflect what David Kennedy has characterized as a newly chastened form of neo-liberalism brought about by disillusion with the political and social results of neo-liberal "market shock" transitions, popular opposition to "structural adjustment" policies in much of the South, and vulnerabilities felt even in the North concerning the impact of globalization[325]. To be sure, the United States has not given up on David Ricardo or the free market. The 2004 US Model still adheres to a capitalist conception of the role of the State vis-à-vis the market. It still adheres to the threefold premises of the original US BIT outlined earlier; that is, it still expects that States will protect the bargains struck by private parties, generally defer to the market, and intervene in the market only insofar as necessary. Its ideology still reflects

---

[324] Thus, even though Chinese BITs traditionally avoided mention of performance requirements, China's accession to the WTO presumably explains why the New Zealand-China Free Trade Agreement of 2008 incorporates, for the first time, the TRIMS agreement into an investment treaty. New Zealand-China Free Trade Agreement, *supra* footnote 316, Article 140.

[325] Kennedy, *supra* footnote 204, p. 150.

what David Kennedy calls the "welfare economics" characteristic of European and American welfare states[326]. But the new US BIT reflects changes in mainstream thinking about economic development since the mid-1990s brought about by criticisms of the Washington Consensus by scholars like Joseph Stiglitz and Amartya Sen[327]. Whereas the original US BIT focused exclusively on reducing forms of governmental overreach or "government failure", more recent US treaties suggest a new-found awareness that merely assuring that assets are in private hands and subject to accurate price signals does not produce the desired beneficial outcomes that the preamble to the US Model BIT of 1987 presumed.

The new model reflects, as Stiglitz recommends, renewed attention to the need for Governments to be able to respond to market failures, that is, to "private rent seeking, private efforts to use the political process to thwart the effects of virtuous deregulatory policies, failures of private decision making and entrepreneurial culture"[328]. The new treaty re-emphasizes the role of government and, as Kennedy suggests, is characteristic of the more recent forms of development thinking, is more open to local solutions, a greater diversity of institutions, and multiple plans involving Government to achieve a range of public goods[329]. Whereas the object and purpose of the 1987 US BIT was to protect the foreign investor at all costs — as if development was defined by market freedom and the protection of property — the 2004 version implicitly recognizes that host States may define freedom (or sustainable devel-

---

[326] Kennedy, *supra* footnote 204, p. 151.
[327] See, e.g., I. E. Stiglitz, *supra* footnote 230; A. Sen, *Development as Freedom* (New York, Anchor, 2000).
[328] Kennedy, *supra* footnote 204, p. 153.
[329] *Ibid*., p. 158, table 7. See also D. Rodrik, *supra* footnote 203.

opment) more broadly, as does Sen, to include other
forms of human flourishing in addition to entrepreneurial freedom[330].

The object and purpose of the 2004 Model is less
about the investor and more about the rule of law itself.
It emphasizes the need to establish stable rules of the
road to guide both the investor and the State. It appears
to presume that building the rule of law itself is "the
essence of good governance, itself a pre-condition for
long-term economic, social and civil development"[331]
and an objective shared by host and parent State
alike[332]. The purposes of the new BITs and FTAs
appear to include, much more explicitly, the goal of
"balancing" the rights of private investors on the one
hand and States on the other[333]. Post-2004 US treaties
emphasize far more than its old BITs the need for
States to regulate in the public interest. While the
focus of the 2004 Model BIT's substantive guarantees
remains on the rights of foreign investors, the old
model's "asymmetries" have been reduced through
reminders of the competing regulatory goals that States
need to be able to exercise. To this end, the newer
treaties permit the State to re-assert its power at crucial

---

[330] Kennedy, *supra* footnote 204, p. 157 (citing Sen,
supra footnote 327).

[331] Wälde, *supra* footnote 287, pp. 106-107, 113.

[332] Cf. Kennedy, *supra* footnote 204, p. 157.

[333] While some have suggested that all BITs should be
presumed to share a common object and purpose, namely
to balance the respective rights of investors and States, this
ignores the textual differences among BITs, including
between treaties as distinct as the 1984 and 2004 US
Models. Cf. C. McLachlan "The Principle of Systemic
Integration and Article 31 (3) *(c)* of the Vienna Convention", 54 *International and Comparative Law Quarterly*
279 (2005), p. 114. While the singular object and purpose
of the 1984 US Model was to protect the foreign investor,
the same cannot be said about its 2004 Model.

intervals, most controversially whenever a State thinks its "essential security" is threatened, when it takes "regulatory" actions that might otherwise be deemed confiscatory, or whenever all the States parties to a treaty decide to issue a clarifying "interpretation" of their agreement.

The new texts of US investment treaties suggest a greater appreciation for the fact that even reliance on customary international law protections such as the "international minimum standard" may, in the hands of arbitrator-interpreters, become more than a "minimal commitment" to liberal, free-market principles and may result instead in politically unacceptable intrusions on the discretion many Governments believe they are entitled to retain. Indeed, some critics of the investment regime believe that vague guarantees such as "fair and equitable" treatment should be eliminated altogether, in favour of investment protections that commit a State only to national treatment or non-discrimination.

Post-2004 US investment treaties reflect a greater appreciation that the BIT's standard protections — now somewhat reduced in scope and number — may be more onerous and controversial than the Reagan era free marketeers, who played a role in designing the 1987 model, assumed. The newer treaties recognize that it may be impossible to erect a "wall of separation" to insulate business from politics and that an investment treaty, even with enforceable dispute settlement, does not provide the total escape from politics sought by early BIT drafters. The new texts, by acknowledging the need to "balance" the competing rights of private parties and the State (as with respect to "indirect" expropriations), recognize that some arbitral decisions, like some decisions by national courts, necessarily implicate political, and perhaps even constitutional, concerns. Awareness of the public policy implications of investor-State dispute settlement is also apparent in the changes to dispute settlement intended to make that process more transparent and predictable, fairer to the host State, more subject to state control, and perhaps even less costly [334].

The US Model BIT of 2004 also reflects a new-found appreciation for the views of Carlos Calvo [335]. At least some of the changes to substantive investor protections in the new Model BIT reflect concerns of members of the US Congress who indicated, in connection with passage of trade promotion authority in 2002, that henceforth the United States should not grant foreign investors "greater" rights than those enjoyed by US nationals [336]. The new Model's attempts to narrow foreign investors' rights such that they

---

[334] For suggestions that such changes respond to broader pressures on Governments to adhere to global standards expected of this and other forms of "administrative" law, see, e.g., B. Kingsbury and S. Schill, "Investor-State Arbitration as Governance: Fair and Equitable Treatment, Proportionality and the Emerging Global Administrative Law", in *El Nuevo Derecho Administrativo Global en América Latina* (Argentina, Univ. Los Andes, 2009), p. 221.

[335] See, e.g., Michael J. Bond, "The Americanization of Carlos Calvo", 22 *Mealey's International Arbitration Report* 1 (2007).

[336] See P.L. 107-210, 19 USC § 3802. The TPA's objectives stated in relevant part:

"[r]ecognizing that United States law on the whole provides a high level of protection for investment, consistent with or greater than that level required by international law, the principal negotiating objectives of the United States regarding foreign investment are to reduce or eliminate artificial or trade-distorting barriers to foreign investment, while ensuring that foreign investors in the United States are not accorded greater substantive rights with respect to investment protections than United States investors in the United States . . .".

See also CIEL note, *supra* footnote 321.

receive no more protections under the treaty than that which they receive under existing US law means that, ironically, the expropriation provisions contained in the Cuba-Cambodia BIT or in some Chinese BITs, for example, now provide investors with greater protections than do contemporary US investment agreements, such as the United States-Morocco FTA[337].

Other countries, such as Norway, have tried to go further in the direction of "re-balancing" the rights of investors and States. This seems self-evident from the lengthy preamble to the Norwegian Model BIT released in December 2007, which provides:

> "Desiring to encourage, create and maintain stable, equitable, favourable and transparent conditions for investors of one Party and their investments in the territory of the other Party on the basis of equality and mutual benefit;
>
> Desiring to achieve these objectives in a manner consistent with the protection of health, safety, and the environment, and the promotion of internationally recognized labour rights;
>
> Emphasising the importance of corporate social responsibility;
>
> Recognising that the development of economic and business ties can promote respect for internationally recognised labour rights; affirming their

---

[337] Compare the text of the expropriation provision of the Cuban BIT cited at *supra* footnote 286 to the expropriation provision in 2004 US Model BIT, *supra* footnote 294, at Article 6. Note that US efforts to reduce the scope of investor protections to those under existing law appear comparable to US efforts to do the same with respect to human rights treaties. See, e.g., US Reservations, Understandings and Declarations to the ICCPR, Senate Comm. on Foreign Relations, Report on the International Covenant on Civil and Political Rights, S. Exec. Rep. No. 23, 1 (102d Sess. 1992), reprinted in 31 *ILM* 645 (1992).

commitment to democracy, the rule of law, human rights and fundamental freedoms in accordance with their obligations under international law, including the principles set out in the United Nations Charter and the Universal Declaration of Human Rights;

Recognising that the promotion of sustainable investments is critical for the further development of national and global economies as well as for the pursuit of national and global objectives for sustainable development, and understanding that the promotion of such investments requires cooperative efforts of investors, host governments and home governments;

Recognising that the provisions of this agreement and provisions of international agreements relating to the environment shall be interpreted in a mutually supportive manner;

Determined to prevent and combat corruption, including bribery, in international trade and investment;

Recognising the basic principles of transparency, accountability and legitimacy for all participants in foreign investment processes;

Have agreed as follows . . ."[338]

As this preamble suggests, this particular BIT was a far-reaching attempt to recognize the competing obligations of host States, including a number of obligations that exist outside the investment regime. While the preamble retains language on the need for stable and favourable "conditions for investors", virtually every other paragraph now hedges on that guarantee, in order to stress the need for such rights to provide "mutual" benefits for both States parties, to protect

---

[338] Norway Model BIT, available at <http://www.regjeringen.no/upload/NHD/Vedlegg/hoeringer/Utkast%20til%20modellavtale2.doc>.

health, safety, the environment, and internationally recognized labour rights, to maximize the sustainable utilization of resources, to embrace corporate social responsibility, protect human rights, and to combat corruption. This broad preamble is virtually a restatement in treaty form of Sen's attempt, in *Development as Freedom*, to redefine human rights not as a tool to facilitate development but as development itself[339]. Assuming these diverse goals are treated seriously as essential to understanding the Norwegian BIT's object and purpose, this preamble could have suggested revolutionary new interpretations of that treaty's substantive guarantees. Note the potentially expansive enquiries arguably accorded to investor-State arbitrators by the suggestion in this preamble, for example, that the promotion of investments may implicate the efforts of both investors and their home Governments – and does not only require the efforts of host States.

But Norway's effort now has to be addressed in the past tense because on 8 June 2009 that Government withdrew this text noting that since its release its effort had drawn polarized critical reactions from both the left and the right. Indeed, the draft text drew the opposition of both the Socialist Left Party (which suggested that the treaty was still imbalanced in favour of investors) and the Centre Party (which argued that the new model did not provide investors with enough protections). Given these reactions, the coalition Government of Norway announced that achieving "a proper balance is too difficult" and it now appears that Norway may be backing away from negotiating any future BITs with the exception of FTA negotiations under way with India, China, Ukraine and Russia[340]. A

---

[339] Sen, *supra* footnote 337.
[340] D. Vis-Dunbar, "Norway Shelves Its Draft Model Bilateral Investment Treaty", *Investment Treaty News*,

similar outcome is not entirely far-fetched even for the erstwhile leader of the investment regime, the United States. As of the spring of 2009, the Obama Administration convened a subcommittee of the State Department to review the 2004 US BIT and the US BIT programme. One of the two co-chairs of that subcommittee, Thea Mei Lee, who is the policy director of the most prominent US labour union (the AFL-CIO), testified before Congress urging further revisions of the "imbalanced" 2004 US BIT Model, including deletions of investor-State arbitration, greater clarifications to narrow the scope of indirect takings, greater scope for government actions to protect themselves from financial instability, and mandatory environmental and labour provisions[341]. As occurred in Norway, others in the United States, including business groups, strongly oppose further modifications to the 2004 US Model which many regard as already insufficiently protective of investors[342].

The subsequent report issued by that subcommittee reflected these sharp divisions and diverges sharply on such crucial questions as whether any new US Model BIT should include investor-State dispute settlement at

---

8 June 2009, available at <http://www.investmenttreaty-news.org/cms/news/archive/2009/06/08/norway-shelves-its-proposed-model-bilateral-investment-treaty.aspx>.

[341] Testimony of T. M. Lee, Policy Director and Chief International Economist, AFL-CIO, in US House of Representatives, Committee on Ways and Means, Subcommittee on Trade, "Hearing on Investment Protections in US Trade and Investment Agreements", Serial No. 111-20 (14 May 2009), available at <http://www.gpo.gov/fdsys/pkg/CHRG-111hhrg11153473/pdf/CHRG-111hhrg11153473.pdf> (hereinafter "Investment Protections Hearing").

[342] Compare the views of A. P. Larson, appointed to serve, along with Ms Lee, on the subcommittee charged with examining the US BIT Programme. See *ibid.*, Statement of A. P. Larson.

all[343]. If this inconclusive report is any indication, the US BIT programme may be, like Norway's, at a cross-roads. In political contexts as distinct as those in the United States and Norway there appears to be a grow-ing partisan divide separating proponents of robust investment treaty protections from a diverse set of critics, including state and local governments, and some NGOs and scholars[344]. Comparable or even more extreme divides appear elsewhere, particularly in Latin America. The future of the investment regime is likely to turn on whether such divides can be suc-cessfully bridged.

* * *

The evolving nature of BITs and FTAs suggest at least three broader lessons.

(1) Lesson No. 1: Beware portrayals of the invest-ment regime through a single lens.

The evolutions in the texts of investment treaties over time demonstrate why it is a caricature to describe the evolving investment regime as a neo-colonialist scheme to protect the capital interests of the metropole. BITs bite the metropole back and even the metropoles of Europe and the United States are becoming aware of

---

[343] Report of the Subcommittee on Investment of the Advisory Committee on International Economic Policy Regarding the Model Bilateral Investment Treaty, 30 Sep-tember 2009, available at <http://www.state.gov/e/eeb/rls/othr/2009/131098.htm>.

[344] For a listing of business groups in the United States that seek to expand investor rights, US state government groups that seek "no greater rights" for foreign investors, and United States-based environmental or public interest groups opposed to aspects of BITs, see Testimony of R. Stumberg, *supra* footnote 341, pp. 6-7, notes 2-4.

it and are reacting. As the US changes to its model suggest, even when the metropole wins the cases filed
against it (as has the United States to date), it finds
itself chafing under the investment regime's reciprocal
constraints[345]. The changes to these treaties over time
tell us that we need to be cautious about describing the
world of BITs and FTAs through any single frame,
whether North/South or other.

(2) Lesson No. 2 : The risks of fragmentation even within the investment "regime" are real.

The evolving nature of BITs and FTAs tell us that it
may be difficult to describe the world of investment
agreements as a single "system" or a coherent regime
of harmonious rules. Despite the prevalence of common standards such as "national treatment" and FET,
perhaps investment agreements constitute only a "framework" at some distance from the coherent "system" of
the WTO or European Community law[346]. If even a
single country like the United States now has concluded treaties as distinct as those based on the 1987
and 2004 US BIT models, one should not underesti-
mate the differences among the nearly 3,000 investment agreements that exist. It is important to remember
that we now have a world in which the United States-
Argentina BIT of 1991 (based on the United States'
most investor protective model of 1987) exists (and by

---

[345] Of course, even during the colonial era, the metropole did not remain unaffected by developments, including
legal developments, resulting from its engagements with
the periphery. See generally Anghie, *supra* footnote 227.

[346] See, e.g., C. H. Brower II, "Legitimacy and
Inconsistency: Is Investment Treaty Arbitration Broken?",
Third Annual Investment Treaty Arbitration Conference:
Interpretation in Investment Arbitration, Washington, DC
(30 April 2009) (copy on file with author).

its terms will remain in effect at least for existing investors for years) alongside agreements like the United States-Uruguay BIT of 2004 (based on the 2004 US Model) and PRC treaties based on these countries' various models over the years. We also have a world where seemingly identical BIT guarantees — such as FET — exist within treaties whose object and purpose may be as different as is suggested by the respective preambles of the proposed Norway BIT of 2007 and that of the US Model BIT of 1987.

As is clear from UNCTAD's latest attempt to survey developments in international investment agreements, there is growing diversity among countries' BITs — and relatively few efforts by leading BIT signatories to replace their older treaties with a single harmonious text[347]. Further, as UNCTAD's survey points out, FTAs, which are part of broader pacts including trade in goods (like the NAFTA), vary in their attention to investor rights; many of these may seek to achieve general economic integration at the expense of investment protection as such[348]. When the diversity of all investment agreements now in effect, along with the evolving (and not always consistent) arbitral decisions interpreting them[349], is considered, it seems clear that the risks of internal fragmentation, that is, of inconsistent international investment law, are real. Given the evident fact that BITs differ, sometimes substantially, and that significant changes are sometimes made even to a single country's preferred negotiating text over rela-

---

[347] See UNCTAD, Recent Developments in Investor-State Dispute Settlement IIA MONITOR No. 2 (2005), UNCTAD/WEB/ITE/IIT/2005/1, 30 August 2005, available at <http://www.unctad.org/en/docs/webiteiit20051_en.pdf>, p. 1 (noting the "increasingly complicated framework of multi-layers and multi-faceted investment rules").

[348] *Ibid.*, pp. 10-13.

[349] This subject will be explored in the next chapters.

tively short periods of time, there is a serious question over whether investment law is truly coalescing into wholly coherent definitions of substantive investment guarantees or residual exceptions for governmental regulatory power. As will be addressed in later chapters, there are clear disputes about how the investment regime as a whole — or at least particular investment treaties — should interact with other international regimes or residual principles of custom. And given the lack of any firm principle of *stare decisis* and the absence of any formal appellate body, the *ad hoc* arbitral tribunals hearing investor-State disputes do not necessarily agree even with respect to the relevant procedural law that governs them[350]. There is no uniform agreement on the rules for initiating or conducting fair investor-State disputes. It is no longer accurate to state unequivocally that these treaties share a single object and purpose or that it is in all cases to benefit foreign investors, certainly not when some of their texts and preambles suggest that their object and purpose may be at least as much to protect certain sovereign prerogatives[351].

> (3) *Lesson No. 3: Despite the risks of fragmentation in the short run, the evolving nature of investment agreements does not preclude the possibility of the eventual harmonization of international investment law.*

The common trends emerging among some recent BITs and FTAs, across nations as different as the

---

[350] Thus, as will be addressed in Chapter IV, the investment regime is now producing controversial decisions by ICSID annulment committees that appear to reflect differences about the role or function of such committees.

[351] See, in particular, the preamble of Norway's latest Model BIT, *supra* footnote 338.

United States, Norway, and China, suggest possibilities whereby the investment regime could eventually coalesce and develop more harmonious, if not entirely stable, law. While few believe that over the short term there will be a successful effort to attempt to negotiate, yet again, a single multilateral treaty text for investment, it is possible that greater coherence over the substantive rights investors and host States enjoy may yet be achieved through a more haphazard route. It is possible, for example, that the positions taken in some recent BITs, particularly those concluded by China and the United States, will come to have greater influence, particularly since the combined capital flows of these two States alone eclipse those of most other States combined. It is possible that the most recent Chinese and US BIT models, which appear to be converging on key points, will exert this influence not only because of the net capital flows they impact but simply because more countries than ever before are, like the PRC and the United States, capital exporters *as well as* capital importers. This reality may also offer confer a form of legitimacy to those countries' most recent model BITs and would, of course, lend considerable power to a United States-China investment agreement should one be concluded.

The position of these countries in the investment regime might be said to approximate that of the individual in John Rawls's "original position", that is, of persons behind a "veil of ignorance" who do not know what social or economic position they occupy within society and are therefore incentivized to articulate principles of justice that are fair to all[352]. The Chinese and US respective BIT programmes might suggest how other countries' investment treaties should evolve, as

---

[352] J. Rawls, *A Theory of Justice* (Cambridge, Harvard University Press, 1971).

they also seek to conclude treaties that balance the rights of private capital versus the rights of sovereign recipients of it[353]. As one Chinese scholar has suggested, a successful Chinese-United States BIT constructed on the basis of the converging trajectory of both States' recent, more "balanced" treaties with others has the potential of overcoming some of the vertical, ideological, and rule of law concerns with the investment regime while the identity of the two parties alone would send a sharp message about the continued relevance of horizontal critiques[354]. Under this scenario for greater harmonization, the States, and not just the arbitrators of the investor-State claims, retain the initiative for change as they conclude investment treaties that contain more provisions in common.

The next chapters examine how the interpretation of these treaties by investor-State arbitrators affects the legitimacy of the investment regime and the prospects for increasingly fragmented or harmonious law.

---

[353] Thus, Congyan's description of China's most recent BITs is strikingly similar to the purposes suggested here for the 2004 US model. Congyan, *supra* footnote 274, p. 462 (indicating that "China has begun to seek a more balanced paradigm of investment treaties with the view to balance the relationship between private invests [sic] and public authority, interests of host state and those of home state").

[354] See *ibid.*, pp. 497-506 (noting how a China-United States BIT could reconstruct the State-State relationship, the public-private relationship between States and investors, and the economic-noneconomic divide by incorporating greater concerns to encourage sustainable development).

CHAPTER III

FAIR AND EQUITABLE TREATMENT:
THE HEART OF THE INVESTMENT REGIME

The last chapter focused on how the international investment regime evolves through changes in investment treaties over time. This chapter addresses another source of change: the evolving interpretations of arbitral tribunals charged with deciding investor-State disputes. In this chapter we will focus principally on how the investment regime's arbitrators have interpreted the fair and equitable obligation and what their efforts tell us about the interaction between investment treaties and non-treaty sources of law, such as customary international law.

Even though those who established the US BIT programme stressed the need for treaty protections against expropriation, the treaty based protection ensuring "fair and equitable treatment" ("FET") is the most important and frequently adjudicated question in international investment law. FET is not only the most frequently invoked claim by investors, it is also the most successful on their behalf[355]. This is so not only because, given the distinct turn to liberal economic regimes and the turn away from the outright expropriations and nationalizations that were once common in the 1960s and 1970s, there are fewer occasions in which investors seek to invoke the expropriation guarantee. FET is as important as it is due to the ubiquity of its infringement.

---

[355] R. Dolzer and C. Schreuer, *Principles of International Investment Law* (New York, Oxford University Press, 2008), p. 119.

Nearly all investment protection treaties have an express reference to FET and some, such as the US Model Treaty of 1987, mention FET in both the text and the preamble, thereby suggesting that granting FET to an investor is both a substantive guarantee and part of that treaty's object and purpose [356]. The pervasiveness of the FET standard among BITs and FTAs is not in doubt. A recent study of 365 BITs found that only 19 of those treaties did not make a reference to FET [357]. That study also concluded that even with respect to treaties having no such reference, it was likely that FET would nonetheless still become relevant — such as a treaty without an FET clause that nonetheless includes a guarantee of treatment "in accordance with international law" [358]. FET might also be relevant in a case where an MFN clause facilitates the use of another treaty's FET clause [359].

This does not mean, however, that all BITs and FTAs treat FET in the identical way. The same study of FET concluded that there were at least five different ways that investment protection treaties made reference to the standard. Consider the following examples of FET clauses, most of which are cited in that study:

---

[356] Even the Multilateral Investment Guarantee Agency ("MIGA") requires FET to be available as a precondition to extending insurance cover. Convention Establishing the Multilateral Investment Guarantee Agency, 1508 *United Nations Treaty Series* 100, signed on 10 November 1985, entered into force on 12 April 1988 (hereinafter "MIGA Convention"), Art. 12.

[357] I. Tudor, *The Fair and Equitable Treatment Standard in the International Law of Foreign Investment* (New York, Oxford University Press, 2008), p. 23.

[358] This is because, as discussed in Chapter III, many assume that a reference to FET is meant to embrace at least the "international minimum standard" of treatment that is accorded to aliens under customary international law.

[359] See Tudor, *supra* footnote 357, pp. 23-24.

(1) Argentina-Australia BIT:

"Each Contracting Party shall at all times ensure fair and equitable treatment to investments." [360]

(2) Argentina-Venezuela BIT:

"Each Contracting Party, in conformity with the norms and criteria of international law, will ensure, a fair and equitable treatment to investments of investors of the other Party; and will not prejudice its management, maintenance, use, enjoyment or disposal thereof through unjustified or discriminatory measures." [361]

(3) France-Guatemala BIT:

"Each one of the Contracting Parties engages to ensure, within its territory, fair and equitable treatment, in conformity with the principles of international law, to the investments of the nationals and of the companies of the other Party and to ensure that the exercise of this recognized right is not limited *de jure* or *de facto*. Especially, even though not exclusively, are considered to limit *de jure* or *de facto* FET, all restrictions on the acquisition and transport

---

[360] Agreement between the Government of Australia and the Government of the Argentine Republic on the Promotion and Protection of Investments, 1997 *Australian Treaty Series*, No. 4, signed on 23 August 1995, entered into force on 11 January 1997, available at <http://www.unctad.org/sections/dite/iia/docs/bits/argentina_australia.pdf> (hereinafter "Argentina-Australia BIT"), Art. 4 (1).

[361] Acuerdo Entre El Gobierno De La República De Venezúela y El Gobierno De La República Argentina Para La Promoción y Protección Recíprocas De Inversiones, signed on 16 November 1993, entered into force on 1 July 1995, available at <http://www.unctad.org/sections/dite/iia/docs/bits/argentina_venezuela_sp.pdf> (hereinafter "Argentina-Venezuela BIT"), Art. 4 (1). Translation by Tudor, *supra* footnote 357, p. 26.

of raw and auxiliary materials, of energy and combustible substances, as well as on the means of production and exploitation of all kinds, all limits to sell and transport products within the country and abroad, as well as all measures having a similar effect." [362]

(4) Bangladesh-Philippines BIT:

"Investments and returns of investors of each Contracting Party shall at all times be accorded fair and equitable treatment and shall enjoy full protection and security in the territory of the other Contracting Party. Neither Contracting Party shall in any way impair by unreasonable or discriminatory measures the management, maintenance, use, enjoyment, extension or disposal of such investments." [363]

(5) United States-Argentina BIT (based on the US Model BIT of 1987):

"Investment shall at all times be accorded fair and equitable treatment, shall enjoy full protection and security and shall in no case be accorded treatment less than that required by international law.

---

[362] Accord entre le Gouvernement de la République française et le Gouvernement de la République du Guatemala sur l'encouragement et la protection réciproques des investissements, signed on 27 May 1998, entered into force on 28 October 2001, available at <http://www.unctad.org/sections/dite/iia/docs/bits/france_guatemala_fr.pdf> (hereinafter "France-Guatemala BIT"), Art. 4 (1). Translation by Tudor, *supra* footnote 357, p. 26.

[363] Agreement between the Government of the Republic of the Philippines and the Government of the People's Republic of Bangladesh for the Promotion and Reciprocal Protection of Investment, signed on 8 September 1997, entered into force on 1 August 1998, available at <http://www.unctad.org/sections/dite/iia/docs/bits/bangladesh_philippines.pdf> (hereinafter "Bangladesh-Philippines BIT"), Art. III (1).

Neither Party shall in any way impair by arbitrary and discriminatory measures the management, operation, maintenance, use, enjoyment, acquisition, expansion, or disposal of investments . . . Each party shall observe any obligation it may have entered into with regard to investments."[364]

These different versions of FET suggest different possibilities. Some like (1) above just refer to FET as a self-standing standard. Some, like (2), cite FET as if this was a mere application of a rule that already exists in customary international law (or maybe general principles of law). Others, like (3), combine a reference to FET with one to international law and also give the FET guarantee some context by providing examples of government actions that would violate that right. Some, like (4), include FET, alongside prohibitions on "unreasonable" and/or "arbitrary" or "discriminatory" measures. And some, like (5), cite FET with or without some of the other elements from 1-4 above, add a reference to "full protection and security" and suggest that investments are entitled to the better of any standard granted under either FET or general international law, as if the two standards were distinct[365].

---

[364] Treaty between the United States of America and the Argentine Republic concerning the Reciprocal Encouragement and Protection of Investment, signed on 14 November 1991, entered into force on 20 October 1994 (hereinafter "United States-Argentina BIT"), Art. II (2) *(a)*, *(c)*.

[365] The examples cited here do not exhaust the possibilities. Thus, UNCTAD identified no less than seven basic FET models: (1) a simple reference to FET; (2) a reference to FET linked to NT or MFN treatment; (3) FET paired with a duty not to impair the investment through unreasonable or discriminatory measures; (4) FET in accordance with international law; (5) number (4) above coupled with a broad definition of international law that goes beyond customary international law; (6) a guarantee

These treatments of the FET standard raise a number of interpretative questions:

(1) What exactly is the intended relationship between FET and "international law"? Does the exact way the particular BIT or FTA is phrased matter to this question?

The France-Guatemala BIT, in using the phrase "in conformity with", appears to presume that FET and international law provide equivalent forms of treatment. The United States-Argentina BIT, on the contrary, appears to assume that full protection and security is a distinct additional guarantee above and beyond FET — and neither of these is the equivalent of the protections accorded under customary international law. Should arbitrators give effect to these textual differences (as they arguably should if they apply the plain meaning rules of the VCLT), even if this means reaching different conclusions as to the meaning of FET (as would be the case if they faithfully applied intertemporal rules as to the meaning of treaties)? Or should they, on the contrary, as they become aware of each others' decisions, strive to give FET the same meaning across BITs and FTAs, in accordance with those who advocate *jurisprudence constante*? And is the latter really an option where a State, such as the United States, altered its FET provision in its later treaties precisely in reaction to arbitral interpretations with which it disagreed?

---

of FET subject to domestic law of the host State; and (7) equating FET with the minimum standard of treatment (as does the NAFTA and the 2004 US Model BIT). See M. Kinnear, "The Fair and Equitable Treatment Standard", in A. K. Bjorklund *et al.* (eds.), *Investment Treaty Law: Current Issues III: Remedies in International Investment Law & Emerging Jurisprudence in International Investment Law* (London, British Institute of International and Comparative Law, 2009), p. 213 (citing UNCTAD).

Note that the question of overlap between FET and custom extends beyond matters dealt with by rules governing State responsibility to aliens. Although the NAFTA Commission's 31 July 2001 Note of Interpretation suggested that FET was equivalent to such rules, other matters of overlap between FET and other general rules may arise. Does a reference to FET only entitle arbitrators to examine the meaning of the "international minimum standard" as owed to aliens or can arbitrators charged with interpreting FET "in conformity with international law" turn to, for example, general principles of law — such as the rule against "unjust enrichment" or against rewarding a party with "unclean hands" — or other general rules of international law — such as the procedural rights or property rights protections recognized under human rights law [366]?

Of course, if FET is functionally the equivalent of the international minimum standard as traditionally applied to aliens, it may be unnecessary for a treaty to make explicit reference to FET, so long as there is another reference stating that investments or investors shall be treated "in accordance with international law". But if FET is treated as the functional equivalent of either the international minimum standard or other general rules applicable to all, such as customary procedural protections accorded under customary human rights, this may enhance the precedential value of investor-State decisions as these would suggest customary international obligations, not limited to the

---

[366] Indeed, even a treaty that does not include express permission to interpret FET "in conformity with international law" might license such references. Consider Vienna Convention on the Law of Treaties, 1155 *United Nations Treaty Series* 331, signed on 23 May 1969, entered into force on 27 January 1980 (hereinafter "VCLT"), Art. 31 (3) *(c)* (licensing resort to "any relevant rules of international law applicable in the relations between the parties").

States parties to BITs and FTAs. To the extent that investor-State arbitrators are issuing interpretations of general international law when they interpret FET or other BIT provisions, their decisions would not be easily dismissed as *lex specialis* limited to the investment regime. To the extent FET implicates or is functionally equivalent to rights generally accorded under international law, the judges of a number of international tribunals — from the European Court of Human Rights to the ICJ — should be referring to investor-State decisions that address, for example, the type of fair process that international law requires of States.

(2) Is it relevant to finding a violation of FET whether a host State is violating other international obligations, such as the rules of the WTO (assuming that it is a WTO member)? Does a reference to "international law", as in the examples from the Argentina-Venezuela or United States-Argentina BITs above, include international obligations that are not generally applicable but apply as between the two particular States in question — e.g., because both States are parties to a BIT and the WTO or the BIT and an environmental convention[367]?

---

[367] Note that those who reach the application of other relevant rules of international law through Article 31 (3) *(c)* face the same uncertainty given the ambiguity in the phrase "in the relations between the parties". *Ibid.* For a broad interpretation of this phrase, see B. Simma and T. Kill, "Harmonizing Investment Protection and International Human Rights: First Steps Towards a Methodology", in C. Binder *et al.* (eds.), *International Investment Law for the 21st Century: Essays in Honor of Christoph Schreuer* (New York, Oxford University Press, 2009), p. 678; but see "Notes of Interpretation of Certain Chapter 11 Provisions", *NAFTA Free Trade Commission* (31 July 2001), available at <http://www.international.gc.ca/trade-agreements-accords-commerciaux/disp-diff/nafta-interpr.aspx?lang=en> (hereinafter "NAFTA Interpretation") (attempting to preclude such interpretations of FET).

(3) Is it relevant to finding a violation of FET whether a State is violating its own law or its own administrative practices or whether its national laws are vague or unclear? Is there a presumption that FET is not violated when the host State has acted in accord with its own law or public administrative practices? Even though these FET clauses usually make no reference to national law, is such reference implicit in the notion of unfairness or perhaps in the international minimum standard itself, to the extent that guarantee embraces the concept of legitimate expectations based on existing law?

(4) Is FET a single guarantee or two, namely a requirement to accord "fair" as well as "equitable" treatment?

(5) Is there a principle that underlies FET and that can serve to give it content or are arbitrators stuck with an amorphous standard that can only be given content with respect to particular facts? Is an FET violation amenable to a definition more specific than "we know a violation when we see it" — like US Supreme Court Justice Stewart's test for obscenity? Or can it be reduced to a promise not to violate the "legitimate expectations" of investors? If so, are those expectations limited to those given to the investor in the form of an investment contract or are other government assurances relevant, such as those made in the host State's laws, by a government agency, or in licences issued at the time the investment was made? If "legitimate expectations" are relevant, are the legitimate expectations of host States relevant as well? And what precisely is the relationship between FET and the separate guarantee made in some BITs, see, for example, the United States-Argentina BIT, that host States "observe any obligation" made to investors — the so-called "umbrella clause"?

(6) As is suggested by some of the questions above,

what is the relationship between FET and other provisions provided in the same treaty? Under the ordinary rules of treaty interpretation, interpreters are urged to pay heed to the context of a provision, that is, the other provisions in the treaty[368]. Does the canon in favour of the "principle of effectiveness" — treaty clauses ought not be superfluous — mean that FET *must* necessarily mean something other than a violation of other BIT provisions, for example those prohibiting discrimination, guaranteeing NT and MFN, or the umbrella clause[369]? Notice that if we follow this approach, a guarantee of FET could serve as the functional equivalent of a "catch-all" or residual investor protection to be used when the treatment investors receive falls short of violating other investment treaty guarantees; that is, when what the State has done is not quite "arbitrary", "discriminatory", in violation of NT or MFN, a violation of the umbrella clause, or insufficiently grave to constitute a direct or indirect expropriation, but is still, somehow, "unfair" and "inequitable". There may also be other provisions in BITs and FTAs that raise the question of possible overlap with FET[370]. What is the

---

[368] VCLT, *supra* footnote 366, Art. 31 (2).

[369] Note, however, that some investment treaties attempt to resolve explicitly some of these questions of overlap between provisions internal to a BIT or FTA. See, e.g., North American Free Trade Agreement, 32 *International Legal Materials* 612, signed on 17 December 1992, entered into force on 1 January 1994 (hereinafter "NAFTA"), Art. 1110 (1) *(c)* (stating explicitly that the benefits of FET (Article 1105) must be accorded when a State expropriates an investment).

[370] Another example of overlap is suggested by the NAFTA's *Metalclad* decision, which found a violation of the FET and the indirect expropriations provisions of the NAFTA on the basis of what appears to be the same governmental actions. *Metalclad Corp.* v. *Mexico*, Award, ICSID Case No. ARB (AF)/97/1 (8 August 2001).

relationship, if any, between a duty to accord FET and the exception in the United States-Argentina BIT, for example, that permits States to take action "necessary" to maintain their public order or to protect their "essential security interests"?

(7) More broadly still, is FET a *de facto* delegation to investor-State arbitrators to apply equitable rules or even to decide a dispute *ex aqueo et bono*, that is, on the basis of equity? If so, does it authorize an arbitrator to consider the equities on both sides, that is the rights of host States being sued as well as those of investors? If that is the case, application of FET might entitle arbitrators to consider the particular circumstances of a host State, including its available resources or its actual capacity to extend the protections of the national rule of law, in the course of determining the level of FET protection that an investor might reasonably expect. This interpretation of FET might go some way towards achieving the re-calibration or re-balancing of State/investor rights that some would urge[371].

Given the fact that references to FET began appearing in United States Treaties of Friendship, Commerce and Navigation ("FCNs") after World War II — in FCNs with Germany, Ethiopia, and the Netherlands — and that a reference to "just and equitable treatment" appeared in Article II (2) of the 1948 Havana Charter for an International Trade Organization that never came into effect, it might be surprising that we have so many fundamental unanswered questions about its meaning. But it is important to remember that even though references to FET in treaties are scarcely new, it was not until 1997 that a tribunal dealt with its interpretation, at least in a public award[372]. Given this, as

---

[371] See *supra* Chap. II.
[372] Tudor, *supra* footnote 357, p. 15.

well as the fact that due to the absence of the doctrine of *stare decisis* in arbitration, investor-State tribunals since then have had the opportunity to interpret FET anew each time that it has come up, it becomes a bit more understandable why we still have no definitive answers to basic questions of interpretation.

It is not as if some States parties have not tried to answer many of these questions. The United States, Canada, and Mexico were among the first group of States facing a number of sophisticated investor-State disputes raising the FET provision. In April 2001, *Pope & Talbot* v. *Canada*, an arbitral tribunal convened under Chapter 11 of the NAFTA, found that Canada's aggressive requests for the corporate data of a firm shortly after that firm had filed its notice of Chapter 11 arbitration violated the NAFTA's FET provision[373]. The relevant NAFTA provision stated:

Article 1105 (1):

"Each Party shall accord to investments of investors of another Party treatment *in accordance with international law, including* fair and equitable treatment and full protection and security."[374]

Notice that this provision is not identical to the one we just saw in the United States-Argentina BIT:

"Investment shall at all times be accorded fair and equitable treatment, shall enjoy full protection and security *and shall in no case be accorded treatment less than that required by international law . . .*"[375]

---

[373] *Pope & Talbot* v. *Canada*, Award on Merits of Phase Two, NAFTA Chap. 11 Arb. Trib. (10 April 2001) (hereinafter "*Pope & Talbot* Phase Two").

[374] NAFTA, *supra* footnote 369, Art. 1105 (1) (emphasis added).

[375] United States-Argentina BIT, *supra* footnote 364, Art. II (2) *(a)* (emphasis added).

As the italicized language from these provisions suggests, the NAFTA's FET language appears to equate FET with international law while the United States-Argentina text appears to assume that FET and international law provide different protections and that the FET (and full protection and security) guarantees may provide additional guarantees to an investor above and beyond that provided by international law. This was the position taken by both Canada and the United States before the *Pope & Talbot* tribunal. Indeed Canada defended its actions in that case on the basis of old cases which indicated that the international minimum standard under international law, as was stated in the *Neer* case of 1927, was satisfied unless the State's conduct was "notoriously unjust" or "egregious"[376].

And yet, despite these differences in language, the *Pope & Talbot* tribunal found that the practice of the United States and other industrialized countries in the course of their FCNs and other BITs reflected their intent to provide investors with additional rights "no matter what else their entitlement under international law [and] . . . free of any threshold that might be applicable to the evaluation of measures under the minimum standard of international law"[377]. The *Pope & Talbot* tribunal rejected, in short, the contention by both

---

[376] *Pope & Talbot* Phase Two, *supra* footnote 373, para. 108. For a recent NAFTA decision on point, see *Glamis Gold Ltd.* v. *United States*, Award, UNCITRAL Arbitration Rules (8 June 2009), available at <http://www.state.gov/documents/organization/125798.pdf>, para. 22 (finding that the *Neer* standard continues to apply to the meaning of FET under the NAFTA but suggesting that what is deemed "egregious" or "shocking" evolves over time).

[377] *Pope & Talbot* Phase Two, *supra* footnote 373, paras. 110-111. For a more thorough telling of the *Pope & Talbot* story, see D. A. Gantz, "International Decision: *Pope & Talbot, Inc.* v. *Canada*", 97 *American Journal of International Law* 937 (2003).

Canada and the United States that they intended more limited investor protection in the NAFTA's version of the FET provision.

Probably as a result of that decision — as well as other arguments raised by other claimants under the NAFTA in prior and on-going cases — the NAFTA parties took action, permitted under that agreement[378], and issued a formal binding "interpretation" of their agreement[379]. The 31 July 2001 Free Trade Commission Interpretation stated in relevant part:

> "(1) Article 1105 (1) prescribes the customary international law minimum standard of treatment of aliens as the minimum standard of treatment to be afforded to investment of investors of another Party.
>
> (2) The concepts of 'fair and equitable treatment' and 'full protection and security' do not require treatment in addition to or beyond that which is required by the customary international law minimum standard of treatment of aliens.
>
> (3) A determination that there has been a breach of another provision of the NAFTA, or of a separate international agreement, does not establish that there has been a breach of Article 1105 (1)." [380]

Since this interpretation was issued before the *Pope & Talbot* tribunal had made its findings of damages, the arbitrators were forced to reconsider their earlier findings with respect to the meaning of FET. They did

---

[378] NAFTA, *supra* footnote 369, Art. 1131 (2).

[379] Note that the NAFTA's specific authorization to issue such Commission interpretations under Article 1131 (2), appears to be distinct from the general power treaty parties have, under customary international law, to adopt subsequent agreements or engage in subsequent practice intended to affect the interpretation of their original agreement. See VCLT, *supra* footnote 366, Arts. 31 (3) *(a)-(b)*.

[380] See NAFTA Interpretation, *supra* footnote 367.

so reluctantly, noting among other things that the NAFTA parties were not authorized to issue "amendments" of the NAFTA, but only "interpretations" and that arbitrators were in principle free to determine whether the parties had exceeded their powers by attempting the latter in the guise of an interpretation[381]. The tribunal even suggested that the purported "interpretation" was in this instance an illegal amendment but held back from so finding because even if FET was equivalent to customary international law, CIL had evolved since the time of the *Neer* case and no longer required "egregious" State conduct[382]. Notably, the *Pope & Talbot* tribunal found that

> "[t]here had been evolution in customary international law concepts since the 1920s. It is a facet of international law that customary international law evolves through state practice. International agreements constitute practice of states and contribute to the grounds of customary international law."[383]

The arbitrators suggested that the concept of fair and equitable treatment was now part of international law and that the more than 1,800 BITs concluded through the time of that decision reflected relevant State practice[384]. That tribunal went on to find that some annoying (but hardly egregious) actions by Canadian bureaucrats violated the NAFTA's FET provision and required compensation[385].

---

[381] *Pope & Talbot* Phase Two, *supra* footnote 373.

[382] *Ibid.*

[383] *Pope & Talbot* v. *Canada*, Damages Award, NAFTA Chap. 11 Arbitral Tribunal (21 October 2002) (hereinafter "*Pope & Talbot* Damages"), para. 59.

[384] *Ibid.*, paras. 60-62.

[385] *Pope & Talbot* Phase Two, *supra* footnote 373. For a considerably narrower, more recent interpretation of the same FET provision by another NAFTA tribunal, see *Glamis Gold*, *supra* footnote 376.

As the episode suggests, at least one prominent effort by some States to answer some of the interpretative questions posed at the beginning of this chapter has not led to the results that those States expected. Even in the context of the NAFTA, where the States parties' formal interpretations are binding on investor-State arbitrators, it is not entirely clear whether dispute settlers are entirely convinced that the meaning of FET remains confined to the "customary international law minimum standard of treatment of aliens" as the NAFTA Interpretation stated. As was pointed out by an expert opinion filed in a later NAFTA case, the actual wording of Article 1105 (1) is not by its terms restricted to that standard but equates FET to "international law" — a term which might include, for example, evolving due process or property rights guarantees that have developed since the *Neer* case for all investors and perhaps all human beings, not just aliens, under modern international law [386]. If the purpose of the NAFTA Interpretation was to cabin FET to a particular narrow meaning and exclude the possibility that FET may evolve over time, that effort did not succeed — including in the *Pope & Talbot* case itself [387].

The limiting effects of paragraph 3 of the NAFTA Interpretation are also dubious. That paragraph was

---

[386] See generally *Methanex Corp.* v. *United States*, Second Opinion of Professor Sir Robert Jennings, QC, NAFTA Chap. 11 Arbitral Tribunal (5 November 2002) (hereinafter "Jennings Opinion"). Note, however, that it might be argued that the disjunctive wording of the relevant NAFTA provision, which anticipates treatment "in accordance with due process of law and Article 1105 (1)", might be read as indicating that these are two distinctive, and not complementary, entitlements.

[387] Indeed, that effort was not entirely successful even with respect to the *Glamis Gold* case, *supra* footnote 376, para. 613 (affirming evolving notions of "shocking" conduct over time).

inspired in part by the arbitral ruling in *Metalclad*, a case which found that Mexico's laws lacked clarity with respect to which governmental entity (state or federal) was entitled to issue building permits and that such an absence of transparency contributed to a violation of FET under the NAFTA[388]. That finding had been reversed by a court in British Columbia charged with determining a challenge by Mexico to the *Metalclad* award under Canadian law because the transparency provisions which the arbitral tribunal had cited for its conclusion were located outside the investment provisions of the NAFTA — outside the competence of investor-State arbitrators[389]. But other arbitral interpretations of FET, including within the NAFTA, as we will see, have tended to find that it indeed includes some obligation of transparency[390].

It is not at all clear that the NAFTA parties will be able to eliminate entirely the possibility that an investor will cite, in support of an FET violation, the fact that the host State has violated other law, whether its own national law or another international obligation in the NAFTA or elsewhere. As an expert in another NAFTA case put it,

---

[388] *Metalclad Corp.* v. *Mexico*, ICSID Case No. ARB (AF)/97/1 (2001), para. 76.

[389] *United Mexican States* v. *Metalclad Corp.*, British Columbia Supreme Court, 2001 *British Columbia Supreme Court Reports* 664 (2001), paras. 71-72 (upholding most of the original award on the basis of expropriation and not FET).

[390] Although there may not be uniform arbitral agreement about what "transparency" entails. See, e.g., *MTD Equity SDN BHD & MTD Chile S.A.* v. *Chile*, Decision on the Application for Annulment, ICSID Case No. ARB/01/7 (21 March 2007) (hereinafter *"MTD annulment"*), paras. 65-67 (criticizing the *TECMED* standard insofar that it implies that investors' expectations, including transparency, are a source of obligations to the host State independent of the relevant investment treaty).

"while a breach of another provision of NAFTA or a separate agreement may not be sufficient in all circumstances to establish a breach of Article 1105 (1), such a breach must surely be relevant evidence concerning whether an investor or an investment has received fair and equitable treatment. The Free Trade Commission does not contend otherwise, and it is thus difficult to understand the utility of this portion of the interpretation." [391]

As we will discuss further, since FET is often read as intended to protect the "legitimate expectations" of the investor, it is relatively easy for an investor to make an argument that those expectations are violated when a host State violates its own law, including obligations imposing transparency. Indeed, notwithstanding the Court of British Columbia's finding in *Metalclad* and paragraph 3 of the NAFTA Interpretation, vagueness and uncertainty in a host State's laws or practices may still be a material fact for determining a violation of FET. This is all the more the case in the typical case where, unlike the NAFTA, States parties to an investment agreement have not specifically addressed the question of the interplay between the FET guarantee and other law.

Interestingly, the NAFTA Interpretation has had one effect on the international investment law that was not necessarily intended by the States that issued it: it has strengthened the contentions of scholars and arbitrators that the international investment regime has affected evolving norms of customary international law — as was suggested by the tribunal in *Pope & Talbot*.

As we have seen, the suggestion that the law of investment treaties and their interpretation has come to affect the obligations of non-parties to such agreements as customary international law (or perhaps general

---

[391] Jennings Opinion, *supra* footnote 386.

principles of law) has divided scholars of the investment regime. As discussed in the last chapter, Andrew
Guzman, among others, has contended that BITs are
lex specialis having no effect on general international
law because, among other things, these treaties are not
intended to have such effects and cannot be relevant
"State practice" (as compared to "legislative" treaties
like the Vienna Convention on the Law of Treaties)
and are motivated only by "economic" reasons, not
opinio juris[392]. Chapter II questioned these premises as
a general matter. The present chapter examines that
contention as it plays out in the interpretation of FET.

But why is this question important?

The interplay between the investment treaty regime
and non-treaty sources of international law is of interest to more than just scholars. It has a potentially huge
impact on the real world of States and investors. With
less than 3,000 investment treaties in existence, the investment regime does not formally extend to every possible
bilateral pairing of States. At present, for example,
there is no BIT or FTA in effect between the United
States and Brazil, Russia, India, or China — despite
the huge capital flows involving the BRICs[393]. Moreover,
investment treaties may be terminated in accordance
with their terms and some States have sought to withdraw from some of the BITs or from ICSID generally

---

[392] A. T. Guzman, "Why LDCs Sign Treaties that Hurt
Them", 38 *Virginia Journal of International Law* 639
(1998), pp. 685-687.

[393] Note, however, that as mentioned in Chapter II, the
United States and China are attempting to negotiate a BIT
at the time of publication. For background on these negotiations and the two countries' respective BIT programmes,
see The Economist Intelligence Unit, "Evaluating A Potential
US-China Bilateral Investment Treaty: Background, Context,
and Implications" (30 March 2010), available at <http://
www.uscc.gov/researchpapers/2010/EIU_Report_on_US-
China_BIT—FINAL_14_April_2010.pdf>.

(or aspects of ICSID jurisdiction). A great number of investors have potentially significant stakes in knowing whether what these treaties say reflects general international law that might be put to use, even when a BIT or FTA is not in play. In addition, the question is important outside the context of investor-State arbitration, as, for example, in old-fashioned diplomatic espousal efforts on behalf of foreign investors, which may still continue notwithstanding investor-State arbitration, or in claims in national courts applying general international law or using it to interpret national law.

Exploring the potential interplay between general international law and investment treaties is also of interest to those attempting to litigate or interpret BITs or FTAs. Despite some commonalities, investment treaties remain limited party agreements with textual variations that reflect differences in States' model negotiating texts and differences in relative bargaining leverage between say, Canada, Mexico and the United States (negotiating the NAFTA's Chapter 11) or the United States and Grenada (where, scarcely 3 years after the United States invasion of Grenada, those States concluded a BIT that is virtually identical to the then US Model[394]). Unlike the trade regime, there is no single, overarching multilateral treaty on investment. There is not even an accepted "model" for an investment protection or promotion agreement, as compared to, for example, the model bilateral extradition treaty adopted by the UN General Assembly[395]. Under the

---

[394] Treaty between the United States of America and Grenada concerning the Reciprocal Encouragement and Protection of Investment, signed on 2 May 1986, entered into force on 3 March 1989, available at <http://www.bilaterals.org/spip.php?article440> (hereinafter "United States-Grenada BIT").

[395] See Model Treaty on Extradition, General Assembly res. A/RES/45/116 (XLV) (1990).

circumstances, there is a huge interest in exploring the possibilities of coherent frameworks for understanding international investment law and for filling gaps in the treaties that exist. The typical BIT is a relatively concise (and perhaps somewhat cryptic) document as compared to the voluminous substantive and procedural details contained in the GATT covered agreements. It is of more than scholarly interest to see to what extent general international law fills in details that the typical investment treaty fails to address.

As we suggested in the last chapter, conclusions that BITs or FTAs are *lex specialis*, are not "legislative", or lack common content, present artificially constrained black/white choices that bear little resemblance to the complexities of the interactions between treaty and non-treaty sources of law or the international legal process. These are not qualities subject to a dichotomous on/off switch. There are aspects of BITs that are *lex specialis*: that is, intended to exclude the applicability of any general rules to the contrary[396]. This seems to be the case, for example, with respect to the particular procedural conditions required by each of these treaties for initiation of investor-State dispute settlement. Some substantive BIT provisions also reflect particular quid pro quos — such as a clause in the United States-Argentina BIT of 1991 providing that Argentina need not provide US auto makers all the benefits that Argentine auto makers get[397]. No one suggests that all the substantive guarantees contained

---

[396] For one example, see the ruling in *United Parcel Service of America* v. *Canada*, Award, UNCITRAL Arbitration Rules (24 May 2007), para. 59 (rejecting the application of the traditional attribution rules stated in the ILC's Articles of State Responsibility and concluding that the NAFTA provided alternative rules).

[397] United States-Argentina BIT, *supra* footnote 364, Protocol.

in BITs and FTAs are part of CIL or general principles of law. Nor would many contend that some of the procedural requisites reflected in these agreements — such as BIT provisions that enable even minority shareholders to make a claim on behalf of a company — reflect general law [398]. On the other hand, there are other provisions in such treaties that explicitly or implicitly rely on general international law or reflect intent by their drafters to affirm such traditional principles.

The proclamation in the NAFTA Interpretation that FET is equivalent to customary international law is not surprising given the fact that at least US investment agreements, and those modelled after them, were always intended in part to reaffirm the customary law that had been challenged by, among other things, developments in the early 1970s at the UN General Assembly. As noted in Chapter II, the US Model of 1987 specifically relies on protections under international law in a number of provisions. As noted in that chapter, this reflects the desire by US negotiators to use such treaties to affirm customary rules and provide for their enforcement, including with respect to using US BITs to defend the "Hull Rule" on compensation for expropriation.

When arbitral decisions equate some BIT protections to those found in customary law, they are not only interpreting a particular treaty-contract between

---

[398] See, e.g., Dolzer and Schreuer, *supra* footnote 355, pp. 56-59 (summarizing disagreements among arbitral and other tribunals over the ability of shareholders to bring such claims); M. Perkams, "Piercing the Corporate Veil in International Investment Agreements", in A. Reinisch and C. Knahr (eds.), *International Investment Law in Context* (Utrecht, The Netherlands, Eleven International Publishing, 2007), p. 93 (comparing the law on shareholder claims under customary international law and under investment treaties).

the parties; they purport to reflect and therefore affect the meaning of general international law. After the NAFTA Interpretation at least, NAFTA arbitral decisions interpreting FET and "full protection and security" are *necessarily* efforts to interpret and apply customary law [399]. As with any effort to apply the law, arbitral efforts to apply law to fact invariably affect the meaning of the law. In this connection, it is significant that many decisions under the NAFTA's investment chapter, including *Pope & Talbot*, have given FET a more expansive meaning that this term had in 1927 when the *Neer* case was decided [400]. There is consider-

---

[399] See, e.g., Dolzer and Schreuer, *supra* footnote 355, p. 128 (noting that "insistence that FET is identical with customary international law may well have the effect of accelerating the development of customary law through the rapidly expanding practice on FET clauses in treaties"). For arguments that BITs affect customary law, see S. M. Schwebel, "The Influence of Bilateral Investment Treaties on Customary International Law", 98 *American Society of International Law* 27 (2004); J. E. Alvarez, "A BIT on Custom", 42 *New York University Journal of International Law and Politics* 17 (2009).

[400] See, e.g., *Mondev International Ltd*. v. *United States*, Award, ICSID Case No. ARB(AF)/99/2 (11 October 2002) (hereinafter *"Mondev"*, paras. 116, 125. That tribunal noted that the Commission's interpretation incorporated international law "whose content is shaped by the conclusion of more than two thousand bilateral investment treaties and many treaties of friendship and commerce". *Ibid*. See also *ADF Group Inc*. v. *United States*, Award, NAFTA Ch. 11 Arb. Trib. (9 January 2003), para. 179 (noting that the customary international law in Article 1105 (1) of the NAFTA is not frozen in time, but evolves, and is not a "static photograph of the minimum standard of treatment of aliens as it stood in 1927 when the Award in the *Neer* case was rendered"). But see *Glamis Gold*, *supra* footnote 376, paras. 612-616 (finding that the *Neer* standard continues to apply but that contemporary views of what is "shocking and outrageous" have evolved).

able evidence that arbitral interpretations of the NAFTA's FET standard and other investment treaties with FET provisions are expanding the reach of customary international law[401].

Notably, as we saw in Chapter II, the language from the NAFTA Interpretation was incorporated into the 2004 US Model BIT and appears in all BITs and FTAs concluded by the United States since 2004. In addition, as we noted, the new US Model BIT now explicitly equates its expropriation guarantees to those provided under customary international law[402]. Interpretations of FET under the NAFTA are also likely to influence those who apply recent Chinese BITs, such as the China-Mexico BIT, which, as noted in Chapter II, defines FET in terms sometimes similar to that of the NAFTA Interpretation and post-2004 US BITs[403].

---

[401] See, e.g., O. K. Fauchald, "The Legal Reasoning of ICSID Tribunals — An Empirical Analysis", 19 *European Journal of International Law* 301 (2008), pp. 310-312 (noting that ICSID tribunals used customary law as a separate legal basis in 34 of 98 decisions), pp. 324-325 (noting that ICSID tribunals explicitly resorted to customary law as an interpretative argument in 24 of 98 decisions and that it is a "significant element in the decisions of ICSID tribunals"). But see *Glamis Gold*, *supra* footnote 376, para. 605 (drawing distinctions between decisions rendered by investor-State arbitrations and traditional evaluations of State practice and *opinio juris* leading to custom).

[402] See US Department of State and US Trade Representative, "2004 US Model BIT", available at <http://www.state.gov/documents/organization/117601.pdf>, Annex B, para. 1 ("Article 6 [expropriation and compensation] is intended to reflect customary international law concerning the obligation of States with respect to expropriation").

[403] . This is particularly significant because prior to the conclusion of the China-Mexico BIT in 2008, the Chinese Government had historically been sceptical of customary international law because of that source's Western provenance. See C. Congyan, "China-US BIT Negotiations and

More significantly, investor-State arbitrators, operating outside the context of the NAFTA or investment treaties that explicitly equate treaty standards to those in CIL, have also tended to blur firm distinctions between an investment treaty's FET guarantee and customary law[404]. Most, but not all[405], of the arbitral decisions issued to date on point explicitly equate the two standards, assimilate the two standards, or at least indicate that the FET treaty standard needs to be informed

---

the Future of Investment Treaty Regime: A Grand Bilateral Bargain with Multilateral Implications", 12 *Journal of International Economic Law* 457 (2009), p. 468. While the text of the China-Mexico BIT still avoids mention of custom as such, its reliance on "state practice" and "opinio juris" comes very close to the United States' text explaining FET in its 2004 Model BIT (see *supra* footnote 402), as well as the NAFTA Interpretation (see *supra* footnote 367).

[404] Nor is this tendency limited to investor-State arbitrators. Some States had suggested, even prior to the issuance of the NAFTA Interpretation, that a reference to FET was intended to be a reference to the international minimum standard. C. McLachlan, "Investment Treaties and General International Law", 57 *International & Comparative Law Quarterly* 361 (2008), p. 381, n. 125 (quoting a 1980 statement by the Swiss Foreign Office).

[405] See, e.g., *Vivendi Universal S.A.* v. *Argentina*, Award, ICSID Case No. ARB/97/3 (21 November 2001) (emphasizing that the FET clause in the France-Argentina BIT — which referred to FET in conformity with international law — was intended to provide protection greater than under the minimum international standard); *Glamis Gold, supra* footnote 376, paras. 606-611 (distinguishing arbitral awards interpreting FET clauses that equate the term to customary law — as does the NAFTA — from those interpreting an autonomous FET principle unconnected to custom). Other cases have suggested that the FET and customary international law standards could diverge in principle, although the differences were not materially relevant to the claims before them. See, e.g., Kinnear, *supra* footnote 365, pp. 219-220.

by the applicable rules of international law such as the international minimum standard (as would be suggested by the interpretation rules in the Vienna Convention on the Law of Treaties)[406]. Even those tribunals interpreting treaties that identify FET and international law as distinct standards and which recognize that in such cases, FET may require treatment above that required by the "floor" set by international law often find that the differences between the two standards, when applied to the specific facts of a case, are more apparent than real[407]. Such determinations also subtly influence the meaning of customary law. Thus, the *Azurix* v. *Argentina Award* suggested that the question of whether or not FET is intended to be an additional guarantee to the investor may be academic, as in substance the rights it accords may now be the same as those under customary law[408]. And in *Sempra Energy*

---

[406] The outlier cases are those that seem to delink FET guarantees in investment treaties from CIL. See, e.g., *Glamis Gold*, *supra* footnote 376.

[407] See, e.g., Dolzer and Schreuer, *supra* footnote 355, p. 126.

[408] This is certainly borne out by Tudor's survey of investor-State arbitral decisions applying the FET standard, which frequently blur firm distinctions between FET as a treaty standard and underlying or related principles of CIL or general principles of law. See generally Tudor, *supra* footnote 357. For specific examples, see *Azurix Corp.* v. *Argentine Republic*, Award, ISCID Case No. ARB/01/12 (14 July 2006), para. 364 ("The question whether fair and equitable treatment is or is not additional to the minimum treatment requirement under international law is a question about the substantive content of fair and equitable treatment and, whichever side of the argument one takes, the answer to the question may in substance be the same"); *Siemens AG* v. *Argentina*, Award, ICSID Case No. ARB/02/8 (6 February 2007), paras. 293, 299 (concluding that customary law has evolved since the *Neer* case and it is no longer necessary to show bad faith or malicious intention on the part of the host State); *MCI Power* v. *Ecuador*,

v. *Argentina*, the arbitrators suggested that the meaning of FET, never precise to begin with, has evolved over the centuries and that "[c]ustomary international law, treaties of friendship, commerce and navigation, and more recently bilateral investment treaties, have all

---

Award, ICSID Case No. ARB/03/6 (31 July 2007), para. 369 (noting that FET "obliges State parties to the BIT to respect the standards of treatment required by international law" and that the BIT's reference to international law "refers to customary international law"); *Saluka Investments BV (The Netherlands)* v. *Czech Republic*, Partial Award, UNCITRAL Arbitration Rules (17 March 2006) (hereinafter *"Saluka"*), para. 292 (noting that the customary international minimum standard is in any case binding and that the FET standard may in fact provide no more than "minimal" protection); *Occidental* v. *Ecuador*, Award, UNCITRAL Arbitration Rules, 12 *ICSID Reporter* 59 (1 July 2004), paras. 189-190 (opining that the FET standard in the treaty and that required by international law is not different "concerning both the stability and predictability of the legal and business framework of the investment"); *CMS* v. *Argentina*, Award, ICSID Case No. ARB/01/8, 44 *International Legal Materials* 1205 (12 May 2005), paras. 282-284 (holding that the treaty FET standard "is not different" from the international law minimum standard and its evolution under customary law). Note that such decisions omit one possible distinction between the customary standards applicable to aliens under the doctrine of State responsibility and FET guarantees under BITs: the former was applicable only at the instigation of the home State of the alien or investor and only arose at the inter-State level in the course of diplomatic espousal. The international minimum standard was therefore a substantive right owed only to States *inter se* and existed only through their intercession. Arbitral tribunals appear to be equating the rights of investors under BITs to those once granted only to States as between themselves without much discussion about whether it matters who is the bearer of the right (and whether BITs are merely an application of diplomatic espousal or provide a unique set of rights to private parties). This broader question is further addressed in Chapter V.

contributed to this development"[409]. That tribunal further muddied the waters by suggesting that FET, like the international minimum standard, was essentially a gap-filler intended to enable arbitrators to fulfil the "principle of good faith" in the course of case-by-case application. Some scholars have read these and other arbitral decisions as giving "modern expression to a general principle of due process" or even the "minimum requirements of the rule of law", and have suggested that "some elements of human rights law may furnish a source of general principle from which the obligation of fair and equitable treatment may be given contemporary content"[410]. While such efforts to draw from disparate treaties and rules of custom might be attributed to sloppy thinking, these interpretations are hardly surprising given other requirements in many BITs or FTAs to accord investors the benefit of "treatment in accordance with international law" and the

---

[409] *Sempra Energy International* v. *Argentina*, Award, ICSID Case No. ARB/02/16 (28 September 2007) (hereinafter *"Sempra"*), paras. 296-297, 300. This portion of the decision is not the subject of the annulment issued in *Sempra Energy International* v. *Argentine Republic*, Decision on the Argentine's Republic's Application for Annulment of the Award, ICSID Case No. ARB/02/16 (29 June 2010) (hereinafter *"Sempra annulment"*)).

[410] McLachlan, *supra* footnote 404, pp. 396-383. See also A. Newcombe and L. Paradell, *Law and Practice of Investment Treaties* (The Hague, Kluwer Law International, 2009), p. 252 (arguing that some measures that affect foreign investors may violate international human rights law and that "[w]ith respect to procedural rights, there may be a significant overlap between claims of human rights violations on the one hand, and claims of denial of justice and due process on the other"); Tudor, *supra* footnote 357, pp. 154-181. Some have also suggested that the FET standard also overlaps with BIT and FTA non-discrimination guarantees. See, e.g., S. Subedi, *International Investment Law : Reconciling Policy and Principle* (Portland, Hart Publishing, 2008), p. 57.

need to render interpretations of FET in this broader context.

As the foregoing suggests, most tribunals charged with interpreting FET have not emphasized the textual differences among FET clauses in investment treaties surveyed at the outset of this chapter. On the contrary, the cases interpreting FET suggest a tendency by arbitrators to look for common general interpretative principles that may underlie FET.

Some arbitrators have suggested that FET is tantamount to a clause requiring good faith on the part of the host State, including good faith efforts by that State to promote legal stability; or a clause that, like the international minimum standard, seeks to avoid "unjust enrichment"[411] or seeks to prevent a party from benefiting from its own wrong (as in the doctrine of "unclean hands"); or, perhaps most commonly, to a provision that protects the "legitimate expectations" of the parties, especially investors[412]. As these different formulations suggest, arbitrators have differed over

---

[411] See, e.g., Dolzer and Schreuer, *supra* footnote 355, p. 13 (discussing the *Lena Goldfields Arbitration*'s reliance on unjust enrichment).

[412] See, e.g., *ibid.*, pp. 122-123. For a thorough discussion of arbitrators' use of "legitimate expectations" for this and other purposes in interpreting investment treaties, see A. Von Walter, "The Investor's Expectations in International Investment Arbitration", in *International Investment Law in Context, supra* footnote 398, p. 173. Note that the concept of "legitimate expectations" may play an interpretative role in connection with other substantive guarantees, such as national treatment or the minimum standard of treatment contained in BITs and FTAs. See, e.g., *International Thunderbird Gaming Corp.* v. *Mexico*, Award, UNCITRAL Arbitration Rules (26 January 2006), paras. 145-167 (discussing the concept of "legitimate expectations" without clarifying whether it was part of the analysis for FET, national treatment or the minimum standard of treatment or all three).

whether FET imposes an affirmative obligation on States to encourage investments (as might be suggested by the object and purpose of many BITs) or merely imposes an obligation of non-interference within a stable environment[413].

Despite the linguistic differences among investment treaties with respect to how FET is incorporated, there is an emerging consensus among arbitral decisions issued to date that FET is a single, unified standard and does not license two separate enquiries (that is a determination of whether a Government's action was "fair" and a separate determination of whether it was "equitable"); that it is an independent absolute standard and not a "relative" standard of treatment such as national treatment or a standard whose application depends on the laws of the host State; but also that it is a fact-specific, flexible, and contextual standard whose application turns on the circumstances of each case[414].

There is also apparent agreement that while a violation of FET may be demonstrated by actions in bad faith taken by a State, FET does not require bad faith, willful action, or malicious intention on the part of the State[415]. And, despite the canon of treaty interpretation (the principle of effectiveness) that urges that every provision be given its own independent meaning and warns against interpretations that render some provi-

---

[413] Kinnear, *supra* footnote 365, pp. 222-223.

[414] See, e.g., Dolzer and Schreuer, *supra* footnote 355, pp. 123, 128.

[415] See, e.g., *ibid*., pp. 146-147; Kinnear, *supra* footnote 365, p. 223. Moreover, even though an FET violation may be demonstrated by intentional discrimination, it does not require it. *Ibid*. Thus, even the arbitral decision that has arguably given the narrowest scope to FET, *Glamis Gold*, accepted that customary law has evolved since the *Neer* case at least to the extent that bad faith is no longer necessary to find a violation of FET. *Glamis Gold*, *supra* footnote 376, para. 616.

sions superfluous, many arbitral decisions have suggested that the FET guarantee may overlap to some extent with other BIT guarantees. Indeed, one tribunal went so far as to state that FET was a

> "more general standard which finds its specific application in, *inter alia*, the duty to provide full protection and security, the prohibition of arbitrary and discriminatory measures and the obligation to observe contractual obligations towards the investor"[416].

These developments do not indicate that the meaning of FET has now been fully clarified and its vagaries eliminated. The seven interpretative questions posed at the beginning of this chapter concerning its meaning remain for the most part unresolved despite a substantial volume of arbitral awards on point. To a considerable extent the meaning of that standard remains as elusive as ever and its meaning triggers significant debates over whether, for example, appliers of FET are supposed to take into account the respondent State's relative state of technological development, social structure, or fiscal resources or whether FET is such a basic absolute standard of civilization that all such differences among States are irrelevant to its application[417]. Others dispute the merits of leaving

---

[416] See Dolzer and Schreur, *supra* footnote 355, p. 123, n. 24 (quoting *Noble Ventures, Inc.* v. *Romania*, Award, ICSID Case No. ARB/01/11 (12 October 2005), para. 182). See also *Saluka*, *supra* footnote 408 (finding a violation of FET because of discriminatory treatment in an instance where an ailing bank in which the foreign claimant was invested was taken over by a competitor that had received financial assistance from the State for the purpose of the takeover and where that assistance was not available to the foreign claimant).

[417] Even scholars have appeared to straddle these two seemingly irreconcilable positions. Thus, Schwarzenberger

FET as a relatively flexible standard that adapts to each case's facts but urge that it be given greater precision and harmonized application[418]. And although arbitrators repeatedly assert the significance of "legitimate expectations", they appear to differ on when these expectations emerge or what is relevant in determining them. It is not clear, for example, whether investors are entitled to rely only on representations made directly to them by the State or whether reliance on publicly available information provided by the State at the time of investing creates legitimate expectations that are protected by FET[419]. It is also not clear whether the

---

stated that "in relations between heterogeneous communities — in varying stages of technological advance, social structure and political organization — and in an age of rapid change, the standard of equitable treatment provides equality on a footing of commendable elasticity". G. Schwarzenberger, "The ABs-Shawcross Draft Convention on Investments Abroad: A Critical Commentary", 9 *Journal of Public Law* 147 (1960), pp. 152-153. Compare *ibid.* with *Glamis Gold*, *supra* footnote 376, para. 615 (finding that FET, when equated to customary law, is an absolute, minimum standard that does not vary from State to State or investor to investor).

[418] Compare C. McLachlan, "Investment Treaties and General International Law", in Bjorklund *et al.* (eds.), *supra* footnote 365, pp. 120-121 (comparing the development of FET as a general standard necessarily subject to case by case application to the development of the law of civil wrongs) with B. Kingsbury and S. Schill, "Investor-State Arbitration as Governance: Fair and Equitable Treatment, Proportionality, and the Emerging Global Administrative Law", Institute for International Law and Justice Working Paper No. 6 (2009), available at <http://www.iilj.org/publications/2009-6Kingsbury-Schill.asp> (criticizing the "I know it when I see it" approach to FET as lacking legitimacy and accountability).

[419] See, e.g., Kinnear, *supra* footnote 365, p. 226. This debate is relevant to whether, for example, the decision reached in *Continental Casualty Co.* v. *Argentina*, ICSID Case No. ARB/03/9 (5 September 2008), a case that will

investor must have actually relied upon the State's representations when deciding to invest in order to succeed in a subsequent claim[420]. There are also a number of uncertainties concerning the extent of the investor's obligations and the extent to which these contribute to setting the threshold for legitimate expectations[421]. Perhaps most significantly, there are doubts about the extent FET is indeed the "absolute" (non-relative) standard it is often said to be, especially if its application varies with the conduct of investors, the reasonableness of their expectations, or conditions within the host State[422].

As is suggested above, that some arbitrators have equated the FET clauses in some investment agreements to non-treaty sources of general obligation (such as custom) — even in the absence of language as explicit as that in the NAFTA Interpretation or in BITs in the mould of the 2004 US Model — indicates that

---

be addressed in Chapter IV, was properly decided. At least one case suggested that a rapid series of legislative changes may create a lack of stability and predictability sufficient to breach investors' legitimate expectations. See *PSEG Global Inc.* v. *Republic of Turkey*, Award, ICSID Case No ARB/02/5 (19 January 2007), para. 250; but see *Glamis Gold*, *supra* footnote 376, paras. 798-802 (finding no violation of FET when the host State had promulgated new rules in a highly regulated environment because the United States had not given specific, unambiguous assurances to the investor and only such assurances, undertaken in order to induce investment, can give rise to the legitimate expectations protected by FET).

[420] See, e.g., Kinnear, *supra* footnote 365, p. 227.

[421] See, e.g., *ibid.*, p. 229 (noting cases that have suggested that the conduct of the claimant may be relevant to: whether a breach is found, whether the breach causes the loss alleged, and the amount of damages to be awarded).

[422] See, e.g., *ibid.*, p. 234; *Glamis Gold*, *supra* footnote 376.

such interpretations are influencing those non-treaty sources in the course of interpreting investment treaties. The prior chapter suggests how the negotiation and conclusion of investment treaties may be contributing to State practice and *opinio juris*. The rest of this chapter returns to this question but explores how investor-State arbitral decisions, particularly those involving FET, may be affecting the content of general international law.

If investor-State arbitral decisions are to be believed, the spread of investment treaties, arbitral decisions, and changes in State laws and practices have not left the state of general public international law unchanged. Many scholars agree and one set of authors have suggested that arbitral interpretations of the FET standard show "a clear progression over time towards more exacting standards for host states"[423]. This conclusion is suggested by the two most often cited arbitral decisions on the meaning of FET.

One of the most frequently cited quotations on point is from the arbitral decision in *Waste Management*:

"[T]he minimum standard of treatment of fair and equitable treatment is infringed by conduct attributable to the State and harmful to the claimant if the conduct is arbitrary, grossly unfair, unjust or idiosyncratic, is discriminatory and exposes the claimant to sectional or racial prejudice, or involves a lack of due process leading to an outcome which offends judicial propriety — as might be the case with a manifest failure of natural justice in judicial proceedings or a complete lack of transparency and candour in an administrative process. In applying this standard it is relevant that the treatment is in breach of representations made by

---

[423] Dolzer and Schreuer, *supra* footnote 355, p. 128.

the host State which were reasonably relied on by the claimant."[424]

Waste Management's restatement of FET eludes any differences between the "international minimum standard" and FET and imposes a discrete (and impressively long) laundry list of regulatory obligations on a host State. Under this view, FET now requires States to avoid arbitrary, grossly unfair, unjust, or idiosyncratic actions. A host State also needs to avoid discriminating against the investor and this duty not to discriminate apparently exists independently of any guarantee of national treatment premised on nationality. Under FET a State is not entitled to treat an investor differently based on the investor's race or even the sector in which its investment is located. Under *Waste Management*'s expansive view, FET also includes the concept of due process — which apparently means something beyond government actions that offend the sense of judicial propriety or infringes concepts of "natural justice" but includes lack of "transparency" and "candour" even with respect to administrative processes. *Waste Management*'s list includes a failure to abide by "representations" — which seems to go beyond specific contractual guarantees offered — so long as the investor reasonably relied on them. As this suggests, *Waste Management* builds onto the old *Neer* standard an impressive array of regulatory obligations, all the while suggesting that all of these are now required not by a specific treaty but by general international law.

Another frequently cited FET standard comes from *TECMED* v. *Mexico*. In that case, the arbitrators declared that FET required a State:

---

[424] *Waste Management, Inc.* v. *Mexico*, Award, ICSID Case No. ARB(AF)/00/3 (30 April 2004), para. 98.

"[T]o provide to international investments treatment that does not affect the basic expectations that
were taken into account by the foreign investor to
make the investment. The foreign investor expects
the host State to act in a consistent manner, free
from ambiguity and totally transparently in its relations with the foreign investor, so that it may know
beforehand any and all rules and regulations that
will govern its investments, as well as the goals of
the relevant policies and administrative practices or
directives, to be able to plan its investment and
comply with such regulations . . . The foreign
investor also expects the host State to act consistently, i.e. without arbitrarily revoking any pre-
existing decisions or permits issued by the state that
were relied upon by the investor to assume its commitments as well as to plan and launch its commercial and business activities." [425]

The *TECMED* standard, which gives credence to the
notion that international investment law is a species of
global administrative law [426], has been criticized for
being an impossible goal and not merely a standard. As
one scholar put it, it describes a state of "perfect public
regulation in a perfect world, to which all states should
aspire but very few (if any) will ever attain" [427]. Others
suggest that the *TECMED* interpretation converts FET
into an old-fashioned stabilization clause that essentially freezes a State's legislation [428].

---

[425] *TECMED S.A.* v. *United Mexican States*, Award,
ICSID Case No. ARB/AF/00/2 (29 May 2003), para. 154.

[426] See, e.g., Kingsbury and Schill, *supra* footnote 418.

[427] McLachlan, *supra* footnote 418, p. 121 (quoting Z.
Douglas, "Nothing if Not Critical for Investment Treaty
Arbitration: *Occidental*, *Eureko* and *Methanex*", 22 *Arbi-
tration International* 27 (2006), p. 28).

[428] See, e.g., A. Falsafi, "The International Minimum
Standard of Treatment of Foreign Investors' Property: A

One does not have to agree with every aspect of *TECMED*'s extensive enumerations of what apparently FET *and* CIL now require to acknowledge that even if some of these requisites are now widely expected of Governments, the general "international minimum standard" of treatment has evolved a great deal since the *Neer* case recognized only the barest duties to aliens. Despite the conclusion reached in one NAFTA case affirming the relevance of the *Neer* standard[429], the suggestion, stemming from *Neer*, that the minimum standard could only be breached by governmental actions involving bad faith, is a limitation few arbitrators appear inclined to impose today[430]. A State's mere failure to act, particularly to provide a remedy for a breach of the State's own representations to an investor, seems capable of grounding a violation of general international law or FET today[431].

Contingent Standard", 30 *Suffolk Transnational Law Review* 317 (2007), p. 341.

[429] *Glamis Gold*, *supra* footnote 376.

[430] See generally J. Paulsson, *Denial of Justice in International Law* (New York, Cambridge University Press, 2005).

[431] See, e.g., *Wena Hotels* v. *Egypt*, Award, ICSID Case No. ARB/98/4 (8 December 2000), para. 885 (noting that "even if Egypt did not instigate or participate in the seizure of the two hotels . . . there is sufficient evidence to find that Egypt . . . took no actions to prevent the seizures or to immediately restore Wena's control over the hotels"); A. F. Lowenfeld, *International Economic Law* (Oxford, Oxford University Press, 2002), p. 476 (citing *Asian Agricultural Products Ltd*. v. *Republic of Sri Lanka*, Final Award, ICSID Case No. ARB/87/3 (27 June 1990) (finding that Sri Lanka had failed to take appropriate precautionary measures to protect the interests of a British company injured in the course of fighting between the Government and rebel forces)). There are parallels here with the growing depth of State commitments with respect to human rights beginning with classic judgments such as *Velásquez Rodríguez* v. *Honduras*, Inter-American Court of Human

Specific applications of the FET standard suggest the many other ways that arbitrators rely on and in turn affect underlying customary norms as well as general principles of law[432]. As the quotations from *TECMED* and *Waste Management* suggest, a number of FET cases stress the need for a *transparent and stable legal framework* and identify these qualities as part of the investors' "legitimate expectations" requiring protection.

Notably, the requirement that Governments provide information about their laws or administrative practices is grounded not only in international investment law. It is a part of certain human rights regimes' emphasis on the public's right to receive (as well as impart) information.

For many, including proponents of high accountability standards for global administrative law, they are necessary elements of the rule of law or even of free-

---

Rights (Ser. C), No. 4 (29 July 1988), paras. 159 *et seq.* (interpreting States' duty to "ensure" the exercise of human rights in the American Convention on Human Rights and finding that duty requires States to investigate atrocities committed by private militias). Note that the emphasis in many FET cases on the need to respect the investors' "legitimate expectations", particularly when these are based on specific promises made by the State to the investor, may suggest that even BITs which do not have an "umbrella clause" protecting the investors' contracts may provide investors with some protection from breaches of their contracts under an FET clause or even under a residual provision protecting the investor "under international law". See, e.g., Tudor, *supra* footnote 357, pp. 193-200.

[432] See, e.g., C. N. Brower and J. K. Sharpe, "The Creeping Codification of Transnational Commercial Law: An Arbitrator's Perspective", 45 *Virginia Journal of International Law* 199 (2004), pp. 209-213 (contending that investor-State arbitrations may be a fertile ground for applying UNIDROIT's Principles (on international commercial contracts) as general principles of law).

dom of expression[433]. Similarly, the proposition common to many FET cases, namely that investors have a right to rely on the specific assurances made to them by the host State, that such expectations cannot be breached by an act taken by a State in its sovereign capacity, and that such assurances are entitled to be respected draws, of course, from such general principles of law as *pacta sunt servanda* and long established principles of estoppel[434]. Taken to its logical conclusion, this proposition suggests that investors may be entitled to the benefit of any assurances made by government officials even when the underlying investment treaty under which they are claiming lacks a specific FET clause or a specific "umbrella clause" like the one in the US Model BIT of 1987. Indeed, this has been suggested by at least one investor-State case. In *SPP* v. *Egypt*, the claimant successfully argued that it was entitled to rely on the acts of Egyptian officials because these "created expectations protected by established principles of international law"[435].

A number of FET cases turn on the failure by a host State to respect the "elementary requirement of the rule of law", namely procedural propriety and due process[436].

---

[433] It is also part of the US "freedom of information" tradition. See, e.g., T. W. Wälde, "Improving the Mechanisms for Treaty Negotiation and Investment Disputes: Competition and Choice as the Path to Quality and Legitimacy", in K. P. Sauvant (ed.), *Yearbook on International Investment Law & Policy 2008-2009* (New York, Oxford University Press, 2009), p. 550.

[434] See, e.g., Dolzer and Schreuer, *supra* footnote 355, pp. 140-142.

[435] *Southern Pacific Properties (Middle East) Ltd.* v. *Egypt*, Award and Dissenting Opinion, ICSID Case No. ARB/84/3, 3 *ICSID Reports* 189 (20 May 1992) (hereinafter "*SPP* v. *Egypt*"), paras. 82-83.

[436] For suggestions that the principle of providing legal protection for legitimate expectations is an aspect of the

FET violations premised on the lack of fair procedure or serious procedural shortcomings, especially in the course of criminal, civil, or administrative adjudicatory proceedings, have much in common with claims by aliens that were once cast as "denials of justice" or violations of the international minimum standard[437]. Current investor-State cases, involving, for example, instances in which investors were denied the opportunity to appear in court or in administrative proceedings are strikingly similar to some human rights cases brought before regional human rights courts involving nearly identical claims. Notably these conceptions of basic human rights entitlements are now increasingly regarded as so fundamental that other international adjudicators are recognizing them. Indeed, claims such as those in *TECMED* v. *Mexico* which found a violation of FET because, among other things, the environmental regulatory authority had failed to notify the foreign investor of its intentions and therefore deprived it of the opportunity to be heard, or *Metalclad* v. *Mexico*, which found a violation of FET because, among other things, the Mexican town council had denied the investor the opportunity to appear before it, resemble the recent *Kadi* case. In *Kadi*, where the European Court of Justice found illegal European Union law implementing Security Council counter-terrorism sanctions precisely because those targeted by such action

---

rule of law, namely the principle of legal certainty, and that the protection of legitimate expectations can be found in local law as well as the practice of international dispute settlers as varied as the European Court of Human Rights, the administrative tribunal of the International Labour Organization, and the WTO, and not only in investor-State tribunals, see C. Brown, "The Protection of Legitimate Expectations as a General Principle of Law: Some Preliminary Thoughts", 6:1 *Transnational Dispute Management* (2009).

[437] See, e.g., McLachlan, *supra* footnote 418, p. 118.

were not given the opportunity to be heard or to confront the evidence against them[438]. Notice that all of these claims — *Kadi*, *Metalclad*, and *TECMED* — dealt with violations of the property rights of private non-State parties, even though only some of them involved claims under investment protection treaties.

And while the overlap between customary law, general principles of law, and the FET treaty standard is most obvious in the case of FET, other treaty protections in BITs and FTAs also evoke non-treaty sources of law. As noted, the NAFTA Interpretation equates that treaty's full protection and security guarantee to that under customary international law and it would not be surprising if other investor-State tribunals outside the NAFTA are influenced by this conclusion, as they have sometimes been with respect to FET[439]. If so, investor-State arbitral interpretations of full protection and security will also, over time, affect the general law, even with respect to non-parties to BITs or FTAs. Accordingly, it will become important whether future investor-State tribunals, under the NAFTA or elsewhere, suggest that the full protection and security clause goes beyond the State's duty to provide police protection to persons and property from physical violence or harassment under customary international law[440]. While some tribunals have suggested that the full protection and security treaty clause ensures only

---

[438] *TECMED*, *supra* footnote 425; *Metalclad*, *supra* footnote 370.

[439] See, e.g., *Noble Ventures*, *supra* footnote 416, para. 164 (suggesting that the duty of full protection and security may not be greater than the general duty to exercise due diligence to protect aliens found in customary international law).

[440] See, e.g., Dolzer and Schreuer, *supra* footnote 355, pp. 150-151.

access to a State's judicial system [441], others have suggested that a

> "host State is obligated to ensure that neither by amendment of its laws nor by actions of its administrative bodies is the agreed and approved security and protection of the foreign investor's investment withdrawn or devalued" [442].

Comparable possibilities exist with respect to the investment regime's impact on the law governing expropriation. As is suggested by the clause in the US Model BIT of 2004, which equates that treaty's expropriation guarantee with that required under customary international law [443], it has been the long-standing position of the United States that customary international law, and not merely its Model BIT, requires "prompt, adequate and effective compensation". Whether or not one accepts this contention — which goes back to the United States' proclamation of the so-called "Hull Rule" early in the twentieth century — the investment regime may be driving a growing consensus about what general international law provides at least with respect to the process investors (and all persons) are entitled to expect when States purport to take their property [444]. This is suggested by international deci-

---

[441] *Lauder* v. *Czech Republic*, Final Award, UNCITRAL Arbitration Rules, 9 *ICSID Rep.* 66 (3 September 2001), para. 314.

[442] *CME Czech Republic B.V.* v. *Czech Republic*, Partial Award, UNCITRAL Arbitration Rules, 9 *ICSID Reports* 121 (13 September 2001), para. 613.

[443] See 2004 US Model BIT, *supra* footnote 402, Annex B, para. 1.

[444] Indeed, both the investment regime and human rights regimes share common due process concerns over such matters. See, e.g., *Kadi* v. *Council & Commission*, Judgment, Grand Chamber of the European Court of Justice, Case No. C-402/05 (2008), paras. 354-371

sions far afield from the investment regime, as in the *Kadi* case discussed above, as well as investor-State awards. There may also be growing consensus, as a result of investor-State case-law, about what the relevant customary rules are with respect to what were once strongly contested other matters — such as whether a formal decree of nationalization or expropriation is necessary to present an issue of a compensable taking[445]. And thanks to the intense focus provided in the course of a number of investor-State arbitrations — filled with expert opinions on point — there may even be an eventual consensus on what are the applicable principles for calculating the "full" value of expropri-

---

(deciding that counter-terrorism sanctions originally imposed by the Security Council and enforced through European Union law violated individuals' due process rights, including their right to property). See also Subedi, *supra* footnote 410, p. 75 ("Taking without due process of law would entail a taking in contravention of the principle of equality before the law, fair hearing and other principles of natural justice generally recognised by the world's principal legal systems"). For debates among scholars about whether, apart from due process, customary international law now recognizes the right to property, compare C. Tomuschat, "Court of Justice: Case T-306/01, Ahmed Ali Yusuf and Al Barakaat International Foundation v. Council and Commission; Case T-315/01, Yassin Abdullah Kadi v. Council and Commission", 43 *Common Market Law Review* 537 (2006), pp. 547-548 (contending that the right to property has evolved into a right under customary law) with J. Hathaway, *The Rights of Refugees under International Law* (New York, Cambridge University Press, 2005), pp. 518-523 (noting that many States are not yet prepared to bind themselves to such a concept).

[445] See, e.g., W. M. Reisman and R. D. Sloane, "Indirect Expropriation and Its Valuation in the BIT Generation", 74 *British Year Book of International Law* 115 (2004), p. 121 (suggesting that what matters is the effect of governmental conduct, not the existence of a formal expropriation decree).

ated property[446]. Despite differences on such matters as whether and when to award expected stream of profits, some would suggest that thanks to the growing practice of investor-State arbitral tribunals, international law now accepts as a general proposition that expropriated investors are entitled to an amount that approximates the "fair market value" of what they lost and that this measure may require going beyond the "book value" of the investment[447]. Of course, the tendency for arbitral decisions interpreting the expropriation guarantees of a BIT or an FTA to equate these to those under CIL is all the greater when the particular treaty explicitly equates the two (as do post-2004 US investment treaties) — but, as with respect to FET and full protection and security, the influence of investor-State decisions on the general law may not be limited to such cases.

The proposition that the investment regime is reflecting and therefore affecting non-parties to BITs

---

[446] See, e.g., Subedi, *supra* footnote 410, pp. 125-129 (summarizing arbitral case-law addressing when the full value of expropriated property is due); *S.D. Myers, Inc.* v. *Canada*, Partial Award on the Merits, UNCITRAL Arbitration Rules (13 November 2000) (finding that future earnings should not be awarded in cases of lawful expropriation).

[447] See, e.g., Subedi, *supra* footnote 410, p. 126. At a minimum, the prevalence of BITs and FTAs with comparable expropriation provisions makes it much less tenable to suggest, as some States did at one time, that the question of compensation in such cases is purely a matter of national law not governed by international law. See, e.g., *CME Czech Republic B.V.* v. *Czech Republic*, Final Award, UNCITRAL Arbitration Rules (14 March 2003), paras. 497-498 ("The possibility of payment of compensation determined by the law of the host State . . . has disappeared from contemporary international law as it is expressed in investment treaties in such extraordinary numbers, and with such concordant provisions, as to have reshaped the body of customary international law itself").

and FTAs is *not* a one-way ratchet in favour of
investors. A number of recent arbitral decisions stand
for the proposition that BITs' substantive guarantees,
including the international minimum standard or FET,
assurances of non-discrimination or national treatment,
and the duty to compensate for indirect expropriations,
must all be interpreted such as to not interfere with
States' ability to regulate in the public interest in a
non-discriminatory fashion, whether or not an "exception" clause to this effect exists in an investment
treaty [448]. Of course, this is all the more the case when

------

[448] See, e.g., *S.D. Myers, Inc.*, *supra* footnote 446,
para. 161 (finding that the international minimum standard is
not a licence to "second-guess government decision-making"); *Saluka*, *supra* footnote 408, paras. 305-306 (noting
that the legitimate expectations concept requires weighing
the investor's legitimate and reasonable expectations as
against States' "legitimate regulatory interest"); *Methanex
Corp.* v. *United States*, Final Award, UNCITRAL Arbitration Rules (3 August 2005), Part IV, Chap. D, para. 7
(citing customary international law for the principle that
economic injury caused by bona fide regulation within the
police powers of a State does not require compensation);
Feldman v. *Mexico*, Award, ICSID Case No. ARB(AF)/
99/1, 42 *International Legal Materials* 625 (16 December
2002), para. 103 (stating that customary international law
recognizes that "governments must be free to act in
broader public interest" and need to be able to undertake
"[r]easonable governmental regulation"). See also Subedi,
supra footnote 410, pp. 173-175 (contending that the FET
standard requires arbitrators to "balance" the competing
rights of States and investors). At the same time, it cannot
be assumed that arbitrators charged with interpreting a
treaty that identifies as one of the goals to ensure a predictable commercial framework for investment and promote development, as does the NAFTA, will always side
with the defendant State and its regulatory objectives. In
Pope & Talbot, for example, the tribunal required the State
to justify its "non-discriminatory policy goals" in relation
to national treatment and suggested that the State's goals
should not "unduly undermine the *investment liberalizing*

the relevant investment agreement recognizes such an
exception — as does Annex B of the US Model BIT of
2004[449]. In some cases, arbitrators reach this conclusion on the premise that only the investors' "legitimate" expectations are protected by FET, and that they
can reasonably expect to be regulated at least in the
same manner and to the same extent as they were when
they first entered the country. Indeed, some arbitral
decisions have been quite explicit that application of
FET and/or legitimate expectations requires "a weighing of the [investor's] legitimate and reasonable expectations on the one hand and the [host State's] legitimate
regulatory interests on the other"[450]. A number of
investor-State arbitral decisions have recognized that
there is a presumption that the investor's legitimate
expectations have *not* been disturbed when the State is
merely adhering to the same regulations that existed at
the time the investment was made[451]. Recognition of
the host State's residual right to regulate may be
grounded in general international law (which can be
applied under the traditional rules of treaty interpretation) insofar as such right is considered part and
parcel of the right of every State to self-determination, that is, to determine its own legal and economic

---

objectives of the NAFTA." *Pope & Talbot* Phase Two,
supra footnote 373, para. 78 (emphasis added).

[449] Which provides: "Except in rare circumstances,
non-discriminatory regulatory actions by a Party that are
designed and applied to protect legitimate public welfare
objectives, such as public health, safety, and the environment, do not constitute indirect expropriations." 2004 US
Model BIT, *supra* footnote 402, Annex B, para. 4 *(b)*.

[450] *Saluka*, *supra* footnote 408, para. 306.

[451] See, e.g., Dolzer and Schreuer, *supra* footnote 355,
p. 134 (citing *Feldman*, *supra* footnote 448; *S.D. Myers,
Inc.*, *supra* footnote 446; *GAMI Investments, Inc.* v. *Mexico*,
Final Award, UNCITRAL Arbitration Rules (15 November
2004); *Mondev*, *supra* footnote 400.

order[452]. As this suggests, when either the text of BITs or the decisions of arbitrators connect or equate certain treaty guarantees to those existing in CIL or general principles of law, both investors and States may face evolving notions of what is relevant "national policy space", the "right to regulate", or residual sovereign rights to provide regulatory "flexibility for development"[453]. Some ICSID tribunals have applied "transnational notions of public policy" or general principles of law to find inadmissible investor claims "not made in good faith, obtained for example through misrepresentations, concealment . . . or corruption, or amounting to an abuse of the international ICSID arbitration system"[454]. In yet other cases, it would appear that the

---

[452] See, e.g., Dolzer and Schreuer, *supra* footnote 355, p. 134.

[453] See generally P. Muchlinski, "Policy Issues", in P. Muchlinski *et al.* (eds.), *The Oxford Handbook of International Investment Law* (Oxford, Oxford University Press, 2008), p. 14. This is all the more apparent given the evolving nature and ideology of the US Model BIT over time, as discussed in the previous chapter. See also J. E. Alvarez, "The Once and Future Investment Regime", in M. Arsanjani *et al.* (eds.), *Looking to the Future: Essays on International Law in Honor of W. Michael Reisman* (The Hague, Martinus Nijhoff Publishers, forthcoming 2010). In some cases, it has been suggested that some arbitrators have gone too far in deploying the residual rules of general international law, resulting in a miscarriage of justice. See, e.g., McLachlan, *supra* footnote 418, pp. 127-128 (criticizing the *Loewen* decision under the NAFTA for imposing a requirement of exhaustion of local remedies as part of the substantive requirement for breach of FET within the context of treaty that had otherwise derogated from the exhaustion requirement).

[454] See, e.g., *Phoenix Action, Ltd.* v. *Czech Republic*, Award, ICSID Case No. ARB/06/5 (15 April 2009), para. 100 (noting that the purpose of BITs is to protect "bona fide" investments); *Plama Consortium Ltd.* v. *Republic of Bulgaria*, Award, ICSID Case No. ARB/03/24 (27 August 2008) (ruling that since the investment was the result of

recourse to CIL to interpret BIT provisions, such as the requirement to extend "full protection and security", may serve to limit the scope of States' duties[455]. Moreover, interpretative principles drawn from either CIL or general principles of law, such as reliance on "legitimate expectations", may also provide a licence for arbitrators to undertake a contextual enquiry of the circumstances in which those expectations are shaped and the respective duties that might be expected of the investor, and not merely the State[456]. Notwithstanding

---

fraud, the substantive protections of an investment treaty were inapplicable under principles of good faith and transnational public policy); *World Duty Free Company* v. *Kenya*, Award, ICSID Case No. ARB/00/17 (4 October 2006) (refusing to enforce a contract procured through a bribe since this would violate transnational public policy). For other investor-State arbitral cases relying on the principle of good faith, see Von Walter, *supra* footnote 412, pp. 195-197. While investor-State arbitral decisions refusing to enforce investments procured through fraud or corruption are sometimes grounded in specific BIT provisions limiting the treaty's coverage to investments made "in accordance with" the host State's law, even those cases may resort to general principles such as the need for the parties to act in "good faith" or the Latin maxim *nemo audittur propriam turpitudinem allegans* — no one can benefit from their own wrong — to come to this conclusion. See, e.g., *Inceysa Vallisoletana* v. *El Salvador*, Award, ICSID Case No. ARB/03/26 (2 August 2006), paras. 231-232, 242-243 (relying on good faith and the above maxim); see also *ibid.*, para. 246 (relying on international public policy); *ibid.*, paras. 254-257 (relying on unjust enrichment).

[455] See, e.g., *Noble Ventures*, *supra* footnote 416, para. 164 (using customary international law to interpret "full protection and security" as providing only for due diligence but not strict liability). A similar suggestion appears in some of the Argentina arbitral decisions. See, e.g., J. E. Alvarez and K. Khamsi, "The Argentine Crisis and Foreign Investors", in Sauvant (ed.), *supra* footnote 433.

[456] See, e.g., P. Muchlinski, " 'Caveat Investor' ? The Relevance of the Conduct of the Investor under the Fair

the "absolute" nature of guarantees such as FET, some arbitrators have taken into account a host State's political or economic instability, for example, in calculating the damages due investors on the premise that these chronic conditions must have been clear to the investor from the outset and shaped his/her legitimate expectations[457].

There is yet another reason why the investment regime sometimes affects the general public law. Like all treaties, BITs and FTAs contain numerous gaps and adjudicators interpreting them need to have recourse to "relevant rules of international law" to fill them[458]. This rule of "systemic integration" means, for example, that investor-State arbitrations are becoming a prominent forum — perhaps the most frequent — for ever more nuanced interpretations of such general public international law rules as those contained in the ILC's Articles of State Responsibility, including rules of State attribution, the meaning of remedies such as "reparation" or "restitution", as well as the scope of excuses from wrongful action, such as the defence of necessity[459]. Moreover, like most international adjudicative forums, investor-State arbitrations are venues

---

and Equitable Treatment Standard", 55 *International & Comparative Law Quarterly* 527 (2006) (contending that investors are now generally expected to avoid unconscionable conduct, reasonably assess investment risks, and operate reasonably).

[457] See, e.g., Von Walter, *supra* footnote 412, pp. 187-191 (discussing *American Mfg. and Trading, Inc.* v. *Zaire*, Award, ICSID Case No. ARB/93/1 (12 Febuary 1997), a decision that suggested that investors' compensation must take into account the realities of a tempestuous climate for investment and not merely some theoretical ideal environment).

[458] VCLT, *supra* footnote 366, Art. 31 (3) *(c)*.

[459] See generally Alvarez and Khamsi, *supra* footnote 455.

for interpreting or elaborating upon many other concepts in public international law, including general principles of law such as the duty to mitigate damages and equitable doctrines such as estoppel, acquiescence, or unclean hands, even outside the FET context. Indeed, the arbitrators in *Pope & Talbot* hesitated in accepting the NAFTA Interpretation in that case, despite an explicit treaty provision authorizing such interpretations, in part because it might offend the general principle that parties should not be permitted to be judges of their own cause[460]. The need to conduct an investor-State arbitration based on the relatively rudimentary procedural rules available (such as the ICSID or UNCITRAL rules) may also require arbitrators to rely on "common rules of international procedure" used by other international tribunals — yet another form of non-treaty law[461].

As the FET case-law suggests, investor-State arbitrators sometimes rely on non-treaty sources of law. Their decisions may nonetheless be unclear as to

---

[460] See *Pope & Talbot* Damages, *supra* footnote 383, paras. 48-51 (indicating that applying a NAFTA interpretation retroactively was a difficult question); C. H. Brower II, "Investor-State Disputes under NAFTA: The Empire Strikes Back", 40 *Columbia Journal of Transnational Law* 43 (2001), pp. 56-57, n. 71 (questioning the enforceability of certain NAFTA Interpretations particularly if these purport to affect pending arbitrations). The possibility that States may issue such interpretations, such as those authorized under investment agreements concluded by the United States after 2004, precisely to affect claims that are already in the process of adjudication may also be offensive to other principles, including perhaps the general *compétence de la compétence* that all international adjudicators are said to enjoy. See *ibid.*

[461] For a survey of how international adjudicators rely on and affect public international law, see, e.g., J. E. Alvarez, *International Organizations as Law-Makers* (New York, Oxford University Press, 2005), pp. 485-502.

whether or to what extent this is occurring; or whether such non-treaty sources are CIL, general principles of law, or even prior arbitral decisions on point[462]. While such ambiguity may be due to careless drafting, there may be good reasons for it. It is not entirely clear, for example, whether the principle of good faith is a principle of CIL or a general principle of law. It may indeed be both.

At the same time, most arbitrators are careful to avoid the suggestion that FET is merely a wide open licence to treat the disputing parties fairly. Many arbitrators stress that what they are applying may be a vague rule but is nonetheless a standard of law. While FET may require the use of equitable principles and is susceptible to case-by-case application, no arbitrator suggests that it is nothing more than a licence to decide a dispute *ex aequo et bono*[463]. As André von Walter has suggested, there is a difference between applying equity as a matter of abstract justice and applying a standard (like FET) that relies on equitable principles like legitimate expectations, good faith, or unclean hands[464].

The rest of this chapter considers three broader implications of evolving investor-State arbitral decisions.

A. The Limits of "Treatification"

'Legalization' in the international realm is defined by rising numbers of international legal obligations, accompanied by increasing precision of those obligations, alongside ever more instances in which States delegate to neutral third parties the power to make,

---

[462] The impact of investor-State arbitral decisions on international law is further addressed *infra*, Chaps. IV-V.

[463] See, e.g., Kinnear, *supra* footnote 365, p. 223.

[464] Von Walter, *supra* footnote 412, pp. 194-195.

interpret, and enforce these obligations[465]. For most observers, legalization is associated with "treatification". International lawyers commonly assume that since we have more treaties than ever before, and these are more ambitious in scope than ever before, treaties are displacing non-treaty sources like custom[466]. Most see treatification as a good thing, since treaties are more precise, more legitimate, and more democratic.

Most international lawyers have praised the move to treaties as demonstrating significant progress over reliance on "vague" custom or general principles of law. The substantive rules contained in custom or general principles are often criticized as fatally vague; worse still, international lawyers are still debating fundamental questions such as what these sources are or exactly how to define them[467]. Unlike a treaty whose beginning and end are usually precisely drawn and whose interpretation is subject to at least some distinct rules, the existence of (and even the distinction between) rules of custom and general principles leads to disagreements. For others, non-treaty sources are

---

[465] See K. Abbott and D. Snidal, "The Concept of Legalization", in J. Goldstein *et al.* (eds.), *Legalization and World Politics* (Boston, MIT Press, 2001).

[466] For the impact of international organizations, see Alvarez, *supra* footnote 461.

[467] Thus, for example, the final report of the International Law Association on customary international law drew considerable controversy when it appeared to suggest that *opinio juris* was no longer needed as a discrete element in addition to State practice. See International Law Association, Committee on the Formation of Customary (General) International Law, "Statement of Principles Applicable to the Formation of General Customary International Law" (2000), available at <http://www.ila-hq.org/download.cfm/docid/A709CDEB-92D6-4CFA-A61C4CA30217F376>.

less legitimate simply because they lack the most obvious forms of State consent and its consequences: clear dates of ratification and entry into force.

Critics of the democratic credentials of international law within the United States, such as John McGinnis, argue that CIL is undemocratic and ought to be rejected as a source of obligation because (1) nations do not assent affirmatively to it and may be deemed to have consented by failing to object; (2) undemocratic, even totalitarian, nations have an equal say in its formation; (3) such rules are merely empty promises that are routinely flouted since there are no or only weak mechanisms to enforce them — unlike rules that are approved by Congress and codified into domestic law; (4) the content and even the existence of these rules is unclear; and (5) these sources are opaque or even unknown to average Americans[468]. From this standpoint, it is therefore a good thing that treaties are increasingly "displacing" the inferior, outdated, or useless alternative sources of international law[469].

The investment regime is an excellent place to test the alleged benefits of treatification and the claimed inferiority of alternatives. Upon closer examination, it turns out that many of the assumptions of advocates of treatification are questionable, at least in the context of the investment regime. Treatification in this regime has not meant that treaties are the pivot around which the regime turns or that changes to the regime rest on changes to them[470]. As all of the most prominent

---

[468] J. O. McGinnis, "The Comparative Disadvantage of Customary International Law", 30 *Harvard Journal of Law & Public Policy* 7 (2006).

[469] J. P. Kelly, "The Twilight of Customary International Law", 40 *Virginia Journal of International Law* 449 (2000).

[470] See T. W. Wälde, "The Specific Nature of Investment Arbitration", in P. Kahn and T. Wälde (eds.), *New*

scholars in the field have suggested, the investment regime is now principally driven by arbitral *jurisprudence constante*. It is also not the case that the nearly 3,000 investment agreements have made customary norms, such as the international minimum standard, or general principles of law, such as the principle of unclean hands or estoppel, less relevant. As we have seen in this chapter, recourse to these non-treaty sources is more prevalent than ever before, because of the vague terms contained in BITs and FTAs (such as FET) as well as those treaties' reliance on non-treaty sources. Given these facts, it is not at all clear to what extent "treatified" investment law constitutes a dramatic improvement, in terms of the familiar rule of law goals of predictability, certainty, and stability.

The investment regime's reliance on arbitral *jurisprudence constante* has other implications for those who examine treatification and its effects. If it is true, as Wälde and many other investment scholars contend, that investor-State arbitrators are now charged with making and not merely interpreting the law, what does this say about the positivist assumptions of advocates of treatification? For such advocates, the appeal of treaties lies precisely in that they apply only to those who have consented to them. The positivist defenders of treatification would like to affirm that BITs and FTAs do not have an impact on the general law. They would like to say that any State other than one that is a party to a particular BIT or FTA need not be concerned with what such treaties provide or what arbitrators say such treaties mean in a particular case. As this chapter and prior chapters suggest, this is probably wrong.

Aspects of International Investment Law (Leiden, Martinus Nijhoff, 2007), p. 46 (contending that the modern international investment law "develops now mainly out of cases, and less out of treaties").

Some rules of custom and general principles of law are indeed affected by what goes on within the investment regime. As this chapter suggests, this is true at least in part because of the impact of arbitral awards.

Strict positivists would also deny that investor-State arbitral decisions can have such general law-making effects. Each of those *ad hoc* panels of three arbitrators is charged, after all, only with interpreting the particular treaty before them and not with pronouncing on the general law. Moreover, the investment regime does not even have a single multilateral treaty text to guide it and no appellate tribunal or process to reconcile conflicting arbitral interpretations of its sources of obligation — unlike the WTO[471]. In any case, even assuming investor-State arbitral decisions can be considered "judicial decisions" mentioned in Article 38 of the Statute of the ICJ, such decisions can only be *subsidiary* places to look for evidence of actual obligations. They are not, under the terms of that article, an authorized source of customary law themselves and cannot be a substitute for State practice and *opinio juris*[472]. To a strict positivist, investor-State arbitral decisions, even a stack of arbitral decisions each relying on earlier ones, is a house of cards, signifying nothing. As some have said is the case with respect to the effect of General Assembly resolutions, having a

---

[471] Chapter IV will address recent decisions that might suggest that ICSID's annulment process may be developing into a full-fledged process of appeal from erroneous findings of law.

[472] Objections to the alleged precedential value of arbitral decisions are legion. See, e.g., P. M. Norton, "A Law of the Future or a Law of the Past? Modern Tribunals and the International Law of Expropriation", 85 *American Journal of International Law* 474 (1991), pp. 475, 486 (discussing objections to reliance on arbitral decisions, including those made by a number of dissenting Iranian judges in the United States-Iran Claims Tribunal).

large number of such resolutions does not give them any more weight as sources of customary international law; the sum of a thousand zeros remains zero.

The investment regime is one more reason why strict positivism of this sort is not viable in the modern world. That arbitral decisions are only "subsidiary" sources of international law is no more relevant with respect to the investment regime than with respect to evaluating the legal impact of judgments of other international tribunals, from those of the WTO to the ICJ. A blinkered view of what those decisions portend would mislead us given the extent to which international lawyers, whether from common law or civil law nations, now resort to and rely on these arbitral awards as guidance indicating the state of the law.

As this suggests, the investment regime is an excellent place to re-examine the ways international law now gets made. Arbitral awards have such an influence on international investment law because they are frequently better than the few alternative places we have to look for guidance with respect to what that law is. They are, at the very least, as influential as are many kinds of "soft" law standards which critics of the investment regime claim are "hardening" and need to be considered when evaluating the international obligations of TNCs[473]. As is clear when international lawyers attempt to codify the relevant rules of interna-

---

[473] For a description of international adjudications, including arbitrations, as "soft law", see, e.g., Alvarez, *supra* footnote 461, pp. 505-506; A. T. Guzman and T. L. Meyer, "International Common Law: The Soft Law of International Tribunals", 9 *Chicago Journal of International Law* 515 (2009). Thus, it is ironic that Peter Muchlinski, who denigrates the impact of the foreign investment regime on the general law, see Muchlinski, *supra* footnote 453, simultaneously relies on "soft law" standards for this purpose. *Ibid.*, pp. 18-19.

tional law, as did the ILC when it elaborated its Articles of State Responsibility and commentaries[474], arbitral and judicial decisions are often the only credible efforts publicly available that apply law to concrete fact. Indeed for a long time, arbitral decisions have been treated as more relevant to determining what custom or general principles are than at least two forms of State practice: lump sum agreements or diplomatic letters or protests. Lump sum agreements tell us only what the last set of States was willing to settle for and not the state of the law[475]. Arbitral awards are also more likely to offer useful guidance than the diplomatic actions of self-interested States. Arbitral awards, at least the public ones, are easier to find. While it is possible for modern interpreters of the law to engage in the kind of historical survey of diplomatic State practice undertaken by, for example, the judges of the US Supreme Court in the famous *Paquete Habana* case, choosing to focus as that court did on the correspondence of States is time-consuming and, given the varied

---

[474] See J. Crawford, *The International Law Commission's Articles on State Responsibility: Introduction, Text, and Commentaries* (Cambridge, Cambridge University Press, 2002).

[475] See, e.g., *Banco Nacional de Cuba* v. *Chase Manhattan Bank*, United States 2nd Circuit Court of Appeals, 658 *Federal Reporter, Second Series* 875 (1981) (rejecting the view that lump-sum agreements had contributed to the development of a partial compensation rule); *Barcelona Traction Light and Power Co. Limited (Belgium* v. *Spain)*, Judgment, *ICJ Reports 1970*, paras. 59-63 (noting that lump-sum agreements were *sui generis* and were at best *lex specialis* — having no significance beyond the special circumstances which give rise to them). For a contrary view arguing for the relevance of lump-sum agreements in the context of custom, see R. B. Lillich and B. H. Weston, "Lump Sum Agreements: Their Continuing Contribution to the Law of International Claims", 82 *American Journal of International Law* 69 (1988).

abilities of States to record their views in this fashion, is likely to lead to charges that only some States' practices are accorded weight[476]. In any case, the self-serving statements of foreign ministries, included in their digests of practice, as cited in the *Paquete Habana* case, arguably do not have the "objectivity" of a neutral forum charged with resolving the same issue.

Many of the alternatives to arbitral decisions simply have less legitimacy. As Patrick Norton indicates, it is scarcely surprising if those charged with resolving disputes turn to how others have resolved comparable disputes[477]. The well-crafted arbitral decision is persuasive. It is rare to find the kind of detailed reasoning and application of law to fact that is found in adjudicative efforts. As Norton points out, reliance on a string of comparable decisions is compelling to advocates and attractive to other arbitrators since the latter typically want to deflect the charge that they are engaged in "judicial legislation"[478]. As Norton concludes, power-

---

[476] Thus, even the widely praised efforts by the US Supreme Court in *The Paquete Habana*, United States Supreme Court, 175 *United States Reports* 677 (1900), have been criticized for that Court's apparent inability to consider the State practices of others apart from the United States and some of its European allies.

[477] Norton, *supra* footnote 472, pp. 499-501. It may be, as was stated by the arbitrators in one case, that investor-State arbitrators rely on prior cases because they believe they have "a duty to seek to contribute to the harmonious development of investment law and thereby to meet the legitimate expectations of the community of States and investors towards certainty of the rule of law". *Saipem S.p.A.* v. *Bangladesh*, Decision on Jurisdiction, ICSID Case No. ARB/05/07, Decision on Jurisdiction (21 March 2007), para. 67.

[478] Norton, *supra* footnote 472, p. 500. See generally M. Shapiro, *Courts: A Comparative and Political Analysis* (Chicago, University of Chicago Press, 1981).

ful cultural and sociological reasons explain the "preference for precedents" seen in this and other international legal regimes[479]. Of course, to the extent all of this is true, it means that international lawyers, from human rights advocates to litigants before other international tribunals, need to pay heed to the rulings issued by investor-State arbitrators — as where they elaborate in ever greater detail what a "denial of justice" or a violation of the "international minimum standard" really means.

As this suggests, the investment regime provides public international lawyers with potent caveats on the relative merits of treaty, custom, and general principles of law — some of which may run counter to accepted wisdom. It may also challenge those who still insist that these positivist sources — and the traditional ways in which they are defined — are the sum total of what is legally relevant in the modern world.

B. The "Democratic" Credentials of the Investment Regime

McGinnis's contentions are not borne out by the investment regime and particularly the way it handles FET — where treaty, CIL, and general principles are inexorably intertwined and hard to disentangle. Given the entanglements among treaty, non-treaty sources of international obligation, and national laws and practices, it would be misleading to suggest that the relevant principles of custom applied in investment disputes have not been subject to consent, have not been scrutinized by legislatures or parliaments, are only characteristic of totalitarian societies, or are only found in rhetorical UN General Assembly resolutions. And if the treaty standard of FET and the customary inter-

---

[479] Norton, *supra* footnote 472, pp. 497-500.

national minimum standard are both unclear (even if the first is contained in a treaty), both are arguably becoming less so as they are applied to concrete fact situations through investor-State dispute settlement. In any case, these standards, whether found in custom or treaty, are no more uncertain or illegitimate than are ageless concepts such as "due process" under national laws or constitutions — which also achieve precision largely as a matter of application, case by case.

Treaties are not the only legitimate or effective sources of international obligation. As the US Government has recently learned from the global reactions to its "war" on terror, allegedly "vague" customary norms prohibiting the ill-treatment of aliens may have as much or even greater legitimacy and power than do treaty obligations and these non-treaty norms exist alongside textual commitments that have been more clearly subject to "democratic" approval, such as those in the Geneva Conventions or the Convention against Torture. It is wrong, in the investment regime, as with respect to human rights, to contend that only treaties are truly capable of influencing the behaviour of States, and that, to quote two leading critics of international law, "CIL as an independent normative force has little if any effect on national behavior"[480].

Critics of custom like McGinnis are right that international law rules are not transparent but the entanglement of treaty and custom makes drawing distinctions between these two sources on this ground a dubious exercise in this regime and one suspects in others as well.

---

[480] J. L. Goldsmith and E. A. Posner, "Understanding the Resemblance between Modern and Traditional Customary International Law", 40 *Virginia Journal of International Law* 639 (2004), p. 641.

C. The Entwined Nature of Treaty
and Non-Treaty Sources

As the investment regime makes very clear, incorporating customary law into a treaty regime that includes a reasonably effective dispute settlement mechanism is not likely to leave the original rules of custom unchanged. Treatification affects what is considered to be customary law or general principles of law.

A more accurate perspective on the entwined nature of treaty and non-treaty sources of international obligation was suggested by Wolfgang Friedman long ago in his Hague lectures.

He argued that all sources of international law are inseparable and lie atop each other in a dense web, particularly as applied within the transnational legal process[481].

Friedman's views are given concrete form in, for example, the canon of interpretation deployed by investor-State and other international tribunals according to which, unless treaty parties explicitly provide to the contrary, treaty interpreters should not presume that a treaty dispenses with the application of fundamental rules of customary international law (such as the principle requiring exhaustion of local remedies)[482].

---

[481] W. Friedman, "General Course in Public International Law", *Recueil des cours*, Vol. 127 (The Hague, Leiden, 1969), pp. 131-136. See also P. C. Jessup, *Transnational Law* (New Haven, Connecticut, Yale University Press, 1956).

[482] See, e.g., *Sempra*, *supra* footnote 409, para. 378; *Elettronica Sicula S.p.A. (United States* v. *Italy)*, Judgment, *ICJ Reports 1989*, 15 (20 July 1989), para. 112; *Amoco Int'l Finance Corp.* v. *Iran*, Award, *Iran-United States Claims Tribunal Reports* 189 (14 July 1987), para. 50; *Legal Consequences for States of the Continued Presence of South Africa in Namibia (South West Africa) Notwith-*

The interpretations issued by investor-State tribunals to date tell us that the move to investment
treaties has not displaced the resort to CIL or general
principles[483].

Treatification, at least in this regime, does not, contrary to the expectations of some, suggest the "twilight
of customary international law"[484]. Indeed, debates
over the content of customary international law are,

---

standing Security Council Resolution 276, Advisory
Opinion, *ICJ Reports 1971* 16 (21 June 1971), p. 47;
Loewen Group, Inc. v. *United States*, Award, ICSID Case
No. ARB (AF)/98/3 (26 June 2003), para. 160. See also G.
Schwarzenberger, *International Law as Applied by
International Courts and Tribunals* (London, Stevens, 3rd
ed., 1957), p. 57 ("Even if the standard of national treatment is laid down in a treaty, the presumption is that it has
been the intention of the parties to secure to their nationals
in this manner additional advantages, but not to deprive
them of such rights as, in any case, they would be entitled
to enjoy under international customary law or the general
principles of law recognised by civilised nations"). This
canon is defended as a valued tool to avoid the risk of
general fragmentation of international law in the International Law Commission's final report on fragmentation.
See International Law Commission, "Fragmentation of
International Law: Difficulties Arising from the
Diversification and Expansion of International Law", UN
doc. A/CN.4/L.702 (18 July 2006) (hereinafter "Fragmentation Report").

[483] Indeed, Campbell McLachlan contends that

"the main route through which practice under investment treaties contributes to the development of general
international law is through the elucidation of general
principles of international law, which illuminate the
province of international law in its supervision of the
conduct of national State officials". McLachlan, *supra*
footnote 404, pp. 364-365.

[484] The same scholar advocates that CIL should be
"eliminated as a source of international law in the modern
era". Kelly, *supra* footnote 469, p. 540.

within the treated investment regime, livelier than ever before[485].

And, despite the suggestions of certain international law sceptics, there is no evidence that States are distinguishing, in terms of their readiness to comply with arbitral rulings, between those based on treaty or non-treaty sources of law[486].

Although the investment regime faces challenges of enforcement and compliance — as do all international

---

[485] As a recent effort of one scholar to canvass the emerging arbitral case-law on the meaning of FET demonstrates. That study necessarily spends considerable time describing the extent to which FET now reproduces and has changed CIL or relevant general principles of law. See Tudor, *supra* footnote 357.

[486] Although some States resist paying arbitral awards rendered against them and compliance may take some time (as it sometimes does with respect to the WTO), investor-State arbitral awards generally achieve routine compliance. Indeed, the relative efficacy of the regime's enforcement scheme is one of its unique characteristics. See, e.g., G. Van Harten and M. Loughlin, "Investment Treaty Arbitration as a Species of Global Administrative Law", 17 *European Journal of International Law* 121 (2006). By comparison, Goldsmith and Posner rely on rational choice theory to contend that compliance with CIL as such does not exist. They write that "CIL is the label that we attach to certain behavioral regularities that result from nations pursuing their self-interest; it does not cause or constrain anything". Goldsmith and Posner, *supra* footnote 480, pp. 662-663. Although Goldsmith and Posner acknowledge that government officials use the language of CIL, they contend that this is merely "cheap talk" that "serves an important coordinating function that can facilitate cooperation". *Ibid*. Their contention that when nations pursue goals in pursuit of power and national interest, CIL as an "independent normative force" drops out of the picture, is inconsistent with the argument here that even if States conclude BITs for "economic reasons", the network of BITs influences CIL and serves to enforce it. *Ibid.*, p. 663.

legal regimes — these appear to have little to do with the sources of obligation being applied.

(1) Treatification does not equal precision

A mordant wit once suggested that a treaty is a dis-agreement reduced to writing[487]. While that may go too far with respect to investment agreements, the turn to BITs and FTAs does not *necessarily* entail a move to more precise, or textually more determinate rules. This is certainly not the case to the extent these treaties affirm that investors are entitled to FET or to the protections of "full protection and security" or of "international law" or to be compensated when they have been subjected to an "indirect" taking of their property — especially when the relevant treaties do not define any of these crucial terms. While some guarantees in BITs and FTAs — such as NT — might be relatively precise in their content, an FET guarantee that not only does not define the term but also (as is typical) fails to indicate what kind of compensation might be due for violating that guarantee, is not, in itself, a move to textual clarity.

(2) The absence of precision in a treaty is not the last word

Those who focus on "treatification" — and its alleged superiority over the customary international law-making process — risk fixating on the source of obligation at the expense of overlooking the processes of dispute settlement and treaty interpretation. As the evolving interpretation of FET by arbitrators suggests, the textual clarity (or lack of it) of BIT or FTA guarantees (or of CIL contained in them) is not as important as the process for resolving interpretative ambiguities

---

[487] P. Allot, "The Concept of International Law", 10 *European Journal of International Law* 31 (1999), p. 43.

that accompany these treaties. The investment regime does not support the proposition that treatification in and of itself constitutes undeniable progress in international law. And the continued interaction between custom and treaty in this regime should make us a bit sceptical of the proposition that States are only likely to abide by what they specifically agreed upon in a treaty. The investment regime supports the proposition that the "judicialization" of international law may be far more significant than its "treatification". Whether the turn to judicialization has legitimated the regime, however, is a distinct question that will be addressed in Chapter V.

Another lesson one might draw from the study of FET is that the absence of textual clarity is not necessarily a bad thing. There are benefits to the law's deployment of standards over rigid rules. There is nothing inherently wrong with applying a case by case FET standard. As suggested above, FET is no less legitimate, no less "democratic", a principle than is due process under US Constitutional law. As Alec Stone Sweet and other advocates of proportionality balancing have noted, to the extent democratic States rely on constitutional proportionality balancing, it can scarcely be argued that such balancing — which is not a mechanical exercise but a fact-laden one — is itself undemocratic [488]. (This is a different question, of course, from the decision on who is given the authority

---

[488] See A. Stone Sweet and J. Matthews, "Proportionality Balancing and Constitutionalism", 47 *Columbia Journal of Transnational Law* 73 (2008), p. 89 (noting that the move to balancing makes clear that, among other things, "determining which value shall prevail is not a mechanical exercise, but is a difficult judicial task involving complex policy considerations" and "that future cases pitting the same two legal interests against one another may well be decided differently, depending on the facts").

to balance — whether national or international authorities, how such persons are chosen, to whom such decision-makers are accountable, and so on.)

The imprecision of FET leads investor-State interpreters to have recourse to supplemental principles, including from CIL or general principles of law, especially when these have been used by prior arbitrators. When such efforts are carefully undertaken, they can give the application of FET greater coherence and legitimacy — even when the underlying standard is acknowledged to be fact-specific. The same is true of other BIT and FTA guarantees that are less than precise, such as the concept of "full protection and security" or of an "indirect" taking. As will be explored further in the last chapters, it may also be the case that the ambiguities of such standards may be necessary, at least to the extent this gives treaty interpreters leeway to avoid the excesses that some associate with market liberalism and strongly investor-protective treaties such as the US Model BIT of 1987[489]. The absence of precision may indeed be a principal reason why the "progressive" evolution of international investment law remains possible.

(3) Fragmentation and its discontents

Chapter II demonstrated how the risk of fragmentation may be exacerbated by the differing texts of investment treaties over time. Are there available remedies?

The ILC's report on fragmentation highlights a number of ways in which the risks of fragmentation

---

[489] See, e.g., K. Polanyi, *The Great Transformation* (Boston, Beacon Press, 1944) (arguing that an excessive focus on correcting government imperfections generates an inevitable countermovement to restore the proper role of government intervention in a market economy).

might be alleviated. The ILC suggested that these risks are lessened to the extent international law is seen as a legal system and not as a set of "self-contained" sub-specialties. Specifically, the ILC's report recommended that in interpreting treaties it would be useful to apply the harmonizing principle suggested by such rules as Article 31 (3) *(c)* of the Vienna Convention on the Law of Treaties (requiring residual application, in the course of interpretation, of "relevant rules of international law"); that the rule of *lex specialis* be given a "contextual" interpretation, particularly since its application "does not normally extinguish the relevant general law"; that the general law be used to fill gaps even with respect to "special" regimes; and that this last is especially appropriate when the relevant treaty rules are "unclear" or "open-textured"[490]. It is striking how many of these recommendations to avoid fragmentation have been deployed by arbitral tribunals in the course of interpreting FET. If these interpretations of FET are any indication, investor-State arbitration may be one mechanism through which the internal fragmentation of the investment regime prompted by disparate BIT texts may be deflected, although not wholly avoided. In the next chapters we will explore this question further in the context of some recent cases brought against Argentina.

D. *Globalization and its Discontents*

That the investment regime is having an impact on the general law should not be seen, as it sometimes is,

---

[490] Fragmentation Report, *supra* footnote 482. Investor-State arbitrators do not appear as reticent as other tribunals (such as WTO dispute settlers) are with respect to relying on such systemic integration devices as Article 31 (3) *(c)* of the Vienna Convention on the Law of Treaties. See, e.g., *Saluka*, *supra* footnote 408, para. 254.

as a triumph of the Global North over the South or of investors over the regulatory power of States. The contemporary investment regime, as is addressed in prior chapters, is now too universal in scope and includes too many prominent first movers from the "Global South" to be credibly portrayed in such terms. It has, to this extent, outgrown its origins[491]. Moreover, as is suggested in this chapter, it is premature to conclude that the investment regime will redound to the benefit of investors or host States. The continued openness of the investment regime to other non-treaty sources of law may help to ameliorate concerns over fragmentation as well as fears that the regime is overly preoccupied with investors' rights over the public good. In principle, the use of non-treaty sources of law is open to all participants in the regime, from host States (from the North and South) facing investor-State claims to NGOs increasingly able to participate as *amici* in investor-State disputes. References to general international law can be deployed by arbitrators appointed by States as well as by States parties to investment treaties like the NAFTA that permit them to issue joint interpretations of their treaty. Given the fact that most investor-State arbitral decisions have been rendered only in the course of the last ten years, it seems premature to draw conclusions about who is most likely to benefit from the regime's reliance on non-treaty sources and what the impacts of these decisions on non-treaty sources will be.

For much the same reasons, it is premature to suggest, as some have, that the investment regime continues to legalize a rigid version of the "Washington Consensus" mode of governance. While that might

---

[491] See generally J. E. Alvarez, "The Contemporary Foreign Investment Regime: Empire of Law or Law of Empire?", 60 *Alabama Law Review* 943 (2009).

have been the case under the US Model BIT of 1987, even the United States has changed its mind since then. Operationalizing the Washington Consensus is not the goal sought by many of the regime's stakeholders today. It is certainly not the goal sought by the many NGOs that are urging States to modify their BITs to include *greater* references to customary principles of human rights or environmental protection or urging arbitrators, through *amicus* briefs, to do the same in the course of deciding disputes. Legalizing "the Washington Consensus", as that term is traditionally understood, would also be an odd way to characterize attempts by the United States or China to recalibrate their BITs in the ways described in Chapter II. The United States' (and others') efforts to equate FET with CIL in its recent treaties evince an intent to make recent investment treaties more, not less, sensitive to the diverse regulatory needs of States. And those investor-State arbitrators who are using (and developing) CIL and general principles to interpret investment treaties to make these "more harmonious with the expectations of the international community" are also not likely to see themselves as engaged in giving effect to *Washington*'s version of that Consensus.

As to the charge made by globalization critics that the investment regime is recognizing more elaborate protections for investors, as it arguably does with respect to FET, a relevant question must surely be what are the alternatives? The ideal some pursue in lieu of the current regime — achieving a multilateral treaty coupled with a single investment court — may in the end prove less flexible in terms of recognizing the diverse needs of claimants and host States than the chaotic, but adaptable, bilateralized regime that we now have. As is suggested by this chapter and the previous one, the current investment regime, for all its flaws and risks of internal fragmentation, is, if nothing else, an instrument that enables the law — through evolving BITs and FTAs and sometimes inconsistent arbitral case-law — to adapt to the changing demands made by the regime's stakeholders. The lack of a single WTO text or a single organization enables more exit and voice in this regime than is true of the trade regime. While most States do not see that they have an option to withdraw from the WTO, some States have and will continue to withdraw from some of their BITs, seek to amend or re-interpret their existing investment treaties, or withdraw from or modify their commitment to international arbitration (as under ICSID). The contemporary investment regime is also surely more accommodating to the rights of LDCs than what preceded it — an era when investment protections were subject to customary rules developed before most LDCs achieved independence, where these rules were enforced by gunboats and crude political tactics, and where few treaties or international adjudicative mechanisms existed to permit orderly change over time.

CHAPTER IV

LESSONS FROM THE ARGENTINA CRISIS CASES

A. Introduction

Recent investor-State claims have described the situation in Argentina during the period of 1999-2002 in the following terms:

> "Towards the end of the 1990's a serious economic crisis began to unfold in Argentina, which eventually had profound political and social ramifications."[492]

> "In the third quarter of 1998, the Argentine economy plunged into a period of recession that was to last four years and triggered, in [the opinion of Argentina], the worst economic crisis since Argentina's inception in 1810 . . ."[493]

> "Argentina's crisis deepened at the end of 2001. The Government experienced increased difficulties in repaying its foreign debt. As poverty and unemployment soared, Argentines feared that the Government would default on its debt and immobilize bank deposits. Therefore, savings were massively withdrawn from the banks. In response, the Government issued Decree No. 1570/01, known as

---

[492] *CMS Gas Transmission Co.* v. *Argentina*, Award, ICSID Case No. ARB/01/8 (12 May 2005) (hereinafter *"CMS"*), para. 59.

[493] *LG&E Energy Corp.* v. *Argentina*, Decision on Liability, ICSID Case No. ARB/02/1 (3 October 2006) (hereinafter *"LG&E"*), para. 54.

'Corralito', on 1 December 2001, restricting bank withdrawals and prohibiting any transfer of currency abroad. Amid widespread discontent and public demonstrations, including violence that claimed tens of lives, President De la Rúa and his Cabinet resigned on 20 December 2001. A succession of presidents took office and quickly resigned." [494]

In response to this crisis, the Argentine authorities took a number of other actions which would ultimately prompt the largest number of investor-State claims directed at a single State in the history of investment treaties. At this writing, Argentina faces some 40 investor-State claims [495]. Although the actual sums sought by investors, especially with respect to claims that have not been made public, are uncertain, the face value of the publicly available claims is said to exceed 80 billion [496].

The actions triggering these claims include Argentina's Emergency Law of 2002, which abrogated the prior one-to-one peg of the Argentine peso to the US dollar and required that all debts arising from public contracts and debts under private agreements would now be paid in pesos and not dollars. Although the switch into Argentine pesos ("pesification") affected the entire Argentine economy and not only foreign investors and was characterized by the Government as

---

[494] *Op. cit., supra* footnote 493, para. 63.

[495] W. W. Burke-White, "The Argentine Financial Crisis: State Liability under BITs and the Legitimacy of the ICSID System", 3 (1) *Asian Journal of WTO and International Health Law and Policy,* 199 (2008), p. 204.

[496] *Ibid.*; Aktion Finanzplatz Schweiz, International Conference on Illegitimate Debts Berne, 3-4 October 2007, *Argentina 1976-2007: The Paradigmatic Case of an Extraordinarily Legitimate Debt,* available at <http://www.aktionfinanzplatz.ch/pdf/kampagnen/illegitime/Keene_handout_en.pdf>.

a necessary step to restore economic stability, these measures triggered BIT claims apart from non-discrimination, such as violations of fair and equitable treatment ("FET") and their umbrella clauses. The vast majority of the claims against Argentina, perhaps as many as 27[497], have involved those who had invested in public services or utilities (namely gas, electricity, water, or telecommunications). These sectors had been privatized over recent years[498]. Most of these claims stemmed from the same emergency law's provisions modifying the underlying public service contracts or other assurances given these utilities under Argentina law, including their licences to operate. The changes made to the law meant that notwithstanding prior assurances made, the tariffs and prices for gas and other public utility services were now to be calculated in pesos. That law also abolished prior arrangements under the pre-existing regulatory framework that had provided that "if tariffs ceased to be fair and reasonable" specific adjustment mechanisms would be triggered; that is, that Argentina and the companies would renegotiate to enable tariffs to be adjusted on a perio-

---

[497] E. Kentin, "Economic Crisis and Investment Arbitration: The Argentina Cases", in P. Kahn and T. Wälde (eds.), *New Aspects of International Investment Law* (2007) p. 635. Of the 36 cases identified by Kentin, 13 involved a US investor and the United States-Argentina BIT. *Ibid.*, p. 636.

[498] For an overview of Argentina's actions in opening its economy to foreign investment and the resulting spate of investor-State claims, see R. Ortíz, "The Bilateral Investment Treaties and the Cases at ICSID: The Argentine Experience at the Beginning of the XXI Century", *Foro Ciduadadano de Participación por la Justicia y los Derechos Humanos* (September 2006) (copy on file with author). This document also contains a listing of all cases pending against Argentina as well as a list of BITs entered into by that Government.

dic basis. The new law also ignored prior guarantees that stated that tariff adjustments would be made in US dollars or other foreign currencies and that contained particular indexing mechanisms; instead, the law unilaterally abrogated these adjustment mechanisms and directed the Executive Branch to renegotiate all public service contracts.

These measures resulted in investor-State claims pursuant to a number of BITs that Argentina had concluded, particularly in the early 1990s, at the height of that country's enthusiasm for market reforms and for privatization urged by, among others, the IMF[499]. The first set of claims resulting in significant awards against Argentina involved invocation of the United States-Argentina BIT of 1991, a treaty based on the US Model BIT of 1987 examined in Chapter I. The four largest awards rendered through the end of 2008 involved US investors in the transportation and distribution of gas: *CMS*, *LG&E*, *Enron*, and *Sempra*. These companies had filed ICSID claims under the United States-Argentina BIT arguing that Argentina's emergency measures violated the FET, umbrella, non-discrimination, and expropriation guarantees of that treaty. In all four cases, the arbitrators found that the investors had successfully shown violation of the FET and umbrella clauses[500] and awarded significant sums: US$133.2 million to CMS, US$106.2 million to Enron, over US$128 million to Sempra, and US$57.4 million to LG&E. All these awards led to annulment proceed-

---

[499] See, e.g., IMF, "Argentina — Letter of Intent, Memorandum of Economic Policies, Technical Memorandum of Understanding" (30 August 2001), available at <http://www.imf.org/external/np/loi/2001/arg/02/index. htm>.

[500] But note that the tribunal in *LG&E* found, in addition, that Argentina's actions were also discriminatory. *LG&E*, *supra* footnote 493, para. 147.

ings, however, and these have significantly affected Argentina's liabilities.

The first annulment committee to reach a conclusion, the *CMS* Annulment Committee, ended up affirming that award in full, although not without overruling its finding of an umbrella clause violation and significant criticism of the original tribunal's reasoning with respect to Argentina's defence of necessity. Whether or not as a result of the annulment committee's criticisms of the original *CMS* award, the *CMS* claimants, to date, have not been able to collect on their award.

The second and third annulment committees, involving *Sempra* and *Enron*, annulled these respective awards in their entirety, determining, albeit for different reasons, that the original decisions had failed to apply correctly Argentina's defence of "necessity" either under the United States-Argentina BIT or customary international law[501]. Argentina scored another relative success with respect to a different US claimant, Continental Casualty, whose claims were considerably different from those of the public utilities involved in the *CMS, Enron* and *Sempra* cases but were also grounded in Argentina's emergency measures taken in the wake of its crisis in 2001. Continental Casualty was an insurance company that maintained a portfolio of investment securities in Argentina, primarily in assets denominated in Argentine pesos. It claimed that its assets suffered losses in value of over US$46 million as a result of Argentina's Capital

---

[501] *Sempra Energy International* v. *Argentine Republic*, Decision on the Argentine's Republic's Application for Annulment of the Award, ICSID Case No. ARB/02/16 (29 June 2010) (hereinafter "*Sempra annulment*"); *Enron Creditors Recovery Corp. Ponderosa Assets, L.P.* v. *Argentine Republic*, Decision on the Application for Annulment of the Argentine Republic, ICSID Case No. ARB/01/3 (30 July 2010) (hereinafter "*Enron annulment*").

Control Regime. The complaint was directed at Argentina's actions, commencing in December 2001, to restrict capital transfers out of its territory, rescheduling of cash deposits, and pesification. The tribunal, which issued its decision after the *CMS* annulment committee's decision was rendered (but before the annulment decisions in *Enron* and *Sempra*), took notice of that committee's criticism of the original *CMS* decision. *Continental Casualty* upheld Argentina's plea of necessity, rejected the bulk of the investor's claims, and awarded only US$2.8 million in compensation for particular actions that Argentina had taken after the Argentine crisis was, in the tribunal's view, over [502].

Argentina has also faced claims growing out of measures it took during its economic crisis under its other BITs, including the United Kingdom-Argentina BIT. In two such claims, involving another gas distribution company, the BG Group, and an electric company, National Grid, the claimants ended up with awards of over US$185 million and over US$53 million respectively [503]. Both of these cases found that, assuming that the customary defence of necessity was still applicable to a BIT that was silent on the question, Argentina had failed to satisfy that defence's rigorous requirements.

Given the huge sums at stake in these cases, it is hardly surprising that the proceedings — both initially and on annulment — have drawn considerable attention, both inside Argentina and abroad. Prior to the recent annulment decisions in *Sempra* and *Enron*, it

---

[502] *Continental Casualty Co.* v. *Argentine Republic*, Award, ICSID Case No. ARB/03/9 (5 September 2008) (hereinafter *"Continental Casualty"*).

[503] *BG Group and the Republic of Argentina*, UNCITRAL Award (24 December 2007) (hereinafter *"BG Group"*); *National Grid P.L.C.* v. *Argentine Republic*, UNCITRAL Award (3 November 2008) (hereinafter *"National Grid"*).

was estimated that Argentina had been ordered to pay some two-thirds of a billion dollars, plus interest, to claimants under investor-State arbitrations[504]. The decisions, particularly those awarding huge sums to investor claimants, have fuelled pre-existing criticisms of the investment regime. For some critics, the potential impact on Governments of some of these awards alone suggest the "public" nature of this kind of litigation, as compared to ordinary commercial arbitration between two private entities. Despite more recent rulings in Argentina's favour, the Argentine investor-State claims are likely to remain a central focus for defenders and critics of the investment regime for years to come.

For critics, the recent annulment decisions in favour of Argentina demonstrate the inadequacy of the original *ad hoc* tribunals — whose "flawed" rulings required years of costly and time-consuming litigation for Argentine officials to "correct". For defenders of the investment regime, especially those in the business community, on the other hand, both the original arbitral awards as well as the annulments issued to date, including those ruling in favour of investors, suggest flaws in a system that was once touted as ensuring an apolitical process, assured compensation, and stable and predictable investment rules.

The Argentina cases have demonstrated that the investment regime's enforcement scheme is not foolproof. To date, Argentina has resisted paying out any of the sums awarded in the cases discussed here — even

---

[504] L. E. Peterson, "Round-up: Where Things Stand with Argentina and Its Many Investment Treaty Arbitrations", *Investment Arbitration Reporter* (17 December 2008) (examining known awards issued through December 2008). In addition, Peterson reports that more than half a dozen other claims against Argentina have been terminated following successful settlement talks between the Government and individual foreign investors.

after failing to secure an annulment of the original *CMS* award. Other ICSID annulment committees are now wrestling with demands by ever more unsatisfied claimants that Argentina demonstrate its good faith by making payments into escrow accounts pending the outcome in those cases[505]. Moreover, the annulment decisions in *Enron* and *Sempra* may well increase the likelihood that other arbitral awards will also be taken through the annulment process or challenged in other respects, thereby delaying the potential for any payments at least in the interim. For the investor community on whose behalf BITs and FTAs were negotiated, Argentina's failure to pay sums legally due demonstrates that the international investment regime shares the common Achilles heel of other international regimes. It too finds it difficult to secure damages from an entity with sovereign immunity. Moreover, as is further addressed in this chapter, the awards issued to date in the Argentina cases surveyed here do not bode well for those who expected that the spread of investment treaties would lead to harmonious and consistent international investment law.

This chapter uses a select slice of the Argentina awards to consider the structural aspects of the investment regime and the legitimacy concerns arising from it. It will draw broader implications for other international regimes and public international law more generally. At the same time, the most recent annulment decisions in *Enron* and *Sempra* suggest the need for caution in using any set of recent arbitral rulings to draw long-term conclusions about what is, by any

---

[505] Peterson, *supra* footnote 504. In addition, successful claimants against Argentina, such as Azurix and CMS, are at this writing pursuing other avenues to secure payment, such as denials of US GSP treatment for Argentine products, see <http://www.mondaq.com/unitedstates/article.asp?articleid=108718>.

measure, a rapidly developing regime. At least prior to the annulment decisions in *Enron* and *Sempra* — whose implications on other pending cases remain speculative — it appeared that Argentina was paying a steep price for becoming a signatory to one of the most pro-investor BITs in the world, namely the US Model BIT of 1987. At least prior to the issuance of those annulments, many scholars (and not a few States) were sympathetic to Argentina's plight and increasingly sceptical of the merits of the investment regime. The original multimillion dollar awards issued in *CMS, Enron* and *Sempra* in particular played into broader criticisms of the "Washington Consensus-inspired" advice that States like Argentina had been getting from experts (as from the IMF)[506]. As is suggested in

---

[506] Others contend, on the contrary, that Argentina's crisis resulted from that country's failure to implement the advice that it received, including from the IMF. Indeed, many of the arbitral decisions discussed here find it necessary to assign blame for the crisis since, as discussed *infra*, at least the customary defence of necessity considers this a relevant question. Most of the arbitral decisions that have addressed the issue have suggested that Argentine government actions substantially contributed to the underlying crisis that that country faced in 2001-2002. The IMF's own conclusions were more tempered. Its report concludes:

"The catastrophic collapse of the Argentine economy in 2001-02 represents the failure of Argentine policy makers to take necessary corrective measures at a sufficiently early stage. The IMF on its part, supported by its major shareholders, also erred in failing to call an earlier halt to support for a strategy that, as implemented, was not sustainable." IMF Independent Evaluation Office, "Report on the Evaluation of the Role of the IMF in Argentina: 1991-2001" (2004), available at <http://www.imf.org/External/NP/ieo/2004/arg/eng/index.htm>, p. 64.

While most arbitrators have assumed that evaluating

Chapter II, those decisions, as well as the wave of
investor claims against Argentina generally, also
encouraged other States, including Canada, China, and
the United States, to make certain changes in their
respective model BITs and FTAs[507]. Some of these,
such as the changes to the treaties' "essential security"
clauses and "clarifications" of their vague FET guarantees discussed in Chapter III, seemed specifically
directed at avoiding some of the outcomes emerging
from the Argentine investor-State case-law[508].

The latest annulment rulings make it more not less
likely that the Argentina cases will remain a Rorschach
test to gauge attitudes towards the investment regime.
Whether or not those annulments will lessen concerns
over the impact of BITs and FTAs on the regulatory
discretion enjoyed by sovereigns, they raise serious
questions about the interaction between international
investment law and the rest of public international law,
the purposes of the ICSID annulment procedure,
including how the annulment process contributes to the
jurisprudence constante expected of the investment

Argentina's necessity defence requires reliance on evidence from economists, the *Enron* annulment committee,
as is discussed *supra*, took a different approach, see *Enron
annulment*, *supra* footnote 501, para. 377 (concluding that
in determining whether a State invoking necessity took the
"only" course of action available to it arbitrators need to
apply the law and not rely on an "expert opinion on an
economic issue").

[507] For suggestions that China's BIT programme has
been influenced by the lessons presented by the Argentina
cases, see, e.g., C. Congyan, "China-US BIT Negotiations
and the Future of Investment Treaty Regime: A Grand
Bilateral Bargain with Multilateral Implications", 12 *Journal
of International Economic Law* 457 (2009), p. 462.

[508] As noted, investors' claims against Argentina were
most successful when based on invocation of the FET
clause. These cases have accordingly brought renewed
attention to the meaning of that guarantee.

regime. These issues are likely to become prominent in discussions of the future of the investment regime and its possible institutional reforms.

The legitimacy complaints that have so far been triggered by the Argentina cases, particularly vociferous among NGOs and scholars, include the following:

(1) The investment regime produces *inconsistent law* and undermines the stability and predictability that is the ostensible goal of the regime.

(2) The investment regime is unduly *intrusive on national sovereignty* or "domestic jurisdiction" as it is insufficiently deferential to the rights of FDI host States to regulate in the public interest.

(3) The investment regime is *biased* in favour of investors and the capital exporting States that they come from.

(4) The investment regime inappropriately adopts arbitral mechanisms normally used for resolving *private* commercial disputes to resolve *public* disputes.

(5) The investment regime constitutes a form of *global administrative law* that fails to contain the guarantees that make such a form of governance accountable.

The Argentina crisis cases have renewed charges that the investment regime contains, as discussed in Chapter I, vertical, horizontal, ideological and rule of law flaws. The first and fifth complaints above reflect dissatisfactions with the regime's rule of law aspects. The original arbitral decisions in cases like *CMS*, *Sempra* and *Enron* were seen as overturning the will of elected officials who enacted emergency legislation intended to benefit all that country's residents. These awards, viewed as vertical assaults on Argentina's democratic decisions, laws, and institutions, inspire the second complaint that the investment regime unduly

intrudes on national sovereignty. This charge is all the
more salient because of the nature of the Argentine
national decisions that have been put under scrutiny.
These investor claims have involved, after all, governmental actions taken in the midst of, and in order to
stem the effects of, a national crisis of substantial
dimensions. If investor-State arbitrators can second-
guess the assertions of emergency power by Governments in the midst of a crisis of dimensions comparable to those of 11 September 2001 — of a catastrophe
implicating a country's political and economic security
— it would appear that nothing that a sovereign does is
immune from supranational arbitral scrutiny. For countries outside of Europe, including the United States, for
whom binding supranational adjudication remains a
rarity, such a development may seem a radical step
for a "rudimentary" international system. Supranational
second-guessing of a country's most fundamental
national laws may appear as a stretch for those who
believe that international law remains grounded in the
Lotus presumption — that is, that States are free to do
whatever they have not barred themselves from doing
through their consent[509].

The third complaint above stems from deep suspicion, spurred on by the early awards against Argentina,
that investor-State arbitration does not rest on a level
playing field. Critics have argued that it seems incon-
ceivable that had the tables been turned, US emergency
legislation (such as that taken in the wake of the 2008
global economic crisis) would have been subject to
comparable arbitral second-guessing — or would have

---

[509] For the most recent apparent affirmation of the
Lotus presumption by the International Court of Justice
(ICJ), see *Accordance with International Law of the Unila-
teral Declaration of Independence in Respect of Kosovo*,
Advisory Opinion (22 July 2010), available at <http://
www.icj-cij.org/homepage/pdf/20100722_KOS.pdf>.

required an appeal to an annulment committee to vin-
dicate the United States' interests as a sovereign[510].
Some have seen evidence of bias simply in the respective win/loss records of the United States as compared
to Argentina's. Whereas claimants against Argentina
have won damages in many of their recent cases, the
United States has yet to lose a single investor-State
claim, even though to date 19 claims have been
brought against it under the NAFTA's investment chapter, and, of course, it has not had to resort to an annulment process in a single instance[511]. As is suggested by
Chapter II, complaints about the horizontal inequities
of the regime have other roots as well. Given the low
level of investment by Argentine claimants in the
United States, the United States-Argentina BIT (or the
United Kingdom-Argentina BIT for that matter) has
been seen as a characteristically asymmetric investment agreement between a rich capital exporter and a
relatively poorer capital importer, where the flows of
capital (and of investor-State claims) are principally in
one direction and where only one State (the FDI host)
bears the treaty's burdens[512].

The fourth complaint, critiquing the "public" nature

---

[510] Indeed, there is speculation that the economic
power of the United States helps to explain why post-2008
US emergency legislation has not yet been challenged in
investor-State dispute settlement. See, e.g., L. Reed, "The
Consequences of Market Regulation", Posting of 11 March
2010, available at <http://kluwerarbitrationblog.com/blog/
2010/03/11/the-consequences-of-market-intervention-by-
lucy-reed-and-phillip-riblett/>.

[511] See NAFTA Claims, available at <http://www.nafta-
law.org/disputes_us.htm>. Only 6 of these cases have
ended with final awards. See *ibid.*; US Department of
State, NAFTA Investor-State Arbitrations, available at
<http://www.state.gov/s/l/c3439.htm>.

[512] Compare the views of Andrew Guzman discussed in
Chapter II.

of investor-State arbitration, is at least partly ideological.

For some critics, the Argentine awards rendered to date — all of which are of undeniable public interest to the people of Argentina no less than would be any decision by that country's constitutional court — are not comparable to routine arbitrations commonly used to resolve ordinary disputes between private companies. The complaint is that such issues should not be adjudicated by *ad hoc* arbitrators appointed by the disputing parties operating on the basis of procedural rules suited to routine business transactions. For scholars like Gus Van Harten, the Argentina claims illustrate how the anti-governmental, pre-deregulatory ethos of the Washington Consensus model of governance prevalent to investment protection treaties has led to the inappropriate *privatization* of public law adjudication[513].

The alleged legitimacy deficits of the investment regime, and what to do about them, are the focus of the last chapter of this monograph. The rest of this chapter examines some of the Argentina awards in light of the first complaint noted above: the problem of inconsistent investment law.

B. *The Inconsistent Argentina Cases*

Many have expressed concerns that neither the investor-State three-person arbitral panels established on an *ad hoc* basis to resolve each investor claim, one at a time, nor the equally *ad hoc* annulment committees established by ICSID are producing the consistent international investment law that States and investors anticipated. They point to a number of different out-

---

[513] G. Van Harten, *Investment Treaty Arbitration and Public Law* (Oxford, Oxford University Press, 2007).

comes produced by the rising number of investor-State arbitral decisions that are now being made public, almost on a daily basis. Apart from differences over the precise meaning of FET suggested by Chapter III — including differences over whether FET is an independent standard or is identical to the customary international minimum standard — investor-State tribunals have differed over such matters as the meaning of "investment" for purposes of deciding whether a BIT extends its protection, whether the most favoured nation treaty guarantee permits a claimant to select a more favourable dispute settlement provision from another BIT (such as one not requiring exhaustion of local remedies), or whether umbrella clauses generally permit claimants to bring an investor-State claim under a BIT even when the breach of contract by the State did not involve any governmental or regulatory action but was merely commercial in nature[514]. These differences in the interpretation of issues vital to determining jurisdiction or the underlying substantive rights of investors trouble the regime's principal stakeholders — States and investors — precisely because both groups assumed that BITs and FTAs would establish stable and predictable legal rules for what are necessarily long-term relationships. Governments also hoped for consistent investment arbitral case-law since this would provide more reliable guidance for rendering

---

[514] See, e.g., P. Acconci, "Most-Favoured-Nation Treatment", in P. Muchlinski *et al.* (eds.), *The Oxford Handbook of International Investment Law* (Oxford, Oxford University Press, 2008), pp. 382-387; E. C. Schlemmer, "Investment, Investor, Nationality and Shareholders", in P. Muchlinski *et al.* (eds.), *The Oxford Handbook of International Investment Law* (Oxford, Oxford University Press, 2008), p. 49. See also A. Newcombe and L. Paradell, *Law and Practice of Investment Treaties* (The Hague, Kluwer Law International, 2009), pp. 437-479.

their national laws and procedures consistent with their international obligations. Such consistency is also politically desirable. To the extent international investment obligations are predictable and consistent, these provide a more reliable answer for executive branches trying to resist protectionist pressures from legislators or others. Further, having harmonious rules applicable to all foreign investors would reduce the prospect of needing to explain to the average taxpayer why some foreign investors need to be treated better than others[515].

Of course, no one could have reasonably expected total consistency from a regime lacking a single constitutive text (as compared to the GATT covered agreements). One reason for inconsistent arbitral decisions is suggested by prior chapters: not all BITs and FTAs are alike and even one country's model BIT may change dramatically over time. Some inconsistencies between arbitral rulings may result from differences among the respective treaties at issue and cannot be blamed on arbitrators who ignore prior rulings by their predecessors. Inconsistent rulings are most troubling when these arise with respect to the same treaty language and involve nearly indistinguishable facts. Also troubling are inconsistent legal rulings by those charged with reconsidering these awards: that is, if annulment committees, when established as they can be under ICSID, for example, not only fail to render the law more consistent but in fact add to the regime's troubles by differing among themselves. The Argentina cases are a wonderful case study for examining the problem of

---

[515] The literature complaining about the lack of consistency in investor-State arbitral awards is substantial. For an example, see, e.g., S. Franck, "The Legitimacy Crisis in Investment Treaty Arbitration: Privatizing International Law through Inconsistent Decisions", 73 *Fordham Law Review* 1521 (2005).

inconsistency precisely because many involve very similar facts, an identical time period in the history of a single country, often comparable investors in the same sector (e.g., public utilities), and often the same or very similar BITs. They are also interesting for this purpose because several of the Argentina awards have now been subjected, as noted, to annulment.

The 10 decisions issued by the tribunals in *CMS, Enron, LG&E, Sempra, BG, National Grid, Continental Casualty* and by Annulment Committees in *CMS, Enron* and *Sempra* create troubling inconsistencies in terms of fact-finding, logic, and the law. All but one of these cases involved a foreign investor in a now privatized public utility and all but two of these involved the United States-Argentina BIT. In all of these, the principal Argentine defence was the same: the measures under challenge were a necessary and excusable response to a serious economic/political crisis. Although Argentina was found liable, sometimes for substantial amounts, by all the original panels that addressed these claims and at least three of the initial arbitral awards (in *CMS, Enron*, and *Sempra*) closely resembled one another, substantial inconsistencies among the cases have emerged over time, as later tribunals (namely *LG&E* and *Continental Causality*) began to reconsider the merits of Argentina's principal defence and later still, as annulment committees revisited the original decisions years after they had been originally issued.

Three differences among the decisions are apparent:

(1) Some of the 10 arbitral decisions considered here, by original panels or annulment committees, diverged with respect to governing law, with at least three of the original tribunals (*CMS, Enron*, and *Sempra*) ruling that, under the ICSID Convention, at least some aspects of the dispute were governed by

both Argentine and international law. The *LG&E* tribunal, on the other hand, did not consider Argentina law at all, while the *Enron* annulment committee, for its part, downplayed the significance of Argentine national law in the *Enron* decision that it was examining[516].

(2) The tribunals' interpretations of the relevant BIT guarantees were not always consistent. Although in all of these cases, the arbitrators rejected allegations of "arbitrary" treatment and allegations of expropriation, not all tribunals came to the same conclusion with respect to the meaning of "discrimination" under the United States-Argentina BIT, with only the *LG&E* tribunal finding that the investors had indeed been subjected to discrimination[517]. Further, the tribunals differed somewhat with respect to their respective interpretations of FET. As is addressed in greater detail later in this chapter, *National Grid* was alone in finding that "[w]hat is fair and equitable is not an absolute parameter" and that "[w]hat would be unfair and inequitable in normal circumstances may not be so in a

---

[516] Compare *LG&E*, *supra* footnote 493, paras. 91-98 with *CMS*, *supra* footnote 492, paras. 115-123; *Enron Corp.* v. *Argentina*, Award, ICSID Case No. ARB/01/3 (22 May 2007) (hereinafter *"Enron"*), paras. 203-209; *Sempra Energy International* v. *Argentina*, Award, ICSID Case No. ARB/02/16 (28 September 2007) (hereinafter *"Sempra"*), paras. 241-246. The relevant portions of the *Enron annulment* include paras. 231-232 (finding that the original *Enron* tribunal did not rely on Argentine national law for its determination that Argentina violated the fair and equitable treatment guarantee except insofar as it relied on that law for its finding that in fact Argentina had given the investor specific guarantees), paras. 235-236 (similar finding with respect to the *Enron* tribunal's finding of a violation of the umbrella clause), but see paras. 242-246 (acknowledging that the *Enron* tribunal appeared to rely in part on Argentine law regarding the principles of "imprevisión" and "state of emergency").

[517] See *LG&E*, *supra* footnote 493, paras. 147-148.

situation of an economic and social crisis"[518]. That tribunal's interpretation of the FET standard (and of the investors' expectations) was apparently affected by the arbitrators' assessment of the impact of the ongoing crisis in Argentina. There is also some disagreement among these decisions with respect to the meaning of the umbrella clause in the United States-Argentina BIT as the *CMS* annulment reversed the *CMS* tribunal's ruling under the umbrella clause and only affirmed on the basis of FET, while the *Enron* annulment committee, on the other hand, left undisturbed the original *Enron* tribunal's determination that the umbrella clause had been breached[519].

(3) But the most significant differences among the Argentina cases that have emerged to date — and the one that is the focus here — have involved Argentina's principal defence, namely that all its actions were excused under either the customary international law doctrine of necessity or the United States-Argentina BIT's measures not precluded clause (Art. XI) which, as noted, permits States parties to take action "necessary" to protect the State's "essential security" or to

---

[518] See *National Grid*, *supra* footnote 503, para. 180. That tribunal found that the investor could not be "totally insulated" from the crisis and that, therefore, the breach of the fair and equitable standard occurred not on 6 January 2002 (when the relevant emergency measures were first imposed at the height of the Argentine crisis) but later, on 25 June 2002 (when Argentina required that the investor "renounce . . . the legal remedies" to which they had recourse).

[519] See *CMS Gas Co*. v. *Argentina*, Decision on Annulment, ICSID Case No. ARB/01/8 (25 September 2007) (hereinafter "*CMS annulment*"), paras. 89-100; *Enron annulment*, *supra* footnote 501, paras. 321-343 (finding that the *Enron* tribunal had sufficiently explained its findings on this point and distinguishing the *CMS* decisions on this point).

maintain public order[520]. This chapter examines this issue in depth.

(1) Inconsistent views of what is "necessary"

There are, to be sure, commonalities among the nine decisions with respect to Argentina's principal defence. To date, all the tribunals that have considered this provision in the United States-Argentina BIT have rejected Argentina's claim that the measures not precluded clause (Art. XI) is "self-judging" and have, instead, gone on to examine for themselves whether this clause or the customary defence of necessity was satisfied[521]. This aspect of the underlying decisions was left undisturbed by the relevant annulment committees[522]. All the arbitrators that addressed the point

---

[520] Article XI of United States-Argentina BIT states:

"This Treaty shall not preclude the application by either Party of measures necessary for the maintenance of public order, the fulfillment of its obligation with respect to the maintenance of restoration of international peace or security, or the protection of its own essential security interests."

See Treaty between the United States of America and the Argentine Republic concerning the Reciprocal Encouragement and Protection of Investment (hereinafter "United States-Argentina BIT"), signed on 14 November 1991, entered into force on 20 October 1994, available at <http://www.unctad.org/sections/dite/iia/docs/bits/argentina_us.pdf>.

[521] Most recently, the contention that a State could judge for itself a claim of necessity was rejected in *Funnekotter* v. *Zimbabwe*, involving the *Netherlands* v. *Zimbabwe BIT*. See *Funnekotter* v. *Zimbabwe*, Award, ICSID Case No. ARB/05/6 (15 April 2009) (hereinafter "*Funnekotter*"), paras. 103-106.

[522] Indeed, even the *Sempra* annulment committee went out of its way to find that the original tribunal's finding on this question was not annullable error. *Sempra annulment*,

have also suggested that major economic crises could, at least in principle, be covered by the language of Article XI of the United States-Argentina BIT or the customary defence of necessity[523]. All have also accepted that, to the extent it is relevant to interpreting a BIT (whether the United States-Argentina BIT or the United Kingdom-Argentina BIT), the customary defence of necessity has been codified in Article 25 of the Articles of State Responsibility promulgated in 2001 by the International Law Commission[524]. As that Article indicates, the customary defence of necessity requires, among other things, that the State making this affirmative defence demonstrate that it faced a sufficiently grave threat, namely a "grave and imminent peril"; that it took the "only way" to safeguard its essential interest; and that it had not "contributed to the situation of necessity"[525]. All the tribunals that con-

---

supra footnote 501, para. 170 (finding no failure on the part of the tribunal to consider the matter of whether Article XI is self-judging and finding its conclusion that this article was not self-judging one that the original panel was "perfectly entitled to reach").

[523] *CMS*, *supra* footnote 492, para. 319; *LG&E*, *supra* footnote 493, para. 251; *Enron*, *supra* footnote 516, para. 334; *Sempra*, *supra* footnote 516, para. 346.

[524] This finding is hardly surprising as it appears that in none of the cases did the parties challenge the proposition that Article 25 reflects the state of customary international law on the matter. As was suggested by the *Enron* annulment committee, this was "common ground" between the parties and was not disputed. *Enron annulment*, *supra* footnote 501, para. 356 (finding that it could not be annullable error for a tribunal "to give an applicable legal rule an interpretation on which both parties were agreed").

[525] Article 25 provides:

"1. Necessity may not be invoked by a State as a ground for precluding the wrongfulness of an act not in conformity with an international obligation of that State unless the act:

sidered the question have agreed that Article 25 states a relevant rule of customary law that applies to all treaties with the exception of those that expressly deviate from it. But the seven tribunals and three annulment committees considered here differed on many other significant questions raised by Argentina's resort to this defence.

Table 2 summarizes these differences.

(2) Is there one defence or two?

The original panels in *CMS, Enron*, and *Sempra* essentially equated Article XI of the United States-Argentina BIT with the customary defence of necessity and applied the same requisites to both[526]. They also suggested that even if Article XI had been successfully invoked, the consequences were the same as under the traditional customary defence of necessity: that is, any

---

   (a) is the only way for the State to safeguard an essential interest against a grave and imminent peril; and

   (b) does not seriously impair an essential interest of the State or States towards which the obligation exists, or of the international community as a whole;

   2. In any case, necessity may not be invoked by a State as a ground for precluding wrongfulness if:

   (a) the international obligation in question excludes the possibility of invoking necessity; or

   (b) the State has contributed to the situation of necessity."

[526] See *CMS, supra* footnote 492, paras. 353, 357-359, 383-393; *Enron, supra* footnote 516, para. 334; *Sempra, supra* footnote 516, paras. 376-378. For a more detailed justification for these conclusions, see J. Alvarez and K. Khamsi, "The Argentine Crisis and Foreign Investors: A Glimpse into the Heart of the Investment Regime", in K. P. Sauvant, *Yearbook on International Investment Law & Policy 2008-2009* (New York, Oxford University Press, 2009), p. 379.

TABLE 2. QUESTIONS PRESENTED IN THE ARGENTINA CASES

Questions	Different Conclusions		
When a BIT contains an "essential security" clause as does the United States-Argentina BIT, does that claim constitute a separate or distinct defence from the excuse of necessity under customary law? That is, does Article XI of the United States-Argentina BIT = Article 25 of the Articles of State Responsibility or is it *lex specialis*?	*CMS, Enron, Sempra*	*CMS* annulment, *Continental Casualty, Sempra* annulment	
Does the customary defence of necessity apply when a BIT is silent as to that defence?	*BG*	*National Grid*	
Assuming that it is applicable, what must the State show in order to successfully invoke the customary defence of necessity?	*CMS, Enron, Sempra, BG, National Grid*	*LG&E*	*Enron* annulment
Assuming that Article XI of the United States-Argentina BIT provides a defence distinct from the excuse of necessity, what exactly does it require in order for it to be successfully invoked?	*LG&E*	*CMS* annulment, *Sempra* annulment	*Continental Casualty*
What is the effect of a successful invocation of Article XI?	*CMS, Enron, Sempra*	*CMS* annulment, *Continental Casualty, Sempra* annulment	*LG&E*

legal duty to compensate for internationally wrongful acts remains in effect[527].

For its part, the *LG&E* tribunal was not altogether clear on whether the two defences were distinct. While it considered Article XI separately, it also suggested that the two defences led to the same result in this case and that Argentina satisfied the requisites of both[528].

The *CMS* annulment, although it did not annul the original *CMS* award, opined in dicta that had it been charged with determining that question it would have decided that Article XI was a separate and distinct "primary" rule capable of excusing Argentina from all liability if properly invoked[529]. Although the *CMS* annulment committee, headed by James Crawford, the ILC Rapporteur responsible for the final version of the Articles of State Responsibility, did not spell out what Article XI actually meant if treated as a distinct defence, it suggested that it did not require Argentina to satisfy the rigorous requisites of the customary defence of necessity[530]. It opined that the customary defence of necessity was a residual excuse that could be applied only if Argentina tried but failed to meet the requirement of Article XI[531]. Given the high burdens imposed by the customary defence of necessity, however, it seems doubtful whether, if this view is accepted, this residual defence could ever prove useful or relevant. Under the *CMS* annulment committee's interpretation, for all practical purposes, Article XI

---

[527] See *CMS*, *supra* footnote 492, paras. 383-394; *Enron*, *supra* footnote 516, para. 344-345; *Sempra*, *supra* footnote 516, paras. 393-397.

[528] See *LG&E*, *supra* footnote 493, paras. 257-258.

[529] See *CMS annulment*, *supra* footnote 519, paras. 124-125.

[530] *Ibid.*, para. 130.

[531] *Ibid.*, paras. 132-134.

operates as *lex specialis* to oust the application of the presumably narrower customary "necessity" defence.

A later tribunal, *Continental Casualty*, applying the rationale suggested by the *CMS* annulment, affirmed that the two defences were distinct. It also found that the requisites of the Article XI defence were significantly easier for Argentina to satisfy than the customary defence. That tribunal concluded that Argentina satisfied the terms of Article XI. It concluded that this was an effective response to those claims presented in that case stemming from Argentina's emergency legislation and absolved Argentina from liability to that extent[532].

The *Sempra* annulment also applied the rationale suggested by the *CMS* annulment and annulled the original award because that tribunal had

> "adopted Article 25 of the ILC Articles as the primary law to be applied, rather than Article XI of the BIT, and in so doing made a fundamental error in identifying and applying the applicable law"[533].

The *Enron* annulment committee, however, annulled the *Enron* award on a different basis, namely because the arbitrators had not properly applied or explained the requisites of the customary defence of necessity as codified in Article XI[534].

---

[532] See *Continental Casualty*, *supra* footnote 502, paras. 175-181.

[533] *Sempra annulment*, *supra* footnote 501, para. 208. That committee found that this failure "constitutes an excess of powers within the meaning of the ICSID Convention" (*ibid.*, para. 209), and that this error was "manifest". *Ibid.*, para. 219.

[534] *Enron annulment*, *supra* footnote 501, paras. 368-395 (determining that the *Enron* tribunal had failed to explain or justify its findings that Argentina had not resorted to the "only way" to address its crisis and had contributed to the situation of necessity within the meaning of Article 25).

As Table 2 suggests, the decisions on this point present diametrically opposing lines of authorities, with the most recently view pronounced by two annulment committees being that Article XI is indeed a distinct defence from that under customary law. Whether subsequent arbitral decisions and other annulment committees will follow this lead, agree with the *Enron* annulment's alternative views, or continue to adhere to the rationales offered by the original *CMS*, *Enron* and *Sempra* tribunals, remains to be seen.

> (3) *Does the customary defence of necessity apply when a BIT is silent, that is, when the BIT does not have an essential security exception or measures not precluded clause?*

BG and *National Grid*, involving claims under the United Kingdom-Argentina BIT, which has no equivalent to Article XI of the United States-Argentina BIT, differed on this point, albeit in dicta — not in their holdings. While *National Grid* assumed that the customary defence of necessity still applied when the BIT was silent and ruled that Argentina had failed to satisfy its requisites[535], *BG* refused to make a definitive finding on this point, suggesting that perhaps the customary defence of necessity was not available as a defence against a private party, such as an investor, since that defence had originated in the State-to-State context. *BG* also suggested that perhaps such a defence was inapplicable in the context of a BIT that failed to

---

[535] See *National Grid*, *supra* footnote 503, paras. 255-262 (determining that the United Kingdom had not limited its sovereign powers to assert the necessity defence by entering into a treaty that did not mention it and that the evidence submitted by Argentina itself demonstrated that Argentina had substantially contributed to its underlying crisis).

address that defence and therefore had sought to disable a State from unilaterally revoking investors' "vested rights" by invoking necessity[536]. *BG* avoided deciding these issues because it found that even if the customary defence had been available, Argentina failed to meet its "very restrictive conditions"[537]. If, as one survey of BITs suggests, nine-tenths of them fail to include a measures not precluded clause[538], the question left unresolved by these two cases is very likely to arise repeatedly.

> *(4) Assuming that it is applicable, what does the customary defence of necessity require States (or claimants) to show?*

The original tribunals in *CMS, Enron* and *Sempra*, as well as the arbitrators in *BG* and *National Grid* all imposed a very high standard of proof on Argentina in terms of resorting to the customary defence of necessity. All of them indicated that they were strictly applying, in quite literal terms, the requisites indicated in Article 25 of the ILC Articles of State Responsibility. All of them also found that Argentina had not successfully proven that it had faced a grave enough threat to constitute a threat to its "essential interest" as required by necessity, or that Argentina had failed to demon-

---

[536] See *BG Group*, *supra* footnote 503, paras. 407-409 (noting, without deciding, that the Article 25 defence may relate exclusively to international obligations between sovereign States and that an investment protection treaty that omits such an exception may intend to derogate from the normal application of the necessity defence).

[537] *Ibid.*, para. 411.

[538] See W. Burke-White and A. von Staden, "Investment Protection in Extraordinary Times: The Interpretation and Application of Non-Precluded Measures Provisions in Bilateral Investment Treaties", 48 *Virginia Journal of International Law* 307 (2008).

strate that its actions were the "only way" to deal with
that threat, or that Argentina had significantly contributed to the underlying economic threat and was
therefore unable to rely on necessity. Some tribunals
found it unnecessary to consider all these requisites
once they had found that Argentina had failed to satisfy
one of them while others found that Argentina had failed
to satisfy all three requirements of the defence[539].

Although the tribunal in *LG&E* agreed with the
others that Article 25 of the Articles of State Responsibility accurately stated the requisites of the customary defence of necessity, it was significantly more deferential to Argentina in applying those requisites,
which it considered only after applying Article XI of
the United States-Argentina BIT. *LG&E* found that an
"essential interest" for purposes of Article 25 need not

---

[539] See *CMS*, *supra* footnote 492, paras. 355-356 (concluding that the Argentinean crisis was not a catastrophe
reaching the level of *force majeure*); *Enron*, *supra* footnote 516, paras. 305-314 (holding that no essential interest
of Argentina had been threatened and that the Argentine
authorities had contributed to some extent to the underlying crisis); *Sempra*, *supra* footnote 516, para. 391 (holding
that the essential interest of the investor would be impaired
by Argentine actions); *National Grid*, *supra* footnote 503,
paras. 260-262 (finding that Argentina's contribution to the
crisis was substantial); *BG Group, supra* footnote 503,
paras. 410-411 (finding that Argentina failed to meet the
"very restrictive conditions" of the defence of necessity).
But even these tribunals appeared to differ on the margins
with respect to their interpretation of the requisites of the
necessity defence. Not all of them suggested, as did the
original *Enron* tribunal, that the "essential interest"
required for invocation of the defence of necessity needed
to "compromise the very existence of the State and its
independence". *Enron*, *supra* footnote 516, para. 306. But
see *Enron annulment*, *supra* footnote 501, para. 359 (indicating that, when read in context, the *Enron* tribunal was
not suggesting that an "essential interest" needed to
threaten the existence of the Argentine State).

involve a threat to the State's existence as some of the other tribunals appeared to suggest, but only a "serious and imminent danger"[540]. That tribunal also found that the totality of Argentina's emergency measures was "the only way" that the State had to respond to the crisis since an "across the board response was necessary" and "tariffs on public utilities had to be addressed"[541]. With respect to the need to prove that the State had not contributed to the situation of necessity, *LG&E* ruled that the *claimants* had failed to prove that Argentina had contributed to the crisis, effectively shifting the burden of proof on this key question[542].

The *Enron* Annulment Committee went considerably farther than the other tribunals (and, as it acknowledged, even farther than the litigating parties[543]) in elaborating what it considered to be the requisites of the necessity defence. It annulled the original *Enron* award precisely because the arbitrators had failed to explain what the "only way" requisite to the defence of necessity meant and because they had apparently relied on the "wrong" type of evidence for their conclusion that Argentina had not met this requisite. It berated the tribunal for not resolving whether that requisite could be satisfied if the State had, at its disposal, no alternative measures other than those involving "a similar or graver breach of international law"[544]; for failing to explain whether the relative effectiveness of possible measures mattered[545]; and for not addressing whether the crucial "only way" determination needed to be

---

[540] See *LG&E*, *supra* footnote 493, paras. 251-254.

[541] *Ibid.*, para. 257.

[542] *Ibid.*, para. 256.

[543] *Enron annulment*, *supra* footnote 501, para. 375 (noting that the parties failed to address many of the points the annulment committee was now raising).

[544] *Ibid.*, paras. 370-379.

[545] *Ibid.*, para. 371.

made with the benefit of hindsight or should have accorded the State a "margin of appreciation" given the available information that the State had at the time the emergency measures were taken[546]. That annulment committee also concluded that the original *Enron* tribunal erred in its apparent reliance on the expert testimony of an economist in resolving this legal question[547].

The *Enron* annulment found comparable flaws in the tribunal's consideration of Article 25 (1) *(b)* (requiring consideration of whether the measures adopted by Argentina seriously impaired an essential interest of the State or States towards which the obligation exists) and its determination that Argentina had contributed to the underlying crisis[548].

As Table 2 suggests, putting aside some other nuances among the decisions[549], at least three distinct

---

[546] *Enron annulment, supra* footnote 501, para. 372.

[547] *Ibid.*, paras. 374-377.

[548] *Ibid.*, paras. 379-384 (determining that the tribunal had failed to make an explicit finding with respect to Article 25 (1) *(b)*) and paras. 385-393 (determining that the tribunal did not explain what Article 25 (2) *(b)* means, such as whether it requires a demonstration of fault, and that as with respect to the tribunal's finding on "only way" it was wrong to rely on an economist's testimony for resolving that legal question). The Annulment Committee also noted that the *Enron* tribunal failed to address whether the BIT excludes the possibility of invoking necessity (*ibid.*, para. 394). That committee found that these errors amounted to a failure to apply the applicable law and a failure to state the reasons for its decisions and were therefore annullable errors. See, e.g., *ibid.*, paras. 377-378.

[549] For example, there appears to be some differences of opinion, among the cases as well as scholars, as to whether at least in the investor-State context, arbitrators need to consider the "essential" or other interests of investors and not just the interests of the State invoking the necessity defence or the interests of other States.

positions emerge from this group of cases: namely (1) that the customary requisites of the defence of necessity need to be literally applied, together constitute an affirmative defence that imposes a high burden of proof on the party asserting them, and that it is notoriously difficult (if not impossible) for the necessity doctrine to justify actions taken in response to a crisis having myriad causes (such as an economic crisis) (the original decisions in *CMS*, *Sempra* and *Enron*); (2) that the requisites of the defence of necessity permit some margin of deference to States taking "necessary" action and that at least with respect to proving the existence of alternative courses of action, the burden of proof lies with the party challenging the State's emergency measures *(LG&E)*; and (3) that arbitral determinations relating to the defence of necessity must rigorously and explicitly consider every requisite of that defence as stated in Article 25 and must also justify every conclusion reached through reliance on appropriate legal (and not merely economic) evidence (*Enron* annulment). Note that while the *Enron* annulment ruling affirmed, as did the others, that Article 25 of the ILC's Articles of State Responsibility accurately reflects the requisites of customary law, the way it interpreted those requisites seems inconsistent with what the ILC had in mind. While the *Enron* annulment did not make an explicit finding with respect to burden of proof, its position, if taken seriously, would turn a defence that the ILC itself had indicated is purposely hard for a State to prove[550], into a ready escape from a determina-

---

[550] See J. Crawford, *The International Law Commission's Articles on State Responsibility: Introduction, Text and Commentaries* (Cambridge, Cambridge University Press, 2002), p. 178 (note 2 to Commentary on Article 25, indicating why the special features of the defence render it rarely available and why strict adherence to its requisites are necessary to "safeguard against possible abuse").

tion of wrongfulness. The *Enron* rulings make it considerably harder for a claimant to challenge a State's invocation of necessity. Position 3 suggests, *de facto*, a considerable "softening" of the defence of necessity[551]. Of course, since that defence presumptively applies to all international obligations, this may represent a considerable "softening" of the binding force of all international treaties.

> *(5) Assuming that Article XI of the United States-Argentina treaty is a distinct defence from the excuse of necessity, what exactly does it require in order for it to be successfully invoked?*

While the original *CMS, Enron* and *Sempra* tribunals concluded (as noted) that what was "necessary" under Article XI was the same as what was "necessary" under CIL, the *LG&E* tribunal was unclear on this point, suggesting both that the two defences were distinct and that their requisites were the same[552]. To the extent that *LG&E* might be read as stating that Article XI contains distinct requirements from that

---

[551] For an argument against such softening, see F. Orrego-Vicuña, "Softening Necessity", in Mahnoush Arsanjani *et al.* (eds.), *Looking to the Future: Essays on International Law in Honor of W. Michael Reisman* (Leiden, Martinus Nijhoff, 2011).

[552] Compare *LG&E, supra* footnote 493, para. 349 ("Article XI refers to situations in which there is no choice but to act") and *ibid.*, para. 257 (finding Argentina's actions justified insofar as they fulfilled the requirements of customary international law because "the evidence before the Tribunal demonstrates that an across-the-board response was necessary"), *ibid.*, para. 258 (distinguishing the analysis under Article XI and customary international law). An alternative interpretation of these passages is that the tribunal took distinct analytical steps with respect to each defence even though it suggested that they were similar.

reflected in Article 25 of the ILC's Articles of State Responsibility, this may explain that tribunal's suggestions that Argentine actions merit a margin of appreciation, that tribunal's shifting the burden of proof to the claimant with respect to some requisites of the defence, or its conclusion that since Article XI was satisfied Argentina was absolved of financial liability at least while its crisis continued. (All of these contentions were rejected by the original tribunals in *CMS*, *Enron* and *Sempra*.)

Both the *CMS* and the *Sempra* annulment committees, as noted, disagreed with the contention that the two defences were identical but neither indicated what exactly needed to be shown to satisfy Article XI if not the requisites of the customary defence of necessity. Under these decisions, an arbitral tribunal faced with interpreting Article XI presumably would be writing on a clean slate. It could turn, for example, to the dictionary (as did early GATT jurisprudence) to interpret critical words in that provision, such as "necessary", "essential security", or "maintenance of public order".

Continental Casualty followed a different path. It agreed with the *CMS* annulment committee that Article XI was a "threshold" requirement or a distinct "primary" rule[553]. Accordingly, unlike the original awards in *CMS, Enron, Sempra* and *LG&E*, that tribunal did not begin by assessing the merits of the investor's claims based on the substantive guarantees in the BIT. It began by examining Argentina's invocation of Article XI since, in its view, that provision could absolve Argentina from all liability and render any consideration of the BIT's guarantees unnecessary.

---

[553] See *Continental Casualty*, *supra* footnote 502, para. 164, n. 236.

Continental Casualty accepted Argentina's contention in that case that the term "necessary" in Article XI ought to be interpreted in accordance with GATT and WTO case law and not, as the claimant suggested, in light of its "ordinary meaning" and in light of the customary defence of necessity, that is, as measures that "cannot be dispensed with or done without"[554]. It therefore found that Article XI could be satisfied even if Argentina contributed to the underlying crisis and even if it failed to show that its measures were the "only" means available[555]. Instead, that tribunal found the relevant test to be the meaning of "necessary" used in the general exceptions clause of the GATT (that is, its Article XX)[556]. It therefore concluded that in order to find whether a measure that was not indispensable could still be "necessary", this required a "weighing and balancing" as applied in GATT cases such as *Korea — Beef*, which had considered the relative importance of the end pursued and the contribution of the means to that end as balanced against the restrictive impact on international trade[557]. Argentina's actions would not be necessary if a "less inconsistent alternative" was reasonably available and under GATT law, an alternative was not to be considered reasonably available if it imposed an "undue burden" or "prohibi-

---

[554] See *Continental Casualty*, *supra* footnote 502, paras. 192-195.

[555] *Ibid*., para. 234 (rejecting the contention that the defence of necessity is unavailable if Argentina contributed to the state of necessity because Article 25 cannot be the "yardstick" as to the application of Article XI of the United States-Argentina BIT and stating that "[a]rguably, under Article XI a Contracting Party may invoke necessity even if the need to protect its essential security interest has materialized as a consequence of a deliberate but still legitimate policy of that very State").

[556] See *ibid*., para. 192.

[557] See *ibid*., para. 194.

tive costs"[558]. Drawing on the economic studies and testimony presented in the case and applying the GATT law on Article XX, *Continental Casualty* found that Argentina had no reasonably available alternatives for its challenged actions and that these emergency actions made a "material or decisive contribution" to protect that country's essential security interests[559].

Having found that Argentina's challenged actions in violation of the BIT were indeed necessary, *Continental Casualty* excused all of Argentina's actions during the period of its crisis. This meant that the bulk of the claims in that case were dismissed and the claimant won damages only with respect to a relatively minor claim involving actions taken by Argentina as its crisis was lifting[560].

As Table 2 indicates, to the extent these cases have considered the question of what Article XI requires, as distinct from the customary defence of necessity, three distinct answers have emerged. First, there is one of the positions suggested by *LG&E*. Under one interpretation of that decision, even if Article XI is seen as a distinct clause, its requisites are effectively the same as under the customary defence of necessity. Second, there is the position, also suggested by *LG&E* (and implied by *CMS* annulment), according to which the arbitrator is free to give Article XI whatever meaning is suggested by that clause's plain meaning, even if the result is considerably different from the requisites of the customary defence. A third possibility is that in *Continental Casualty*: Article XI ought to be read in light of the GATT's Article XX. If subsequent tribunals follow the lead of the *Sempra* annulment and the opin-

---

[558] See *Continental Casualty*, *supra* footnote 502, para. 227, n. 343.

[559] See *ibid.*, para. 197.

[560] *Ibid.*, paras. 222, 304-305.

ions expressed in the *CMS* annulment, resolving this interpretative question will become ever more crucial for those arbitrators facing a measures not precluded clause like Article XI of the United States-Argentina BIT.

(6) What is the effect of a successful invocation of Article XI?

In dicta, the original tribunals in *CMS, Enron* and *Sempra* all suggested that even if Article XI of the United States-Argentina BIT had been successfully invoked, compensation would still have been due to the investor if this had been required under the substantive law of the BIT as this would have been the result under the customary defence of necessity under Article 27 of the Articles of State Responsibility[561]. This is because, as Article 27 of the Articles of State Responsibility indicates, defences such as necessity are "without prejudice to . . . [t]he question of compensation for any material loss caused by the act in question"[562]. *LG&E* found, on the contrary, that the successful invocation of Article XI permanently excused Argentina from any liability but only during the period of the crisis; it suggested that liability re-emerged for any continuing harms occurring once the crisis was over[563].

Since they took the view that Article XI of the United States-Argentina BIT was a distinct defence, the *CMS* and *Sempra* annulment committees both sug-

---

[561] See *CMS, supra* footnote 492, para. 390; *Enron, supra* footnote 516, para. 344; *Sempra, supra* footnote 516, paras. 392-397.

[562] International Law Commission, "Draft Articles on Responsibility of States for Internationally Wrongful Acts", 22 *Yearbook of the International Law Commission* 1 (2001) (hereinafter "Draft Articles"), Article 27.

[563] See *LG&E, supra* footnote 493, para. 261.

gested that Article 27 of the Articles of State Responsibility was not relevant. Indeed, the *CMS* annulment committee stated that the impact of a successful invocation of Article XI was "clear enough" — that is, it operates as a primary rule excluding the application of any of the substantive guarantees of the BIT such that no compensation would be due to the investor for any actions excused by Article XI. The same conclusion appears to be implicit in the *Sempra* annulment[564].

For its part, *Continental Casualty* took seriously the *CMS* annulment committee's views as to the effect of application of a "primary rule" and rejected all claims of compensation for any actions taken during the period of Argentina's crisis[565]. It therefore agreed that applying Article XI renders the protections of the BIT entirely ineffective.

As Table 2 suggests, at least three possible results are suggested by the cases. A successful invocation of Article XI may not change a State's financial liability at all, either because that provision itself only "precludes" measures but does not exempt a State from liability or because to this extent the residual rule in Article 27 of the Articles of State Responsibility should continue to apply[566]. On the other hand, if Article XI is indeed a primary rule that precludes any and all liability, perhaps it absolves a State permanently from any liability once the clause is invoked, whether or not the underlying crisis is over[567]. Finally,

---

[564] See *CMS annulment*, *supra* footnote 519, para. 146.

[565] See *Continental Casualty*, *supra* footnote 502, para. 304.

[566] For an argument that this indeed is the proper result given the plain meaning, object and purpose and negotiating history of the United States-Argentina BIT, see Alvarez and Khamsi, *supra* footnote 526, pp. 407-460.

[567] While none of the decisions expressly came to this conclusion, the rationale in the *CMS* annulment might sug-

there is the middle ground taken in *LG&E* and *Continental Casualty*: it is a clause that absolves a State from liability when successfully invoked but only for as long as the underlying crisis continues.

C. Broader Problems

(1) The fragmentation of international investment law

Which of these tribunals was correct with respect to the five interpretative questions arising from Argentina's defence to these claims is the subject of a growing literature[568]. This author has taken the position that, with respect to the defence of necessity, the original findings made in the *CMS-Enron-Sempra* trilogy of cases more accurately reflect the plain meaning, object and purpose and negotiating history of the strongly

---

gest this outcome. This also appears to be the result if a measures not precluded clause is found to be "self-judging" such that its invocation renders a claim non-justiciable or inadmissible. See, e.g., United States-Peru Trade Promotion Agreement, signed on 12 April 2006, entered into force on 1 February 2009, Article 22.2, n. 2 (stating that "[f]or greater certainty, if a Party invokes [the measures not precluded clause] in an arbitral proceeding . . . the tribunal or panel hearing the matter shall find that the exception applies").

[568] See, e.g., Alvarez and Khamsi, *supra* footnote 526; Burke-White and von Staden, *supra* footnote 538; Jürgen Kurtz, "Adjudging the Exceptional at International Law: Security, Public Order and Financial Crisis", Jean Monnet Center Working Paper (8 June 2008), available at <http://centers.law.nyu.edu/jeanmonnet/papers/080601.pdf>; C. McLachlan, "Investment Treaties and General International Law", 57 *International & Comparative Law Quarterly* 361 (2008); Théodore Christain, "Quel remède à l'éclatement de la jurisprudence CIRDI sur les investissements en Argentine? La decision du Comité *ad hoc* dans l'affaire CMS c. Argentine", 111 *RGDIP* 879 (2007).

investor-protective United States-Argentina BIT[569]. Others, including most obviously the annulment committees in *CMS* and *Sempra*, disagree, but the merits of these cases are not my central concern here. More interesting for our purposes is what these disparities reveal about the investment regime and criticisms addressed to it.

Most of the interpretative questions mentioned above concerning the meaning of the necessity defence turn on whether one views the investment regime as *lex specialis* or as a set of rules that, absent express derogation, need to be read in light of the rest of public international law. This question is familiar to international lawyers, and in particular to WTO lawyers, who have long wrestled with the appropriateness of turning to non-GATT rules in the course of WTO adjudication[570]. This question has also led the International Law Commission to make proposals about the interpretation of treaties to avoid the further "fragmentation" of international law[571].

Even prior to the recent annulment decisions in *Enron* and *Sempra*, international investment lawyers expressed considerable angst about the disparate legal findings concerning the interpretation of Argentina's necessity defence. That the five categories of questions set out in Table 2 remain unresolved and subject to differing results despite repeated consideration by distinguished groups of arbitrators, many of whom purported to seriously consider the results reached by their pre-

---

[569] See Alvarez and Khamsi, *supra* footnote 526, pp. 407–460.

[570] See generally "Symposium: The Boundaries of the WTO", 96 *American Journal of International Law* 1 (2002).

[571] See ILC, *Fragmentation of International Law: Difficulties Arising from the Diversification and Expansion of International Law*, A/CN.4/L.702 (18 July 2006).

decessors, is not a positive development for those who believe that the turn to BITs and FTAs would render the law more certain than in the days when it was governed solely by the vagaries of custom and only rarely resulted in public decisions by neutral decision-makers. But these concerns pale in significance given the issuance of the annulment decisions in *CMS, Enron* and *Sempra*. Few observers would have predicted that the ICSID annulment process, never intended to constitute a form of appellate review, would have a *detrimental* impact on the harmony of international investment law and yet, if these three decisions are any guide, this is precisely what has occurred.

The trend in the most recent Argentina cases surveyed above, including in two of the three annulment rulings, to interpret Article XI of the United States-Argentina BIT as a provision whose effect and purpose is distinct from the customary defence of necessity is a troubling development that exacerbates the potential for greater internal and external fragmentation of the law. The annulment decisions issued in *CMS, Enron* and *Sempra* are troubling on a number of levels.

The *CMS* and *Sempra* annulment rulings dissociate the United States-Argentina BIT, or at least its measures not precluded clause, from other countries' investment agreements which typically do not contain such a clause. As this author has argued elsewhere[572], distinguishing the customary defence of necessity from Article XI of the United States-Argentina BIT is a perverse result for a treaty which, like the US Model BIT on which it is based, was intended to affirm, not deviate from, relevant principles of custom, and which explicitly sought to provide investors with the

---

[572] See Alvarez and Khamsi, *supra* footnote 526, pp. 408-417.

strongest set of protections then in existence relative to other existing BITs[573]. The result of these cases is that a treaty that, like the United Kingdom-Argentina BIT, has no clause on essential security or public order provides covered investors with much stronger protections — at least vis-à-vis a State invoking "necessity" — than the US Model of 1987, whose Article XI was precisely intended to affirm the traditional defences of *force majeure*, distress and necessity[574]. But the troubling aspect of these decisions goes far beyond the possibility that they, with all due respect, misconstrue a particular clause in a specific treaty.

The annulment decision in *Sempra* in particular, which renders the silence of some BITs on this point critical to the success or failure of a claim, fragments international investment law. Under the rationale in that case, BITs and FTAs which either do or do not have a measures not precluded clause are given radically different meanings. This result, which also creates much greater incentives for investors covered by treaties with measures not precluded clauses to seek the "higher" protections accorded by those treaties which are silent on the matter through MFN guarantees, is bound to sow confusion and uncertainty for both investors and States.

Moreover, the position of investors covered by treaties like the United Kingdom-Argentina BIT which do not have measures not precluded clauses have now been rendered much more precarious by the *Enron* annulment. If that decision is taken seriously, it means

---

[573] Alvarez and Khamsi, *supra* footnote 526, pp. 427-440. See also Article X of the United States-Argentina BIT, *supra* footnote 520 (providing investors with the better treatment accorded, whether under the BIT, national law, or general public international law).

[574] See Alvarez and Khamsi, *supra* footnote 526, pp. 428-433.

there were annullable errors committed in *BG* and *National Grid* since neither of those tribunals' laconic findings determining that Argentina had failed to satisfy the requisites of the customary defence of necessity satisfy the now far more exacting requirements imposed under the *Enron* annulment. The single paragraph in *BG,* for example, in which the arbitrators found that Argentina had not met the "very restrictive conditions" for that defence is far less detailed or reasoned that the comparable findings in the annulled *Enron* decision. That finding, as well as all those previously issued in the Argentina cases applying the traditional requisites of the customary defence of necessity, would appear to contain annullable errors if the *Enron* annulment's elaborate pre-conditions are taken seriously. None of the prior decisions considering Argentina's defence have explicitly addressed the precise legal and factual questions spelled out for the first time in *Enron*. This is hardly surprising since neither the ILC Commentaries nor the numerous decisions cited therein consider the questions that were deemed crucial by the *Enron* annulment committee. Indeed, even the deferential *Continental Casualty* award would appear to run into trouble under the newly pronounced *Enron* standard for the defence of necessity. As noted, that tribunal relied essentially on economic data for its crucial findings on point – an annullable error under *Enron*. Every one of the earlier cases' findings with respect to the customary defence of necessity raises serious annulment questions if the *Enron* annulment is taken as the applicable standard.

Quite apart from whether the *Enron* annulment committee was correct as a matter of law or procedure to impose such conditions when these were never originally argued by either side in the underlying case, the uncertainty and increased litigation (at least in terms of additional requests for annulment by either party) engendered by these findings are likely to add considerably, at least in the short run, to the internal fragmentation of international investment case-law.

The *Sempra* and *Enron* annulments also pose considerable risks for external fragmentation. Those decisions pose the risk that the world of BITs and FTAs will become, over time, a world apart from the rest of public international law[575]. The *Sempra* annulment decision says not one word about why Article XI of the United States-Argentina BIT constitutes an express derogation from a fundamental principle of law, namely the defence of necessity. (Indeed, that tribunal's discussion of the underlying *Sempra* decision appears to confuse the established principle that there needs to be clear evidence that the parties intended to repudiate from an important rule of customary international law, such as the rule requiring exhaustion of local remedies[576], with the completely different notion that preemptory or *jus cogens* norms prevail over treaties[577].) Nor does that

---

[575] For a persuasive critique of the notion of "self-contained" regimes, see B. Simma and D. Pulkowski, "Of Planets and the Universe: Self-Contained Regimes in International Law", 17 *European Journal of International Law* 483 (2006).

[576] See, e.g., *Sempra*, *supra* footnote 516, para. 112 (tacit repudiation of an "important principle of customary international law not favoured"). See also *Amoco Int'l Finance Corp.* v. *Iran*, 14 July 1987, *Iran-United States Claims Tribunal Rep.* 189 (1987), para. 50; *Legal Consequences for States of the Continued Presence of South Africa in Namibia (South West Africa) Notwithstanding Security Council Resolution 276*, Advisory Opinion, *ICJ Reports 1971* 16 (21 June), para. 96; *The Loewen Group, Inc.* v. *United States*, ICSID Case No. ARB(AF)/98/3 (26 June 2003), 42 *ILM* 811 (2003), para. 160.

[577] Cf. *Sempra annulment*, *supra* footnote 501, paras. 197, 200, and 202 (disputing the proposition that necessity is a "mandatory" principle or that *jus cogens* requires States to avoid forgoing the principle of necessity in their treaties).

tribunal consider the interpretation of Article XI in light of standard rules of interpretation under the Vienna Convention on the Law of Treaties, including Article 31 (1) _(a)_ (urging consideration of the plain meaning of a treaty given its context and object and purpose), Article 31 (2) (defining context to include a treaty's other provisions), Article 31 (3) _(c)_ (authorizing recourse to "any relevant rules of international law applicable in the relations between the parties), and Article 31 (2) (permitting subsidiary resort if needed to negotiating history). Those arguments about the interpretation of Article XI of the United States-Argentina BIT were presented to the original tribunal by the parties [578].

The _Sempra_ annulment committee addresses none of these interpretative contentions. It simply sets out the respective terms of Article XI of the BIT and Article 25 of the Articles of State Responsibility, and indicates that it is "apparent" that these are not the

---

[578] See, e.g., _Sempra_, _supra_ footnote 516, paras. 370, 373, 375, 378 and 388. See also Alvarez and Khamsi, _supra_ footnote 526, pp. 408-460. Consideration of the context of the United States-Argentina BIT, _supra_ footnote 520, would include, of course, examination of what its Articles X and IV (3) tell us about the meaning of Article XI. As this author has elaborated elsewhere and, more importantly, as was argued before the original _Sempra_ tribunal, Article X anticipates that investors get the benefits of, among other things, customary international law (which includes presumably the defence of necessity), while Article IV (3) provides investors with additional protections, against non-discrimination, should a State provide compensation to other persons following a serious crisis, such as a state of national emergency or civil disturbance. The _Sempra_ annulment decision does not explain why a treaty, which anticipates the continuation of investor protections, including those under customary law and including in cases of crisis, would simultaneously eliminate such protections under Article XI.

same[579]. This mechanical approach to interpretation fails to address the problem that Article XI, whose text stems from at least the US Model BIT of 1984, could not possibly have replicated the text of Article 25, which was not finalized until 2001[580].

As this suggests, the *Sempra* annulment appears to dismiss or disregard other relevant principles of international law, apart from the customary defence of necessity. Quite apart from the basic interpretative principles noted above, the findings in the original *Sempra* case concerning Argentina's contribution to the underlying crisis is based on the general principle of unclean hands or estoppel, and not merely the customary defence of necessity as codified under Article 25 of the Articles of State Responsibility. Does the *Sempra* annulment stand for the proposition that this general principle of law, as well as the customary defence of necessity, is inapplicable to the interpretation of BITs or that it too can be disregarded when a treaty does not expressly mention it?

Equally troubling, at least for frequent users of ICSID, is what these annulment decisions may mean for the ICSID annulment process and what they appear to say about the ICSID rules limiting annulment to instances where the tribunal "manifestly exceeded its powers" or "failed to state the reasons" for its award[581]. Contrary to the hopes of those who established the pro-

---

[579] *Sempra annulment*, *supra* footnote 501, paras. 198-199.

[580] For a detailed discussion of this point, see Alvarez and Khamsi, *supra* footnote 526, pp. 430-433.

[581] Convention on the Settlement of Investment Disputes between States and Nationals of Other States, Washington, 575 *United Nations Treaty Series 259,* signed on 18 March 1965, entered into force on 14 October 1966, available at <http://icsid.worldbank.org/ICSID/StaticFiles/basicdoc/CRR_English-final.pdf>, Articles 52 (1) *(b)* and 52 (1) *(e)* (hereinafter "ICSID Convention").

cedures for ICSID and its limited grounds for annulment, the annulment decisions in *CMS*, *Sempra* and *Enron* sow confusion with respect to other international rules, apart from the interpretation of BITs or the customary defence of necessity. This may in turn undermine confidence in and the legitimacy of ICSID (and possibly other venues for investor-State arbitration).

States and investors now face three distinct annulment outcomes arising from strikingly similar cases. In one case, *CMS*, an annulment committee severely criticizes but does not annul a decision contending that to do so would be to confuse a wrongful application of the law from an act that fails to apply the correct law. The second, *Sempra*, goes ahead and annuls a comparable decision for failing to distinguish customary law from Article XI of the United States-Argentina BIT, ignoring the earlier annulment committee's warning against acting as an appellate court. The third, *Enron*, affirms the very same legal findings annulled in *Sempra* but annuls the underlying award for failing to apply the customary defence that *Sempra* found to be improper!

These results, while perhaps not entirely surprising given the *ad hoc* nature of the annulment committees formed in each case, confuse instead of providing consistent guidance to future arbitrators, investors and States. The decisions send decidedly mixed messages about the naure of the annulment process. They threaten to turn a limited annulment process into a *de facto* appellate process by arbitral fiat, and they undermine *jurisprudence constante*[582]. Note that even the

---

[582] Ironically, the *Enron* annulment committee itself recognized the need for annulment decisions to render consistent decisions. *Enron annulment*, *supra* footnote 501, para. 66 ("Although there is no doctrine of binding precedent in the ICSID arbitration system, the Committee con-

annulment committee that ruled in favour of investors *(CMS)* was possibly the least pleasing to both disputing parties: Argentina was told to pay an award that the annulment committee itself suggested was wrongly decided, while the "winning" investor was put in the position of trying to enforce an award that had been delegitimized by the annulment committee.

And although the *Enron* annulment committee repeatedly stressed the restrictive nature of its enquiries given the limited nature of the annulment process under the ICSID Convention and the relevant arbitral case law[583], its extraordinary decision annulling an award for failing to articulate legal grounds that were never argued before it and second-guessing that tribunal for relying on a particular kind of expert witness, appears to be a prime example of an annulment committee acting as a full-fledged court of appeal, irrespective of the plain meaning of the ICSID Convention and the limits of its own jurisdiction[584]. Indeed, the *Enron* annulment — to the extent it overturned the fact-finding of the earlier tribunal — seemed to assume powers that are denied even to the WTO Appellate Body (which cannot reconsider an earlier panel's fact-finding). Similarly, the *Sempra* annulment committee proceeded to do exactly what the *CMS* annulment committee warned against, that is, substitute its view of the law for that of the Tribunal[585].

---

siders that in the longer term there should develop a jurisprudence constante in relations to annulment proceedings").

[583] See, e.g., *Enron annulment*, *supra* footnote 501, paras. 63-65, 69 and 74.

[584] Compare *CMS annulment*, *supra* footnote 519, para. 136 (recognizing that the committee "cannot simply substitute its own view of the law and its own appreciation of the facts for those of the Tribunal").

[585] *Ibid.*

Are these annulments to be treated as unique to investor-State arbitration and not meant to be considered as relevant jurisprudence with respect to other annulment procedures anticipated by ICSID, or national court reviews under the New York Convention or national arbitration laws? If so, why is this fragmentation of applicable arbitration law justifiable?

And most obviously, to the extent that these decisions — from *LG&E* to the *Enron* annulment — appear to be suggesting that the customary defence of necessity is now subject to a deferential margin of appreciation, are they suggesting that this too is unique to the investment regime? The alternatives are not attractive. Either these cases stand for the general proposition that, notwithstanding the ILC's and others' traditional understanding of that exceedingly and purposely narrow defence, necessity is now considerably easier to invoke as a defence to all international obligations or they suggest that this broadened excuse applies only in the BIT context. The former position has the potential to radically undermine all international obligations, particularly if the burden is now on those who resist a State's argument that a "crisis" made it violate international law[586]. And no justification has yet been offered for the latter outcome — which has the effect of depriving injured third parties from compensation that would otherwise be due and turns the defence of necessity itself into a fragmented doctrine, whose differing applications depend on whether it is invoked in favour of an investor or not.

In the view of this author, the better outcome would have been to interpret Article XI of the United States-Argentina BIT in light of the customary defence of necessity which inspired it but remain sensitive to

---

[586] See, e.g., Orrego-Vicuña, *supra* footnote 551.

the regulatory needs of States in the course of applying (and interpreting) the substantive guarantees in such treaties, including FET, as is further addressed below.

But even if this conclusion is incorrect, one would have hoped at least for a second best outcome: namely that repeated arbitral consideration of the same question would have achieved greater clarity with respect to the underlying necessity/Article XI defence. For now, the opposite appears to be occurring.

Why?

The annulment decisions in *Sempra* and *Enron* appear, at least to this observer, to be outcome-driven. Neither is a model of legal reasoning. Neither provides a plausible, non-result oriented rationale for annulling the respective underlying awards. If one were to explain why these annulment committees seemed bent on handing a victory to Argentina, irrespective of the effects on international investment law or public international law more generally, a likely explanation lies in the global economic crisis that occurred after the original arbitral decisions in these cases were issued. That crisis, and the reactions of important economic players such as the United States, cast into doubt the very premises of the underlying United States-Argentina BIT, including the use of that instrument as a credibility device to tie the hands of a State that had demonstrated a repeated proclivity to declare an emergency and escape from its promises to investors[587]. The annulment committees in *Sempra* and *Enron* may have thought that affirming Argentina's liability in the midst of the new political realities — where a number of Governments have taken "emergency" measures in response that arguably violate BIT or FTA commit-

---

[587] See Alvarez and Khamsi, *supra* footnote 526, pp. 414-415.

ments[588] — would alienate even the erstwhile backers of the investment regime. They may have annulled the earlier decisions because to do otherwise would have exacerbated long-standing criticisms of the investment regime, prompted concerns about regulatory sovereignty even among developed States, and possibly even threatened the continued viability of BITs and FTAs.

Of course, such political concerns should not, in principle, affect neutral arbitrators charged with enforcing the terms of a treaty that at the time it was negotiated presumed that it would continue to protect investors precisely when they needed such protections the most, namely during a proclamation of "emergency". This had been the case, after all, when the United States had proclaimed the Hull Rule in defence of compensation for properties expropriated during a Mexican political and economic crisis[589]. That arbitrators — or members of annulment committees — should be influenced by such political concerns casts into doubt some of the assumptions of those who drafted and negotiated the US BIT and possibly other BITs as well as some critics of the investment regime.

As discussed in Chapter I, proponents of BITs assumed that investor-State arbitration would "depoliticize" such disputes. The Argentina cases suggest, on the contrary, that far from removing political concerns, using the arbitration process to resolve investment disputes may politicize arbitration. Even if the

---

[588] See A. Van Aaken and J. Kurtz, "Emergency Measures and International Investment Law: How Far Can States Go?", in K. P. Sauvant (ed.), *Yearbook International Investment Law & Policy 2009-2010* (Oxford, Oxford University Press, forthcoming 2011).

[589] See, e.g., A. F. Lowenfeld, *International Economic Law* (Oxford, Oxford University Press, 2002), pp. 397-403.

results in none of the Argentina cases were influenced by political factors, no one would suggest that the resort to investor-State dispute settlement has "de-politicized" the underlying disputes. The political concerns that have always driven international investment matters — from the days of gunboat diplomacy through diplomatic espousal to the fraught battles over the New International Economic Order — are now being waged over the terms of investment treaties and how these are interpreted in investor-State cases. Politics has not been eliminated. It has just changed venue.

And if the recent Argentina victories are any indication, some criticisms of the regime may also need to be reconsidered. The ideological critique discussed in Chapter I suggests that investor-State arbitrators are not automatons mechanically and neutrally applying the law but human beings whose views of the law reflect to some extent their backgrounds and perhaps even the appointing authorities to whom they owe their positions. Some, such as Gus Van Harten, have taken this point further to suggest that the entire system of investor-State arbitration, including ICSID, is structurally rigged in favour of the interests of investors[590]. But contentions according to which those who serve as adjudicators in these cases are systematically biased in favour of investors ignores the fact that at least two of the arbitrators appointed in each of these cases owe their appointments to someone other than the investor-claimant and that none of those chosen to serve on annulment committees owe their positions to the business community or to the disputing parties to a particu-

---

[590] Van Harten, *supra* footnote 513, pp. 167-175 (describing the problem of the independence of investor-State arbitrators as the "most troubling issue that arises from the use of private arbitration to resolve regulatory disputes"). See also Chapter I's discussion of "ideological" critiques.

lar dispute[591]. The results in the Argentina cases surveyed here, particularly but not exclusively on annulment, do not support the systematic bias charge, either as a matter of fact or even from the standpoint of perceptions of a lack of independence. But if, as is suggested here, those who annulled *Enron* and *Sempra* tweaked the law in order to avoid sovereign threats to the regimes of international investment or arbitration, the broader ideological critique may be at least partly right. Investor-State arbitrators and those who serve on annulment committees, consciously or not, take into account the views of the investment regime's relevant stakeholders. The mistake is to assume that those stakeholders are limited to investor-claimants; in fact, thanks to the increasingly public nature of this regime, these diverse stakeholders also include richer and poorer sovereign States, international financial organizations, NGOs (who increasingly intervene as *amici*), as well as the taxpayers of many nations (who may need to be convinced that providing compensation to injured foreign investors serves their long term interests). A second mistake may be to assume that permanent judges, including those who serve on prominent national supreme courts, are not influenced by political considerations[592].

---

[591] ICSID annulment committees are appointed by the President of the World Bank, see ICSID Convention, *supra* footnote 581, Article 52 (3) (also barring nationals from the disputing parties from such appointments). Whatever one's views about the political sympathies of the World Bank's President, it is surely misleading to suggest that this individual is *de facto* the agent of private businesses, as opposed to an agent of the collectivity of States that established the Bank.

[592] See generally B. Friedman, *The Will of the People : How Public Opinion Has Influenced the Supreme Court and Shaped the Meaning of the Constitution* (New York, Farrar, Straus and Giroux, 2009).

None of this is intended to justify the legal opinions issued in the annulments in *Enron* or *Sempra*. Even if investor-State adjudicators are right to seek to avoid politically suicidal awards (whether in favour of States or investors), the provisions contained in BITs and FTAs contain interpretative possibilities that were left unexplored by these decisions.

The results in the Argentina claims were not pre-ordained even under the strongly investor-protective United States-Argentina BIT. The possibilities of decisions that would have been more sensitive to the proper interpretation of the underlying law as well as to the risks of fragmentation are addressed in the next section, which critiques a third Argentine decision, *Continental Casualty*.

(2) The hazards of premature de-fragmentation

The fragmentation risks presented by the inconsistent Argentina decisions are more obvious than a second risk: that investor-State arbitrators may prematurely and wrongly reach to non-investment rules in order to "harmonize" investment law with other international regimes. Of the Argentine decisions discussed here, *Continental Casualty* falls into the alternative trap of premature de-fragmentation.

Continental Casualty is dramatically at odds with the original arbitral awards issued in *CMS, Sempra* and *Enron*.

The GATT-type balancing test applied in *Continental Casualty* is, on its face, starkly different from the tight requirements imposed on any State seeking to invoke the customary defence of necessity that were applied in those earlier cases by way of interpreting Article XI. As noted, under the customary defence, States must take any alternatives to illegal action available, even those that are more costly or less convenient[593]. States must not have substantially contributed to the underlying situation provoking the necessity defence, they must resume compliance with their underlying obligations as soon as the crisis situation has passed, and must, in any case, pay any compensation normally due. Necessity, in other words, is hard to prove and has limited consequences even when demonstrated since even a successful invocation of it merely excuses a temporary breach but does not terminate the underlying legal obligation. This is different from the GATT approach under Article XX which essentially permits the least restrictive, and also reasonably available, measure that makes a material contribution to meeting the legitimate end pursued[594]. As is suggested in the GATT case of *Brazil Tyres*, "necessary" measures under Article XX need not be the "only" means; they are those that are "reasonably available" once unduly burdensome alternatives are discarded[595].

---

[593] See, e.g., Draft Articles, *supra* footnote 562, Article 25, Commentary, para. 15.

[594] The relevant text of GATT Article XX states:

"Subject to the requirement that such measures are not applied in a manner which would constitute a means of arbitrary or unjustifiable discrimination between countries where the same conditions prevail, or a disguised restriction on international trade, nothing in this Agreement shall be construed to prevent the adoption or enforcement by any contracting party of measures:

(a) necessary to protect public morals;
(b) necessary to protect human, animal or plant life or health . . ."

[*(c)*-*(j)* follow].

[595] *Brazil: Measures Affecting Import of Retreaded Tyres*, Report of the Appellate Body, World Trade Organization Case No. WT/DS332/AB/R (3 December 2007), para. 156.

Continental Casualty went far beyond the earlier Argentina awards discussed here in giving content to the meaning of Article XI, if viewed as a defence distinct from necessity. It decided that Article XI should be interpreted in light of how WTO adjudicators have interpreted the GATT's Article XX and not in light of the customary defence of necessity.

That tribunal's sole justification for turning to GATT law was a single sentence:

> "Since the text of Article XI derives from the parallel model clause of the U.S. FCN treaties and these treaties in turn reflect the formulation of Article XX of GATT 1947, the Tribunal finds it more appropriate to refer to the GATT and WTO case law which has extensively dealt with the concept and requirements of necessity . . . rather than to refer to the requirement of necessity under customary international law." [596]

Even those who disagree with the conclusion that Article XI reflects the customary defence of necessity are likely to find this justification unsatisfactory as a matter of straightforward treaty interpretation. Why should interpreters of the United States-Argentina BIT turn to trade law rather than, as directed by the Vienna Convention on the Law of Treaties, the ordinary meaning of the terms "necessary to", "public order", and "essential security" in light of the context, object and purpose, and if needed, the negotiating history of that BIT? Apart from the quotation above, the *Continental Casualty* award makes no attempt to compare the

---

[596] See *Continental Casualty*, *supra* footnote 502, para. 192. For a comparable leap to GATT Article XX, see, e.g., *S.D. Myers, Inc.* v. *Canada*, Separate Opinion of Schwartz, UNCITRAL Arbitration Rules (12 November 2000), para. 129 (reading Article XX *(b)* into the NAFTA).

actual texts of Article XI of the United States-Argentina BIT with the GATT's Article XX or to consider the histories of these respective provisions. It merely assumes, with little textual and even less actual historical support, that the two provisions are comparable and share common objectives[597]. Nothing could be farther from the truth. As is clear from comparing their texts (see Table 3), if any clause in the GATT covered agreements is comparable to Article XI of the BIT, that clause is GATT Article XXI, not its Article XX. The model for the essential security clause of the FCNs was, naturally enough, the essential security clause of the GATT (Article XXI) and not its "general exceptions" clause at Article XX. Nothing comparable to the GATT's Article XX exists in the US BITs of this period.

Note that even when the drafters of FCNs drew from the GATT's limited security exception at Article XXI, they made a telling change suggestive of the wholly different purposes of FCNs, as compared to the GATT. The typical FCN dropped the critical phase "which it considers" which had appeared in GATT, Article XXI *(b)*. The significance of this omission became clear in the *Nicaragua* case where the ICJ properly noted that the omission meant that, unlike in the context of GATT, when it came to interpreting the "essential security" clause of FCNs, the States parties to FCNs did not have the authority to determine for themselves whether their essential security was at issue, but rather this question, like every other interpretative issue in the FCN, was subject to independent assessment by any third-party adjudicator tasked with

---

[597] To this extent, its mechanistic comparison of texts is reminiscent to that adopted in the *Sempra annulment* decision, as discussed above, albeit to very different effect, see *Sempra annulment*, *supra* footnote 501.

TABLE 3. DISTINGUISHING ARTICLE XXI

Article XXI of the GATT	*Article XXI of FCN*
Nothing in this Agreement shall be construed . . .	1. The present Treaty shall not preclude the application of measures:
(b) to prevent any contracting party from taking any action which it considers necessary for the protection of its essential security interests	*(a)* regulating the importation or exportation of gold or silver;
(i) relating to fissionable materials or the materials from which they are delivered;	*(b)* relating to fissionable materials, to radioactive by-products of the utilization or processing thereof or to materials that are the source of fissionable materials;
(ii) relating to the traffic in arms, ammunition and implements of war and to such traffic in other goods and materials as is carried on directly or indirectly for the purpose of supplying a military establishment;	*(c)* regulating the production of or traffic in arms, ammunition and implements of war, or traffic in other materials carried on directly or indirectly for the purpose of supplying a military establishment;
(iii) taken in time of war or other emergency in international relations; or	*(d)* necessary to fulfill the obligations of a Party for the maintenance or restoration of international peace and security, or necessary to protect its essential security interests . . .
(c) To prevent any contracting party from taking any action in pursuance of its obligations under the United Nations Charter for the maintenance of international peace and security.	

interpretation and application[598]. Now why would FCN drafters opt to make the essential security clause not self-judging, unlike the GATT? The reasons lie in the structural differences between the trade and FCN/BIT regimes that were briefly introduced in Chapter I.

Unlike the GATT regime, which seeks to prevent certain actions by States (if necessary by authorizing trade retaliation until the offending measure is removed) but does not attempt to provide recompense to injured traders, FCNs, like BITs, are treaties that crucially seek to provide remediation for past injury and permit those who are injured to bring claims for damage caused by treaty breach. To this end, FCNs are deemed "self-executing" under US law and permit eligible traders and investors to bring claims directly in local US courts[599]. A self-judging essential security clause was in all likelihood deemed to be inconsistent with this remedial aspiration or with recognizing FCNs as giving a cause of action to private litigants.

By comparison, a self-judging essential security clause in the context of the GATT — where only States could file complaints against one another and where all GATT contracting parties needed to join consensus to

---

[598] But note that the absence of cases in the GATT renders speculative the extent to which GATT Article XXI is wholly self-judging. Compare A. Emmerson, "Conceptualizing Security Exceptions: Legal doctrine or Political Excuse?", 11 *J. International Economic Law* 135 (2008), p. 145 (arguing that the specific exceptions embraced by Article XXI *(b)* (i-iii) indicate that "[w]hile a member may have scope to determine what constitutes its own essential security interests — perhaps including human rights — the adequacy of the measure cannot be removed from judicial review") (citations omitted).

[599] See, e.g., *Asakura* v. *City of Seattle*, 265 US 332 (1924) (recognizing an FCN treaty as self-executing and upholding a Japanese pawn-broker's claim over a discriminatory local ordinance).

accept an adverse GATT panel decision (at least in the pre-1994 GATT system) — was likely to cause considerably less damage. The GATT remedial scheme put States in the driver's seat when it came to deciding the scope of, or even whether to accept, third-party interpretations of their GATT obligations. Further, unlike parties to FCNs (or the later BITs), GATT parties had not given any third parties legitimate expectations that their rights as traders were individually protected. The GATT parties may also have believed that members of the GATT would be far more likely to self-police their respective assertions of essential security within the context of a multilateral regime since each GATT party would recognize that such assertions would be reciprocally claimed by other contracting parties. Indeed, like other purely interstate dispute settlement systems, the WTO's system anticipates that States will consider the broader political relationships between them as well as the fact that such considerations will discourage the filing of some interstate claims because of the risk of retaliatory claims by others[600].

Indeed, the GATT regime, unlike the investment regime, is constructed on notions of tit-for-tat (or specific) reciprocity. Reciprocity operates from the imposition of trade rules — when prospective GATT members are required to change their existing trade laws and quotas in order to satisfy existing GATT parties that they are adopting truly reciprocal trade obligations — to the concluding enforcement stage, where the only authorized remedies for breach of the GATT are proportionate tit-for-tat trade countermeasures[601]. As this

---

[600] See, e.g., J. Kurtz, "The Use and Abuse of WTO Law in Investor-State Arbitration: Competition and Its Discontents", 20 *European Journal of International Law* 749 (2009), p. 756.

[601] As Thomas Franck has pointed out, the GATT requires that counter-measures authorized by the WTO

suggests, from the outset, the drafters of FCNs (and the later BITs) recognized distinctions between the rights accorded third parties under those treaties as compared to the interstate remedial scheme and remedies of the GATT (and later the WTO).

Continental Casualty ignored these distinctions when it chose to use GATT law to interpret Article XI of the United States-Argentina BIT. Five critical flaws undermine this decision.

Failed history

Continental Casualty was correct insofar as it compared the typical FCN's exceptions clause to that in the United States-Argentina BIT. Table 4, comparing the texts of the two, makes this clear:

TABLE 4. ESSENTIAL SECURITY CLAUSES

Article XI of United States-Argentina BIT	*Article XX (1)* (d) *of FCN*
This Treaty shall not preclude the application by either Party of measures necessary for the maintenance of public order, the fulfillment of its obligation with respect to the maintenance of restoration of international peace or security, or the protection of its own essential security interests.	... necessary to fulfill the obligations of that Party for the maintenance or restoration of international peace and security, or necessary to protect its essential security interests ...

Dispute Settlement Body be "equivalent" to the "nullification and impairment" resulting from the trade law violation. T. M. Franck, "On Proportionality of Countermeasures in International Law", 102 *American Journal of International Law* 715 (2008), p. 742. As he writes, "[t]he

But that tribunal's further contention that Article XI of the United States-Argentina BIT is comparable to the general exceptions clause of the GATT, namely its Article XX, makes little sense. GATT Article XX provides as follows:

"Subject to the requirement that such measures are not applied in a manner which would constitute a means of arbitrary or unjustifiable discrimination between countries where the same conditions prevail, or a disguised restriction on international trade, nothing in this Agreement shall be construed to prevent the adoption or enforcement by any contracting party of measures:

(a) necessary to protect public morals;
(b) necessary to protect human, animal or plant life or health;
(c) relating to the importations or exportations of gold or silver;
(d) necessary to secure compliance with laws or regulations which are not inconsistent with the provisions of this Agreement, including those relating to customs enforcement, the enforcement of monopolies operated under paragraph 4 of Article II and Article XVII, the protection of patents, trade marks and copyrights, and the prevention of deceptive practices;
(e) relating to the products of prison labour;

---

violation of a reciprocal obligation creates an opportunity for the injured party to seek relief by the imposition of a countermeasure. That the counter-measure does not exceed limits imposed by proportionality is superintended by the dispute settlement procedure" (*ibid.*, p. 743). Note that the measure of proportionality in the GATT regime is determined by the amount of trade retaliation that is deemed necessary to bring about a State's removal of the GATT-offensive measure (*ibid.*, pp. 743-744).

(f) imposed for the protection of national treasures of artistic, historic or archaeological value;

(g) relating to the conservation of exhaustible natural resources if such measures are made effective in conjunction with restrictions on domestic production or consumption;

(h) undertaken in pursuance of obligations under any intergovernmental commodity agreement which conforms to criteria submitted to the CONTRACTING PARTIES and not disapproved by them or which is itself so submitted and not so disapproved;*

(i) involving restrictions on exports of domestic materials necessary to ensure essential quantities of such materials to a domestic processing industry during periods when the domestic price of such materials is held below the world price as part of a governmental stabilization plan; *Provided* that such restrictions shall not operate to increase the exports of or the protection afforded to such domestic industry, and shall not depart from the provisions of this Agreement relating to non-discrimination;

(j) essential to the acquisition or distribution of products in general or local short supply; *Provided* that any such measures shall be consistent with the principle that all contracting parties are entitled to an equitable share of the international supply of such products, and that any such measures, which are inconsistent with the other provisions of the Agreement shall be discontinued as soon as the conditions giving rise to them have ceased to exist. The CONTRACTING PARTIES shall review the need for this subparagraph not later than 30 June 1960."

There is nothing in the typical FCN which looks

like Article XX and of course nothing in the United States-Argentina BIT that contains such a laundry list of general regulatory exceptions. Article XI of the United States-Argentina BIT is a far more limited clause. Like the FCN's Article XX (1), this provision is not self-judging and anticipates evaluation by an independent third-party adjudicator so that the rights of investors could not be lightly disregarded by a State inclined to act as a judge in its cause.

There is no connection between Article XX of the GATT — which includes measures for a number of regulatory purposes not identified in the United States-Argentina BIT and does not include exceptions for either "public order" or "essential security" — and the measures not precluded clause of the United States-Argentina BIT. There is nothing in the historical evolution of the text of Article XI that supports the conclusion that the interpretation of GATT Article XX, including the meaning of the word "necessary" in that article, is relevant to the interpretation of Article XI of the BIT.

The failure to consider the chapeau clause of Article XX

Turning to GATT law on this point is also inapposite insofar as Article XX of the GATT includes an important dimension not addressed by the tribunal in *Continental Casualty*. Under Article XX of the GATT, a treaty interpreter only gets to evaluate whether a measure is "necessary" for purposes of evaluating measures under *(a)* or *(b)* of that clause if a State's measure is "not applied in a manner which constitute[s] a means of arbitrary or unjustifiable discrimination" or a "disguised restriction on international trade" under the famous chapeau clause. This subjects State measures to additional guarantees not contained in Article XI of the United States-Argentina BIT. Since the "balancing" that occurs under the GATT's Article XX already screens out the most objectionable type of actions against foreign business — namely protectionist, arbitrary, or discriminatory measures — the GATT's adjudicators can afford to accord considerable deference to *remaining* non-discriminatory measures that States try to justify as "necessary" for the enumerated legitimate regulatory purposes contained in sections *(a)* through *(j)* of that article. The chapeau clause of Article XX necessarily affects the meaning of that entire provision and especially what should be deemed to be "necessary" under that article. Indeed, as commentators have suggested, giving effect to the chapeau has also undoubtedly affected how the national treatment provisions of the GATT have been read[602].

Under the United States-Argentina BIT, there is a separate guarantee protecting investors against "arbitrary and discriminatory" action (in Article II) — but ironically, under *Continental Casualty*'s interpretation of Article XI as a "primary rule" excluding all other BIT provisions, this guarantee, along with all others contained in the rest of the BIT, is of no use to the investor. *Continental Casualty* fails to consider the full text of Article XX as well as the different contexts of the GATT covered agreements and the BIT. Under *Continental Casualty*'s interpretation of Article XI, there is no screening of measures that are arbitrary or discriminatory; instead the arbitrator proceeds directly to "balancing" with due deference to the State taking the offending actions. Its resort to the deferential "balancing" aspects of GATT Article XX absent that provi-

---

[602] See, e.g., Kurtz, *supra* footnote 600, pp. 756-757 (noting the relevance of having the "fail-safe" provisions of Article XX for the purpose of correcting for any legal errors in interpreting "national treatment").

sion's chapeau screening clause carves out a much bigger hole in the investment protections of the United States-Argentina BIT than Article XX does for purposes of the GATT.

The chapeau of Article XX of the GATT and the absence of anything comparable to it in Article XI of the United States-Argentina BIT also suggests other relevant differences between the trade and investment regimes that make *Continental Casualty*'s leap to trade law illogical. As the chapeau to Article XX suggests, the trade regime's principal objectives are narrower than those of the typical BIT as it seeks to encourage trade liberalization and therefore to prevent government actions of a particular kind, namely those that are protectionist in intent or effect[603]. The trade regime needs to be able to distinguish legitimate regulation from GATT-illegal measures that are intended to protect national industry from foreign competition or that have that effect. This explains not only the chapeau of Article XX but the felt need in the GATT to enumerate permissible types of regulation in the rest of that provision, namely Article XX *(a)* through *(j)*. While some BIT guarantees (such as its protections against non-discrimination and providing for compensation for indirect takings) also require distinctions between types of regulation, investment treaties seek to protect and more importantly to provide remedial relief to particular investors harmed as a result of a full range of governmental action, and "protectionist" intent or effect is not

---

[603] This is made explicit in GATT Article III (1) which requires that internal taxes or other internal charges should not be applied "so as to afford protection to domestic production". See also Kurtz, *supra* footnote 600, p. 753 (noting that this obligation ensures that "conditions of competition within the state are not modified by government intervention so as to advantage a domestic product over its foreign competitors").

a condition for the illegality of such action. Substantive guarantees like FET, full protection and security, compensation upon direct expropriation, or upholding contractual obligations (umbrella clauses) are *not* based on the relative treatment foreign investors receive and may be violated without a showing of bad faith and irrespective of "protectionist" intent or effect. In many instances, as was discussed in the context of FET, the absolute guarantees provided in BITs may be violated irrespective of the intent or purpose of the government measures at issue.

The failure to consider the differing regulatory purposes identified in GATT Article XX

Continental Casualty's blithe assumption that GATT Article XX and Article XI of the United States-Argentina BIT are comparable ignores the fact that the laundry list of exceptions in Article XX has engendered an increasingly rich jurisprudence unique to the trade regime about the *relative* importance of measures undertaken for the different regulatory purposes enumerated [604]. The relative weight of the regulatory purposes identified in *(a)-(j)* affects the balancing that trade adjudicators apply under Article XX [605]. As

---

[604] The relative importance of the regulatory purposes reflected in sections *(a)* through *(j)* of Article XX is suggested by the text of that provision itself. Thus, for example, Article XX *(g)* anticipates that members may take measures that merely "relate" to the conservation of exhaustible natural resources but Article XX *(b)* anticipates an exception only for measures "necessary" to protect human life or health.

[605] Despite the text of Article XX *(b)*, Franck notes that when the State's regulatory objective relates to a highly valued interest such as the protection of human life, the challenged regulation will likely be upheld "if there is any doubt as to the ability of the proposed alternative to

Continental Casualty acknowledges, by quoting the test of "reasonable availability" deployed in a GATT case, the "reasonable available measures" under that regime are those that would preserve the State's "right to achieve its desired level of protection *with respect to the objective pursued . . .*"[606].

No such nuance exists among the types of actions identified in Article XI of the United States-Argentina BIT — all of which are presumably of equal importance to the State invoking them — or in the deferential "balancing" that *Continental Casualty* applies. Accordingly, no such nuance dulls the blunt impact of what that tribunal does with GATT Article XX balancing in the radically different context of investor-State arbitration.

The failure to consider the prevalence of political/ economic crises in investment disputes

Like other US BITs of its time, the United States-Argentina BIT seeks to provide investors with a remedy for damages that they suffer including particularly

---

achieve the same level of efficacy". See Franck, *supra* footnote 601, p. 751 (quoting Alan O. Sykes, "The Least Restrictive Means", 70 *University of Chicago Law Review* 403 (2003), p. 416, and noting that a less rigorous standard of review applies when the regulatory objective is to protect "some lesser interest than life or health"). See also Kurtz, *supra* footnote 600, p. 754 (noting that the GATT drafters incorporated these regulatory purposes as "targeted departures" from the operative commitments and in order to elevate particular values over and above the project of trade liberalization).

[606] See *Continental Casualty*, *supra* footnote 502, para. 195 (citing *United States — Measures Affecting the Cross-Border Supply of Gambling and Betting Services*, Report of the Appellate Body, World Trade Organization Case No. WT/DS285/AB/R (7 April 2005) (hereinafter *"US Gambling"*)).

when such damages are most likely to occur, namely
during periods of perceived economic or political crisis
in host States. A BIT such as the United States-
Argentina treaty, unlike the GATT, presumes that its
protections continue — indeed may be most significant
— during a period of host State crisis[607]. This is most
clearly demonstrated by Article IV (3) of that treaty,
which grants investors from either party the right of
non-discriminatory treatment should a State compensate any investor for harm "owing to war or other
armed conflict, revolution, state of national emergency,
insurrection, civil disturbance or other similar events".
Continental Casualty, like the *Sempra* annulment, does
not consider how its interpretation of Article XI may
affect the scope or operation of the investor's rights
provided in Article IV (3) — or what its interpretation
does to the parties' original understanding of the types
of measures from which they were agreeing to protect
their respective investors. As the history of BITs
described in prior chapters implies, States enter into
treaties like the United States-Argentina BIT to reas-
sure investors, particularly in the case of a volatile or
unstable economy when their rights are most vulnera-
ble. *Continental Casualty* ignores this salient fact —
which is also part of the context of the BIT it was
interpreting. Instead, it opts to rely on a wholly different (trade) regime that anticipates that such crises, as

---

[607] See, e.g., *CMS, supra* footnote 492, para. 354
(although noting that a crisis leading to the "disintegration
of society" might obviate such protections); Alvarez and
Khamsi, *supra* footnote 526, pp. 414-417. Also see *Patuha
Power Ltd. (Bermuda)* v. *PT (Persero) Perusahaan
Listruik Negara (Indonesia)*, Final Award, 14 *Mealey's
International Arbitration Report* (1999), para. 325 (noting
that the effect of "macro-economic events" on contractual
obligations "far from being 'unprecedented', has a long
history").

auto-interpreted by the States invoking them, are permissible derogations from trade liberalization.

The failure to consider the relevance of "primary" versus "secondary" rules

The distinction between primary and secondary rules so crucial to the *CMS* annulment decision does not exist in the GATT, even though a WTO panel would never, as *Continental Casualty* does, apply Article XX before finding a substantive breach of the GATT. *Continental Casualty* fails to consider whether its insistence that Article XI is a "primary" rule excusing all liability ought to affect its equal insistence that GATT law is relevant to Article XI's interpretation.

The question of comparability between the trade and investment regimes is relevant first with respect to burden and standard of proof. Those relying on a primary rule ordinarily have the burden of proof, whereas those asserting a secondary rule, especially one that is an affirmative defence to primary liability, ordinarily face the burden of proof.

Continental Casualty's decision to interpret Article XI as a primary rule to be interpreted in light of GATT Article XX presumes that the standard and burdens of proof can be simply extrapolated from one regime to the other. Yet, as Kurtz points out, the interstate GATT regime presumes a certain form of informational symmetry between the complaining parties simply because both are States[608]. Under that regime, a measure will be found more restrictive than necessary (that is, disproportionate) when the complaining party proves that another measure is reasonably available, this alternative would achieve the appropriate level of protection,

---

[608] Kurtz, *supra* footnote 600, pp. 757-758.

and would be less restrictive of trade [609]. This approach
to burden of proof makes some sense when both parties to a dispute are States and can be presumed to be
able to sustain such a burden. By contrast, informational asymmetries abound in the investor-State context, where the complaining non-State party generally
lacks the resources and access to government documents that the respondent State is rightly presumed to
have. As between these two parties, it makes far more
sense to impose the burden of showing, for example,
that other government measures were reasonably available on the State that ought to have, consistent with its
treaty obligations, considered such alternatives. Investor-
State arbitration is available not only to large TNCs but
to individual investors and small companies, that is,
parties who face the highest risk of discriminatory or
other abusive conduct on the part of host States in
which they operate and which, like most foreign
investors, have no right to influence host State action
(as do local investors) through political participation [610].
As Kurtz suggests, these asymmetries

> "should inform our thinking on how to properly and
> fairly allocate both the burden of proof (the respon-
> sibility to adduce evidence before an adjudicator)
> and the requisite standard of proof (the type and
> quantum of evidence necessary to persuade an adju-
> dicator) on particular substantive questions . . ." [611].

The arbitrators in *Continental Casualty* do not
address this point or why jurisprudence produced in a

---

[609] Franck, *supra* footnote 601, p. 751-752.
[610] See, e.g., Kurtz, *supra* footnote 600, p. 758;
T. Wälde, "Introduction: International Investment Law
Emerging from the Dynamics of Direct Investor-State
Arbitration", in Kahn and Wälde (eds.), *supra* footnote 497,
p. 11.
[611] Kurtz, *supra* footnote 600, p. 758.

regime that makes no distinction between primary and secondary rules can be fruitfully extrapolated to one that, at least as those arbitrators believed, does make such a distinction.

The distinction between primary and secondary rules is most directly relevant to remedies. As noted, the individualized retrospective remedies anticipated in the world of BITs raise a number of issues that simply do not come up in the WTO context. When it comes to remedies, investor-State arbitrators are principally concerned with measuring the extent of the harm suffered by the investor as this will determine the measure and proportionality of damages. In doing so, those arbitrators need to address numerous temporal issues. As noted, they need to resolve whether past compensation is permanently and completely excused (as apparently found in *Continental Casualty*) or resumes once the crisis is resolved (as apparently found in *LG&E*), or is merely delayed while the crisis lasts (as might be suggested by Article 27 (1) *(a)* of the Articles of State Responsibility).

These remedial issues, which obviously divided some of the arbitrators hearing the Argentina claims, simply do not arise in the GATT regime. Since WTO remedies are prospective only and, in any case, are not measured by the harm to any private party, WTO dispute settlers are not concerned with measuring the damage caused to anyone in the past. The only question for these adjudicators is whether at the time a State seeks to get their authorization for trade retaliation there is a continuing breach of the GATT and whether any trade remedies that they ultimately authorize are likely to induce future compliance with GATT rules. These limited queries shape the way the "proportionality" of WTO remedies is addressed. As Franck indicates, the need to induce State compliance may lead WTO adjudicators to authorize a trade remedy that is not equivalent to the wrong likely to be inflicted on traders provided this remedy is deemed likely to make the offending State react by becoming GATT compliant. Unlike BIT remedies which aim to compensate, WTO-authorized-countermeasures need to "take into account the need to overcome evident reluctance of the wrongdoer to comply with its legal obligation" and may involve considerations that are, strictly speaking, extraneous in the context of a BIT, such as the prior record of the offending party in resisting GATT-illegal behaviour[612].

And given the fact that trade retaliation may be more akin to a punishing sanction, it is no surprise that it is rarely authorized. As many trade law scholars have suggested, trade retaliation is an understandably rare concession granted only in order to "discipline" a Government that refuses to remove an offending measure. Such remedies are, in the context of a regime otherwise devoted to trade liberalization, an admission of failure that runs counter to that regime's ethos. BITs are, on the contrary, "tools for obtaining compensation for loss"[613]. They are precisely designed to provide damages to injured investors and not, as such, to "discipline" or punish States. The arbitrators in *Continental Casualty* do not ask themselves whether these differences in the nature and desirability of remedies in the respective regimes might matter to any attempt to graft trade law onto the wholly different remedial context of BITs.

Continental Casualty's interpretation of Article XI of the United States-Argentina BIT as a "primary" rule excusing all treaty obligations ignores the possibility

---

[612] Franck, *supra* footnote 601, p. 747.
[613] M. Orellana, "Science, Risk and Uncertainty: Public Health Measures and Investment Disciplines", in Kahn and Wälde (eds.), *supra* footnote 497, p. 757.

that Article XI is, as this author has suggested elsewhere, a far more nuanced tool that distinguishes legal from illegal actions, lessens or delays an award of damages, or avoids the imposition of non-monetary remedies[614]. None of these are possibilities in the GATT regime. Moreover, that tribunal's decision that Article XI of the United States-Argentina BIT is, on the contrary, a blanket permission to violate that treaty ignores another salient difference between the trade and investment regimes. Whereas GATT balancing, including under GATT Article XX, necessarily involves weighing the interests of two States, investor-State arbitrators need to consider the primarily financial interests of a third party, namely the foreign investor, as well. *Continental Casualty* assumes, without explaining why this is appropriate, that the purely interstate balancing tests used in interpreting GATT Article XX ought to and can be extrapolated to weigh the very different concerns of a very different (non-State) investor.

Continental Casualty's decisions (1) that Article XI is distinct from the customary defence of necessity, (2) that it embodies a primary rule excusing all possible liability, and (3) that it needs to be interpreted along the differential standard suggested by the GATT's interpretation of "necessary" in its Article XX jurisprudence, turn Article XI from a rarely applicable provision of negligible significance into a doomsday trump card for host States[615]. Whatever might be said for the

---

[614] Alvarez and Khamsi, *supra* footnote 526, pp. 458-460.

[615] See, e.g., C. H. Brower, "Balancing the Rule of Law and National Interests", *Symposium on Preventing and Managing Conflict in Energy and Other Natural Resource Investment Relations : Columbia University School of Law* (13 May 2009) (suggesting that Article XI of the United States-Argentina BIT "functions like a doomsday button ;

merits of each of these three determinations individually, it cannot be denied that, in combination, they
render the United States-Argentina BIT a far less effective instrument of investment protection than it was
intended to be.

Of course, arguing that *Continental Casualty* was
wrong in turning to GATT law does not resolve how
Article XI ought to be interpreted assuming that it is
not functionally equivalent to the customary defence of
necessity. The difficulty that the *Continental Casualty*
arbitrators faced is clear: by its terms, Article XI does
not tell us what "necessary" means or which, of many
possible analogies with international law or national
law, might be helpful by presenting a meaningful comparison[616].

Continental Casualty provides a valuable lesson
about the risks of premature de-fragmentation: to the
extent analogies to other regimes are used by investor-

---

difficult to engage, but filled with the potential to unleash
terrible force"). Of course, under *Continental Casualty*'s
interpretation, this "doomsday button" is far easier to
engage but remains equally devastating in its effect, at
least to investors.

[616] The arbitrators in *Continental Casualty* do not
explain why, for example, the interpretation of derogation
clauses such as Article 4 (1) of the International Covenant
on Civil and Political Rights does not provide a more
relevant analogy for purposes of interpreting Article XI.
That provision states:

"In time of public emergency which threatens the
life of the nation and the existence of which is officially
proclaimed, the States Parties to the present Covenant
to the extent strictly required by the exigencies of the
situation, provided that such measures are not inconsistent with their other obligations under international law,
and do not involve discrimination solely on the grounds
of race, colour, sex, language, religion or social origin."
International Covenant on Civil and Political Rights,
999 *UNTS* 171, entered into force on 23 March 1976.

State arbitrators, these need to be attentive to context, including the precise object and purpose of treaties like the United States-Argentina BIT. Care should also be exercised lest the balancing tests used in other contexts (and sometimes alluded to in the course of investor-State arbitration) — whether the margin of appreciation as used by the European Court of Human Rights, the use of "proportionality" in a multitude of contexts, or the "least restrictive alternative" test deployed in the GATT — blur or elude the distinctions among these regimes[617].

Continental Casualty's implicit assumption that the general regulatory exceptions of Article XX are somehow comparable to those in Article XI of the United States-Argentina BIT may lead to other troublesome misunderstandings. As this author has argued elsewhere, Article XI's reference to "public order" was not intended as a general reference to the power all States have, as part of their inherent jurisdiction to prescribe law, to make all relevant laws, such as to protect the environment or the health of their inhabitants[618]. There is no general exceptions clause in the United States-Argentina BIT (or in most BITs), probably because their drafters saw no need to enumerate a specific list

---

[617] Compare Franck, *supra* footnote 601, p. 761 (noting that the "margin of appreciation" seems to shift the burden of proof away from the constraining authority to the complaining party regardless of the facts of the case while the principle of proportionality is, on the other hand, case and fact specific). Franck also notes that proportionality is used by the European Court of Human Rights in order to limit the "margin of appreciation" *(ibid.)*. See also Alvarez and Khamsi, *supra* footnote 526, pp. 440-449 (warning against the extrapolation of "margin of appreciation" analysis into the interpretation of Article XI of the United States-Argentina BIT).

[618] Alvarez and Khamsi, *supra* footnote 526, pp. 450-451.

of legitimate non-protectionist measures. Unlike the case of the trade regime, BITs do not have as their predominant purpose outlawing governmental measures with an impermissible protectionist intent. BIT drafters assumed that legitimate regulation, for whatever purpose, that did not violate FET or the other specific minimal guarantees of the BIT was not in violation of the BIT[619].

---

[619] With all due respect, Kurtz is wrong to suggest that the absence of general exceptions clause such as the GATT's Article XX in BITs means that no such exceptions apply in the context of BITs (except to the extent they can be embraced by a measures not precluded clause such as Article XI of the United States-Argentina BIT). Kurtz argues that BIT drafters sacrificed the right to regulate to the "immediate and dominant goal of investment protection". Kurtz, *supra* footnote 600, p. 755. This ignores the usual canon of interpretation, applied by the ICJ among others, that in the absence of explicit treaty provision, States ought not to be presumed to intend to deviate from a norm of fundamental importance such as their general residual right to engage in legitimate regulation. Such a residual right would appear to be embedded in such basic international legal principles as the right to non-interference with "domestic jurisdiction". BIT guarantees, such as the international minimum standard, presuppose States' continuing ability to exercise their general police powers. See, e.g., *Methanex Corporation* v. *United States*, Final Award, UNCITRAL Arbitration Rules (3 August 2005), IV (D), para. 7 ("as a matter of general international law, a non-discriminatory regulation for a public purpose, which is enacted in accordance with due process and, which affects, *inter alios*, a foreign investor or investment is not deemed expropriatory and compensable"). See also S. Schill, "Enabling Private Ordering — Function, Scope and Effect of Umbrella Clauses in International Investment Treaties", IILJ Working Paper, 2008/9, p. 59, available at <http://www.iilj.org/publications/documents/2008-9.Schill.pdf> (contending that umbrella clauses are directed at protecting investors from "opportunistic behaviour" and do not interfere with a host State's exercise of its usual police powers). As this suggests, the United States'

Accordingly, it would be wrong to attempt to pigeon-hole States' residual right to regulate into the three specific types of measures contained in Article XI — public order, essential security, or threats to the international peace. It would be difficult, for instance, to contend that legitimate labour regulations are part of a State's police powers to deal with civil disorders and therefore ought to be included in the "maintenance of public order". It would be equally untenable to contend that since, for example, post 2004 US investment treaties no longer refer to "public order", those newly rebalanced agreements now exclude host States' ability to regulate in the public interest. Nor should a State's general right to regulate, inherent to its right to self-determination, be conditioned on a determination of whether its actions are "necessary" — as would be the case if the right to regulate in BITs is put on the same plane as it is under GATT Article XX or is assumed to be protected by a "measures not precluded" clause such as Article XI of the United States-Argentina BIT[620].

---

effort to make this explicit with respect to expropriation was merely a clarification of existing law. See 2004 US Model BIT, US Department of State and US Trade Representative, US Model BIT 2004, Annex B, available at <http://www.state.gov/documents/organization/117601.pdf>. Such a clarification was probably desirable given the unique vagaries attached to the meaning of indirect takings. See, e.g., D. Schneiderman, *Constitutionalizing Economic Globalization: Investment Rules and Democracy's Promise* (Cambridge, Cambridge University Press, 2008), p. 80 (noting the *Pope & Talbot* tribunal's recognition that the line between takings and regulations is sometimes uncertain in US law).

[620] Compare Schneiderman, *supra* footnote 619. p. 91 (criticizing the separate opinion of Schwarz in *S.D. Myers*, *supra* footnote 596, precisely for relying on the GATT Article XX *(b)* test of necessity to justify environmental regulation under the NAFTA despite the traditional difficulty in satisfying this strict test).

Moreover, BITs that lack a general exceptions clause should not be interpreted as agreements to restrict the parties' right to regulate or to restrict this right to the enumerated purposes contained in a far more limited "measures not precluded" clause[621]. Such a colossal derogation from the general right to regulate must be express. Treaties that do not contain such an explicit derogation — such as the nine out of ten BITs that apparently do not include an explicit "measures not precluded" clause — should be interpreted to mean what their plain meaning suggests, namely that States can regulate for any and all purposes so long as their actions do not violate a substantive guarantee in the BIT[622]. Indeed, it is for this reason that BITs do not

---

[621] For a contrary view, see M. Sornarajah, "The Neo-Liberal Agenda in Investment", in Shan *et al.* (eds.), *Redefining Sovereignty in International Economic Law* (Portland, Hart Publishing, 2008), p. 203 (suggesting that BITs consciously sought to "destroy" host States' ability to prevent environmental pollution or to protect the interests of their citizens "so that the interests of property protection could trump all other interests").

[622] Note also the provision, now common to US BITs after 2004, stating that "except in rare circumstances, non-discriminatory regulatory actions by a Party that are designed and applied to protect legitimate public welfare objectives, such as public health, safety, and the environment, do not constitute indirect expropriations". This attempt to replicate existing US takings jurisprudence, clarifies what the United States, and most States, always intended based on existing international and national law. 2004 US Model BIT, *supra* footnote 619, Annex B. Notably, other BIT negotiators are taking notice and adopting the same clarification in their model BITs. Consider the protocol in the China-India BIT of 2006, which contains a very similar provision (cited in C. Congyan, *supra* footnote 507, p. 478, n. 120). It would, however, be perverse to suggest that the sovereign right to regulate in the public interest disappears where, as is true in the case of nine out of ten BITs, a "measures not precluded" clause

necessarily derogate from the long-standing rule, cited by sources as diverse as Brownlie and the arbitrators in *Saluka* v. *Czech Republic*, that States do not owe compensation for bona fide regulatory measures[623].

A more proper way to recognize States' right to engage in legitimate regulation is to do so in the course of applying and interpreting the substantive guarantees in the BIT, where the residual right to regulate can be properly balanced and weighed, as might be necessary when a violation of FET or a claim of indirect taking is asserted[624]. Some regulations may not be confiscatory,

---

like Article XI of the United States-Argentina BIT does not exist in an investment treaty. Such a silent derogation from such an important right should not be presumed. Yet this perverse outcome seems dictated by decisions that equate that clause providing for the right to regulate — as *Continental Casualty* implicitly does.

[623] See, e.g., U. Kriebaum, "Privatizing Human Rights", in A. Reinisch and U. Kriebaum (eds.), *The Law of International Relations: Liber Amicorum Hanspeter Neuhold* (Utrecht, Eleven International Publishing, 2007), pp. 178-179, 182 (quoting Brownlie and the *Saluka* decisions). This would be the result if such bona fide regulations do not violate the substantive provisions of BITs, irrespective of the view one takes of whether compensation remains due under Article XI of the United States-Argentina BIT. It would also mean that the States' ability to engage in such regulation would remain unaffected, even if the BIT does not include an explicit essential security clause (as is the case with the United Kingdom-Argentina BIT).

[624] The right of States to engage in legitimate regulation also seems implicit in the concept of legitimate expectations, now frequently deployed by investor-State arbitrators in the course of applying the FET guarantee. What makes such expectations "legitimate" may be, among other things, bona fide regulatory needs. As McLachlan points out, the idea of legitimate expectations "supports the application of host State law, and the liberty of the host State to determine the content of that law", C. McLachlan, "Investment Treaties and General International Law", in A. K. Bjorklund *et al.* (eds.), *Investment Treaty Law:*

but may be unfair and inequitable. Some measures may not violate any relevant rights of investors precisely because the underlying measures should have been anticipated by them — as they would be if these were bona fide regulatory measures[625]. This has everything to do with the interpretation of the substantive rights in these BITs and, in most instances, probably nothing to do with a measures not precluded clause limited to "essential security" and the "maintenance of public order". The general right to regulate should not be a sword of Damocles that threatens to come down as a primary rule excusing all of a State's wrongful actions, as it would be if one treated it the way *Continental Casualty* treats Article XI.

Consider *National Grid*'s altogether different approach to Argentina's economic/political crisis. In *National Grid*, a foreign investor engaged in electricity transmission presented similar claims to those made in the gas sector cases (*CMS, LG&E, Enron* and *Sempra*). The investor claimed that Argentina's Public Emergency and Exchange Rate Reform Law of 6 January 2002 — which abolished the currency board previously established, terminated the right to calculate public utility tariffs in dollars and the right to adjust these on

---

Current Issues III (London, British Institute of International and Comparative Law, 2009), p. 122.

[625] As a former US BIT negotiator and strong advocate of investor protections, Daniel Price has noted, in connection with both the international minimum standard as well as the guarantee of compensation for regulatory takings, general non-discriminatory measures are not threatened by these provisions. D. Price, "NAFTA Chapter 11 Investor-State Dispute Settlement: Frankenstein or Safety Valve?", 26 *Canada US Law Journal* 107 (2001), Supplement p. 4. ("if a government measure is a generally applicable, bona fide and legitimate exercise of regulatory authority (and there is no indication that the measure is discriminatory or has an illicit purpose), the measure will be upheld").

the basis of international price indices, and converted public service tariffs into Argentine pesos — violated the pre-existing undertakings and assurances that National Grid had received when it invested in the country[626]. This case involved, as noted, the United Kingdom-Argentina BIT, which does not contain an "essential security" or "public order" clause, and therefore the customary defence of necessity was assumed to apply. The tribunal found (predictably) that Argentina could not invoke the defence of necessity since it had substantially contributed to the underlying crisis triggering its invocation[627]. This did not mean, however, that the tribunal otherwise ignored Argentina's crisis in interpreting the United Kingdom-Argentina BIT.

National Grid concluded that Argentina had breached the FET standard because it had "fundamentally changed the legal framework" which it used to solicit the underlying investment and on which the claimant had relied, because no "meaningful negotiations" took place in the two years between Argentina's adoption of its measures and the sale of the claimant's shares, and because Argentina had required the renunciation of the investors' anticipated legal remedies[628]. At the same time, however, that tribunal concluded that Argentina's breach "must be qualified in time"[629]. The *National Grid* award narrowed the extent of Argentina's liability given the context in which the measures were taken. As the tribunal stated:

> "The determination of the Tribunal must take into account all the circumstances and in so doing cannot be oblivious to the crisis that the Argentina

---

[626] *National Grid*, *supra* footnote 503, paras. 63-64.
[627] *Ibid.*, para. 260.
[628] *Ibid.*, para. 179.
[629] *Ibid.*, para. 180.

Republic endured at that time. What is fair and equitable is not an absolute parameter. What would be unfair and inequitable in normal circumstances may not be so in a situation of an economic and social crisis. The investor may not be totally insulated from situations such as the ones the Argentine Republic underwent in December 2001 and the months that followed. For these reasons, the Tribunal concludes that the breach of the fair and equitable treatment standard did not occur at the time the Measures were taken on 6 January 2002 but on 25 June 2002 when the Respondent required that companies such as the Claimant renounce . . . the legal remedies they may have recourse as a condition to re-negotiate the Concession."[630]

That tribunal also concluded that 25 June 2002 was the relevant date when Argentina breached its undertaking to accord the investors "constant protection and security" under the United Kingdom-Argentina BIT[631]. Since 25 June 2002 was established as the date for evaluating the value of the claimant's shares, this finding decreased the extent of the claimant's subsequent damages.

National Grid might be criticized insofar as the award fails to explain exactly why or how the existence of Argentina's crisis affected the analysis of the substantive guarantees of the relevant BIT. There are several ways one can attempt to explain the arbitrators' conclusion. The easiest but least satisfactory is simply to suggest that FET and "constant protection and security" are case-specific standards or rules of equitable treatment and that Argentina's actions on 25 June 2002 mysteriously crossed an undefined line into "unfair-

---

[630] *National Grid*, *supra* footnote 503, para. 180.
[631] *Ibid.*, para. 190.

ness". As we noted in the last chapter, this analysis plays into criticisms of the FET standard as rudderless and unpredictable.

There might be a different rationale based on the underlying legitimate expectations principle which, as we have noted, is often used to explain the FET and was relied upon in *National Grid* itself. As the arbitrators suggested in this case, the protection of the investors' legitimate expectations under the FET standard is limited in two respects: the investor cannot be shielded from the ordinary business risk of the investment and the legitimacy of the investors' expectations depends on the particular context in which the investment is made[632]. It might be argued that given the history of Argentina and economic conditions prevailing there at the time the investment was made, passage of an emergency law such as the one passed on 6 January 2002 was within the anticipated "business risk" that investors ought to have considered or that this possibility was within the investors' reasonable expectations. One could argue that investors assumed the risk that Argentina would pass emergency legislation of this kind and therefore did not have a legitimate expectation that all the assurances they had been provided with under pre-existing Argentine law would not be subject to occasional interruption or interference. On this view, investors should have reasonably anticipated that even though they had been given assurances of good faith tariff negotiations should circumstances change, the initiation of negotiations might be subject to some reasonable delay — particularly should Argentina suffer from one of its periodic (and predictable) economic crises. On this view, it was not until Argentina definitively renounced any effort to engage in those bargained for negotiations — and not when it initially

---

[632] *National Grid*, *supra* footnote 503, para. 175.

passed its emergency law — that the investor's legitimate expectations were breached. At this point,
Argentina's behaviour became unfair and inequitable
and also clearly in violation of its obligation to provide
constant protection and security. But while this explanation may provide a rationale for the conclusion
reached in *National Grid* it does come close to suggesting that investors cannot take the word of a State at
face value but must always discount promises made in
the present because of the fragility of the State's
former promises. States attempting to turn a new leaf
against the bad practices of the past and that use BITs
to make credible commitments might find this rationale troubling.

Another explanation for the conclusion in *National
Grid* might be that under the relevant substantive rights
in the BIT, such as FET, Argentina continued to enjoy
an implicit right to take proportionate action directly
responsive to the underlying economic crisis. It might
be argued that Argentina's actions did not become "disproportionate" (and therefore a violation of FET) until
it renounced the investors' legal remedies in 25 June
2002. Yet another way of reaching the same result
might be to consider that under the relevant substantive
guarantees Argentina needed to demonstrate a clear
nexus between the actions that it took and the underlying crisis that it faced and its decision to walk away
from all negotiations with the claimants lacked that
clear nexus.

All of these rationales involve a kind of balancing
reminiscent of that deployed in *Continental Casualty*
but without the need to rely on far-fetched, implausible
connections to the law under GATT Article XX.

Notably even the much criticized original awards
in *CMS*, *Enron* and *Sempra* turned to some of these
rationales. In all of those cases the arbitrators were
prepared to accept the premise that Argentina needed

to take measures in order to respond to the crisis but, as in *National Grid*, all ultimately concluded that Argentina had failed to adhere to the contractual adjustment mechanisms to which it had specially agreed and had instead acted unilaterally and in defiance of its prior commitments. The original *CMS* tribunal canvassed at length the "pertinent mechanisms" for addressing the crisis in the licence and under Argentine law, concluding that, as the "necessary adjustments could be accommodated within the structure of the guarantees" made to CMS, unilateral action by Argentina was "unnecessary"[633]. The original *Enron* tribunal acknowledged that the dramatic change to economic conditions that occurred in Argentina could have "a profound effect on the economic balance of contracts and licenses"[634], accepted that adjustment might be appropriate as a consequence[635], but noted that "the real problem underlying the claims" was that Argentina had acted unilaterally[636]. It found that under the regulatory framework "if tariffs ceased to be fair and reasonable, the regulatory framework provided for specific adjustment mechanisms, tariff reviews on periodic basis and even the possibility of an extraordinary review"[637]. The original *Sempra* tribunal even appears to have been prepared, if the implementation of the contractual review mechanism had taken some time, to accept that the Government might have taken unilateral measures "pursuant to a limited time schedule while reviews were carried out"[638]. Those tribunals also con-

---

[633] See *CMS*, *supra* footnote 492, at paras. 228-238.

[634] See *Enron*, *supra* footnote 516, para. 143.

[635] *Ibid.*, para. 104.

[636] *Ibid.*, para. 144.

[637] *Ibid.*, para. 143. See also *CMS*, *supra* footnote 492, paras. 228-238; *Sempra*, *supra* footnote 516, paras. 259-260.

[638] *Sempra*, *supra* footnote 516, para. 261.

sidered the implications of Argentina's crisis when it came time to assess the investors' damages[639]. Indeed, an alternative to the approach taken in *National Grid* would be to incorporate the Argentine crisis into the "equitable circumstances" that many believe are already in play in any assessment of remedies in investor-State arbitration[640].

Unlike *Continental Casualty*, all the Argentina cases studied in this chapter recognized that alternatives to permitting total derogation from a BIT exist. Notably these alternatives result in a closer alignment among the BIT's substantive rights, its object and purpose, and the goals of achieving a fair and politically acceptable result[641]. Unlike the blunderbuss approach followed in *Continental Casualty*, which rendered all BIT rights futile, these alternatives permit arbitrators to consider both the needs of a host State in crisis *and* the rights of investors as spelled out in BITs. Whether or not one agrees with the amounts awarded in these cases, the legal conclusions reached in all except *Continental Casualty* were more in line with what the States parties originally intended when they entered into the BITs at issue and with the expectations generated in the business community by these agreements.

A larger lesson suggested by the Argentina cases discussed here is that balancing investor/host State rights in the course of applying the substantive provisions of a BIT or awarding damages is not unusual and well within the expected rules of treaty interpretation. Balancing in the course of applying substantive BIT

---

[639] See Alvarez and Khamsi, *supra* footnote 526, p. 406.

[640] See, e.g., T. W. Wälde, *supra* footnote 610, pp. 64-68 (enumerating "compensation-reducing" elements that arbitrators have applied, including the controversial proposition that arbitrators should consider the State's capacity to pay).

[641] See, e.g., Brower, *supra* footnote 615, p. 2.

guarantees (e.g. the FET obligation or the umbrella clause) and in determining damages is increasingly evident in investor-State arbitrations[642], is not directly connected to the defence of necessity as either a primary or secondary rule, and is, as a result of its subtlety, less likely to result in unjust enrichment[643]. The risk that a host State may be unjustly enriched clearly emerges in the contrary approach followed in *Continental Casualty* — which by its terms eschews any explicit consideration of the legitimate expectations of the investor vis-à-vis the host State. Under *Continental*

---

[642] See, e.g., McLachlan, *supra* footnote 624, p. 121 (identifying investor-State cases where the arbitrators have used balancing to uphold the legitimate public interests of the host State to preserve regulatory flexibility, to deny claims not based on rights in national or international law, to uphold administrative decisions that have an objective basis, and to uphold those that do not have a disproportionate impact on foreign investors); M. Endicott, "Remedies in Investor-State Arbitration: Restitution, Specific Performance and Declaratory Awards", in Kahn and Wälde, *supra* footnote 497, pp. 547-548 (identifying proportionality as the "key principle" in determining the appropriateness of remedies).

[643] Ironically, even the European Court of Human Rights, which gives effect to a far more constrained right to property than that recognized by most BITs, has found that even in cases involving a public emergency or regulations undertaken in the course of fragile economic circumstances, a State cannot totally deny compensation or engage in confiscation and thereby force one particular individual or group to shoulder a disproportionate share of the burden prompted by such a government crisis. C. Tomuschat, "The European Court of Human Rights and Investment Protection", in C. Binder *et al.*, *International Investment Law for the 21st Century : Essays in Honor of Christoph Schreuer* (New York, Oxford University Press, 2009), p. 653 (discussing *Driza* v. *Albania*). Such confiscation would be totally permissible, on the contrary, under *Continental Casualty*'s view of the consequences of successful invocation of Article XI.

Casualty's interpretation of Article XI, successful invocation of that provision serves to entirely remove any
possibility of State liability, even when the State is
openly breaching through its action specific guarantees that it previously entered into, in a contract or
otherwise, and even if the underlying crisis used to
justify its breaches was entirely due to the State's own
actions [644].

It is important, however, to be clear that the criticisms of *Continental Casualty* made here are not
intended to suggest that the result reached in that case
is necessarily wrong. As is suggested in Chapter III,
one of the most striking principles that defines the
international investment regime across diverse BITs
and irrespective of whether such treaties include an
express umbrella clause is derived from the principle
of *pacta sunt servanda*: namely that a State's prior
binding written commitment to the investor, whether
made by contract, licence, or other document sanctioned by its law, ought to be respected [645]. This prin-

---

[644] Notice that this would mean that the United States-
Argentina BIT, *supra* footnote 520, once considered
among the strongest instruments for investor protection
ever concluded, would provide a State with an excuse
from *pacta sunt servanda* not otherwise found in customary international law. See generally J. W. Yackee, "*Pacta
Sunt Servanda* and State Promises to Foreign Investors
before Bilateral Investment Treaties: Myth and Reality",
32 *Fordham International Law Journal* 1550 (2008) (discussing a number of arbitral decisions affirming the
enforcement of investor-State contracts.).

[645] Indeed, even the New Zealand-China Free Trade
Agreement of 2008, which, following the 2004 US Model,
carefully narrowed the scope of indirect takings, goes out
of its way to state that

"[a] deprivation of property shall be particularly likely
to constitute indirect expropriation where it is either:
(a) discriminatory in its effect, either as against the particular investor or against a class of which the investor

ciple is essential to understanding the results reached under FET guarantees in a number of treaties. It certainly explains the original awards rendered in the public utility cases against Argentina, all of which appeared to involve, as these tribunals determined, breaches of distinct promises made to the investors. It is not clear that the investor in *Continental Casualty*, by contrast, which apparently had *not* been given specific prior assurances by Argentina had, unlike the public utility claimants, a legitimate expectation that Argentina's capital control regime would have remained unchanged. The analysis of these questions was short-changed due to the tribunal's reliance on Argentina's defence of necessity [646].

Nor are comparisons to trade law always wrong in the context of investor-State arbitration. There may be investment treaties for which such analogies are appropriate and indeed this may even be true of other portions of the United States-Argentina BIT, such as its

---

forms a part; or *(b)* in breach of the state's prior binding written commitment to the investor, whether by contract, license, or other legal document". See Free Trade Agreement between the Government of New Zealand and the People's Republic of China, signed on 7 April 2008, entered into force on 1 October 2008, available at <http://www.chinafta.govt.nz/1-The-agreement/2-Text-of-the-agreement/0-downloads/NZ-China FTA-Agreement-text.pdf>, Annex 13, para. 4.

[646] As Stephen Schill has argued, determining whether a host State's legislative commitments constitute the equivalent of a specific promise made to an investor in a contract requires a fact-specific enquiry. Determining whether such a breach constitutes a violation of BIT turns not only on the specific guarantees provided in the BIT at issue but may also turn on whether, for example, the legislative commitment made was given as an inducement to get an investor to invest and was specifically relied upon by the investor. S. Schill, *supra* footnote 619, p. 72.

provisions on national treatment or MFN[647]. Scholars and arbitrators are still working through the complex trade jurisprudence on national treatment to see if, for example, the interpretations given to "like product" in GATT law can be applied in whole or in part to determining the meaning of "in like situations" for purposes of a clause like the NT provision in the United States-Argentina BIT[648]. Moreover, *Continental Casualty*'s efforts to draw from the GATT's Article XX would probably have been appropriate if the treaty at issue had included a "general exceptions" clause like the one that now appears in the most recent Canadian Model BIT or in the investment chapter of the Comprehensive Economic Co-operation Agreement between India and Singapore[649]. And if there should ever be trade

---

[647] See generally Kurtz, *supra* footnote 600.

[648] *Ibid*., p. 755.

[649] Comprehensive Economic Cooperation Agreement between the Republic of India and the Republic of Singapore, signed on 29 June 2005, entered into force on 1 August 2005, Article 6.11; Foreign Affairs and International Trade Canada, "Foreign Investment Promotion and Protection Agreement Model" (2003) (hereinafter "Canada Model BIT"), Article 10, available at <http://ita.law.uvic.ca/documents/Canadian2004-FIPA-model-en.pdf>. Article 10 provides in relevant part:

"1. Subject to the requirement that such measures are not applied in a manner that would constitute arbitrary or unjustifiable discrimination between investments or between investors, or a disguised restriction on international trade or investment, nothing in this Agreement shall be construed to prevent a Party from adopting or enforcing measures necessary:

(a) to protect human, animal or plant life or health;
(b) to ensure compliance with laws and regulations that are not inconsistent with the provisions of this Agreement; or
(c) for the conservation of living or non-living exhaustible natural resources."

jurisprudence interpreting the GATT's self-judging essential security in Article XXI, that case law might well come into play with respect to some recent BITs and FTAs, including with the United States, containing comparably explicit self-judging essential security clauses[650].

Note, however, that Canada has made its new general exceptions clause considerably more investor-pro-

---

[650] See, e.g., United States-Peru Trade Promotion Agreement, *supra* footnote 567, Article 22.2, n. 2 (requiring a tribunal to apply the essential security exception to find a claim inadmissible if that exception is invoked by a party). Recent Japanese treaties contain the "which it considers" language with respect to essential security. See, e.g., Agreement between Japan and the Lao People's Democratic Republic for the Liberation, Promotion, and Protection of Investment, signed on 16 January 2008, entered into force on 3 August 2008, Article 18; Agreement between Japan and the Republic of Uzbekistan for the Liberalization, Promotion and Protection of Investment, signed on 15 August 2008, Article 17 (1) *(d)*; Agreement between Japan and the Republic of Peru for the Liberation, Promotion, and Protection of Investment, signed on 21 November 2008, entered into force on 10 December 2009, Article 19 (1) *(d)*. The prospect that such clauses could eviscerate all BIT protections is suggested by *Funnekotter* where Zimbabwe attempted to defend Dutch landowners' claims based on an "emergency" or "necessity" that had not even been declared under its national law. See *Funnekotter*, *supra* footnote 521, paras. 103-107. On the other hand, according to a minority view expressed by some judges on the ICJ, such self-judging reservations within a treaty should be found devoid of all legal validity, see, e.g., *Certain Norwegian Loans (France* v. *Norway)*, Dissenting Opinion of Judge Guerro, *ICJ Reports 1957* 69; *Interhandel (Switzerland* v. *United States)*, Dissenting Opinion of Sir Hersch Lauterpacht, *ICJ Reports 1959*, pp. 101-102. But see *Certain Norwegian Loans (France* v. *Norway)*, Judgment, *ICJ Reports 1957*, p. 27 (giving effect to such a reservation since both parties had accepted it and where the parties had continued to rely upon it).

tective than *Continental Casualty*'s interpretation of
Article XI of the United States-Argentina BIT permits.
Canada has included a chapeau clause comparable to
that in the original GATT Article XX in order to screen
out arbitrary or discriminatory government actions
which cannot be justified [651]. Canada has also limited
its list of legitimate regulatory measures to those it
identifies at *(a)-(c)* in Article 10 of its Model BIT and
has not made invocation of any of these general exceptions self-judging [652]. (There is no "which it considers"
language — unlike its model treaty's Article 10 (4)
(dealing with security issues), which contains such language [653].) In a case dealing with this new general
exceptions clause (absent in most BITs), GATT law on
the interpretation of Article XX might indeed be relevant, but even in such a case, interpreters of this new
clause would still need to consider the potential significance of the difference in remedies and purpose of
the trade versus investment regimes. Of course, in *Continental Casualty*'s analysis, the strikingly different
Article XI of the United States-Argentina BIT was
treated as if its text looked like Article 10 of the latest
Canadian Model BIT.

The larger point is simple enough. Investor-State
arbitrators have to interpret the particular treaty before

---

[651] See text of Article 10, Canada Model BIT, *supra*
footnote 649.

[652] *Ibid*.

[653] Article 10 (4) of the Canadian Model BIT *(ibid.)*
provides in relevant part that:

"Nothing in this Agreement shall be construed:
(a) to require any Party to furnish or allow access to
any information the disclosure of which it determines to
be contrary to its essential security interests; *(b)* to prevent any Party from taking any actions that it considers
necessary for the protection of its essential security
interests . . ."

them, given its plain meaning, its object and purpose, its context, and, if needed, its negotiating history. The accepted rules of interpretation anticipate using "other relevant rules of international law" but do not define or delimit the meaning of "relevant". This residual rule of interpretation assists in the creation of harmonious public international law but not at the expense of ignoring the other, more primary rules of interpretation; that is, not at the expense of a treaty's plain meaning in light of its context and object and purpose. The text and intent of the particular treaty matters — and may lead to divergent results.

The next chapter places the Argentina cases discussed here — and the international investment regime itself — in a wider context.

CHAPTER V

THE ONCE AND FUTURE INVESTMENT
REGIME

A. *The Investment Regime in Transition*

In May 2009, a subcommittee of the US Congress
held hearings to consider changes to the future BIT
programme of the United States. The notice for that
meeting indicated what some US politicians had in
mind. Members of Congress were, at that time, solicit-
ing views on whether US BITs should henceforth allow
for more "policy space" for Governments vis-à-vis foreign investors and whether such treaties should provide
"no greater rights" than that provided to US investors;
the last even contemplated the possibility that foreign
investors should only have recourse to national courts,
like national investors, and no longer have treaty-based
access to investor-State arbitration[654]. One year later,
37 academics from around the world, nearly all professors of law, issued a "public statement" — reminiscent
of a resolution issued by an international organization
— that essentially called for an end to the investment
regime. That statement, which originated from discussions at Osgoode Hall Law School in Canada, and was
signed by eminent authorities, including Martti
Koskenniemi, evinced a "a shared concern for the
harm done to the public welfare by the international

---

[654] See US House of Representatives, Committee on
Ways and Means, Subcommittee on Trade, "Hearing on
Investment Protections in US Trade and Investment Agree-
ments", Serial No. 111-20 (14 May 2009) (hereinafter
"Investment Protections Hearing"), pp. 2 and 34.

investment regime" and, in particular, its "hampering of the ability of governments to act for their people in response to the concerns of human development and environmental sustainability"[655]. The Osgoode Hall

---

[655] See "Public Statement on the International Investment Regime" (31 August 2010), available at <http://www.osgoode.yorku.ca/public_statement/> (hereinafter "Osgoode Hall Statement"). The full text of this extraordinary statement is worth citing in full:

"We have a shared concern for the harm done to the public welfare by the international investment regime, as currently structured, especially its hampering of the ability of governments to act for their people in response to the concerns of human development and environmental sustainability.

WE AGREE THAT:

General principles

1. The protection of investors, and by extension the use of investment law and arbitration, is a means to the end of advancing the public welfare and must not be treated as an end in itself.

2. All investors, regardless of nationality, should have access to an open and independent judicial system for the resolution of disputes, including disputes with government.

3. Foreign investment may have harmful as well as beneficial impacts on society and it is the responsibility of any government to encourage the beneficial while limiting the harmful.

4. States have a fundamental right to regulate on behalf of the public welfare and this right must not be subordinated to the interests of investors where the right to regulate is exercised in good faith and for a legitimate purpose.

Pro-investor interpretations of investment treaties

5. Awards issued by international arbitrators against states have in numerous cases incorporated overly expansive interpretations of language in investment treaties. These interpretations have prioritized the protection of the property and economic interests of trans-

Statement contended that investor-State arbitral awards
created an "overly expansive interpretation" of treaty

national corporations over the right to regulate of states
and the right to self-determination of peoples. This is especially evident in the approach adopted by many arbitration tribunals to investment treaty concepts of corporate
nationality, expropriation, most-favoured-nation treatment, non-discrimination, and fair and equitable treatment, all of which have been given unduly pro-investor
interpretations at the expense of states, their governments,
and those on whose behalf they act. This has constituted
a major reorientation of the balance between investor
protection and public regulation in international law.

6. The award of damages as a remedy of first resort
in investment arbitration poses a serious threat to
democratic choice and the capacity of governments to
act in the public interest by way of innovative policy-
making in response to changing social, economic, and
environmental conditions.

Legal framework and dispute resolution

7. The primary legal framework for the regulation
of investor-State relations is domestic law.

8. Investment treaty arbitration as currently constituted is not a fair, independent, and balanced method
for the resolution of investment disputes and therefore
should not be relied on for this purpose. There is a
strong moral as well as policy case for governments to
withdraw from investment treaties and to oppose
investor-State arbitration, including by refusal to pay
arbitration awards against them where an award for
compensation has followed from a good faith measure
that was introduced for a legitimate purpose.

9. Private citizens, local communities and civil
society organizations should be afforded a right to participate in decision-making that affects their rights
and interests, including in the context of investor-State
dispute settlement or contract renegotiation. The international investment regime, by not allowing for full
and equal participation of such parties alongside
the investor where their interests are affected, fails to
satisfy this basic requirement of procedural fairness.

10. Although not without flaws, investment con-

rights accorded investors and "prioritized the protection of the property and economic interests of transna-

----

tracts are preferable to investment treaties as a legal
mechanism to supplement domestic law in the regulation of investor-State relations because they allow
for greater care to be taken and greater certainty to
be achieved in the framing of the parties' legal rights
and obligations. This is only so, however, if the investment contract precludes resort by either the investor
or the state to an investment treaty claim so as to
permit it to avoid its contractual commitments, including commitments on dispute settlement and choice of
law.

11. Investment contracts should be concluded and
implemented in accordance with the principles of public accountability and openness and should preserve the
state's right to regulate in good faith and for a legitimate purpose.

12. Investment contracts should provide a mechanism for managed renegotiation by the investor and
state, based on a fair and balanced process in which
adequate support and resourcing is available to both
parties, so as to accommodate significant changes in the
circumstances of the underlying agreement.

13. Proposals to conclude a multilateral investment
agreement or to restate international investment law
based on recent arbitration awards are misguided
because they risk entrenching and legitimizing an
international investment regime that lacks fairness and
balance, including basic requirements of openness
and judicial independence.

WE THEREFORE RECOMMEND THAT:

14. States should review their investment treaties
with a view to withdrawing from or renegotiating them
in light of the concerns expressed above; should take
steps to replace or curtail the use of investment treaty
arbitration; and should strengthen their domestic justice
system for the benefit of all citizens and communities,
including investors.

15. International organizations should refrain from
promoting investment treaties and should conduct
research and make recommendations on the serious

tional corporations over the right to regulate of states
and the right to self-determination of peoples"[656]. It
also asserted that these "pro-investor" interpretations
had occurred at the expense of States, Governments,
and "those on whose behalf they act", and that awarding damages "as a remedy of first resort . . . poses a
serious threat to democratic choice and the capacity of
governments to act in the public interest . . ."[657]. It also
asserted that investment treaty arbitration "is not a fair,
independent, and balanced method for the resolution of
investment disputes" and there is

> "a strong moral as well as policy case for govern-
> ments to withdraw from investment treaties and to
> oppose investor-State arbitration, including by
> refus[ing] to pay arbitration awards against them

> risks posed to governments by investment treaty arbi-
> tration; on preferred alternatives to investment treaty
> arbitration including private risk insurance and con-
> tract-based arbitration; and on strategies for states to
> pursue withdrawal from or renegotiation of their invest-
> ment treaties.
> 16. The international business community should
> refrain from promoting the international investment
> regime and from resorting to investment treaty arbitra-
> tion. Instead, it should promote fair and balanced adju-
> dicative processes that satisfy the requirements of open-
> ness and judicial independence in accordance with the
> principles of procedural fairness and the rule of law.
> The international business community should also seek
> to resolve disputes in a co-operative spirit with recourse
> to adjudication only as a last resort.
> 17. Civil society should continue to take steps to
> inform its constituents and society at large of the fail-
> ures of and threats posed by the international invest-
> ment regime and to oppose the application of that
> regime to governments that undertake legislative or
> general policy measures for legitimate purposes."

[656] Osgoode Hall Statement, *supra* footnote 655.
[657] *Ibid.*

where an award for compensation has followed from a good faith measure that was introduced for a legitimate purpose"[658].

This last, an apparent call (by international law professors no less) for States to openly defy their treaty obligations to abide by investor-State awards, apparently on a self-judging basis and as an act of civil disobedience, suggests the vitriolic opposition generated in some quarters by the investment regime.

These two events encapsulate the harsh cross-currents now buffeting the investment regime. Developments at the highest levels of the United States suggest how far that Government has come from the days when it was the foremost defender of investor rights and the drafter of what is described in Chapter I as the most investor-protective treaty in the world. Given the revisions to the US BIT over the course of the 1984-2004 period which, as noted, have narrowed investors' protections and generally expanded the scope of host States' discretion[659], it is striking that at least some

---

[658] Osgoode Hall Statement, *supra* footnote 655.

[659] See C. Lévesque, "Influences on the Canadian FIPA Model and the US Model BIT: NAFTA Chapter 11 and Beyond", 44 *Annuaire canadien de droit international* 249 (2006), p. 249; G. Gagné and J. Morin, "The Evolving American Policy on Investment Protection: Evidence from Recent FTAs and the 2004 Model BIT", 9 *Journal of International Economic Law* 357 (2006), p. 358; United Nations Conference on Trade and Development ("UNCTAD"), "De-Mystifying the 2004 United States Model BIT", Draft (25 February 2008). See also W. Burke-White and A. Von Staden, "Investment Protection in Extraordinary Times: A Reply to Professor Franck", *Opinio Juris* (30 January 2008), available at <http://opiniojuris.org/2008/01/30/investment-protection-in-extraordinary-times-a-reply-to-professor-franck/> (describing BITs, particularly the US BIT, as a balance between investment protections and State freedom of action); J. E. Alvarez, "The

members of Congress continue to believe that even more sovereign-protective changes are needed. As one former US BIT negotiator pointed out in reaction, the demand by some members of the US Congress that foreign investors get "no greater rights" than domestic entrepreneurs appears to ask the United States to renounce its heretofore success-ful battle against the Calvo Clause[660]. A model BIT that does not contain absolute rights on behalf of investors, that is, rights that are not reducible to whatever is contained from time to time in national law, or that merely anticipates enforcement in national courts contradicts the raison d'être of such treaties. The whole premise of the investment regime had been, after all, that host States' national laws and national courts were insufficient protections and that both international guarantees and neutral third-party arbitrators were needed to protect those who had put at risk millions of dollars in sunk costs.

The Osgoode Hall Statement is also a striking departure from the not-so-distant past when comparable academics based in the West had strongly defended resort to international arbitration against attacks by supporters of the "New International Economic Order". Few would have predicted that within 20 years of the fall of the Berlin Wall and the ostensible "victory" of the capitalist West, a group of prominent academics based in rich capital exporting countries would call for the dismantling of a system to protect the interests of capital that had been used since at least the days of the

---

Evolving Foreign Investment Regime", *American Society of International Law : IL.post* (29 February 2008), available at <http://www.asil.org/ilpost/president/pres080229. html> (discussing trends and prospects of investment and the shifting attitudes of several States).

[660] See D. M. Price, "Keep International Protections", *Washington Times* (14 May 2009), p. A17.

Jay Treaty concluded in the administration of George Washington[661].

And much has happened beyond these two events to suggest the global backlash in the wake of the relatively recent proliferation of investment treaties and investor-State arbitral decisions[662]. While at this reading we do not yet know where the United States' review of its BIT programme will lead, it is clear, as discussed in Chapter II, that many of the changes to the early US Model BIT are being emulated by other countries. Other changes in relevant US law and practice, not addressed in the US Model BIT, are also being exported. The world has become aware that the United States has decided, due to post 9/11 security concerns, for example, to strengthen its governmental mechanisms to screen in-coming foreign investment that may threaten its "essential security" interests and that the number of foreign companies being screened for this purpose has increased[663]. Other countries are now adopting comparable screening mechanisms to protect their own — usually undefined — "national" or "essential

---

[661] See generally B. Legum, "The Innovation of Investor-State Arbitration under NAFTA", 43 *Harvard International Law Journal* 531 (2002).

[662] For discussion of the post-Cold War expansion of investment treaties and the reasons for it, see *supra* Chap. I. Evidence of the recent rise in investor-State disputes and arbitral decisions is suggested by the latest statistics on arbitral cases released by ICSID. ISCID, the most used forum for resolving investor-State disputes, has seen the registration of cases go from an average of 1-4 a year from 1972-1996 to over 20 a year from 2003-2009. See *The ICSID Caseload — Statistics*, Issue No. 2010-2, p. 7. According to ISCID, from 2005 to 2010, it has registered 147 cases (of the total of 319 registered since 1972). *Ibid.*

[663] See, e.g., M. E. Plotkin and D. N. Fagan, "The Revised National Security Review Process for FDI in the US", *Columbia FDI Perspectives* No. 2 (2009), available at <http://www.vcc.columbia.edu/content/fdi-perspectives>.

security" interests, especially, though not only, when such foreign investors have a governmental connection — as is the case with State-owned enterprises and sovereign wealth funds[664].

Other forms of backlash against the regime include a decrease in the number of negotiations of new BITs and FTAs and an apparent increase in national laws that disfavour the rights of foreign investors in some respect[665]. Even clearer markers are Bolivia's May 2007 notice to ICSID that it was withdrawing from the ICSID Convention[666], Venezuela's threats to limit

---

[664] Sovereign wealth funds ("SWFs") are typically funds created or controlled by a Government that have been built up as a result of budgetary surpluses or excess foreign exchange reserves. States deploy them much as individuals make use of diversified portfolios of stock holdings; that is, to diversify their exposure to risk, maximize their income, and insulate their budgets and economies from volatility by investing in a broad range of assets in other countries. Among the world's largest SWFs are the Abu Dhabi Investment Authority and Corporation, the Government of Singapore Investment Corporation, (Norway's) Government Pension Fund (Global), and the Saudi Arabia Monetary Agency. Concerns over SWFs are comparable to those prompted by State-owned enterprises: namely that SWFs will invest for political and not economic reasons, that their investment objectives are not transparent, or that their acquisitions may pose national security risks for the host State. See generally United States Government Accountability Office, "Sovereign Wealth Funds: Laws Limiting Foreign Investment Affect Certain US Assets and Agencies Have Various Enforcement Processes", GAO-09-608 (2009), available at <http://www.gao.gov/new.items/d09608.pdf>.

[665] See, e.g., K. P. Sauvant, "Driving and Countervailing Force: A Rebalancing of National FDI Policies", in K. P. Sauvant (ed.), *Yearbook on International Investment Law & Policy 2008-2009* (New York, Oxford University Press, 2009).

[666] ICSID, "ICSID News Release: Bolivia Submits a Notice under Article 71 of the ICSID Convention"

ICSID jurisdiction, Ecuador's recent denunciation of nine of its own BITs and its legislature's vote, on 12 June 2009, to withdraw from the ICSID Convention[667]. Many expect an even greater political backlash against the investment regime should Governments' responses to the global economic crisis — such as United States' emergency legislation granting government assistance to beleaguered industries such as national automakers or national banks but generally excluding foreign investors — come under challenge through BITs, FTAs or even old-fashioned FCNs[668].

Explanations for the investment regime's current predicament abound. Underlying some of the discontent with the regime are growing doubts about its underlying premise that free capital flows raise all boats. While few Governments or academics openly dispute David Ricardo's theory of comparative advantage, there are disparate views, including within developed States of the West and among some economists, about the relative merits of incoming and outgoing

---

(16 May 2007), available at <http://ics*ibid*.worldbank.org/ICSID/StaticFiles/Announcement3.html>.

[667] J. L. Gardiner *et al.*, "Ecuador Moves to Denounce and Leave the ICSID Convention, Attempts to Curtail Investor-State Arbitration Rights", *Skadden, Arps, Slate, Meagher and Flom LLP* (17 June 2009), available at <http://www.skadden.com/content/Publications/Publications1810_0.pdf>. Earlier, Ecuador had announced that it would not recognize ICSID jurisdiction over oil, gas and mining investment disputes. J. L. Gardiner *et al.*, "Ecuador Attempts to Withdraw Consent to ICSID Jurisdiction for Natural Resource Disputes", 16:1 *Latin American Law & Business Report* (2008), available at <http://www.skadden.com/content/Publications/Publications1377_0.pdf>.

[668] See, e.g., A. van Aaken and J. Kurtz, "The Global Financial Crisis: Will State Emergency Measures Trigger International Investment Disputes?", *Columbia FDI Perspectives* No. 3 (2009), available at <http://www.vcc.columbia.edu/content/fdi-perspectives>.

capital flows in particular contexts. Many Governments worry about the alleged "export" of jobs brought about by outgoing businesses or about whether foreign mergers and acquisitions (particularly by State-controlled entities or by nationals of certain States) are driven only by market concerns[669]. Empirical studies have not uniformly supported the proposition that the conclusion of BITs or FTAs encourages greater FDI flows than would otherwise occur. Some studies suggest that even when such flows emerge, these may be accompanied by a number of negative externalities, including wage inequalities or regional disparities of income[670]. While, as Chapter I suggests, many of these concerns reflect perennial worries that have always been prompted by foreign investment, the relatively recent rise of investment treaties and arbitral case-law has brought new force to old complaints. Second thoughts about the regime's fundamental purpose are also prompted by greater concerns over "national" or "essential" security along with more expansive notions of what "security" entails, deeper or more pervasive worries over terrorist acts by "aliens", or the perception that States need to respond to economic crises with greater flexibility than is anticipated by investment treaties.

The more legalistic concerns of the Osgoode Hall Statement suggest that the regime has also become the

---

[669] See, e.g., K. P. Sauvant and J. E. Alvarez, "International Investment Law in Transition", in K. P. Sauvant and J. E. Alvarez with K. G. Ahmed and G. del P. Vizcaíno (eds.), *The Evolving International Investment Regime: Expectations, Realities, Options* (Oxford University Press, forthcoming 2010).

[670] *Ibid.*; see also K. P. Sauvant and L. E. Sachs (eds.), *The Effect of Treaties on Foreign Direct Investment: Bilateral Investment Treaties, Double Taxation Treaties and Investment Flows* (Oxford, Oxford University Press, 2009).

victim of its own success. The proliferation of investment treaties and the arbitral decisions in their wake
have raised the visibility of the regime and conse-
quently drawn attention to it from States, NGOs, and
academics[671]. Adverse reactions to the Argentina
claims and awards feature prominently in the current
backlash. These cases are frequently cited to demonstrate that private commercial arbitral mechanisms are
inappropriate for resolving "public policy" disputes
that, in the view of some, require adjudication by
national judges, or at least permanent judges, whose
independence and neutrality is assured by lengthy
tenure[672]. The Argentina cases are seen as proof that
the current body of investment law and the method for
enforcing it has displaced the "gunboat diplomacy" of
old with "gunboat arbitration" that equally privileges
one set of rights and one group of interests over
competing national and international values and rule of
law[673]. For critics, the plight of Argentina before
ICSID tribunals provides concrete evidence that the
investment regime, far from promoting the rule of law
and democratic governance, threatens both by creating

---

[671] Osgoode Hall Statement, *supra* footnote 655.

[672] Thus, Gus Van Harten begins his book-length critique of the investment regime, which embraces all of
these concerns, by referring to the *CMS* v. *Argentina* arbitral award. G. Van Harten, *Investment Treaty Arbitration
and Public Law* (New York, Oxford University Press,
2007), pp. 1-2.

[673] See, e.g., S. Montt, "What International Investment
Law and Latin America Can and Should Demand from
Each Other: Updating the Bello/Calvo Doctrine in the BIT
Generation", 3 *Res Publica Argentina* 75 (2007), available
at <http://www.iilj.org/GAL/documents/SantiagoMontt.GAL.
pdf>, pp. 82-83 (identifying the danger that BIT jurisprudence concretizes into concrete rights beyond constitutional norms — even within the United States and Europe
— and damages the equality of nations).

legal enclaves available only to those who need it the least (that is wealthy TNCs), while producing inconsistent rulings that do not satisfy its own constituents' needs for predictability[674].

This final chapter uses the Argentina decisions as the linchpin to begin to explore these and other concerns with the investment regime, as well as proposed solutions. It concludes by enumerating the many points of intersection between the investment regime and the challenges to it and much broader concerns now facing other public international law regimes.

B. *The Argentina Cases and the Regime's Alleged Legitimacy Deficits*

(1) The problem of inconsistent arbitral awards

The stakeholders of the investment regime are understandably troubled by decisions as disparate in outcome and rationale as those discussed in Chapter IV, namely the arbitral award in *LG&E*, the initial awards and later annulment rulings in *CMS*, *Enron* and *Sempra*, and the award in *Continental Casualty*. These decisions suggest that investor-State dispute settlement does not produce the stable and predictable rules of the road that some had anticipated. For those who value

---

[674] See, e.g., T. Ginsburg, "International Substitutes for Domestic Institutions: Bilateral Investment Treaties and Governance", 25 *International Review of Law and Economics* 107 (2005) (arguing that the spread of investment agreements permitting powerful players to bypass national courts may help to explain the intractability of LDC's efforts to improve such courts); Susan Franck, "The Legitimacy Crisis in Investment Treaty Arbitration: Privatizing Public International Law through Inconsistent Decisions", 73 *Fordham Law Review* 1521 (2005) (discussing the problems emerging from inconsistent arbitral decisions).

stability and predictability above all else, these inconsistent decisions on the existence, scope, or implications of the "necessity" defence are distressing. It is
disheartening that, despite years of litigation and
numerous opportunities to revisit the underlying issues,
arbitral panels and annulment committees still differ
with respect to the meaning of a single clause in a
single BIT as well as with respect to more systemic
issues, including how to interpret investment treaties
vis-à-vis general rules of international law. These worries have not been reduced through the opportunities
accorded under annulment. On the contrary, to date the
emerging Argentina annulment decisions raise other
unsettling uncertainties (perhaps of greater interest to
private international lawyers), such as the appropriate
level of review envisioned in the course of ICSID
annulment[675].

At the same time, the Argentina cases suggest that
the problem of inconsistency should not be overstated.
Although Chapter IV focuses on the extent of disagreement among the cases, there is a great deal of agreement among the relevant decisions with respect to the
relevant law. For all the disagreements among these
tribunals concerning the meaning or applicability of
Argentina's Article XI defence, there is considerable
arbitral common ground when it comes to the meaning

---

[675] This is certainly suggested by the differing outcomes in the *CMS*, *Enron* and *Sempra* annulments discussed in Chapter IV. While these annulment committees
all cited the same rules governing their respective annulment proceedings, they differed widely in how to apply
them in circumstances involving comparable facts.
Whereas the *CMS* annulment committee did not see itself
as empowered to "second-guess" the legal determinations
rendered by the original *CMS* panel, neither the *Enron* nor
the *Sempra* annulment committees took the same view.
See Chapter IV.

of the relevant substantive investment guarantees, from fair and equitable treatment to protection against expropriation[676]. It is also important to recognize that even with respect to the rulings concerning the customary defence of necessity and/or the measures not precluded clause of the United States-Argentina BIT, some of the arbitral disagreements came in the form of dicta and were not critical to the outcome.

Critics of the differing outcomes in these cases should also exercise care in distinguishing differences that reflect genuine disagreements over the interpretation of the law — and reflect differing legal rationales — as opposed to those that emerge from understandable differences in findings of fact. Although it is true that the awards in *LG&E* and *Continental Casualty* appeared to differ from those originally issued by the *CMS*, *Enron* and *Sempra* tribunals concerning whether Argentina faced a grave enough threat to its "essential security interests", for example, the differences in this critical finding may have had more to do with the evidence presented in these respective arbitrations. Some of these findings may have had something to do with differing credibility assessments with respect to the expert witnesses presented on this point, for example. It is not necessarily true that these tribunals — or the subsequent annulment committees — reached differing legal interpretations of what "essential security interests" are, either for purposes of interpreting the United States-Argentina BIT or the customary defence of necessity. Indeed, all of these tribunals appear to agree that, even if the Article XI or necessity defence

---

[676] See, e.g., J. E. Alvarez and K. Khamsi, "The Argentine Crisis and Foreign Investors", in Sauvant (ed.), *supra* footnote 665, pp. 393-395 (discussing commonalities among the original tribunals in *CMS, LG&E, Enron* and *Sempra*).

requires an exceptional state of affairs tantamount to the threatened collapse of a State, that threat could emerge from either a natural environmental calamity or an economic crisis.

The Argentina cases should, more usefully, direct attention to the type of "inconsistency" that ought to give rise to concern. The mere fact that Argentina faced multi-million dollar judgments in some of these cases — *CMS* — a great deal less in others — *LG&E, Continental Casualty* — and no finding of wrongdoing in others — *Enron* and *Sempra* annulments — is politically troublesome (particularly for Argentina) but not necessarily worrisome for those who care about the rule of law. It is admittedly easier for a Government to pay such awards to foreign investors when the underlying awards are comparable — especially if comparable sums would also be due in similar circumstances to national investors — but mere differences in outcomes — or win/loss records in investor-State dispute settlement more generally — should not be as worrying to lawyers. The application of law to fact in arbitral or any judicial setting regularly produces differing outcomes. Such differences may have been the result of the different skills of the advocates or differences in the evidence presented in each case.

Even when arbitral outcomes differ because of different applications of law to fact, all such differences are not equally troubling. As all lawyers know, not all legal rules are equally precise or intended to produce entirely harmonious outcomes. As is suggested in Chapter IV, the vague rules governing liability reflected in investment treaties have an open texture that may produce equally legitimate, though disparate, awards. To cite one example: neither investment law nor the underlying rules of State responsibility on reparations has yet elaborated precise rules governing how adjudicators must determine the meaning of appropriate com-

pensation, even when a treaty requires "fair market
value" as the standard (as only the expropriation provisions of some BITs provide). While some might regret
this "gap" in the underlying treaty law or the subsequent arbitral case-law, others might suggest that this
"give in the joints" is a necessary or legitimate concession to arbitral discretion. As is also suggested in
Chapter IV, some investment guarantees, such as fair
and equitable treatment, arguably anticipate that those
applying the standard will "balance" the rights of
investors and Governments without indicating with
precision what that "balancing" entails. It is possible
that those who drafted investment treaties intended to
delegate some discretion to arbitrators in applying such
guarantees, perhaps anticipating the difficulty of
assessing precisely the many factual circumstances that
may give rise to an FET claim.

    None of this seeks to belittle the very real and troub-
ling inconsistencies of legal reasoning reflected in the
Argentina decisions surveyed in Chapter IV. There is
no hiding the fact that both *LG&E* and *Continental
Casualty* stated that their damage awards to the respective claimants were affected by the applicability of
Article XI — a result at odds with what we have urged
ought to have been the proper interpretation of that
provision. There is also no denying that in *LG&E*, and
possibly *Continental Casualty*, and in some but not all
the subsequent annulment decisions, the burden of
proof with respect to an affirmative defence appears to
have been put on the claimant and not Argentina. The
original panels and even annulment committees in these
cases obviously did not come to uniform conclusions
with respect to the relationship between Article XI of
the United States-Argentina BIT and customary international law. Moreover, even though all these tribunals
formally agreed that Article 25 of the Articles of State
Responsibility accurately restates the customary defence

of necessity, the *Enron* annulment tribunal's expectations of what needs to be shown with respect to that defence suggests that underneath the surface disagreement exists on what that defence means or when it should apply. There is also little dispute that these inconsistencies render the prospect of enforcing awards against Argentina more difficult, complicate the prospect of settlements with respect to Argentina and possibly elsewhere, and create uncertainties with respect to those who have already filed claims against Argentina. As a result, the law with respect to the interpretation of Article XI of the United States-Argentina BIT, other investment treaties with comparable "measures not precluded" clauses, and even with respect to investment treaties that rely only on customary defences is probably more uncertain now than it was in 1991, when the United States and Argentina concluded their BIT[677].

There are other investor-State arbitral decisions that have produced comparable concerns about inconsistent investment law. Interpreting the meaning and scope of the most-favoured-nation clause has given rise to serious differences of opinion[678], as has the interpretation

---

[677] See, e.g., J. L. Gardiner *et al.*, "New ICSID Annulment Decision Exposes Possible Gap in United States Investment Treaty Protection", *Skadden, Arps, Slate, Meagher and Flom LLP* (19 July 2010), available at <http://www.skadden.com/Index.cfm?contentID=51&itemID=2159> (noting that the *Sempra* annulment decision ruling on the "measures not precluded" clause of the US BIT may undermine the degree of protection many investors assumed that they enjoyed under such treaties).

[678] See, e.g., Y. Banifatemi, "The Emerging Jurisprudence on the Most-Favoured-Nation Treatment in Investment Arbitration", in A. K. Bjorklund *et al.* (eds.), *Investment Treaty Law: Current Issues III: Remedies in International Investment Law and Emerging Jurisprudence in International Investment Law* (London, British Institute

of umbrella clauses — including the one applied in some of the Argentina cases involving the United States-Argentina BIT, for example[679].

There are even differences among arbitral rulings with respect to the type of "investment" embraced by BITs, FTAs, or the ICSID Convention[680].

Nor do investor-State tribunals agree as to when or if an investment protection agreement can be invoked by a foreign investor which has established a "paper" presence in a jurisdiction precisely in order to take advantage of a particular BIT or FTA[681]. On the other hand, there is considerable evidence that investor-State

---

of International and Comparative Law, 2009), p. 242 (noting that divergences of opinion arise particularly regarding the application of the MFN clause to dispute resolution provisions in treaties).

[679] See, e.g., A. C. Sinclair, "The Umbrella Clause Debate", in Bjorklund *et al.* (eds.), *supra* footnote 678, pp. 311-312; S. Schill, "Enabling Private Ordering — Function, Scope and Effect of Umbrella Clauses in International Investment Treaties", Institute for International Law and Justice Working Paper, 2008/9, available at <http://www.iilj.org/publications/documents/2008-9.Schill.pdf>.

[680] See, e.g., *Saba Fakes* v. *Republic of Turkey*, Award, ICSID Case No. ARB/07/20 (14 July 2010), available at <http://ita.law.uvic.ca/documents/Fakes_v_Turkey_Award.pdf> (finding that protectable "investment" under the ICSID convention requires a contribution of certain duration that entails an element of risk but need not be shown to constitute a contribution to the host State's economic development as was found in the *Salini* tribunal).

[681] See, e.g., R. Aguirre Luzi and B. Love, "Individual Nationality in Investment Treaty Arbitration: The Tension between Customary International Law and *Lex Specialis*", in *Current Issues III*, *supra* footnote 678, pp. 196-199 (highlighting the problems of nationality under customary international law as opposed to effective nationality and identifying a double standard between individuals and corporations).

arbitrators generally pay close attention to prior arbitral awards and that — at least within the world of publicly available ICSID awards — prior ICSID rulings are the most frequently cited source of authority within those awards themselves [682].

Given these conflicting signals, just how serious is this "legitimacy deficit" of the regime?

Much depends on the expectations one has. As Charles Brower II has suggested, if one expects BITs and FTAs to produce a "system" and not merely an ambiguous "regime" or merely a "framework", even a small handful of inconsistent arbitral rulings, especially arising in the context of comparable or identical treaty language and comparable facts (such as the Argentina cases surveyed in Chapter IV), is a source of serious concern. This is especially true within a "system" that has relatively few methods to correct mistakes, given the narrowness of review by national courts and, at least prior to the recent annulment rulings in the Argentina context, the comparable narrowness of review by ICSID annulment procedures. Disagreement among scholars and annulment committees as to the legitimate scope of annulment

---

[682] See O. K. Fauchald, "The Legal Reasoning of ICSID Tribunals — An Empirical Analysis", 19 *European Journal of International Law* 301 (2008), p. 335 (indicating that ICSID cases were cited in 92 of the 98 decisions surveyed and that "this was by far the most widely used and most important interpretative argument"). Indeed, in one recent case, the arbitrators stated that they had a "duty" to respect precedent. *Saipem* v. *Bangladesh*, Decision on Jurisdiction and Recommendations on Provisional Measures, ICSID Case No. ARB/05/7 (21 March 2007), para. 67 ("[I]t has a duty to seek to contribute to the harmonious development of investment law and thereby meet the legitimate expectations of the community of States and investors towards certainty of the rule of law").

certainly does not lessen the concerns over "inconsistency"[683].

If one believes, on the other hand, that investor-State arbitration is merely in its "state of adolescence" and will, over time, prove capable of correcting its own mistakes as erroneous decisions are discarded while the fittest survive, either through later arbitral corrections or through changes made to investment treaties by States, inconsistent arbitral rulings issued from time to time are neither troubling nor surprising[684]. How

---

[683] Compare *CMS Gas Co.* v. *Argentina*, Decision on Annulment, ICSID Case No. ARB/01/8 (25 September 2007) (hereinafter *"CMS annulment"*) with *Enron Creditors Recovery Corporation (formerly Enron Corporation) and Ponderosa Assets, L.P.* v. *Argentine Republic*, Decision on the Application for Annulment of the Argentine Republic, ICSID Case No. ARB/01/3 (30 July 2010) (hereinafter *"Enron annulment"*); *Sempra Energy International* v. *Argentine Republic*, Decision on the Argentine Republic's Application for Annulment of the Award, ICSID Case No. ARB/02/16 (29 June 2010) (hereinafter *"Sempra annulment"*) as discussed in Chapter IV. See also T. H. Cheng, "Precedent and Control in Investment Treaty Arbitration", 30 *Fordham International Law Journal* 1014 (2007), p. 1016 (noting that the informal system of precedent is being tested by an increased diversity of arbitrators); S. A. Alexandrov, "On the Perceived Inconsistency in Investor-State Jurisprudence", in *The Evolving International Investment Regime: Expectations, Realities, Options, supra* footnote 669 (cautioning against overstating the degree of inconsistency that is now evident among investor-State awards).

[684] See, e.g., "The Forum Panel Discussion: Precedent in Investment Arbitration", in Bjorklund *et al.* (eds.), *supra* footnote 678, pp. 314-315 (B. Stern suggesting that the process of arbitral decision-making produces a "hierarchy of reason" rather than of precedent as such); *ibid.*, pp. 318-319 (F. Ortino praising the "dialectic process" emerging from the jurisprudence of investor-State tribunals and the political treaty-making arm of States); T. W. Wälde, "Improving the Mechanisms for Treaty

much should we worry if, for example, a MFN clause in a BIT is unexpectedly applied to dispute settlement provisions such that an investor who would normally have to wait six months prior to initiating an ICSID case can resort to a different BIT that permits immediate recourse? For some, such a ruling, even assuming it is an incorrect interpretation of the relevant treaty, is not particularly troubling even without an appellate mechanism permitting correction, because of the remaining possibilities for exit and voice left in the investment regime. China, for example, has lessened the impact of precisely this development by including, in its most recent treaties, a clause that explicitly states that the MFN clause does not extend to dispute settlement[685]. Of course, this assumes that the investment regime should remain firmly within the control of the States that established it and that protecting States' expectations — and not those of foreign investors — should remain the regime's central focus.

The extent of concern over "inconsistency" may also reflect something of a common law/civil law divide, with the common lawyers predictably expressing greater support for the view that arbitration should remain a site for interpretative experimentation. Many lawyers based in the common law express confidence that arbitral decisions will eventually coalesce over the

Negotiation and Investment Disputes: Competition and Choice as the Path to Quality and Legitimacy", in Sauvant (ed.), *supra* footnote 665, pp. 506-512 (categorizing the investor-State arbitrations as an "unmitigated success" that provide "a legal foundation to help the current process of global economic integration run more smoothly" marred by only minor flaws).

[685] See, e.g., C. Congyan, "China-US BIT Negotiations and the Future of Investment Treaty Regime: A Grand Bilateral Bargain with Multilateral Implications", 12 *Journal of International Economic Law* 457 (2009), p. 474 (citing Article 139 (2) of the China-New Zealand FTA).

long term[686]. Debates over whether "inconsistent" arbitral awards are a serious problem may also turn on observers' differing levels of tolerance for deploying "standards" over more precise "rules". Some of these disagreements — as with respect to whether the underlying right to property contained in BITs and FTAs ought to be subject to an imprecisely defined "sovereign right to regulate" — may in turn reflect disagreements concerning the underlying values that the regime ought to protect[687].

And what explains why investor-State arbitrators and annulment panels, despite their respect for *jurisprudence constante*, sometimes render inconsistent decisions even when interpreting identical treaty provisions?

---

[686] See generally "Symposium Issue: Proliferation of International Tribunals: Piecing Together the Puzzle", 31 *New York University Journal of International Law and Politics* 679 (1999) (particularly J. Charney, "The Impact on the International Legal System of the Growth of International Courts and Tribunals", 31 *New York University Journal of International Law and Politics* 697 (1999)); J. Katz Cogan, "Competition and Control in International Adjudication", 48 *Virginia Journal of International Law* 411 (2007).

[687] To the extent that investor-State arbitrators are elaborating concepts of property rights that approximate the balancing inherent to the definition of property rights in the European Convention on Human Rights or other nationally defined constitutional rights, differing results will be the norm. But see A. Stone Sweet and J. Matthews, "Proportionality Balancing and Constitutionalism", 47 *Columbia Journal of Transnational Law* 73 (2008), pp. 91-92 (describing a trend among most post-World War II constitutions to provide for non-absolute rights that are limited by another value of constitutional rank); M. Tushnet, "The Inevitable Globalization of Constitutional Law", 49 *Virginia Journal of International Law* 985 (2009) (contending that international adjudicative processes may be encouraging a trend towards the harmonization of national constitutional norms).

Apart from the self-evident fact that the imprecision of many investment provisions — most especially FET — inevitably produces differing interpretations, another less obvious explanation looks to possible differences in outlook among investor-State arbitrators. Those who adjudicate investment disputes may not always agree on what their job is. Consider the fact that Judge Francisco Rezek was a member of the panels in both *LG&E* and the original *CMS* award or that Professor Albert Jan van den Berg was able to sign both the award in *LG&E* and the strikingly different award in the original *Enron* decision. How is it that these two individuals were able to sign these awards, without separate dissenting or concurring opinions? Although we do not have an explanation from either of these two arbitrators, it is possible that both of them consider that it is more important to render a unanimous decision than it is to explicate their own (presumably consistent) views, through a separate concurring or dissenting opinion. Arbitrators who take this view presumably believe that their signature on an award "certifies no more than their confirmation that they participated in the deliberations and now confirm that this is the decision of the tribunal"[688]. As the experienced arbitrator Jan Paulsson suggests, this reflects an assumption — based on commercial arbitration practices — that there is no reason to issue a dissent as the principal duty of an arbitrator is to resolve the particular dispute and to do so in a manner that will make it easier for the winning party to enforce a presumptively more legitimate, unanimous decision[689]. At the

---

[688] J. Paulsson, "Awards — And Awards", in Bjorklund *et al.* (eds.), *supra* footnote 678, pp. 101-102 (arguing there is no reason in most commercial arbitrations for an arbitrator to issue a dissent).

[689] As Paulsson has noted, unanimous decisions are also harder to overturn — and less likely to be questioned

same time, not all investor-State adjudicators take the view that the most critical factor is encouraging States to comply with a particular award[690].

This suggests that those worried about inconsistent arbitral awards should pay closer attention to the background or relevant expertise of investor-State arbitrators. There may be divides among investor-State adjudicators, some of whom see themselves as engaged in the same task as commercial arbitrators, that is, merely resolving a particular dispute, and some of whom see investor-State arbitrations as a species of "public law" adjudication. As Thomas Wälde has suggested, the first group may place more emphasis on the literal wording of legal texts, in-depth examination of factual issues, and the formal equality of the parties before them[691]. Such arbitrators may be somewhat less worried over whether their particular assessment of what a treaty means differs from another prior tribunal and more concerned with rendering a decision that the disputants before them are inclined to accept and comply with. The second group of adjudicators see their role as more like those engaged in interstate claims commissions or even the International Court of Justice[692]. As Wälde

---

by a national court or an annulment committee — and will likely be regarded as more legitimate. *Supra* footnote 688, p. 100.

[690] The *CMS* annulment, which severely criticizes but did not annul the underlying award, apparently was not worried that its dicta would render the resulting award more difficult to enforce.

[691] See T. W. Wälde, "Remedies and Compensation in International Investment Law", 2:5 *Transnational Dispute Management* (2005), p. 11.

[692] See, e.g., Van Harten, *supra* footnote 672; Wälde, *supra* footnote 691, pp. 2-15; T. W. Wälde, "The Specific Nature of Investment Arbitration" in P. Kahn and T. W. Wälde (eds.), *New Aspects of International Investment Law* (Leiden, Martinus Nijhoff, 2007), pp. 112-

has suggested, the second group might be more aware or sensitive to the systemic asymmetries of investor-State dispute settlement, irrespective of formal adherence to "equality of arms". Adjudicators who see themselves as solving "public" law disputes might tend to focus more on the fact that one of the parties before them is a Government that enjoys, at least at the point of compliance with any award and possibly before, asymmetric power over a private party who has engaged in sunk costs[693]. Whereas the more commercially attuned arbitrator is principally interested in settling the concrete dispute before her, even at the risk of ignoring or disturbing "precedents" set by prior arbitrators[694], the public adjudicator is at least equally interested in setting out the law in a public, reasoned decision that States parties might generally accept and that coheres with the expectations of a broader community,

---

117. See also Wälde, *supra* footnote 684, pp. 549-555 (discussing the divide in the context of debates over the merits of transparency over confidentiality for purposes of investor-State arbitration). But see Wälde, *supra* footnote 691, pp. 14-15 (noting differences between investor-State arbitrations and historic claims commissions).

[693] See Wälde, *supra* footnote 691, p. 13.

[694] See, e.g., "The Forum Panel Discussion: Precedent in Investment Arbitration", in Bjorklund *et al.* (eds.), *supra* footnote 678, p. 320 (C. Schreur citing Bernardo Cremades's dissenting opinion in *Fraport* v. *Philippines*, Dissenting Opinion, ICSID Case No. ARB/03/25 (16 August 2007), para. 7 ("[T]he integrity of this interpretative process must not be compromised by the pronouncements of other arbitral tribunals in their interpretation of different treaties in wholly unrelated factual and legal context"); *ibid.*, pp. 327-328 (W. Rowley noting that the disputants have a right to a clear, reasonably timely and cost-efficient, and un-annullable decision and that his job as a arbitrator "is not to make precedent, but to make a decision"). Rowley notes that as an arbitrator he discourages dissent and seeks to build unanimity since the parties are "inevitably happier with a unanimous result".

including perhaps the invisible college of (public) international lawyers[695]. Some suggest that these divides reflect the differing perspectives of commercial lawyers as opposed to those trained in public international law.

Whether these alleged divides between "commercial" and "public" adjudicators actually exist or are caricatured exaggerations of reality, there is little question that the broader literature on adjudication, even among those who write principally about national courts, reflects these distinct perspectives[696]. Thus, Martin Shapiro, an eminent scholar on the role of courts generally, describes national judges as dispute settlers who are principally engaged in settling a triadic dispute[697]. Owen Fiss, an equally renowned scholar of US judicial review, on the other hand, portrays judges as not mere dispute settlers but as policy-makers consciously engaged in giving meaning to public values[698]. International forms of dispute settlement engage both of these traditions[699]. Since both are represented in the hybrid form of dispute settlement that is investor-State dispute settlement, it should not surprise that both types of scholarship are reflected in the investment law literature.

---

[695] See Wälde, *supra* footnote 684, p. 552.

[696] For a somewhat different two-fold distinction between dispute settlement mechanisms, see D. D. Caron, "Towards a Political Theory of International Courts and Tribunals", 24 *Berkeley Journal of International Law* 401 (2006), p. 403 (distinguishing between "community-originated" institutions and "party-originated" mechanisms).

[697] See M. Shapiro, *Courts: A Comparative and Political Analysis* (Chicago, Chicago University Press, 1981).

[698] See, e.g., O. M. Fiss, "Foreword: The Forms of Justice", 93 *Harvard Law Review* 1 (1979).

[699] For applications of the insights of both Shapiro and Fiss to international dispute settlement, see J. E. Alvarez, *International Organizations as Law-Makers* (New York, Oxford University Press, 2005), pp. 528-545.

(2) Is the investment regime a threat to sovereignty?

The decisions rendered in the course of the Argentina cases discussed in Chapter IV suggest that high profile decisions taken by a Government in the midst of a crisis can be second-guessed by persons at some geographical and temporal distance from that crisis. Moreover, the Argentina decisions highlight the fact that investor-State adjudicators are tasked not with resolving how the Government should have responded to such a crisis but with deciding whether that Government has injured a single foreign investor, irrespective of whether the "emergency" actions of the Government were the most beneficial to the greatest number or whether the investor truly contributed to the economic development of the host State in the past. It is no surprise if such single-minded decisions — the product of a single-minded pro-investor treaty such as the United States-Argentina BIT — should elicit the concerns over sovereignty and sovereign discretion suggested by the Osgood Hall Statement described at the outset of this chapter.

Of course, "sovereignty" is a political and not a legal term of art. As the Osgoode Hall Statement itself suggests, the sovereignty objection to the investment regime is not directed at legalistic concerns that BITs or investor-State dispute settlement constitutes unlawful interference with the legal rights of States. Although the Osgoode Hall Statement suggests that arbitral rulings have "prioritized the protection of the property and economic interests of transnational corporations over the right to regulate of states and the right to self-determination of peoples", the principal argument against the investment regime is not a claim that the underlying treaties violate *jus cogens* or constitute unlawful interference in States' "domestic jurisdiction"[700]. BITs and FTAs are, of course, agreements that permit others, including individuals, to have rights as against States that they would normally not have, such as the right to non-discriminatory treatment. They are also agreements that permit third parties to have relatively effective international remedies for violations of customary international law obligations that pre-date such agreements. Neither of these qualities violate international law or intrude on a nation's right of self-determination, particularly since this latter right has been restrictively interpreted in modern international law[701]. Nor are these qualities unique to the investment regime. Regional human rights courts, the European Court of Justice, and war crimes tribunals that exercise "primary" jurisdiction, such as the ICTR and ICTY, all might be said to be equally "intrusive" with respect to sovereign rights, although perhaps none are as willing to impose large financial penalties on states as some investor-State awards.

The "sovereignty" concern is a bit of a red herring. As the Permanent Court of International Justice

---

[700] See, e.g., Charter of the United Nations, 1 *United Nations Treaty Series* 16, signed on 26 June 1945, entered into force on 24 October 1945, Art. 1 (3) (regarding self-determination of peoples) and Art. 2 (7) (regarding respect for domestic jurisdiction).

[701] It is difficult to argue that the regime established by BITs and FTAs is contrary to the rights of self-determination. See, e.g., *Reference re Secession of Quebec*, Supreme Court of Canada, 2 *Supreme Court Reports* 217 (1998) (distinguishing internal versus external self-determination rights under international law and restricting the latter to colonial situations and other extreme cases where a "people" is blocked from meaningful participation in its own governance). It is of course possible that particular applications of BITs or FTAs might, in particular circumstances, violate human rights, including the self-determination rights of indigenous peoples.

pointed out in the *S.S. Wimbledon* case in 1923, entry into a treaty is an exercise of a State's right of self-determination; it is in effect an exercise of sovereignty, not a renunciation of it[702]. We cannot expect investor-State arbitrators to do anything other than interpret the investment treaty that a State ratified in accordance with the ordinary rules of treaty interpretation. If a State — such as Argentina — is no longer content with the BITs that it has signed, it should terminate or amend them in accordance with their terms; until then, *pacta sunt servanda* demands compliance, even when the treaties impose (as many human rights treaties have done) unanticipated obligations on their signatories. At the same time, as the Osgoode Hall Statement suggests, the legitimacy of the investment regime is undermined to the extent that BITs and FTAs are not interpreted in strict accordance with their terms and are applied, for example, to *sub silentio* disable a State from exercising its normal power to regulate in the public interest[703].

As Chapter IV contends, even the pre-annulment rulings of the *CMS*, *Enron* and *Sempra* awards were sensitive to Argentina's right to regulate and did not

---

[702] *Case of the S.S. "Wimbledon" (United Kingdom, France, Italy, Japan v. Germany)*, Permanent Court of International Justice, 1923 (Ser. A), No. 1, p. 25.

[703] Compare M. Orellana, "Science, Risk, and Uncertainty: Public Health Measures and Investment Disciplines", in *New Aspects of International Investment Law*, *supra* footnote 692, p. 727 (arguing for a "presumption of regularity" with respect to governmental actions) with Wälde, *supra* footnote 692, p. 117 (arguing that given the relative economic and political weakness of foreign investors vis-à-vis domestic competitors and host States and the explicit function of investment agreements, the risks of ambiguity should be borne by the host State, which ought to be required to demonstrate a "higher level of good faith").

purport to disable that State from regulating in the public interest. Ironically, the decision that arguably interferes the most with the sovereign right to regulate is the one that on the surface appears to be most deferential to it, namely *Continental Casualty*. That decision erroneously appears to presume that all regulatory actions need to be explained as "necessary" under Article IX of the United States-Argentina BIT. As is discussed in Chapter IV, the harshly criticized original awards in *CMS*, *Sempra* and *Enron* were not instances in which arbitrators failed to recognize a State's residual power to regulate; the heart of those decisions was that Argentina failed to abide by the specific assurances that it had made, under its own law, to the respective foreign investors and that this failure violated specific guarantees to which Argentina had acceded in the United States-Argentina BIT. Of course, even those inclined to disagree with that assessment should see the annulment rulings in *CMS*, *Enron* and *Sempra* as alleviating at least some of the "sovereignty" based concerns with the regime.

(3) Is the investment regime a threat to human rights?

Even if the "sovereignty" objections to the investment regime are overblown, do investment treaty obligations pose a challenge to States' compliance with their international human rights obligations? While human rights concerns did not play a prominent role in Argentina's responses to the claims discussed in Chapter IV, more recently Argentina and other respondent States in investor-State arbitrations have attempted to mount such defences in the course of investor-State dispute settlement.

In the context of claims by privatized utility companies such as those discussed in Chapter IV, it has now been suggested that Argentina's contested emergency legislation was a defensible action needed to fulfil that country's human rights obligations, such as its citizens' rights to access to basic necessities, or to protect the right to a stable constitutional order that respects rights to public security and safety, assuming that emergency action was justified to avoid public disorder stemming from higher utility prices[704]. In the original *CMS*, *Enron* and *Sempra* claims, these contentions only emerged obliquely in the course of Argentina's contentions that its BIT obligations could not prevail as against its own Constitution. In the *CMS* case, for example, Argentina argued that certain human rights are sanctioned by its Constitution and that, under its law, treaties are not above its own Constitution. It contended that

"as the economic and social crisis that affected the country compromised basic human rights, no investment treaty could prevail as it would be in violation of such constitutionally recognized rights"[705].

The original *CMS* award did not find a "collision" between BIT rights and constitutionally protected rights, explaining

"[f]irst, because the Constitution carefully protects the right to property, just as the treaties on human rights do, and secondly because there is no question

---

[704] See generally *Öneryildiz* v. *Turkey*, Grand Chamber of the European Court of Human Rights, App. No. 48939/99 (30 November 2004), paras. 89-90 (interpreting the positive obligation to take all appropriate steps to impose a primary duty on the State to "put in place a legislative and administrative framework designed to provide effective deterrence against threats to the right to life"); see also Orellana, *supra* footnote 703, pp. 716-718.

[705] *CMS Gas Transmission Co.* v. *Argentina*, Award, ICSID Case No. ARB/01/8 (12 May 2005), para. 114.

of affecting fundamental human rights when considering the issues disputed by the parties"[706].

While this cursory dismissal has been criticized as insensitive to Argentina's legitimate human rights concerns, it is not at all clear that, in this or the other gas sector cases discussed in Chapter IV, Argentina made a serious effort to show how its failure to continue to negotiate the level of gas tariffs with the investors as it promised to do under its law was, in and of itself, required by either its Constitution or its international human rights obligations. Under the circumstances, the *CMS* arbitrators may have thought it sufficient to point out that Argentina's constitutional defence was belied by the fact that its own Constitution would appear to protect the investors' property rights and that a specific defence to the precise measures challenged in that case, grounded in Argentina's other human rights obligations, simply had not been made.

In more recent cases, particularly involving foreign investors in the privatized water sector, Argentina and other respondent States appear to be making the human rights defence more forcefully. In the context of a system of dispute settlement that is heavily reliant on the issues raised by the disputing parties, this means that investor-State arbitrators are likely to take the intersection between human rights and the investment regime more seriously as well. It is therefore possible that some investor-State claims will become vehicles for potentially innovative decisions concerning how States are supposed to comply with both their human rights and their BIT or FTA obligations.

The potential for conflict between investment and human rights obligations has been getting increased scholarly attention and need only be briefly summa-

---

[706] *Op. cit., supra* footnote 705, para. 121.

rized here. It has been suggested that the investment regime, including its resort to investor-State arbitration poses the following human rights challenges:

Lack of equal access to the international rule of law

For countries like the United States and much of Asia that have not adhered to any human rights treaty that commits the nation to binding international dispute settlement, as under a regional tribunal such as the Inter-American Court of Human Rights, investment treaties, which permit foreign investors to have such unique access, present an embarrassing lack of parity. Investor-State arbitrations are limited to examining foreign investors' rights under the BITs and are not forums to adjudicate all the harms that a foreign investor might have inflicted on local populations, local consumers, or its locally hired employees. A nation that permits itself and its laws to be subject to supranational adjudicative review when it comes to how it treats foreign investors but does not permit such independent impartial review with respect to actions that may harm the human rights of others exposes itself to the charge that it values foreign investors' property rights more than it does any other civil, political, economic or social rights[707].

The lack of equal access to an international remedy for human rights violations is problematic for both political as well as legal reasons. This is especially so when, for example, a foreign investor brings a claim

---

[707] See J. E. Alvarez, "Foreword: The Ripples of NAFTA", in T. Weiler (ed.), *NAFTA Investment Law and Arbitration: Past Tissues, Current Practice, Future Prospects* (Ardsley, New York, Transnational Publishers, 2004), p. xxi.

against a State and that State cannot assert, even as a counterclaim before that same arbitral body, that the investor has violated its laws relating to human rights, labour rights or the protection of the environment — even when such laws implement or enforce the host State's international obligations under a treaty or customary law. For many it is not an answer that local courts remain available to adjudicate such complaints. If foreign investors are entitled to internationalized venues to resolve their disputes precisely because local courts are deemed insufficiently professional or independent to protect their rights, it can hardly be a sufficient answer to contend that such courts should be the sole venue to protect other common values of the international (and local) community.

Lack of equal remedies

Even with respect to States that otherwise submit themselves to international adjudication with respect to human rights and are, for example, parties to the American or European Conventions on Human Rights, there is another reciprocity gap. Scholars and NGOs point out that there are awkward inequities with respect to the international remedies available to foreign investors as compared to other rights holders. While violations of human rights under regional human rights conventions are generally subject to exhaustion of local remedies, foreign investors under some BITs, including those negotiated by the United States with "fork in the road" jurisdictional provisions, do not face such a hurdle. Moreover, while the remedies awarded by regional human rights courts tend to focus on preventing future harm by forcing the State to remove laws that offend human rights, the remedies accorded foreign investors under BITs seek to compensate for prior injury. Investor-State arbitrations can result in multi-million dollar damage awards, often far in excess of any compensation awarded in human rights cases, even with respect to those who have suffered the most grievous harms[708].

Threats to other human rights

The third type of human rights concern is suggested by the Argentina claims: the potential for BITs or FTAs to prevent States that are hosts to foreign investment from taking remedial measures needed to abide by widely accepted human rights values or obligations. BIT claimants might challenge, as a violation of NT, a Government's affirmative action programmes that, for example, permit employers to prefer certain minorities in hiring. Indeed, the threat posed to South Africa's Black Economic Empowerment programmes by that country's BITs has led that State to modify its more recent BITs to expressly permit such actions[709]. Of course, international treaties, such as the Convention Eliminating All Forms of Discrimination against Women ("CEDAW") anticipate that such affirmative action programmes may not only be legal but may be necessary to promote equality[710]. Other measures,

---

[708] See, e.g., G. Van Harten and M. Loughlin, "Investment Treaty Arbitration as a Species of Global Administrative Law", 17 *European Journal of International Law* 121 (2006).

[709] See, e.g., L. E. Peterson, "South Africa's Bilateral Investment Treaties: Implications for Development and Human Rights" (Friedrich-Ebert-Stiftung, 2006), available at <http://library.fes.de/pdf-files/iez/global/04137-20080708.pdf>.

[710] See Convention on the Elimination of All Forms of Discrimination against Women, 1249 *United Nations Treaty Series* 13, 19 *International Legal Materials* 33, signed on 18 December 1979, entered into force 3 September 1981 (hereinafter "CEDAW"), Art. 4.

intended to correct inequities in income or job distribution, such as requirements on investors to hire local workers, invest in disadvantaged regions, or transfer advanced technology might be deemed inconsistent with some BITs' prohibitions on performance requirements or bans on "discriminatory" treatment[711].

To the extent BITs protect the rights of foreign investors who have now taken over formerly Government-owned utilities and are now supplying basic commodities such as water or gas to large portions of a nation's citizens, an internationalized commitment to protect these utilities' right to property or prior contractual obligations may pose conflicts with the evolving set of positive international obligations States have undertaken under the International Covenant on Economic, Social and Cultural Rights ("ICESCR")[712]. Thus, a number of BIT claims involving privatized utilities are seen as conflicting with a nation's duty to respect its citizens' rights to water or to health[713].

Alleged conflicts with the residual sovereign right to regulate

As the preceding suggests, it is not hard to recast contentions that the investment regime interferes with the sovereign right to regulate in human rights terms. To the extent, for example, that BIT guarantees ensuring "fair and equitable treatment" are interpreted broadly to protect investors from regulations that

---

[711] See L. E. Peterson, "Human Rights and Bilateral Investment Treaties: Mapping the Role of Human Rights within Investor-State Arbitration" (Montreal, Quebec, International Centre for Human Rights and Democratic Development, 2009), available at <http://www.dd-rd.ca/site/_PDF/publications/globalization/HIRA-volume3-ENG.pdf>.

[712] *Ibid.*

[713] *Ibid.*

change over time because of changing information about health risks or changes in a Government's abilities to defend such interests — on the premise that such changes violate investors' "legitimate expectations" or specific assurances that were made by the Government at the time the investment was first made — such constraints are likely to be as controversial as were comparable attempts to protect investor rights through stabilization clauses in investor-State contracts[714]. BITs and FTAs are particularly likely to be perceived as unjust to the extent that they prevent Governments from taking any of a number of actions — to regulate the environment, protect against child labour, insure labour rights, protect the public from infectious diseases — that are increasingly demanded by other international legal regimes, including evolving interpretations of the ICESCR or even the World Health Organization's International Health Regulations.

Failure to respect differentiated responsibilities

Another alleged human rights flaw emerges from the potential for international investment rights to be interpreted in absolutist terms that do not respond to the differing conditions that prevail in poorer nations. Critics of some arbitral interpretations of fair and equitable treatment, such as that delineated in the

---

[714] See, e.g., P. Kuruk, "Renegotiating Transnational Investment Agreements: Lessons for Developing Countries from the Ghana-Valco Experience", 13 *Michigan Journal of International Law* 43 (1991). For evidence that stabilization clauses continue to be included in current investor-host State contracts, see International Finance Corporation, "Stabilization Clauses and Human Rights" (27 May 2009), available at <http://www.ifc.org/ifcext/sustainability.nsf/Content/Publications_LOE_Stabilization>.

TECMED case (discussed in Chapter III), contend that such interpretations of BITs or even the customary "international minimum standard" do not address the relative resources, technical and otherwise, available to particular nations. For some the problem is that arbitral interpretations of BITs and FTAs do not acknowledge an emerging general principle that is increasingly common to other international regimes such as those governing the global commons or trade, namely differentiated levels of responsibility corresponding to, among other things, differing national capacities. For critics, a regime that forces a Government that cannot feed, educate, or provide minimal health care to its people to pay millions of dollars to a multinational enterprise for violating a contract that may have been concluded under unequal bargaining conditions is simply not just — whether or not it is justified by *pacta sunt servanda*.

But, as is suggested by the origins of the investment regime discussed in Chapters I and II, defenders of the investment regime also resort to human rights values in defending BITs and FTAs. This appeal usually takes the form of one or more of the following contentions.

Support for the rule of law

Since BITs were, after all, designed to support the national and the international rule of law, it is not surprising that its defenders contend that when investors' rights are protected, others' rights tend to be as well. There are various versions of this argument — from the contention that free markets and respect for human rights are part and parcel of a virtuous circle to more specific contentions about the rule of law effects of BITs and FTAs. Some argue that the effective implementation of BITs and FTAs into local law usually requires reforms to national law and courts such that the rights of domestic investors (and others) are better protected as well. It is alleged that States that comply with their BIT obligations are more likely to have functioning and independent local courts or that entering into such treaties creates powerful incentives for States to improve access to national remedies or to improve the quality of their judiciaries. BITs provide, after all, an incentive for Governments to avoid instances where investors have cause to file international complaints because of the State's actions or inactions. Defenders of the investment regime also rely on familiar contentions in defence of *pacta sunt servanda*, namely the contention that a Government that is capable of violating its word to a foreign investor — and breaches solemn promises — is capable of doing the same to its own citizens, whether with respect to its own laws or other international obligations.

The development of fair process

To the extent investor-State decisions elaborate on concepts such as "fair and equitable treatment", they may be engaging in the same enterprise as are international courts engaged in interpreting human rights treaties[715]. It is therefore no surprise that some investor-State awards are now drawing from decisions rendered in human rights courts and some suggest that

---

[715] For one example, see the widely noted decision by the European Court of Justice in *Kadi* v. *Council and Commission*, Judgment, Grand Chamber of the European Court of Justice, Case No. C-402/05 (2008), available at <http://eur-lex.europa.eu/LexUriServ/LexUriServ.do?uri=CELEX:62005J0402:EN:HTML>. For a detailed exploration of the overlap between international investment law and international human rights law, see J. D. Fry, "International Human Rights Law in Investment Arbitration: Evidence of International Law's Unity", 18 *Duke Journal of Comparative and International Law* 77 (2007).

it will not be long before human rights courts, in turn, draw from investor-State awards. Such transnational judicial conversations, it is argued, engage in ever more detailed formulations of what international due process requires, including progressively clearer interpretations of what the "right to be heard" means.

Protecting the rights of non-State actors such as NGOs

A more concrete benefit to human rights defenders may occur to the extent BITs or FTAs extend their protections to a foreign enterprise whether or not it operates for a profit. Many BITs, including those negotiated by the United States, appear to extend their protections to, for example, the offices of Amnesty International located abroad[716]. Given the recent tendency of many Governments to regulate in order to limit the activities of NGOs within their borders[717], environmental and human rights NGOs may need the assistance of a BIT to protect their own interests, including their property, abroad.

Protecting other human rights

Of course, the most direct defence of the investment regime in human rights terms treats the right to prop-

---

[716] See, e.g., "US Model BIT of 1984", in S. Zamora and R. A. Brand (eds.), 1 *Basic Documents of International Economic Law* 655 (Chicago, Illinois, Custom Clearing House International, 1990) (hereinafter "1984 US Model BIT"), Art. I (1) *(a)* (defining eligible "company of a Party" to include "associations . . . whether or not organized for pecuniary gain").

[717] See, e.g., M. Davis, "China's New Nonprofit Regulations: Season of Instability", *Asia Catalyst: Economic and Social Rights in Asia* (14 June 2010), available at <http://asiacatalyst.org/blog/2010/06/chinas-new-nonprofit-regulations-season-of-instability.html#more>.

erty as itself a human right worthy of recognition. As is suggested by the diplomatic exchanges between Mexico and the United States which led to the Hull Rule, BIT and FTA provisions providing for compensation upon expropriation are grounded in all persons' rights to own property as well as their rights not to be arbitrarily deprived of it. This right is recognized by the Universal Declaration of Human Rights as well as customary international law and remains one of the enumerated rights under the European Convention on Human Rights[718]. Quite apart from the right to property, protecting the rights of investors may sometimes be hard to distinguish from protecting their human rights. This may be the case, for example, when the foreign investor is a publisher or broadcaster attempting to remain in business despite government efforts to silence its views[719] or where what a Government does in order to drive an investor out of the country involves acts or threats of violence to the investor or its employees[720]. Human rights defenders of the regime point out that the foreign investors entitled to file claims under BITs or FTAs are not always corporations but may be natural persons. Claimants in investor-State claims are sometimes minority or majority shareholders seeking recompense in their personal capacity. For example,

---

[718] See Universal Declaration on Human Rights, General Assembly res. 217A (III), UN doc. A/777 (1948), Art. 17; European Convention on Human Rights, 213 *United Nations Treaty Series* 222, signed on 4 November 1950, entered into force on 3 September 1953 (hereinafter "ECHR"), Protocol 1.

[719] See, e.g., L. E. Peterson, "International Investment Law and Media Disputes: A Complement to WTO Law", *Columbia FDI Perspectives* No. 17 (2010), available at <http://www.vcc.columbia.edu/content/fdi-perspectives>.

[720] See, e.g., *Desert Line Projects LLC* v. *Republic of Yemen*, Award, ICSID Case No. ARB/05/17 (6 February 2008).

Raymond Loewen, who unsuccessfully tried to file a
NAFTA claim against the United States, is no less an
individual complainant than is anyone else who seeks a
personal remedy before a human rights court. Indeed,
Loewen's claim that he had been discriminated against
or treated inequitably or unfairly by a US court is
strikingly similar to many contemporary human
rights claims. His claim is a direct descendant of the
Chattin and *Neer* cases that helped establish the international minimum standard and helped usher in the
rise of human rights regimes[721].

What are ways to bridge or harmonize the competing human rights contentions surveyed above? One
possible response relies on the regime's continuing
capacities for exit and voice. As is suggested by
Chapter II, the mostly bilateral nature of the investment regime enables State intervention to anticipate,
prevent, or ameliorate conflicts between the rights of
investors and others. To the extent emerging arbitral
case-law threatens States' residual capacity to regulate
on behalf of the public interest, States retain some discretion to resist the further conclusion of such treaties
or to demand changes to existing agreements (as
through the issuance of joint interpretations). As is
suggested by the evolution of the US Model BIT over
time, more recent investment treaties include provisions discouraging races to the bottom by States anxious to attract foreign investors and willing to sacrifice
their regulatory options in order to do so. Accordingly,
some BITs and FTAs now include provisions indicat-

---

[721] *Loewen Group, Inc.* v. *United States*, Award, ICSID
Case No. ARB (AF)/98/3 (26 June 2003); *United States
(Chattin)* v. *United Mexican States*, General Claims
Commission, 4 *Reports of International Arbitration
Awards* 282 (23 July 1927); *United States (Neer)* v. *United
Mexican States*, General Claims Commission, 4 *Reports of
International Arbitration Awards* 60 (15 October 1926).

ing that States should not reduce their existing commitments regarding labour rights or environmental protection in order to attract FDI[722]. In other cases, new preamblar language in such treaties may make it easier for treaty interpreters to find that the "object and purpose" of such treaties include advancing States' ability to fulfil their human rights and other international obligations. As is discussed in Chapter II, recent BITs and FTAs also permit interpretative actions by their States parties *ex post*. Specific provisions, as under the NAFTA, permit the parties to issue interpretations that are binding on investor-State arbitrators. Other recent changes in BITs and FTAs, including demands that investor-State arbitrations be more transparent and open to *amici*, respond, at least in part, to human rights concerns[723].

The second and third possibilities for "re-balancing" the rights of investors and others rest with the other major source of change and law-making within the regime: investor-State arbitrators.

Arbitrators have a ready tool that permits BITs and FTAs to be read harmoniously with host States' ability to regulate in the public interest and comply with their other international obligations: the inherent elasticity of most of the substantive investment guarantees. The vagueness (and relative novelty) of many of the substantive investment guarantees make them supple instruments that could embrace States' legitimate regu-

---

[722] See, e.g., North American Free Trade Agreement, 32 *International Legal Materials* 612, signed on 17 December 1992, entered into force on 1 January 1994 (hereinafter "NAFTA"), Art. 1114. Note, however, that Article 1114 anticipates only "consultations" among the States parties to resolve disputes involving this clause and not investor-State dispute settlement. *Ibid.*, Art. 1114 (2).

[723] See discussion of the evolving texts of contemporary BITs in Chapter II.

latory concerns. This is certainly one implication of the *National Grid* decision discussed in Chapter IV. In that case, the vagueness of FET proved useful to arbitrators who decided that fairness and equity required considering the timing of the challenged Argentine actions relative to the crisis that it faced. The "legitimate expectations" principle that many see as underlying a number of BIT guarantees, from FET to national treatment, is potentially a malleable tool that could lead to the same kind of balancing[724]. As is clear from some of the emerging arbitral decisions, that concept may embrace the reasonable expectations of both the investor — who may be assumed to anticipate the needs of States to respect their international obligations — and the host State. After all, an expectation that is "legitimate" is one that reflects what the investor was only reasonably entitled to assume – based in part on what the Government has done in that sector or technological developments that can be reasonably expected in the particular context. Host States, it has been suggested, have not silently traded away their inherent

---

[724] See, e.g., A. Roberts, "Power and Persuasion in Investment Treaty Arbitration: The Dual Role of States", 104 *American Journal of International Law* 179 (2010), pp. 214-215 (describing legitimate expectations as an underlying principle to FET, though not a general principle of international law); J. Alvarez and T. Brink, "Revisiting the Necessity Defense in the Argentina Cases", *Yearbook on International Investment Law and Policy 2010-2011* (2011), also available on Investment Claims Database (Oxford), see <http://www.investmentclaims.com/subscriber_article?script=yes&id=/ic/Journal%20Articles/lawiic-journal052&recno=20%searchType=browse> (arguing that the principle of proportionality or other forms of balancing are more appropriately applied through applications of substantive guarantees such as FET rather than attempting to do the same through the customary defence of necessity).

rights to regulate in the public interest merely because they have ratified an investment treaty. The principle of "legitimate expectations" may also be a potent tool in the hands of a host State that wants to defend its existing law, particularly when that law was in effect when the investor originally came into the country. As numerous arbitral decisions suggest, it is nearly impossible for an investor to prevail in an investor-State claim when the host State is able to show that its actions are consistent with its law or the regulatory regime that applied at the time the investor made its investment[725]. If those laws incorporate a State's human rights obligations, a State probably need not fear a BIT claim that is grounded on its good faith implementation of such obligations.

Giving due weight to a host State's human rights obligations might also occur through sensitive applications of the national treatment or expropriation guarantees. This may occur, for example, where rules barring discrimination rely on equal treatment "in like circumstances" as under the NAFTA[726]. A host State that distinguishes among investors for purposes of implementing its human rights obligations arguably has not violated the ban on equal treatment in "like" circumstances. Similarly, BITs' expropriation guarantees may permit consideration of the host States' legitimate human rights, as where such provisions provide, as do post-2004 US BITs that "non-discriminatory regulatory actions . . . designed and applied to protect legitimate public welfare objectives" do not normally constitute

---

[725] See, e.g., C. McLachlan *et al.*, *International Investment Arbitration: Substantive Principles* (Oxford, Oxford University Press, 2007), pp. 236-237 (summarizing the gist of many arbitral decisions interpreting FET as "the investor must take foreign law as he finds it").

[726] NAFTA, *supra* footnote 722, Art. 1102.

indirect expropriations[727]. Human rights concerns
might also be accommodated to the extent arbitrators
enjoy some flexibility in determining what constitutes
"fair market value". In these and other ways substantive investment guarantees might be "balanced" to take
account of a host State's residual right to regulate in
order to implement its human rights (or other) international obligations[728].

Third, and perhaps most importantly, arbitrators
may be able to resort to the suppleness of traditional
principles of treaty interpretation. These principles
include the canon of interpretation that unless a treaty
includes explicit language so providing, it should not
be presumed to derogate from fundamental principles
of law, including States' normal capacity to pursue
public welfare objectives. Of course, traditional interpretative principles also include Article 31 (3) *(c)* of
the Vienna Convention on the Law of Treaties which
permits consideration, along with a treaty's context, of
"any relevant rules of international law applicable in
the relations between the parties". As Judge Bruno
Simma and his co-author have argued in a recent
scholarly contribution, the wording of Article 31 (3) *(c)*
is extremely malleable and may permit interpretations
of BITs and FTAs that are not in conflict with a host
State's human rights obligations[729]. A non-dogmatic

---

[727] US Department of State and US Trade Representative, "2004 US Model BIT", available at <http://www.
state.gov/documents/organization/117601.pdf>, Annex B,
Art. 4 *(b)*.

[728] For an attempt to make the same case with respect
to environmental obligations, see, e.g., T. Weiler, "A First
Look at the Interim Measures Award in *S.D. Myers, Inc. v.
Canada*: It Is Possible to Balance Legitimate Environ-
mental Concerns with Investment Protection", 24 *Hastings
International and Comparative Law Review* 173 (2001).

[729] See generally B. Simma and T. Kill, "Harmonizing
Investment Protection and International Human Rights:

reading of that license would permit an investor-State arbitrator to consider "relevant" rules that exist at the time a BIT is interpreted (and not only when it was concluded), international obligations that apply not only between the States parties to the particular BIT but to only one of them, *erga omnes* obligations (as are most human rights) that need not be within the same subject matter as the BIT, and even "soft law" norms "applicable" (but not necessarily binding) between the treaty parties [730].

Of course, there is no guarantee that the Article 31 (3) *(c)* interpretative licence will be treated in the human-rights-friendly way that Simma advises or as the tool for "systemic integration" that others have recommended [731]. Much depends on whether the particular disputing parties in an arbitration make such arguments as arbitrators are not likely to reach for such contentions on their own. While we can imagine a human rights NGO that is permitted to intervene in such disputes readily making the case that, for example, Argentina should have been able to violate its pre-existing tariff obligations with respect to a privatized

---

First Steps Towards a Methodology", in C. Binder *et al.* (eds.), *International Investment Law for the 21st Century: Essays in Honor of Christoph Schreuer* (New York, Oxford University Press, 2009). Simma's work follows on his earlier path-breaking effort to demonstrate why "self-contained regimes" in international law are rare, if they exist at all. See B. Simma and D. Pulkowski, "Of Planets and the Universe: Self-Contained Regimes in International Law", 17 *European Journal of International Law* 483 (2006).

[730] See generally Simma and Kill, *supra* footnote 729.

[731] See *ibid.*, pp. 528-529 (advising interpretation in line with a systemic framework that includes application of general international law, including human rights); see generally C. McLachlan, "The Principle of Systemic Integration and Article 31 (3) *(c)* of the Vienna Convention", 54 *International & Comparative Law Quarterly* 279 (2005).

water company to the extent these become inconsistent
with that country's duties to protect its citizens' access
to water, we can see why Argentina or other respondent
States might well hesitate in relying on such a defence
to an investor-State claim. Not all respondent States in
investor-State arbitration may welcome a widely publi-
cized legal precedent obligating them to respect such
human rights as a matter of international law. Both
investor claimants and respondent States may have
other reasons to resist expanding the substantive
domain of investor-State arbitration. Both might have
an interest in keeping this mechanism as a relatively
expeditious, less expensive, and less politicized forum
for the resolution of economic disputes.

And even when human rights claims are made a
central point of the parties' contentions, there is no
guarantee that investor-State arbitrators will make
these the central point of their decisions. Investor-State
arbitrators selected to resolve what they believed was a
relatively narrow "economic dispute" under an "economic" treaty and worried about challenges to their
limited jurisdiction might well hesitate to enter into a
detailed elucidation of a human rights issue — such as
what it means to have an entitlement to water — that is
at the cutting edge of human rights law[732]. This may be

---

[732] The cutting edge nature of these enquiries is not
limited to international investment law. See, e.g., A. A. Dhir,
"Of Takeover, Foreign Investment and Human Rights:
Unpacking the Noranda-Minmetals Conundrum", 22
Banking & Finance Law Review 77 (2006) (indicating the
controversy when a Chinese company implicated in human
rights violations attempted to purchase a Canadian company and the relevant Canadian laws authorizing the
Government to interfere did not explicitly consider such
issues to be relevant); A. A. Dhir, "Realigning the Corporate Building Blocks: Shareholder Proposals as a Vehicle
for Achieving Corporate Social and Human Rights
Accountability", 43 *American Business Law Journal* 365

all the more the case to the extent the particular arbitrator has an expertise only in private international law or commercial arbitration but even public international lawyers who specialize in investment or trade law may not be comfortable interpreting human rights treaties or customary law.

(4) Is the investment regime "biased" in favour of investors?

Concerns over the asymmetrical obligations in favour of investment protection that are undoubtedly (and purposely) imposed by first generation BITs, like the US Model BIT of 1987 discussed in Chapter II, need to be distinguished from worries that investor-State arbitration is itself biased. The evolution of model BITs discussed in Chapter II suggests that some States, including the United States, have come to believe that their own earlier treaties might have underestimated the scope of obligations assumed. There is much less evidence, however, to support the proposition that investor-State arbitration is itself necessarily biased in favour of pro-investor outcomes.

The largest statistical analysis of publicly available investment treaty arbitral awards, Susan Franck's examination of all publicly available awards issued before 1 June 2006, indicates that respondent Governments won in 58 per cent of the cases while investors won in 39 per cent; that despite the fact that investors claimed on average US$343 million in damages, tribunals awarded only US$10 million on average; and that arbitral outcome was not reliably associated with the development status of the respondent State, the development status of the arbitrator, or some interac-

---

(2006) (proposing changes in Canadian corporate law or its interpretation to permit consideration of evolving human rights concerns).

tion between the two[733]. Franck concludes that there is no empirical evidence to support the proposition that the developing world is treated unfairly in investor-State arbitration or that arbitrators from the developed and developing worlds decide cases differently[734].

Franck's studies do not prove that investor-State arbitration is fair. No one is quite sure what the universe of non-publicly available awards would show in comparison to the awards that she examined or whether pro-investor outcomes are more likely when it comes to settling claims in the shadow of threats to take disputes to arbitration[735]. It is also hard to evaluate what the comparison of awards rendered versus amounts claimed or the win/loss record that Franck records actually demonstrates. That claimants get, on average, much less than they sought might only demonstrate that investors seek vastly inflated or frivolous claims. If so, average awards of US$10 million might not be such a bad outcome from the claimants' standpoint. Similarly, a win record of 39 per cent for investors tells us nothing about whether, objectively,

---

[733] See, e.g., S. D. Franck, "International Investment Arbitration: Winning, Losing and Why", *Columbia FDI Perspectives* No. 7 (2009), available at <http://www.vcc.columbia.edu/content/fdi-perspectives>.

[734] See *ibid*. See also S. D. Franck, "Development and Outcomes of Investment Arbitration Awards", 50 *Harvard International Law Journal* 435 (2009); S. D. Franck, "Empirically Evaluating Claims about Investment Treaty Arbitration", 86 *North Carolina Law Review* 1 (2008).

[735] There are also reported cases where States' public policy or proposed legislation were affected by the threat of investor-State arbitration. See, e.g., D. Schneiderman, *Constitutionalizing Economic Globalization: Investment Rules and Democracy's Promise* (Cambridge, Cambridge University Press, 2008), pp. 127-129 and 132-133 (arguing that NAFTA discouraged "plain packaging" regulations for cigarettes and a national ban on the toxic gasoline additive MTBE).

investors deserved to win these cases or only half as many. Nonetheless, Franck's numbers pour cold water on unexamined assertions by many critics of the regime who have sometimes asserted that the "typical" outcomes in these cases are "multi-million" dollar awards or that States rarely win. More difficult to evaluate are contentions, by Governments such as Ecuador's or scholars such as Gus Van Harten, that irrespective of the actual outcomes in arbitral awards, there is a *perception* that investor-State arbitration is inherently biased in favour of claimants. The argument for the perception of bias rests on two assertions: (1) that the investor-State arbitral mechanism is sustained only to the extent claimants continue to have confidence to bring claims and (2) that arbitrator appointing authorities, such as ICSID, are pre-disposed toward protecting investor rights. Both of these realities, it is claimed, lead to selecting arbitrators who are inclined to rule in favour of investors in order to perpetuate their own continued appointment and investor-State dispute settlement generally. This is contestable. Some suggest, on the contrary, that arbitrators are motivated by maintaining a reputation for fairness, not for sustaining any particular party's claims, and that the market for arbitrators — which includes a market for presidents of tribunals as well as for arbitrators appointed by respondent States — in and of itself protects the system from crude forms of pro-investor (or pro-State) bias [736]. Others would not deny that specific arbitral

---

[736] See, e.g., T. W. Wälde, "Introduction", in Kahn and Wälde (eds.), *supra* footnote 692, p. 51 (noting that investor-State arbitrators are motivated by reputational standing and that perhaps in the long run, "self interest and virtue coalesce"); Caron, *supra* footnote 696, p. 415 (arguing that the motivations of arbitrators extend beyond future retention and include a desire to maintain or increase their reputations).

outcomes might indeed have been influenced by extraneous concerns, including politics or ideology, but suggest that this does not reflect a systemic bias one way
or another with respect to investor-State dispute settlement but lapses in judgment to which all adjudicators,
including judges, sometimes succumb.

The mixed Argentine outcomes discussed in
Chapter IV provide fodder for all sides. While the
wave of annulment decisions in favour of Argentina
would appear to belie claims of endemic pro-investor
bias, those annulment rulings may have been influenced by political concerns — including worries by
members of these annulment committees that upholding the multi-million dollar awards initially rendered
would exacerbate the backlash against the regime
and even threaten its future. If that is the case and political concerns tilted the results reached in the *Enron*
and *Sempra* annulments in favour of Argentina, we
should now expect worries over the "politicization" of
investor-State disputes to come from the business community.

C. Reform Proposals

Given the legitimacy concerns expressed concerning
the investment regime, it is no surprise that a number
of reforms have been suggested[737]. Table 5 groups

---

[737] For more comprehensive surveys of legitimacy con-
cerns and reform proposals, see Organisation for Economic
Co-operation and Development ("OECD"), "Improving the
System of Investor-State Dispute Settlement: An Overview",
Working Papers on International Investment No. 2006/1
(2006), available at <http://www.oecd.org/dataoecd/3/59/
36052284.pdf>; UNCTAD, Trade and Development Board,
Investment, Enterprise and Development Commission,
"Report of the Multi-year Expert Meeting on Investment for
Development on Its First Session" (2009), available at <http
://www.unctad.org/en/docs/ciimem3d3_en.pdf>.

these proposals under the particular legitimacy gap that each primarily seeks to address.

TABLE 5. PROPOSALS FOR CHANGE
IN THE REGIME

Rule of Law	*Vertical Concerns*	*Horizontal Concerns*
(1) Increased resort to doctrines of deference to other fora	(1) Narrow investor rights	(1) Establish an investment law assistance facility
(2) Greater transparency of documents/ awards/ proceedings	(2) Broaden host States' "policy space"	(2) Strengthen ethical and conflict of interest rules for regime participants
(3) Increased third party participation	(3) Consider TNC responsibilities	(3) Encourage "systemic integration" of international investment law
(4) Limiting claims	(4) Include home State responsibilities	(4) Change the appointing authority for arbitrators
(5) Methods to promote more consistent arbitral interpretations	(5) Narrow arbitrators' discretion	(5) Resume negotiations on a multilateral investment treaty
	(6) Encourage greater proportionality balancing	(6) Impose limits on costs or damages awarded in investor-State dispute settlement

Those concerned with the rule of law challenges faced by the regime, from the possibility of inconsistent interpretations of the law to the risk of "forum shopping" among diverse forums by claimants, urge increased resort to doctrines of deference with respect to other adjudicative bodies. Concerns that host States now find themselves facing multiple investor-State claims under different investment treaties, by different groups of investors or subsidiaries or shareholders based on the same claim, under claims filed before different international venues (e.g., in both the European Court of Human Rights and in investor-State arbitration) or in international venues as well as national courts, have prompted proposals for increased resort to stronger doctrines of *res judicata*, *lis pendens* or abstention by investor-State arbitrators to avoid the most egregious cases of forum-shopping [738].

Even more prevalent among reformers are proposals for greater transparency in the course of investor-State arbitration. Those who believe that investor-State arbitrations are so distinct from commercial arbitration that they merit departures from the confidentiality that often characterizes the latter urge that all claims, briefs by the disputing parties, awards, and arbitral hearings be publicly available or open to the public. As noted, NGOs like the International Institute for Sustainable Development are now pressuring arbitral venues, from ICSID to UNCITRAL, to open the arbitral process much more than in the past and abandon the rule that would leave it solely to the parties to a dispute to determine what, if any, part of the process or the underlying

---

[738] See, e.g., A. K. Bjorklund, "Private Rights and Public International Law: Why Competition among International Economic Law Tribunals Is Not Working", 59 *Hastings Law Journal* 241 (2007), pp. 300-304.

documents should be made public[739]. Advocates of transparency point to the NAFTA as the salutary example as the NAFTA parties have gone further than most parties to investment treaties in encouraging transparency, insofar as the three NAFTA Governments have committed themselves to make all documents, including briefs and awards, publicly available — subject only to protecting certain confidential data[740]. The NAFTA example may also have inspired ICSID to change its rules to provide for greater transparency and to permit the admission of *amicus* briefs[741]. ICSID's principal rival body for investor-State disputes, UNCITRAL, is now considering changes in the same direction[742]. At the same time, it must be kept in mind that some States as well as investor claimants want to retain the discretion to settle their disputes quietly, outside the public eye, and it is hard to see how this option can be fully excluded where the underlying BITs or FTAs enable the parties to select arbitral forums or arbitral rules that still permit confidentiality.

As the NAFTA example illustrates, those urging transparency also contend that greater openness co-

---

[739] See, e.g., International Institute for Sustainable Development ("IISD"), "Revising the UNCITRAL Arbitration Rules to Address Investor-State Arbitrations" (2007), available at <http://www.iisd.org/pdf/2008/investment_revising_uncitral_arbitration_dec.pdf> (hereinafter "IISD UNCITRAL Report").

[740] See, e.g., J. J. Coe, "Transparency in the Resolution of Investor-State Disputes — Adoption, Adaptation, and NAFTA Leadership", 54 *University of Kansas Law Review* 1339 (2006).

[741] See, e.g., M. Kantor, "New Amendments to ICSID Arbitration Rules", 2006:1 *Stockholm International Arbitration Review* 213 (2006).

[742] See "UNCITRAL Revised Rules Adopted", United Nations Information Service (29 June 2010), available at <http://www.unis.unvienna.org/unis/pressrels/2010/unis l139.html>.

incides with and, indeed, is a necessary step towards, permitting a greater number of voices to be heard during the course of investor-State dispute settlement and in determining countries' investment policies generally[743]. While rights to participate other than as one of the disputing parties — as *amicus* — are not explicitly provided for in most arbitral rules, some arbitral tribunals, including those operating under the UNCITRAL rules (which generally leave such matters to the arbitrators' discretion), have permitted certain NGOs to submit *amicus* briefs[744]. For some NGOs, however, *amicus* participation is only the first step. Some NGOs are demanding, thus far without success, a right to demand documents from the parties or to participate in oral argument. Demands for greater participation may also encourage more provisions in FTAs permitting other States parties to an FTA, other than the respondent State, to express views on a claim. Such third-party participation rights exist under the NAFTA, for instance, on the premise that all three NAFTA parties have interests in how their joint treaty is interpreted[745].

The problem of inconsistent arbitral rulings has led to other "rule of law" proposals. The motivation to harmonize international investment law explains efforts by individual scholars to elaborate black letter restatements and commentaries on international investment law drawing from both the body of treaties and arbitral decisions[746]. Suggestions for comparable efforts by

---

[743] See, e.g., IISD UNCITRAL Report, *supra* footnote 739.

[744] See *Methanex Corp.* v. *United States*, Final Award on Jurisdiction and Merits, UNCITRAL Arbitration Rules (3 August 2005), paras. 26-30.

[745] NAFTA, *supra* footnote 722, Art. 1128.

[746] See, e.g., Z. Douglas, *The International Law of Investment Claims* (Cambridge, Cambridge University Press, 2009).

groups of scholars, as within UNCITRAL, are driven by a perception that only credible multilateral efforts could exert the degree of influence on investor-State arbitrators, who are the principal target (apart from States parties capable of issuing "joint" treaty interpretations as under the NAFTA) for such efforts.

Such "statements of investment law" by a respected group of experts, whether or not based within an international institution, might even include recommendations for harmonizing the law analogous to those issued by the ILC in the course of its recent Fragmentation project[747]. Like the ILC's study of the challenges produced by the proliferation of treaty regimes and specialized courts, a "restatement of international investment law" could direct investor-State arbitrators to apply the harmonizing principles reflected in Article 31 (3) *(c)* of the Vienna Convention on the Law of Treaties; the canon of interpretation that even *lex specialis* rules need to be given a "contextual" interpretation on the premise that their application "does not normally extinguish the relevant general law"; or general rules of interpretation that permit recourse to general principles of law even with respect to "special" regimes, especially when the relevant treaty rules are "unclear" or "open-textured"[748].

Another way to secure possibly more consistent arbitral decisions would be to consider changes in the

---

[747] International Law Commission ("ILC"), "Fragmentation of International Law: Difficulties Arising from the Diversification and Expansion of International Law", UN doc. A/CN.4/L.702 (18 July 2006) (hereinafter "ILC Fragmentation Report").

[748] *Ibid*. Investor-State arbitrators are not reticent about relying on such systemic integration devices as Article 31 (3) *(c)* of the Vienna Convention on the Law of Treaties. See, e.g., *Saluka Investment Group B.V.* v. *Czech Republic*, Partial Award, UNCITRAL Arbitration Rules (17 March 2006), para. 254.

ways investor-State arbitrations are conducted. This could involve, for example, providing legal assistance to the arbitrators, perhaps drawn from ICSID staff, such that relevant prior rulings are always brought to their attention, irrespective of whether these are relied upon by the disputing parties[749]. Less controversially, there could be more modest changes to the ways in which investor-State arbitrators, or at least the president of three person panels, are selected such as to provide greater continuity among cases involving the same respondent State or comparable legal or factual issues. Greater resort to consolidating related claims, now specifically anticipated under some investment treaties, is yet another possible procedural device that may facilitate the production of a more coherent *jurisprudence constante*.

Some contend that the only or best way to secure consistent interpretations of international investment law is to make sure *ad hoc* panels of arbitrators do not get the last word on what the law is. Some advocate enhanced review of investor-State awards by expanding the ability of annulment committees to overrule arbitral decisions or by changing applicable treaty and national rules so that national courts charged with enforcing arbitral awards also have the power to overturn them on the basis of erroneous findings of law or fact. Others prefer establishing centralized appellate bodies (as within the WTO) or some kind of appellate mechanism for particular BITs or FTAs[750]. Indeed,

---

[749] The WTO dispute settlement system, for example, reportedly relies to a considerable extent on permanent WTO staff for this purpose.

[750] See, e.g., D. McRae, "The WTO Appellate Body: A Model for an ICSID Appeals Facility?", 1 *Journal of International Dispute Settlement* 1 (2010), available at <http://jids.oxfordjournals.org/content/early/2010/07/01/jnlids.idq003.full>.

while discussions of establishing such a body within ICSID have floundered[751], at the urging of the US Congress, contemporary US BITs and FTAs now expressly contain a commitment by the States parties to eventually establish such a mechanism[752]. Others, such as Gus Van Harten, advocate the creation of a single permanent International Investment Court on the assumption that the security of tenure provides adjudicators with the legitimacy and the independence to proclaim coherent and unbiased investment law[753]. Others make proposals inspired by European precedents, including mechanisms by which investor-State arbitrators are entitled to ask for advice from another entity, whether national courts or a political body of trade ministers[754].

Resistance to many of these proposals usually stems from fears that this will make investor-State dispute settlement, which is already becoming more costly and time consuming, even more so. Others fear that some-

---

[751] For an account of the state of play of that proposal, concluding that chances for establishing such a mechanism are "elusive", see D. A. Gantz, "An Appellate Mechanism for Review of Arbitral Decisions in Investor-State Disputes: Prospects and Challenges", 39 *Vanderbilt Journal of Transnational Law* 39 (2006), p. 39.

[752] US Trade Promotion Act of 2002, Public Law No. 107-210 § 2102 (b) (3) (G) (iv) (codified as 19 USC § 3802 (2004)).

[753] G. Van Harten, "A Case for an International Investment Court", *Society for International Economic Law* Working Paper No. 22/08 (2008), available at <http://papers.ssrn.com/sol3/papers.cfm?abstract_id=1153424> (making the case largely on the need to establish perceived guarantees of independence and impartiality).

[754] T. W. Wälde, "Alternatives for Obtaining Greater Consistency in Investment Arbitration: An Appellate Institution after the WTO, Authoritative Treaty Arbitration or Mandatory Consolidation?", 2:2 *Transnational Dispute Management* 71 (2005), pp. 75-77.

thing like a permanent appellate body or an international investment court with tenured judges might be more emboldened (not less) to proclaim principles or rules (as with respect to the rights of investors versus States in the context of access to water or health care) that go beyond where the relevant stakeholders of the regime want to go.

As reactions to proposals for an appellate body suggest, proposed rule of law reforms may not always be consistent with the goals of those whose main concern lies with protecting the rights of sovereigns, that is, those worried about the regime's "vertical" or "democratic" deficits. There is some tension among those who want investor-State arbitrators to establish consistent law, which is presumably more faithful to prior precedents, and those who worry about what that case-law says about the rights of States. Not all agree that the investment regime should remain driven by arbitral "law-making" or that it is desirable to empower arbitrators further, as by establishing a single or a number of appellate bodies. Some reformers would prefer procedural or other rules that would restrain arbitral discretion[755]. This is certainly what happens now under the US Model BIT of 2004 where, as discussed, the States parties to such treaties are able to issue binding interpretations that the arbitrators must respect or

---

[755] There are also some who would stress parallel procedures that improve the efficiency of formal arbitration, including mandatory forms of mediation that are typically conducted away from public scrutiny. See, e.g., T. W. Wälde, *supra* footnote 684, pp. 534-536. Wälde also responds to those proposing a permanent international court by citing research explaining why States prefer *ad hoc* dispute settlement mechanisms that permit them to exercise greater control over permanent bodies. *Ibid.*, pp. 559-560 (citing E. Posner and J. Yoo, "A Theory of International Adjudication", University of Chicago Law School, Olin Working Paper No. 206 (2004)).

through special provisions that empower the States' respective tax authorities to get first crack at deciding whether a challenged tax measure is indeed an expropriation[756].

Most of the other "vertical" reform proposals to lessen the "democratic deficit" of BITs and FTAs listed in Table 5 are self-explanatory. Those seeking to narrow investor rights have ready models on hand based on the efforts by the United States and emulators that would, as discussed in Chapter II, limit the scope of FET or the concept of a "regulatory taking"[757]. Those interested in more explicit changes in BITs to permit greater host State "policy space" have other precedents, such as the recent Canadian Model BIT, which as noted in Chapter II, includes a general exceptions clause similar to that in GATT Article XX or the defunct Norwegian Model BIT's more sovereignty-protective preamble. Efforts to "re-balance" investment treaties such that they contain duties on multilateral enterprises and not merely rights or anticipating residual duties on home States of such investors, are contained in the International Institute for Sustainable Development Proposed Model International Agreement on Investment for Sustainable Development[758]. That

---

[756] 2004 US Model BIT, *supra* footnote 727, Arts. 30 (3), 31 (2) (authorizing joint decisions by the States parties); *ibid.*, Art. 21 (special provisions applicable to challenges to the States parties' taxation measures).

[757] For a useful survey of changes in OECD countries' recent investment treaties, see OECD, "Novel Features in OECD Countries' Recent Investment Agreements: An Overview" (2005), available at <http://www.oecd.org/dataoecd/42/9/35823420.pdf>.

[758] The IISD Model Treaty is an attempt to use the investment regime to remedy a perceived "accountability" or "enforcement" gap with respect to the alleged duties of TNCs. See, e.g., N. L. Bridgeman and D. B. Hunter, "Narrowing the Accountability Gap: Toward a Foreign

proposed model includes extensive pre- and post-estab-
lishment obligations on investors, including an environmental impact assessment, prohibitions on corruption, duties to uphold human rights in the workplace
and in the host State generally, and with respect to corporate governance and social responsibility[759]. It also
proposes enforcing such obligations in some cases by
withholding access to investor-State dispute settlement
for an enterprise that has failed to live up to its obligations or host State laws[760]. That proposed model treaty
even includes an innovative provision that makes
investors subject to civil actions in their home State
courts where their acts or decisions lead to "significant damage, personal injuries or loss of life in the
host State"[761]. This provision, inspired by the Bhopal
disaster of 1984, is intended to reverse a purported
asymmetry, namely that while foreign investors have
special rights accorded to them, they may escape
the jurisdictions of both home and host States on
certain occasions[762]. It is not clear how many of the

Investor Accountability Mechanism", 20 *Georgetown
International Environmental Law Review* 187 (2008),
p. 233 (identifying the IISD Model Treaty as an example
of a method of imposing an accountability mechanism on
investors as a precondition to investment).

[759] See H. Mann *et al.*, *Model International Agreement
on Investment for Sustainable Development: Negotiator's
Handbook* (International Institute for Sustainable Development, 2nd ed., 2006), available at <http://www.iisd.
org/pdf/2005/investment_model_int_handbook.pdf> (hereinafter "IISD Model Treaty"), Arts. 12-15.

[760] *Ibid.*, Art. 18.

[761] *Ibid.*, Art. 17.

[762] *Ibid.*, Art. 17, Commentary. For explanations about
why host States might in principle attempt to file counter-
claims in response to an investor's claim under a BIT or an
FTA, though it is rarely done, see H. E. Veenstra-Kjos,
"Counter-claims by Host States in Investment Dispute
Arbitration 'without Privity'", in Kahn and Wälde (eds.),

stakeholders of the investment regime would support these more radical changes to investment treaties.

Reform proposals intended to address the perceived inequities as between States, namely the "horizontal" inequalities between the rich capital exporters that originally designed the regime through their model BITs and the LDCs that adhered to them, fall along predictable lines. These are also listed in Table 5.

The proposal to establish an independent assistance or advisory facility that would help LDCs both with respect to future BIT negotiations as well as with respect to implementing these treaties has had the most serious attention in Latin America and is the closest to fruition[763]. The goal would be to establish a facility comparable to that which now exists with respect to the WTO[764] which would assist respondent States facing investment claims[765]. Far less likely to occur,

---

supra footnote 692 (also discussing legal obstacles to counter-claims such as the definition of "investment dispute" in the investment treaty and the narrowness of the investor's consent to arbitral jurisdiction).

[763] See UNCTAD, "Consultation Report on the Feasibility of an Advisory Facility on International Investment Law and Investor-State Disputes for Latin American Countries" (2009) (on file with author) (hereinafter "UNCTAD Advisory Facility Report"). See also E. J. Gottwald, "Leveling the Playing Field: Is it Time for a Legal Assistance Center for Developing Nations in Investment Treaty Arbitration?", 22 *American University Law Review* 237 (2007).

[764] See Understanding on the Rules and Procedures Governing the Settlement of Disputes, 1869 *United Nations Treaty Series* 401, 33 *International Legal Materials* 1226, in Marrakesh Agreement Establishing the World Trade Organization, Annex 2, signed on 15 April 1994, entered into force on 1 January 1995 (hereinafter "WTO:DSU"), Art. 27.

[765] See UNCTAD Advisor Facility Report, *supra* footnote 763.

at least in the short term, is a proposal to re-launch multilateral negotiations on a global investment protection treaty along the lines of the failed (and much maligned) MAI discussed in Chapter I. Most observers believe that another attempt to negotiate a multilateral investment treaty, presumably outside the OECD, is not likely over the near term[766]. Efforts to establish more enforceable and coherent conflict of interest rules among investor-State participants, particularly but not only its arbitrators, might be seen as either a "rule of law" initiative or one that seeks to redress North/South imbalances. These grow out of a perception that the existing arbitration world is essentially too cozy and consists of a small number of repeat players dominated by prominent legal academics in Europe and the United States, along with a handful of law firms in London, Paris, New York and Washington, DC, with a specialized practice and expertise[767]. The reformers argue that this group needs to be closely supervised to prevent self-serving behaviour and conflicts of interest that would not be tolerated in the context of most national courts.

As this last suggests, the proposals identified in Table 5 reflect certain assumptions that may prove

---

[766] This does not mean that forward movement on multilateral rules regarding some aspects of investment is not possible. See, e.g., P. Sauvé, "Multilateral Rules on Investment: Is Forward Movement Possible?", 9 *Journal of International Economic Law* 325 (2009). For consideration of the potential for a *de facto* multilateral agreement to emerge through the network of BITs and FTAs (or "multilateral bilateralism"), see E. Chalamish, "The Future of Bilateral Investment Treaties: A De Facto Multilateral Agreement", 34 *Brooklyn Journal of International Law* 304 (2009).

[767] For empirical data supporting such claims, see Franck, "Empirically Evaluating Claims about Investment Treaty Arbitration", *supra* footnote 734.

unwarranted. Those advocating "integrative" interpretations of BITs and FTAs (such as under an expansive view of what Article 31 (3) *(c)* of VCLT entails) may be assuming that recourse to other international regimes or multilateral treaties will redound to the benefit of LDCs. Some assume that harmonized international investment law will lessen the asymmetric impact of relying exclusively on an investment treaty that is likely to be based on a model text drafted by a rich State. Such assumptions may prove unwarranted if, for example, the integrative interpretation is inspired by the GATT or other regimes that are subject to their own horizontal asymmetries. On the other hand, an integrative interpretation that embraces GATT law might further the goal of some reformers who want the investment regime to embrace, as did the GATT, differential responsibilities for States with respect to investment protection based on level of development [768]. Presumably this was the goal sought by those who decided *Continental Casualty*, discussed in Chapter IV. Similarly, those urging that the appointing authority be changed in the case of ICSID arbitrations are presumably guided by the assumption that arbitrators not beholden to a World Bank appointing authority will be more sympathetic to the plight of LDCs in investor-State disputes. But even if a change in appointing authorities results in a greater number of arbitrators from developing States, it is not clear, based on the empirical evidence that we have, that such persons are more likely to rule in favour of LDCs [769].

These reform proposals suggest the possible futures of the investment regime. They are also useful points of departure for addressing the broader connections

---

[768] See, e.g., Congyan, *supra* footnote 685, p. 500.
[769] See Franck, *supra* footnote 733, text accompanying n. 8.

between that regime and the rest of public international law. The next section enumerates these while revisiting some of the broader themes of this monograph.

D. *Points of Intersection between the Investment Regime and Public International Law*

Table 6 identifies ten points of intersection between the international investment regime and other regimes in public international law[770]. This might also be seen as the top ten reasons why the investment regime merits inclusion within the "public" side of the Hague Academy of International Law. The first six points on Table 6 identify phenomena that now characterize many if not all public international law regimes; the last four suggest distinct descriptions of the kind of "global governance" a number of international legal regimes portend.

TABLE 6. POINTS OF INTERSECTION WITH OTHER REGIMES
IN PUBLIC INTERNATIONAL LAW

1	"Treatification" and other positivist sources
2	Fragmentation
3	Impact of non-States parties
4	Globalization and its discontents
5	The profession of international law
6	The move to judicialization
7	Hegemonic international law
8	Global administrative law
9	Constitutionalization
10	Humanity's law

---

[770] For others who have drawn these connections, see, e.g., G. Olivares, "The Essence of Economic Globalization: The Legal Dimension", 36:1 *Revue belge de droit international* (2003).

(1) Treatification and other positivist sources

Chapter III introduced the challenges the investment regime poses for advocates of treatification. As noted at the end of that chapter, the "move to treaties" does not invariably make the law more complete. The proliferation of BITs and FTAs has not necessarily made international investment law clearer, more precise, or less amenable to varying interpretation. The turn to the treaty source of obligation has not freed the regime from relying on "vague" rules of custom or general principles of law[771]. These treaties have not made the underlying rules more legitimate or more democratic. Contrary to the views of some, a treaty has never been a totally discrete law-making effort divorced from supposedly "less legitimate" efforts to distil CIL from the practices of States or to find general principles of law by engaging in comparative law[772]. On the contrary, the "treatified" investment regime provides an excellent vantage point for those seeking to consider the real world impact of "soft law", including arbitral *jurisprudence constante*.

(2) Fragmentation

Fragmentation is the dark side of treatification. As the ILC's Fragmentation project evinces, there is growing concern that as international legal regulation has

---

[771] See, e.g., J. O. McGinnis, "The Comparative Disadvantage of Customary International Law", 30 *Harvard Journal of Law & Public Policy* 7 (2006). See also J. P. Kelly, "The Twilight of Customary International Law", 40 *Virginia Journal of International Law* 449 (2000); J. W. Salacuse, "The Treatification of International Investment Law: A Victory of Form over Life? A Crossroads Crossed?", 2006:3 *Transnational Dispute Management* (2006).

[772] See, e.g., Kelly, *supra* footnote 771.

expanded to cover all kinds of activity (through the proliferation of treaties especially), it has experienced functional differentiation. Many fear that as public international law has become a curriculum and not merely a discrete subject dealing with "foreign affairs" it has produced specialized and relatively autonomous treaty regimes, sometimes with discrete dispute settlement mechanisms to interpret and enforce them. The growing numbers of BITs and FTAs, along with the rise of other regimes such as the WTO, provide other examples of specialization-cum-fragmentation; that is, growing disconnects not only as between international economic law and public international law but between "subspecialties" like human rights, trade, and investment.

The ILC's Fragmentation project began by identifying a number of specialized topics to be prepared by its various members[773]. At least three of these — the function and scope of the *lex specialis* rule, the interpretation of treaties in light of general principles of international law, and the application of successive treaties — are directly implicated by the investment regime. As prior chapters of this monograph illustrate, while that regime might be seen as relatively "self-contained", it repeatedly requires for its interpretation consideration of the possible role of background rules of international law. Despite repeated assertions that individual BITs and FTAs contain *lex specialis* rules[774], the mere fact that a web of such treaties exist and that their

---

[773] See ILC Fragmentation Report, *supra* footnote 747, para. 1.

[774] See, e.g., Fauchald, *supra* footnote 682 (arguing that ICSID tribunals tend to contribute to homogenous development of international law, especially through heavy reliance on prior ICSID awards, but that they could do more to align their approaches with those of other international tribunals, apart from ICSID).

rights overlap and are interpreted by a small group of repeat (arbitral) players requires consideration of how these treaties overlap with each other as well as other conventions and non-treaty sources of international obligation. Such multilateral concerns exist despite the bilateral nature of the regime. As Chapter IV in particular demonstrates, to the extent these treaties and the underlying rules they contain are treated simply as *lex specialis*, this does indeed pose a threat to the *coherence* of international law.

Worries about fragmentation particularly concern NGOs. Many NGOs argue that the operation of the investment regime could lead to conflicts with other treaties, whether within the WTO, or involving regimes governing the environment or human rights[775]. For certain NGOs, one way to deal with the risks of fragmentation is to appoint as investor-State arbitrators experts from fields other than commercial or investment law. It is assumed that such individuals, especially if trained in public international law, will be more willing to build bridges to other parts of public international law. Others stress, on the contrary, the need to adhere to the standard rules of treaty interpretation and to abide by the BITs and FTAs that States have concluded — even if the result is to exclude other rules of international law.

This monograph, and especially Chapter IV, has tried to suggest that adherence to the traditional rules of treaty interpretation is not necessarily incompatible with developing a harmonious jurisprudence that recog-

---

[775] See, e.g., L. E. Peterson and K. R. Grey, "International Human Rights in Bilateral Investment Treaties and in Investment Treaty Arbitration", *International Institute for Sustainable Development* (2003), available at <http://www.iisd.org/pdf/2003/investment_int_human_rights_bits.pdf>; L. Liberti, "Investissements et droits de l'homme", in Kahn and Wälde (eds.), *supra* footnote 692.

nizes that international investment law remains part of public international law. It has tried to suggest that the proposed solutions recommended by the ILC to promote the harmonization of international law — such as greater recourse to general rules of international law to fill in the gaps of discrete legal regimes — need to be contextually applied. Rules of "systemic integration" should not be applied, as attempted in the *Continental Casualty* case, in ways that fundamentally misconstrue the treaties being interpreted. Premature or inappropriate harmonization, contrary to the intent of those who deploy it, may create greater havoc with the system of international law if it comes at the expense of ignoring a treaty's object and purpose or other established rules of treaty interpretation. One of the few principles that unifies international law is that treaties must be grounded in what they say, not what their interpreters want them to have said.

(3) Impact of non-State actors

The investment regime is a prime example of the ways that international law is increasingly turning to non-State actors not only as objects of the law but as law-making or law-influencing subjects[776]. As Chapter II makes clear, that regime is itself arguably a product of non-State actors, at least to the extent that the State

---

[776] See, e.g., R. McCorquodale, "An Inclusive International Legal System", 17 *Leiden Journal of International Law* 477 (2004); L. Catá Backer, "Multilateral Corporations as Objects and Sources of Transnational Regulation", 14 *International Law Students Association Journal of International and Comparative Law* 499 (2008); L. Catá Backer, "Economic Globalization and the Rise of Efficient Systems of Global Private Law-Making: Wal-Mart as Global Legislator", 39 *Connecticut Law Review* 1739 (2007).

originators of BITs were responding to demands from private entrepreneurs dissatisfied with diplomatic espousal and seeking increased forms of international protection[777]. Thanks to BITs and FTAs non-State actors have been transformed into third-party beneficiaries charged with directly enforcing their treaty rights. It is also clear that BITs and FTAs are influencing the behaviour of others, some of whom are now structuring their transactions in order to take advantage of a particular BIT or particular BIT guarantees. The investment regime, no less than tax or corporate rules (national and international), are influencing private ordering[778]. Moreover, the regime has transformed at least some other stakeholders into active participants. This is the case with respect to NGOs that have been permitted to participate as *amici* in a number of investor-State disputes, for example.

There is also increasing recognition that another group of non-State actors, namely party-appointed investor-State arbitrators, have joined other international adjudicators as *de facto* law-makers. Yet other non-State actors, such as international organizations like the IMF, which generally imposes conditions on its loans that are compatible with those of the investment regime, as well as risk assessors in the market who

---

[777] See generally R. Putnam, "Diplomacy and Domestic Politics: The Logic of Two-Level Games", 42 *International Organizations* 427 (1988); Wälde, *supra* footnote 692, pp. 78-81.

[778] See, e.g., *Aguas del Tunari, S.A.* v. *Republic of Bolivia*, Decision on Respondent's Objections to Jurisdiction, ICSID Case No. ARB/02/3 (21 October 2005), paras. 315-323 (accepting the eligibility of an investor whose company incorporated in the Netherlands and triggered the Netherlands-Bolivia BIT — even though there were no other connections to the Netherlands — because the specific ownership structure had an apparent purpose beyond obtaining jurisdiction under the BIT).

rank countries on the basis of their "political risk" or "business environment", also play important roles in making the investment regime effective. Certainly the extent to which losing States in investor-State arbitration routinely comply with the awards rendered against them has something to do with the possibility of adverse action by others – from the IMF to market risk assessors.

The investment regime, like other contemporary international regimes, is unquestionably an agent of non-State empowerment. Public international lawyers have generally applauded this as yet another strike against the "S" word (namely sovereignty)[779]. Most have applauded the increased involvement of non-State actors in the elaboration and enforcement of international obligations, especially those involving human rights. They have argued, for example, that these "transnational norm-entrepreneurs" have made international law less sovereignty-centric, more "inclusive" and more "democratic"[780]. There is an entire scholarly

---

[779] L. Henkin, "That 'S' Word: Sovereignty and Globalization and Human Rights, et cetera", 68 *Fordham Law Review* 1 (1999).

[780] See, e.g., McCorquodale, *supra* footnote 776. For a contrary view that questions the accountability of NGOs, see P. Spiro, "Accounting for NGOs", 3 *Chicago Journal of International Law* 161 (2002). On the impact of "transnational" dispute settlement mechanisms that, like investor-State arbitrations, are open to non-State claimants, see, e.g., C. Borgen, "Transnational Tribunals and the Transmission of Norms", 39 *George Washington International Law Review* 685 (2007). A generally positive view of non-State actors goes back at least to the New Haven School and is not exclusive to more contemporary "liberal" international relations scholars such as Anne-Marie Slaughter, whose *A New World Order* (Princeton, Princeton University Press, 2004) embraces a variety of non-State actors, as does A. Slaughter, "Breaking Out: The Proliferation of Actors in the International System", in Y. Dezalay and B. G. Garth (eds.), *Global Prescriptions* (Ann Arbor,

body of work, inspired by those who study international relations, namely "liberal theory," that contends that international law can best be understood in terms of the interests of non-State actors both within and outside the State[781]. It too generally celebrates the development of transnational networks, from those operating within government bureaucracies (such as the central bankers of the Basel Committee) to transnational communications among national and international judges. This scholarship even suggests that "liberal" States (i.e. "democratic" States), which are more open to such influences, may be more likely to comply with international law[782]. The rise of non-State actors and the pre-

---

Michigan, University of Michigan Press, 2002). See also T. Braun, "Globalization: The Driving Force in International Investment Law", in M. Waibel *et al*. (eds.), *The Backlash against Investment Arbitration : Perceptions and Reality* (Netherlands, Kluwer Law International, 2010), p. 505 (suggesting the investment regime portends the dawning of a "much more inclusive and broader notion of international law in which a reasonable balance exists between the rights of States and respect for the individual"). See also R. Teitel, "Humanity's Law: Rule of Law for the New Global Politics", 35 *Cornell Journal of International Law* 355 (2001).

[781] See, e.g., A. Moravcsik, "Taking Preferences Seriously: A Liberal Theory of International Politics", 51 *International Organizations* 513 (1997).

[782] See, e.g., A. Slaughter, *A New World Order*. *supra* footnote 780; A. Slaughter, "International Law in a World of Liberal States", 6 *European Journal of International Law* 503 (1995). For a sceptical view of whether disaggregationists who examine the role of non-State actors inside and outside the State do a better job of predicting compliance with international law, see E. A. Posner, "International Law and the Disaggregated State", 32 *Florida State University Law Review* 797 (2005); J. E. Alvarez, "Do Liberal States Behave Better?: A Critique of Slaughter's Liberal Theory", 12 *European Journal of International Law* 183 (2001).

sumptive decline of State power is usually seen as part of international law's persistent progress narrative.

The investment regime is an ideal test case for these propositions. Today, not everyone is convinced that the investment regime is a laudatory example of the "democratization" of international law. For some, the regime has in fact privileged some non-State actors (principally large wealthy TNCs, with the wherewithal to bring an investor-State claim) over the wider public interest. As the emerging backlash against strong investor protections suggests, for its critics the regime reveals the dark side of liberal theory's empowered non-State actors. Critics of the investment regime now want to restore the role of Governments as the central actors and defenders of their populations from external interference [783]. Those seeking to restore sovereign "policy space" now see BITs and FTAs as cautionary tales of what happens when States delegate too much of their "sovereign" powers and give up too much power to non-State actors, including to those who are principally motivated by their own financial self-interest.

For those concerned with its "democratic deficits", the investment regime is more a threat than a boon to "democratic" governance. For those worried about "horizontal equity", the empowerment of investors, although premised on the need for free FDI flows to promote development, may threaten sustainable development at least to the extent that the investment regime discourages pro-development policies (such as export promotion schemes now banned by some investment agreements) [784].

---

[783] See, e.g., B. Kingsbury, "Sovereignty and Inequality", 9 *European Journal of International Law* 599 (1998).

[784] See generally T. H. H. Moran, *Foreign Direct Investment and Development* (Washington, DC, Institute

Whether or not such concerns are meritorious, what is clear is that affording some non-State actors (namely foreign investors) direct access to international adjudicative forums is prompting a political backlash against the investment regime — at least to the extent comparable access is denied to other non-State actors adversely affected by foreign investment[785].

The role of non-State actors in the investment regime raises other, more legalistic questions, particularly for its interpreters. Although some urge increased resort to general rules of international law in the course of deciding investor-State disputes, for others there are serious questions about whether the general rules of "inter-State" or international law, while useful to avoid fragmentation, are really appropriate in the context of disputes between private parties and States[786]. If

---

for International Economics, 1999) (discussing the merits of performance requirements). For a survey of the arguments on the investment regime's possible impact on sustainable development, see A. Newcombe, "Sustainable Development and Investment Treaty Law", 8 *Journal of World Investment & Trade* 357 (2007).

[785] See, e.g., N. Gal-Or, "The Investor and Civil Society as Twin Global Citizens: Proposing a New Interpretation in the Legitimacy Debate", 32 *Suffolk Transnational Law Review* 271 (2009) (describing the international investment regime as affecting the "privatization of the public sphere, undermining the power of the State, and contrasting a privileged investor [non-State actor] against a marginalized impacted [non-State actor]").

[786] See, e.g., C. Brown, "The Protection of Legitimate Expectations as a General Principle of Law: Some Preliminary Thoughts", 6:1 *Transnational Dispute Management* (2009) (contending that whereas the principle of estoppel applies as between two equal parties, such as two private parties to a contract or two States, the principle of legitimate expectations applies as between a State agency and a private actor); M. Endicott, "Remedies in Investor-State Arbitration: Restitution, Specific Performance and Declaratory Awards", in Kahn and Wälde (eds.), *supra*

investor-State dispute settlement is not merely another
venue for giving effect to old-fashioned diplomatic
espousal (where the law assumed that the home States
of investors were engaged in defending harms done to
their own interests) but is instead more analogous to
modern human rights regimes, where the rights of non-
State parties are given priority, why should the substantive rules governing inter-State liability, including
the defence of necessity, be relevant to investor-State
arbitration? Indeed, why should even the residual procedural rules governing inter-State claims practice used
by inter-State dispute bodies like the WTO Appellate
Body, from burdens of proof to rules governing
adverse inferences, be relevant to this hybrid form of
dispute settlement[787]? Is investor-State arbitration, in

---

footnote 692, p. 531 (arguing that the Articles of State
Responsibility may provide guidance but do not "formally
apply" to investor-State disputes, including with respect to
remedies).
    [787] See, e.g., T. W. Wälde and B. Sabahi, "Compen-
sation, Damages, and Valuation", in P. Muchlinski *et al.*
(eds.), *The Oxford Handbook of International Investment
Law* (New York, Oxford University Press, 2008),
pp. 1056-1057, n. 22 (questioning whether the measure of
damages identified in the *Chorzów Factory* case is really
appropriate to the measure of damages suffered by an
individual investor and noting that the *Chorzów* award
itself noted that "the damage suffered by an individual is
never . . . identical in kind with that which will be suffered
by a state"); Wälde, *supra* footnote 691, pp. 14-15 (questioning the relevance of prior claims commissions to modern investor-State arbitration given differences in jurisdiction, types of claims and applicable law); *ibid.*, pp. 19-20
(noting the ILC's remedies in its Articles of State
Responsibility were designed for inter-State relationships
and take "little account of the hybrid, mixed form of
investor-State disputes"). See also *Argentinien-Anleihen:
Staatsnotstand berechtigt nicht zur Zahlungsverweigerung
gegenüber privaten Gläbigern (F.R.G.)*, Bundesverfassungsgericht [Federal Constitutional Court of Germany],

short, a form of inter-State dispute settlement where inter-State rules should be presumed to govern, or a new kind of forum for resolving new international rights accorded directly to non-State parties? If it is the latter, perhaps it is subject to unique residual or gap-filling rules.

The hybrid nature of investor-State dispute settlement raises unresolved questions that may be relevant to other international adjudicative forums. Even assuming that investor-State arbitrators should respect principles such as the "equality of arms" upheld by other international tribunals, how does that principle apply when the parties are a State on the one hand and a private party on the other, as is the case in regional human rights courts [788]? Or consider the application of traditional rules governing waiver, for amending treaties, or for their interpretation based on the subsequent practice of their (States) parties. Should the subsequent practice of States really determine the rights of third-party beneficiaries to such treaties? Alternatively, can investors now waive their BIT rights *ex ante* by settling their claims such that their home States can no

---

75/2007 (5 July 2007) (finding the defence of necessity not applicable to permit Argentina to suspend or modify its contractual obligations to a private person as this was governed by national and not international law).

[788] Seeing investors as functionally equivalent to States for purposes of investor-State arbitration may also make it easier for arbitrators to find that these non-State parties also have duties, and not just rights. See, e.g., P. Muchlinski, "'Caveat Investor'? The Relevance of the Conduct of the Investor under the Fair and Equitable Treatment Standard", 55 *International & Comparative Law Quarterly* 527 (2006); see also *Methanex*, *supra* footnote 744, Part II, Chap. I, para. 59 (reprimanding claimant for obtaining evidence by trespass because these "offended basic principles of justice and fairness required of all parties in every international arbitration").

longer complain about the harms done to their nationals [789] ?

If BITs intend to accord directly enforceable rights
to non-State third parties, should not arbitrators take
this seriously so that, for example, once these parties
have vested treaty rights these cannot be waived or
altered by the States as through a new inter-State interpretation of the treaty [790] ? Does it matter if the BIT parties' new interpretation is being issued in the course of
a pending investor-State dispute and is intended to
influence its outcome [791] ? How much power do or
should Governments retain once they establish treaties
to protect investors' settled or legitimate expectations
against their own actions and have accepted the
competence of third-party arbitrators to decide such
matters ?

Should we presume that States parties to BITs or

---

[789] See, e.g., O. Spiermann, "Individual Rights, State
Interests and the Power to Waive ICSID Jurisdiction under
Bilateral Investment Treaties", 20 *Arbitration Interna-
tional* 179 (2004).

[790] See, e.g., C. H. Brower II, "Investor-State Disputes
under NAFTA : The Empire Strikes Back", 40 *Columbia
Journal of Transnational Law* 43 (2001) (questioning the
enforceability of certain NAFTA Commission Interpretations particularly if these purport to affect pending arbitrations). Tillmann Braun posits the challenge as one
pitting those who see investors as having "direct" rights
under BITs and FTAs versus those who see them as having
only "derivative" rights. Braun, *supra* footnote 780. For
discussion of NAFTA cases whose diverging conclusions
appear to turn on whether or not an investment treaty con-
fers direct rights on investors or only rights that derive
from inter-State obligations, see L. E. Peterson, "Analysis :
Arbitrators Diverge as to whether Mexican Tax Is Performance Requirement, and a Legit Counter-measure",
Investment Arbitration Reporter (6 April 2009) (discussing
CPI v. *Mexico* and *ADM* v. *Mexico*).

[791] For a critique of the NAFTA for appearing to authorize such interpretations, see Brower, *supra* footnote 790.

FTAs retain rights to deny their arbitrators' *compétence de la compétence*?

The question of whether States retain certain rights vis-à-vis the third-party beneficiaries of BITs and FTAs may also be relevant with respect to the procedural rules that apply in the course of dispute settlement. In at least one case, an investment arbitral tribunal held that it had the power to accept *amicus* briefs from other non-State actors, including environmental NGOs, even if one of the States parties to the treaty (in this case the NAFTA) did not agree to such submissions[792]. In other cases, they have, however, insisted that investor-State arbitration remains a "consensual" venue subject to State control and have denied making the proceedings or underlying documents open to the public without the State parties' consent[793].

(4) Globalization and its discontents

As the embodiment of how economic globalization takes place, the investment regime serves as a Rorschach test of attitudes towards globalization and international law's contribution to it[794]. There are bur-

---

[792] See *Methanex Corp.* v. *United States*, Decision on Amici Curiae, UNCITRAL Arbitration Rules (15 January 2001) (hereinafter "*Methanex* Amici"), paras. 9-10, 17-23 and 47 (in that instance, while the United States and Canada agreed with admitting the *amici*, Mexico did not).

[793] See, e.g., *Aguas del Tunari* v. *Bolivia, supra* footnote 778, para. 17.

[794] See generally J. Merolla *et al.*, "Globalization, Globalización, Globalisation: Public Opinion and NAFTA", 11 *Law and Business Review of the Americas* 573 (2005). Critical views of the consequences of economic globalization and of the contribution of international lawyers to it abound. See, e.g., B. S. Chimni, "A Just World under Law: A View from the South", 22 *American University International Law Review* 199

geoning studies of the impact of investment agreements on FDI flows and other indicators of economic

---

(2007), pp. 205-208 (contending that the unified global economic space is being established through the international legalization of property rights and that the "enforcement agenda of global capital" bypasses democratic institutions). There is a strong connection between critiques of globalization and efforts to "regulate" multinational enterprises. For a specific example, see, e.g., S. Anderson and S. Grusky, *Challenging Corporate Investor Rule : How the World Bank's Investment Court, Free Trade Agreements, and Bilateral Investment Treaties Have Unleashed a New Era of Corporate Power and What to Do About It* (Institute for Policy Studies, 2007), available at <http://www.ips-dc.org/reports/challenging_corporate_investor_rule>. See generally J. G. Ruggie, "Taking Embedded Liberalism Global : The Corporate Connection", in J. G. Ruggie, *Embedding Global Markets : An Enduring Challenge* (Burlington, Vermont, Ashgate, 2008); D. Held *et al.*, *Global Transformations : Politics, Economics and Culture* (Stanford, Stanford University Press, 1999). However, critical views towards globalization need not manifest themselves as directed against the traditional capitalist West. See, e.g., Y. Trofimov, "In Africa, China's Expansion Begins to Stir Resentment", *Wall Street Journal* (2 February 2007) (reporting on local resentments directed against Chinese investments in Zambia); Dhir, *supra* footnote 732 (detailing Canadian concerns over a proposed takeover by a State-owned Chinese company that purchased inputs from Chinese suppliers that used forced labour). Moreover, critiques of economic liberalization are not limited to concerns over its impact on income distribution or equity. See, e.g., D. M. Goldstein, "Neoliberal Violence and 'Self-Help' Security in Bolivia", 25 *Critique of Anthropology* 389 (2005), p. 389 (contending that lynchings in Bolivia can be understood "as a kind of neoliberal violence, produced both by the scarcities and deficiencies of the privatizing State, and by the logic of transnational capitalism itself, which has saturated civil society and public culture"). For one attempt to explain "globalization backlash", see Ruggie, *op. cit. supra* (suggesting that the backlash is prompted by the fact that its benefits are distributed unequally, that the global rules

development[795]. Determining whether BITs really do contribute to FDI flows and, if they do, whether this really is a positive development for the host State are part of much broader debates about whether international legal regimes designed to facilitate the operation of the free market, from the WTO to international financial institutions, are actually desirable, particularly for LDCs[796].

The investment regime is also at the heart of con-

---

governing it elevate and enforce some goals more than others, and that it has come to be associated with unpredictable forces such as economic instability and economic dislocation).

[795] See Sauvant and Sachs (eds.), *supra* footnote 670 (containing most of the significant analytical and empirical studies on point). Investor-State arbitral awards that have been asked to dismiss, on jurisdictional grounds, an investor's ICSID claim on the basis that the underlying investment did not make a significant contribution to the host State's economic development are apt reminders of these broader debates. Compare *Phoenix Action Ltd.* v. *Czech Republic*, Award, ICSID Case No. ARB/06/5 (15 April 2009) (dismissing a claim for lack of jurisdiction on this basis) with *Malaysian Historical Salvors, SDN, BHD* v. *Malaysia*, Decision on Application for Annulment, ICSID Case No. ARB/05/10 (16 April 2009), paras. 61, 71, 80-81 (divided award annulling an earlier ruling that had denied a claim for not being an eligible investment); *Saba Fakes* v. *Republic of Turkey*, *supra* footnote 680, paras. 107-114 (finding that eligible investment under the ICSID Convention does not require a showing that the investment contributed to the host State's economic development).

[796] The complexity of such determinations is suggested by studies of public perceptions of the merits of developments such as the NAFTA or particular countries' resort to BITs and other tools for capital liberalization. See, e.g., Merolla, *supra* footnote 794; R. Dolzer *et al.* (eds.), *Foreign Investment: Its Significance in Relation to the Fight against Poverty, Economic Growth, and Legal Culture* (Singapore, Konrad-Adenauer-Stiftung, 2006) (particularly chapters by Markus Taube (on China), José E. Alvarez (on Mexico), and Anjan Roy (on India)).

tentious questions about what the "rule of law" means and whether its promotion is a *necessary* component of modernization[797]. Is the establishment of the international rule of law along with institutions defending free markets necessary in order to achieve worthy goals such as protecting the environment or human rights, as proponents of the investment regime assume[798]? Some challenge this presumed wisdom[799]. Critics of the presumptive "virtuous circle" connecting the protection of alien property rights to protecting the rights of other host country citizens point out that, for example, neither the Asian "Tigers" of today nor the historical experiences of the United States in the period of indus-

---

[797] See generally *World Development Report 2005: A Better Investment Climate for Everyone* (New York, World Bank and Oxford University Press, 2004), available at <http://siteresources.worldbank.org/INTWDR2005/Resources/complete_report.pdf> (identifying the "rule of law" as a key component of good governance and contending that investment treaties are part of it).

[798] See, e.g., Wälde, *supra* footnote 684, pp. 583-584 (noting that a major purpose of modern international law, not just the investment regime, is to improve "sustainable development" and arguing that combating climate change, for example, requires massive, high-risk investments in alternative energy). For a view that the potential contribution of the investment regime to goals such as improvement in human rights and environmental protection is "not automatic", see Orellana, *supra* footnote 703, p. 789.

[799] See, e.g., Schneiderman, *supra* footnote 735, pp. 205-222 (presenting different visions of the rule of law). There is also growing criticisms of the ways institutions that support the investment regime, such as the World Bank, purport to measure the efficacy of the rule of law in LDCs. See, e.g., K. E. Davis and M. B. Kruse, "Taking the Measure of Law: The Case of the Doing Business Project", 32 *Law and Social Inquiry* 1095 (2007); K. E. Davis, "What Can the Rule of Law Variable Tell Us about Rule of Law Reforms?", 26 *Michigan Journal of International Law* 141 (2004).

trialization faithfully complied with this model but, on the contrary, these countries achieved fast economic growth while adhering to a far less open, even protectionist, legal framework[800].

Finally, the investment regime highlights concerns about the *kind* of globalization international law ought to endorse and enforce. As discussed in Chapter II, the changes to some countries' BITs and FTAs parallel the changing attitudes among policymakers and many economists towards the once lauded "Washington Consensus". Recent US, Canadian and Chinese investment treaties exhibit a chastened view of the wisdom of the deregulation and privatization that have often accompanied the ratification of such treaties. As is suggested by the changing attitudes towards Argentina as a respondent State discussed in Chapter IV, the same might be said with respect to the evolving interpretations of investment treaties in some investor-State awards. In some cases, arbitrators have attempted to "balance" the rights of investors with those of host States, as in the *National Grid* decision involving the meaning of FET. And even the most investor-protective awards issued against Argentina, discussed in Chapter IV, have adopted views of the expropriation guarantee of the United States-Argentina BIT that seem not all that different from the explicitly hedged property right highlighted in Chapter I from the European Convention on Human Rights[801].

---

[800] See, e.g., A. Perry, "An Ideal Legal System for Attracting Foreign Direct Investment?: Some Theory and Reality", 125 *American University International Law Review* 1627 (2000); Schneiderman, *supra* footnote 735, pp. 16, 223-230 (describing the active role of government in both East Asia and throughout periods in US history).

[801] For a description of the balancing of interests that the European Court of Human Rights has developed to interpret the European Convention on Human Rights' First

That both investment treaties and arbitral interpretations of them are now coming to reflect the changing views of States and others concerning economic globalization and how best to achieve "development" should not surprise anyone. Politics has always influenced the law after all. In retrospect, what was misleading and naive was the assumption of some — including possibly those who drafted the first set of US Model BITs in the 1980s — that investor-State dispute settlement could thoroughly "displace" the politics involved in the espousal of investor claims.

Many of the proposed reforms for the investment regime, identified in the prior section, reflect a belated recognition of the continued significance of maintaining political support for that regime among all its stakeholders, and not only potential investor claimants. At the same time, some reform proposals — such as the International Institute for Sustainable Development's Model Treaty for Sustainable Development — appear to go much farther than politics (and especially States) would dictate. Under that model — or under some proposals for the systemic integration of investor-State dispute settlement — investor-State arbitrations would effectively become general courts of globalization, that is, principal venues for addressing directly or indirectly a full gamut of international obligations owed by States to their peoples, TNCs, and even by TNC home countries[802]. At present there is no evidence that States like the United States or China

---

Protocol, see, e.g., T. Allen, "Compensation for Property under the European Convention on Human Rights", 28 *Michigan Journal of International Law* 287 (2007). As Allen points out, since the Convention does not refer to a right to compensation for those whose property rights have been taken, even the right to compensation itself is a judicial creation in that regime. *Ibid.*, p. 288.

[802] See, e.g., IISD Model Treaty, *supra* footnote 759.

want to go that far. It would be perverse for countries that have so far resisted supranational scrutiny over their national laws (particularly with respect to human rights) to accept such a delegation of sovereign control merely because it would be occurring in the course of investor-State claims. Nonetheless, the changes to US and Chinese investment treaties go some way to redressing the perceived "governance gap" as between States and foreign investors. Over time it is possible that the investment regime will come to address an even greater number of issues that are today prominent among globalization's proponents and detractors[803].

The investment regime also provides opportunities for those inclined to "grand theory". Trends towards "re-balancing" the investment regime might be read within the larger historical framework provided by Karl Polanyi in his highly influential work, *The Great Transformation*[804]. One might see the US Model BIT of 1984 as the embodiment of Polanyi's concept of "utopian market liberalism", that is, an effort, grounded in the historical laissez-faire movement, to expand the scope of the market, reduce government interventions through privatization and liberalization, and get prices right. In this picture the new model BITs of the United States, Canada, and China suggest Polanyi's inevitable

---

[803] For an overview of host and home country "enforcement gaps" with respect to foreign investors and the legal doctrines that underlie them, see N. L. Bridgeman and D. B. Hunter, "Narrowing the Accountability Gap: Toward a New Foreign Investor Accountability Mechanism", 20 *Georgetown International Environmental Law Review* 187 (2008), pp. 195-207.

[804] K. Polanyi, *The Great Transformation* (Boston, Massachusetts, Beacon Press, 2001 ed., 1944). Others have drawn comparisons between Polanyi's insights and the investment regime. See, e.g., Schneiderman, *supra* footnote 735, p. 4 (comparing the regime's constitutional dimensions to Polanyi's work).

protective counter-movement — an evolution stemming from perceptions that earlier models were excessively beholden to market liberalism. Polanyi would have predicted that old BITs would face a backlash, where States would seek to reassert some of their prior powers to regulate the market[805]. At the same time, today's struggles over BIT texts, over conflicting interpretations of these treaties, and over the enforcement of controversial arbitral awards suggest Polanyi's deeper point, namely that what is at work is a *dialectical process* that is inherently unstable. While it might be nice to presume that the investment regime is evolving in one direction — towards an eventual stable point where both the treaties and arbitral case-law reflect a perfect calibration and proportional balancing between the competing goals of stakeholders — this may never occur.

The regime may be — like globalization itself — a site of continued contestation and struggle. The current trend towards less investor-protective BITs and FTAs may be reversed. This may occur if these changes are resisted (as by Norwegian business interests who thought that the most recent model proposed by their Government no longer protected their interests). A backlash to the backlash may be instigated not only by powerful multilateral enterprises based in the West but by emerging market TNCs. Both of these may seek to restore the vision that once saw these treaties as promoting a harmonized vision of the "rule of law" that applies both in the places they invest *and* in their home countries[806].

---

[805] See generally, J. Stiglitz, "Foreword", in Polanyi, *supra* footnote 804 (connecting Polanyi's original insights to the disenchantment with the "Washington Consensus" model of governing and development after the Asian crisis).

[806] For consideration of what emerging TNCs might desire from the investment regime, see, e.g., J. E. Alvarez,

(5) The international law profession

The role of US Government lawyers in, for example, authorizing the use of "enhanced interrogation techniques" in conducting the "war on terror" has focused attention on how international lawyers behave as professionals, particularly when they provide advice to sovereigns about whether to comply with international law[807]. The investment regime, and particularly investor-State dispute settlement, raises unsettled (and unsettling) questions concerning the professional responsibilities of advocates and adjudicators who, while subject to national codes of conduct, engage with each other as advocates in a transnational setting.

Those who participate in international dispute settlement as judges or advocates, whether in the ICJ or *ad hoc* tribunals established under BITs and FTAs, tend to come from a relatively small group of repeat players. And yet, there is some question about whether even this group has a common understanding of, for example, the rules for preparing witnesses; for determining what is a conflict of interest among those who may be acting as scholars one day, arbitrators the next, and expert witnesses thereafter; or about what should remain confidential and unavailable for public scrutiny. It is not clear that arbitrators charged with settling investor-State claims have a common view of their own role; that is, whether they see themselves princi-

---

"The Rise of Emerging Market Multinationals: Legal Challenges Ahead", in W. Mascheck *et al.* (eds.), *Thinking Outward: Global Players in Emerging Markets* (forthcoming).

[807] See, e.g., J. Waldron, "The Rule of International Law", 30 *Harvard Journal of Law & Public Policy* 15 (2006) (arguing that legal advisers to Governments need to hold their Governments to their international legal responsibilities under the rule of law).

pally as agents to the disputing parties before them or, more broadly, as agents of the international community[808]. There are also serious debates about whether there really are "common rules of international procedure" or of professional conduct that all international adjudicators have in common or whether a hybrid form of dispute settlement, involving non-State and States parties as litigants, poses special problems meriting unique solutions. There are also clear divisions between those who think that we can trust the competitive market for international arbitrators, and for investor-State arbitrators in particular, to produce ethical outcomes and those who think more top-down regulation of the international legal profession is required[809].

These professional questions, which overlap with the subject of "judicialization" that will next be addressed, are now emerging as never before in the course of public debates about the legitimacy of the investment regime. Outcomes reached in the investment regime may well be of interest to other international regimes experiencing judicialization.

---

[808] For consideration of some of these matters, see, e.g., H. Mann, "The Emperor's Clothes Come Off: A Comment on *Republic of Ghana v. Telekom Malaysia Berhard*, and the Problem of Arbitrator Conflict of Interest", 2:1 *Transnational Dispute Management* (2005), p. 3 (arguing that arbitrators are more likely to delve into broad issues of public policy when they decide specific disputes); Wälde, *supra* footnote 684, pp. 544-546.

[809] See, e.g., S. D. Franck, "The Role of International Arbitrators", 12 *International Law Students Association Journal of International and Comparative Law* 499 (2006). There is a growing literature relating to the professional ethics of commercial and investor-State arbitrators. See, e.g., C. A. Rogers, "The Ethics of International Arbitrators", in L. W. Newman and R. D. Hill (eds.), *The Leading Arbitrators' Guide to International Arbitration* (Huntington, New York, Juris Publishing, 2nd ed., 2008), p. 621.

(6) Judicialization

With at least 300 known investor-State claims initiated as of 2008, the investment regime is handling a nearly unprecedented number of international adjudications[810].

The States that established investor-State dispute settlement as a commitment device intended to enable more credible commitments to investors probably did not anticipate the broader implications of their turn to third-party adjudication.

Today investor-State arbitration is of interest, alongside other *ex post* control and governance mechanisms in other regimes, to those who explore compliance questions generally in international law[811] or wonder what drives States to establish mechanisms that effectively deprive them of considerable governmental discretion[812].

---

[810] Sauvant, *supra* footnote 665, pp. 259-260 (contrasting the recent increase in investment disputes with the lower number of disputes in the international trade regime). The only internationalized forums with comparable number of claims are the UN Claims Commission (which handled claims against Iraq) and the United States-Iran Claims Tribunal.

[811] As Wälde indicates, the discretion arbitrators deploy to adjust compensation given a State's capacity to pay may reflect awareness of the need to facilitate enforcement of their awards. Wälde, *supra* footnote 691, p. 66.

[812] See generally Z. Elkins *et al.*, "Competing for Capital: The Diffusion of Bilateral Investment Treaties: 1960-2000", 60 *International Organizations* 811 (2006); A. Stone Sweet, "Judicialization and the Construction of Governance", 32 *Comparative Political Studies* 147 (1999); J. M. Smith, "The Politics of Dispute Settlement Design: Explaining Legalism in Regional Trade Pacts", 54 *International Organizations* 137 (2000); A. T. Guzman, "The Cost of Credibility: Explaining Resistance to Interstate Dispute Settlement Mechanisms", 31 *Journal of Legal Studies* 303 (2002).

Many of the questions addressed in prior chapters — such as whether investor-State arbitrators view themselves as having a "duty" to adhere to prior arbitral decisions — can be recast in terms that would be familiar to those who study compliance. To the extent the regime's arbitrators are in fact producing *"jurisprudence constante"* by relying on their predecessors' rulings[813], this may be of interest to those who debate whether or to what extent international law relies on mimesis or "normative isomorphism" to ensure compliance[814].

Of course, since the investment regime relies more than in most international regimes on third-party adjudication for its continuing elaboration, the regime should be of particular interest to those who examine other judicialized international venues, such as the WTO or the European Court of Justice. The judicialized investment regime provides an excellent case study for those who consider how States chose between distinct forms of "law-making" — from informal network regulatory processes to more formal insti-

---

[813] For empirical evidence of the increasing citation to prior investor-State arbitral decisions in such decisions, see, e.g., J. P. Commission, "An Analysis of a Developing Jurisprudence in International Investment Law — What Investment Treaty Tribunals are Saying and Doing", 6:1 *Transnational Dispute Management* (2009).

[814] See, e.g., Stone Sweet and Matthews, *supra* footnote 687, p. 163 (noting that as courts adopt proportionality balancing the "dynamics of diffusion became subject to logics of mimesis and increasing-returns (band-wagon effects): courts began copying what they took to be the emerging best-practice standard . . ."). See also R. Goodman and D. Jinks, "International Law and State Socialization: Conceptual, Empirical, and Normative Challenges", 54 *Duke Law Journal* 983 (2005); R. Goodman and D. Jinks, "How to Influence States: Socialization and International Human Rights Law", 54 *Duke Law Journal* 621 (2004).

tutionalized venues[815]. It provides a vantage point to consider whether all international adjudicators or only some face pressures to adopt balancing techniques, to be more transparent, or to admit amici; or whether States that establish such mechanisms ultimately face pressures to establish forms of appellate supervision of awards[816]. (As noted, the leading forum for investor-State claims, ICSID, and leading countries in the regime, such as the United States and Canada, have responded positively to such pressures but it remains to be seen whether other investor-State forums will follow suit[817].) The investment regime is, accordingly, an excellent case study for exploring whether international judges are immune from the accountability techniques and pressures being faced by other international regimes[818].

The investment regime also provides a powerful demonstration of how "judicialization" deepens when

---

[815] See, e.g., D. Zaring, "Rulemaking and Adjudication in International Law", 46 *Columbia Journal of Transnational Law* 563 (2008). See generally Alvarez, *supra* footnote 699, pp. 458-520 (surveying distinct areas of law affected by institutionalized judicial law-making).

[816] See, e.g., A. Stone Sweet, "Investor-State Arbitration: Proportionality's New Frontier", 4.1 *Law & Ethics of Human Rights* 47 (2010).

[817] For a survey of the level of transparency anticipated under ICSID and other arbitral rules regularly used in investor-State proceedings, see IISD Working Paper on Transparency, draft distributed at the Barcelona Conference on 6 July 2010 (forthcoming).

[818] See, e.g., B. Kingsbury and S. Schill, "Investor-State Arbitration as Governance: Fair and Equitable Treatment, Proportionality and the Emerging Global Administrative Law", in *El nuevo derecho administrativo global en América Latina: desafíos para las inversiones extranjeras, la regulación nacional y el financiamiento para el desarrollo* (Buenos Aires, Ediciones RAP S.A., 2009), p. 221.

individuals and companies and not only States are permitted to file claims. It is therefore a good place to consider the relative values of "transnational" dispute settlement, as compared to the classic inter-State models followed by the ICJ and, to a lesser extent, the WTO[819].

Investor-State arbitration is also a leading exemplar of the proliferation of international courts and tribunals and a good place to examine the question of whether this phenomenon is normatively desirable[820]. At least since the League of Nations attempted to compel States to settle their disputes without recourse to war, most international lawyers have assumed that the turn to neutral third parties to decide international disputes constitutes a victory for the "rule of law" over "power

---

[819] See R. O. Keohane *et al.*, "Legalized Dispute Settlement: Interstate and Transnational", 54 *International Organizations* 457 (2000) (contending that dispute settlement mechanisms that grant *locus standi* to individuals provide incentives for such actors to mobilize, increase the legitimacy of such claims, promote law generation, and expand adjudicative power).

[820] See generally "Symposium Issue: The Proliferation of International Tribunals: Piercing Together the Puzzle", 31 *New York University Journal of International Law and Politics* 679 (1999); Katz Cogan, *supra* footnote 686. For an attempt to explain why forms of "arbitration" including investor-State dispute settlement are more attractive to States and are more "legitimate" than international courts such as the ICJ, see M. L. Movesian, "International Commercial Arbitration and International Courts", 18 *Duke Journal of Comparative & International Law* 423 (2008). See also R. Alford, "International Arbitrators vs. International Judges", *Opinio Juris* (5 October 2007), available at <http://opiniojuris.org/2007/10/05/international-arbitrators-vs-international-judges/> (noting that the legitimacy and professionalism of an international court of tenured judges turns on how such judges are selected and that the present politicized system for selecting international judges does not inspire confidence).

diplomacy". We have tended to assume that, whether for purposes of settling a boundary or deciding a trade or investment dispute, adjudicative forums "level the playing field" between disputing States and are tools to promote sovereign equality. Others say that this progress narrative applies, if at all, only to permanent international courts with permanent judges[821] or that even those serving on established courts need checks on the exercise of the authority that is delegated to them, especially if they may second-guess those with greater democratic legitimacy, including national judges and legislators[822]. Others argue that competition among dispute settlers or forms of inter-court dialogue can be trusted to improve the quality of justice achieved through international adjudication[823].

Whether investor-State dispute settlement is seen as part of these broader concerns with the "judicializa-

---

[821] See, e.g., Van Harten, *supra* footnote 753.

[822] For consideration of possible conflicts between investor-State arbitrations and national courts, see, e.g., P. H. F. Bekker, "The Use of Non-Domestic Courts for Obtaining Domestic Relief: Jurisdictional Conflicts between NAFTA Tribunals and US Courts", 11 *International Law Students Association Journal of International and Comparative Law* 331 (2005). As noted, some address this point by recommending greater deference among internationalized courts or between them and national courts. See, e.g., Bjorklund, *supra* footnote 738 (arguing that the risks of forum shopping in the investment regime suggest the need for greater attention to such doctrines as *res judicata*, *lis pendens*, and abstention).

[823] See, e.g., Katz Cogan, *supra* footnote 686 (urging "competition-friendly" procedures). For a more general response to critiques of the legitimacy of investor-State arbitration, see D. S. Meyers, "In Defense of the International Treaty Arbitration System", 31 *Houston Journal of International Law* 47 (2008) (disputing Gus Van Harten's critique and concluding that investor-State arbitration has acceptable levels of accountability, openness, coherence, and independence).

tion" of international law may depend on whether it is regarded as a modern form of inter-State adjudication not dramatically different from the ICJ, other international courts, or older claims commissions such as the United States-Mexican Claims Commission[824] or whether we see it as merely a form of private commercial arbitration dependent on its procedures and using its practitioners[825]. Whether investor-State arbitration belongs to the private or the public side of the aisle is therefore not solely a question of interest to academics. It has real world political implications. For those who see the investor-State mechanism as a variant on private commercial dispute settlement, goals such as building up harmonious (and of course public) law pleasing to the academy, influencing future jurisprudential trends, making the process more transparent, enhancing access to non-parties, or presenting a fully elaborated judicial decision that would please law professors may be less important[826]. It is possible that differing views of investor-State dispute settlement underlie differing views among arbitrators about what their role is. Commercially trained arbitrators uncomfortable with economic analysis may be more comfortable, particularly when it comes to determining damages, in

---

[824] Such comparisons are encouraged when investment disputes have emerged in other tribunals, including (rarely) within the International Court of Justice and the previous Permanent Court of International Justice ("PCIJ"). See examples in Wälde, *supra* footnote 684, p. 561, n. 186.

[825] As noted, investor-State disputes are usually conducted using the rules originally intended for commercial disputes such as those of ICSID, UNCITRAL, the PCA, the Stockholm Chamber of Commerce, the ICC, or the London Court of International Arbitration and many of its arbitrators are commercially trained lawyers.

[826] See, e.g., Cheng, *supra* footnote 683 (suggesting that differences exist among arbitrators with respect to their attitude towards respect for prior arbitral decisions).

rendering oft-condemned "split the baby" decisions[827]. Those more attuned to the need to establish judicial precedents satisfying to a wider international community, and not only the litigants before them, may be, by contrast, more likely to prefer elaborately reasoned decisions, perhaps including separate concurring or dissenting opinions (as in the ICJ).

As prior chapters suggest, some investor-State arbitrators may be content to settle the particular dispute before them while others see themselves as part of a grander enterprise in the construction of general harmonious law. The latter might see themselves as akin to some constitutional court judges charged with expressing public values or, at the very least, with enhancing the credibility or legitimacy of the adjudicative system in which they are participating[828]. This may explain why some arbitral results appear to reflect political or pragmatic concerns not reflected in the investment treaty being applied. Chapter IV has suggested that this may have been the case with respect to some of the recent annulment rulings arising from the Argentina claims and it may have been the case in more routine instances, such as decisions that have narrowed the scope of the umbrella clause out of expressed concerns with "flooding" ICSID's dockets with contract claims[829]. Questions about the propriety of such decisions or other allegations of "judicial activism" are no stranger to this regime and obviously relate with others raised above, including the problems of fragmentation, the role of non-State actors, and questions relating to professional ethics. All of these

---

[827] See, e.g., Wälde, *supra* footnote 691, pp. 42-43.
[828] For general discussion of these roles among other international dispute settlers, see Alvarez, *supra* footnote 699, pp. 521-584.
[829] See, e.g., Schill, *supra* footnote 679, p. 34.

familiar issues connect international investment lawyers to the broader public international law of which it is a part. Investment lawyers are not the only ones asking whether their adjudicators ought to be seen as agents only of the parties that appointed them, trustees of a relatively self-contained legal regime, or autonomous members of a broader amorphous international community consciously engaged, consistent with the ILC's recommendations in its Fragmentation Project, in bridging the law among discrete international regimes [830].

(7) Hegemonic or imperial international law?

For some critics of contemporary international law and its "progress narrative", the expanding domain of international regulation does not constitute a victory for the equal application of the apolitical rule of law. For some, international law remains what it was during from the age of Grotius through the colonial age: yet another tool that powerful States use to get their way [831]. For these critics, having recourse to a forum established through multilateral co-operation — whether it is ICSID or the UN Security Council — provides no

---

[830] Such questions lie very close to the surface of the arguments raised by some third parties in the course of recent investor-State disputes. See, e.g., *United Parcel Service of America, Inc.* v. *Government of Canada*, Decision of the Tribunal on Petitions for Intervention and Participation as Amici Curiae, UNCITRAL Arbitration Rules (17 October 2001), para. 24; *Glamis Gold Ltd.* v. *United States*, Quechan Indian Nation Application for Leave to File a Non-Party Submission, UNCITRAL Arbitration Rules (16 October 2006) (hereinafter "*Glamis* Quechan Submission").

[831] See, e.g., Chimni, *supra* footnote 794 (contending that the world is moving towards a "Global State" that is imperial in character).

escape from "hegemonic" international law[832]. Others see multilateral institutions as part and parcel of an "imperial" State in the making, one which intends to impose the will of its most powerful members on those who are in no position to resist[833]. This is one way that the IMF's resort to conditionality on its structural assistance loans has been described.

As is evident from the horizontal and some of the ideological critiques made with respect to the investment regime, this is also how some see this regime. To what extent can this regime, which operates without benefit of a single institution subject to weighted voting, be accurately described as part of an imperial or hegemonic enterprise no less than the IMF or the UN Security Council?

Or if one prefers to stay within the same subject matter: to what extent is contemporary international investment law caught in the same North/South imperial dynamic that characterized old (pre-BIT) rules governing international investment?

This author has contended elsewhere that the forms of hegemony imposed under the investment regime are no longer usefully described, as during the colonial

---

[832] This seems evident from the abundant scholarship critiquing the UN Security Council's assumed post 9/11 "legislative" powers to expand the rules on the use of force, wage the war on terror, control the spread of weapons of mass destruction ("WMDs"), and perhaps even change the rules of occupation. See, e.g., J. E. Alvarez, "Hegemonic International Law Revisited", 97 *American Journal of International Law* 873 (2003); N. Krisch, "International Law in Times of Hegemony: Unequal Power and the Shaping of the International Legal Order", 16 *European Journal of International Law* 369 (2005).

[833] See, e.g., U. Mattei, "A Theory of Imperial Law: A Study of US Hegemony and Latin Resistance" (2003), available at <http://works.bepress.com/ugo_mattei/1/>.

era, as territorially based empire[834]. As the evolving
BITs and FTAs described in Chapter II suggest, it is
no longer accurate or sufficient to describe BITs and
FTAs as tools of the North to extract resources from
the South — not at a time when FDI flows both
ways, BITs bite the "empire" back, nations like Egypt,
China and Cuba are leading BIT proponents, and
emerging market TNCs are part of the investment community.

Today's investment regime has a distinct pro-market
ideology that originated in the North but is no longer
defined by it. The "hegemony" of the investment
regime today is non-territorial and de-racionated.
Today, most countries, including those that are ostensibly Communist, worship at the shrine to David
Ricardo and his theory of comparative advantage.

Participation in regimes like that for investment, the
United Nations' collective security scheme, or the
WTO is no longer a choice for most States. All of these
regimes aspire to, or are on their way to securing,
universality. Participation and compliance with them
is, increasingly, the only option States have. These
regimes have no clear rival. To refuse to participate in
them — or to respect the underlying investment rules
of the road even while not being parties to such BITs
— is tantamount to political or financial suicide. As
Abe and Antonia Chayes pointed out long ago, to be
allowed to participate in regimes like this is to be
allowed to enjoy the newly defined "sovereignty" left
to States[835]. While one could describe the investment
regime as an "empire of capital", it is more plausibly

---

[834] J. E. Alvarez, "The Contemporary Foreign Investment Regime: Empire of Law or Law of Empire?", 60
Alabama Law Review 943 (2009).

[835] See A. Chayes and A. Chayes, *The New Sovereignty:
Compliance with International Regulatory Agreements*
(Cambridge, Harvard University Press, 1995), p. 27.

described as an empire of law[836]. This connotes that it is both a tool of empire in its underlying ideology but that it is not the law of empire as it was understood during the colonial age. Despite the emerging differences among BITs and FTAs, the empire of investment law continues to contain a highly political and ideological conception of how States and markets ought to relate to one another that now takes the form of increasingly universal rules of law.

This characterization shares much with that of Michael Hardt and Antonio Negri. In their book, *Empire*[837], they describe a "global market and global circuits of production", a new "global order", that has "a new logic and structure of rule — in short a new form of sovereignty"[838]. Hardt and Negri write of a post-sovereign world that "encompasses the spatial totality" and knows no territorial boundaries[839]. Their version of empire joins societies across spatial political boundaries and makes such boundaries less relevant. As Hardt and Negri indicate, empires of law reflect the fact that old notions of sovereignty and the exercise of sovereign power are no longer sufficient to describe contemporary international law[840]. Regimes like that

---

[836] Alvarez, *supra* footnote 834.

[837] See M. Hardt and A. Negri, *Empire* (Cambridge, Harvard University Press, 2000), pp. xiv-xv (arguing that "the rule of Empire operates on all registers of the social order extending down to the depths of the social world"); see also S. Marks, "Empire's Law", 10 *Indiana Journal of Global Legal Studies* 449 (2003), p. 461 (asserting that globalization reconfigures political authority to create a new system of sovereignty).

[838] See Hardt and Negri, *supra* footnote 837, p. xi.

[839] *Ibid.*, p. xiv.

[840] *Ibid.*, pp. xii-xiii (arguing that empire is not an extension of imperialism which worked to enrich European colonizers, but a decentralizing and deterritorializing force); compare Marks, *supra* footnote 837, p. 461

governing investment have outgrown their origins. They are no longer the product of territorially demarcated empire — even as they enable the pursuit of the ideologies favoured by the powerful[841]. Regimes like the investment regime or that of collective security under the United Nations are not mere figleafs for old-fashioned imperialist power. Even the United States has discovered that the shift to using global law has consequences and imposes limits on its action. These limits include unanticipated checks and balances on the exercise of hegemonic power, such as the international courts that are now attempting to check the power of the UN Security Council[842]. Other limits, such as the new forms of "balancing" emerging within BITs and FTAs, result from the fact that any law worthy of the name (even empires of law) needs to be reciprocally applied.

(8) Global administrative law?

There are other ways to describe the investment regime and its larger implications. Led by Benedict Kingsbury and Richard Stewart at New York University School of Law, some have described myriad international regimes as producing global administrative law[843]. For these scholars, global administrative

---

(asserting that globalization creates a new form of sovereignty).

[841] Marks, *supra* footnote 837, pp. 461-464 (drawing comparisons between international lawyers' perspectives and those by Hardt and Negri).

[842] For a chart of international courts and tribunals, see Alvarez, *supra* footnote 699, pp. 404-405.

[843] Kingsbury and Schill, *supra* footnote 818. See also B. Kingsbury *et al.*, "The Emergence of Global Administrative Law", 68 *Law and Contemporary Problems* 15 (2005); Van Harten and Loughlin, *supra* footnote 708. See generally, Wälde, *supra* footnote 691, p. 74 (noting that certain guarantees in BITs "create external disciplines" on

action occurs through rule-making, adjudications, and other decisions that are neither treaty-making nor simple dispute settlements between States and are not confined to either the processes or the international legal persons of public international law as traditionally understood[844]. They focus on administration undertaken by formal international organizations, on collective action by transnational networks between national regulatory officials of Governments, on distributed administrative arrangements conducted by those officials or hybrid inter-governmental-private arrangements, or on the action of private institutions with regulatory functions[845].

The investment regime shares many of the features of global administrative law[846]. By accepting the investor guarantees accorded in BITs and FTAs, States have accepted an internal form of supervision. They accept that their own laws, courts, and administrative

---

government regulation and administrative conduct that are characteristic of national judicial review and distinct systems of administrative law and courts and urging investor-State arbitrators to adapt their remedies to this reality).

[844] Kingsbury, *supra* footnote 843, p. 17.

[845] *Ibid*.

[846] See Kingsbury and Schill, *supra* footnote 818. This description of the investment regime is not limited to Kingsbury and others writing about "global administrative law". See, e.g., T. W. Wälde, *supra* footnote 736, p. 87 (noting that investment arbitration differs from commercial arbitration as it is a "particular form of international quasi-judicial review of governmental conduct"); *ibid*., p. 101 (comparing investor-State dispute settlement to administrative or general courts). But Wälde also points out that while the typical national administrative action usually seeks to correct defects in procedures and rarely leads to monetary damages, calculating damages in instances involving flaws in administrative action is one of the arguably unique features of investor-State arbitration. Wälde, *supra* footnote 691, p. 74.

agencies can be judged by objective international standards[847].

There are distinct parallels between the most widely cited interpretation of FET — the *TECMED* standard discussed in Chapter III — and the standards deployed for judging administrative action in, for example, relevant US administrative law[848]. The *TECMED* standard is effectively a global administrative law standard.

Thanks to the *"jurisprudence constante"* produced by investor-State arbitrations, the guarantee of fair and equitable treatment in particular has emerged as a singularly effective test for contesting the legality of governmental action, comparable in scope to demanding that States adhere to the rule of law itself[849]. As the *TECMED* standard suggests, what we ask investor-State arbitrators to do is strikingly similar to what we demand of national administrative law-makers and enforcers. Investor-State arbitral tribunals tasked with reviewing whether the actions of governmental agencies are, for example, "fair and equitable", are expected to review and control public regulatory actions. As Gus Van Harten and Martin Loughlin have argued, this is a system akin to national review of administrative action "in that it keeps public authorities within the bounds of legality and provides enforceable remedies to individuals harmed by unlawful state conduct"[850]. Whether or not these authors are correct in describing investor-State arbitration as the "only case

---

[847] C. McLachlan, "Investment Treaties and General International Law", in Bjorklund *et al.* (eds.), *supra* footnote 678, p. 125.

[848] See Kingsbury and Schill, *supra* footnote 818.

[849] See, e.g., McLachlan, *supra* footnote 847, p. 125 (suggesting that the FET principle owes much to the overarching concept of the rule of law).

[850] Van Harten and Loughlin, *supra* footnote 708, p. 149.

of global administrative law in the world today"[851], what is clear is that investor-State arbitrators purport to rule on the legality of national laws, on the legality of how national law is enforced at every level of government (including through agency action), on customary law and general principles of law, and, at times, on the applicability and interpretation of other treaty regimes, such as those involving trade.

More extraordinary still is that enforcement of this supranational supervision over the administration of national law is handed over to private attorneys general and that this acceptance of "governance" extends beyond bilateral investment treaties to include the participation of international financial institutions. The IMF and other international financial institutions engage in what one author has described as "international investment regulation" through actions as different as the enforcement of "guidelines" on infrastructure projects undertaken by the World Bank, structural adjustment conditionality on IMF loans, or "soft" forms of regulation (such as the technical advice accorded Governments under the World Bank's International Finance Corporation)[852]. These actions, together with those of political risk insurers and market participants, which indirectly serve to enforce the strictures of investment treaties and investor-State arbitral rulings, constitute a "hybrid" public/private form of transnational regulation.

The characterization of the investment regime as a form of global *public* administrative law has normative implications insofar as it suggests that investment rules must be wrought "by the whole society" since they

---

[851] Van Harten and Loughlin, *supra* footnote 708, p. 149.

[852] D. Kalderimis, "IMF Conditionality as Investment Regulation: A Theoretical Analysis", 13 *Social & Legal Studies* 103 (2004).

address "matters of concern to the society as such"[853].
This characterization also suggests that governance
standards being elaborated in the investment regime
should, in principle, engage with other bodies of rules
concerning the good administration of the laws and the
promotion of the rule of law, whether these are
imposed by the WTO for trade-related actions, by
international human rights courts, or by international
financial or aid agencies by way of technical advice[854].
Describing the investment regime as global administrative law implicitly suggests that every effort ought to
be made by the treaty's interpreters to render its rules
compatible with those in relevant international regimes
and may even suggest which regimes or rules are in fact
relevant[855]. Like the other forms of global administrative law described by Kingsbury and his colleagues,
the investment regime is facing comparable pressures
to promote greater transparency and participation.
Rules that seek to make host States adhere to the "rule
of law" need themselves to adhere to the rule of law.

Some of the suggested reforms to the regime are
inspired by the global administrative law perspective.
If investor-State arbitration is a form of governance,
this is all the more reason to distinguish its procedures
from those governing ordinary commercial arbitration.
Kingsbury and others have argued, for example, that
investor-State arbitrators' role in governance requires
them to provide far more reasoned decisions than those

---

[853] Kingsbury and Schill, *supra* footnote 818.

[854] See, e.g., *ibid.*, p. 229.

[855] Indeed, Kingsbury and Schill even imply that as a
form of governance, international investment mechanisms
need to be seen not merely as means to economic growth
and development, but, at a deeper level, as promoting
"democratic accountability and participation, the promotion of good and orderly State administration, and the protection of rights and other deserving interests". *Ibid.*, p. 231.

issued in some of the original Argentina decisions — where, as we have discussed, the arbitrators did not always explain in detail why they were turning to either WTO law or customary international law[856]. This critique might indeed have influenced the annulment decision in *Enron* which found the reasoning in the original award inadequate. On the other hand, this criticism may not be very convincing or compelling to many of the regime's stakeholders — who turned to this method of dispute settlement in the hope that it would be more expeditious, cheaper, and less political than the likely alternatives[857]. Some may question whether the original nearly 150-page *CMS* award, for example, is truly less well reasoned or detailed in articulating its legal rationale than is the recent *Kadi* decision issued by the European Court of Justice. The latter, the typical product of the least common denominator approach to opinion writing that characterizes that Court, addresses the human rights flaws of the counter-terrorism legislation challenged in that case in rudimentary, even cursory fashion[858]. It is not clear that

---

[856] Kingsbury and Schill, *supra* footnote 818, pp. 247-250.

[857] See, e.g., Wälde, *supra* footnote 684, p. 581 (noting that the push for more complex and transparent investor-State procedures is likely to be resisted by its primary users, namely investors, home and host States). Schneiderman notes that Governments pay an average of US$1-2 million in legal fees to defend investor-State claims, while the total costs can go to about US$3 million; claimants allege that they spend far more (such as US$11-12 million to litigate Methanex's case). Schneiderman, *supra* footnote 735, p. 77 (also noting that this is why some international trade lawyers dispute that NGO submissions are "effectively 'for free'").

[858] See R. Alford, "The Inferior Quality of ECJ Decisions", *Opinio Juris* (31 October 2007), available at <http://opiniojuris.org/2007/10/31/the-inferior-quality-of-ecj-decisions/>.

investor-State decisions would invariably suffer by comparison to that court, to recent decisions of the ICJ, or to other international courts.

(9) Constitutionalization?

Some international lawyers are now debating whether the juridification or legalization of some parts of international law have gone so far that it is possible to ascribe aspects of "constitutionalization" to what is occurring, particularly within international institutions and tribunals. Those who ascribe "constitutionalization" to diverse international regimes have the advantage that the term is hardly a term of art but can be defined to suit one's purposes. For Habermas, for example, the UN Charter, as it has evolved over time, now evinces "prima facie" constitutional features insofar as it, like national constitutions, connects its broad political purposes to securing the protection of human rights and can credibly claim universal validity for law enacted pursuant to it[859]. Others contend that the GATT has been "constitutionalized" through the establishment and the subsequent evolution of the WTO[860]; while others aspire to make constitutionalism real in

---

[859] T. Giegerich, "The Is and the Ought of International Constitutionalism: How Far Have We Come on Habermas's Road to a 'Well-Considered Constitutionalization of International Law'?", 10 *German Law Journal* 31 (2009), p. 37 (discussing Habermas's conception of constitutionalization).

[860] For a thorough consideration and critique of those who would describe the WTO in constitutional terms, see generally D. Z. Cass, *The Constitutionalization of the World Trade Organization* (New York, Oxford University Press, 2005). See also J. L. Dunoff, "Constitutional Conceits: The WTO's 'Constitution' and the Discipline of International Law", 17 *European Journal of International Law* 647 (2006).

that context through the recognition of an individual right to trade[861]. For those for whom the key to "constitutionalization" is judicial norm-generation, the investment regime would appear to be even more "constitutionalized" than is the WTO since BITs and FTAs produce far more judicialized case-law than the WTO.

Others see "constitutionalization" occurring through adjudication when the adjudicators attempt to balance the rights of a private party vis-à-vis the State, whether through the application of proportionality or other forms of "balancing". If this is the measure of "constitutionalization", there is little question that investor-State arbitrators are engaging in it as forms of balancing are now apparent with respect to the application of virtually every substantive guarantee contained in investment treaties, from FET to national treatment, and, at least in the views of some arbitrators, with respect to defences such as "necessity" and the calculation of damages[862]. There is also some evidence

---

[861] See, e.g., E. U. Petersmann, "Theories of Justice, Human Rights, and the Constitution of International Markets", 37 *Loyola of Los Angeles Law Review* 407 (2003).

[862] See, e.g., Wälde and Sabahi, *supra* footnote 787, p. 1089 (discussing the balancing that occurs with respect to applying the principle of legitimate expectations and with respect to the calculation of damages — as where adjudicators must apply principles like the duty to mitigate); *ibid.*, pp. 1056, 1100 (discussing the role of proportionality in assessing the "egregiousness" of the breach for purposes of calculating damages); *ibid.*, pp. 1103-1105 (discussing the role of "equitable circumstances" in determining damages). The *TECMED* tribunal even considered whether the negative financial impact suffered by the investment was proportional to the public interest protected by the Government's regulatory measures and police powers and found these to be reasonable. *Tecnica Medioambietales, TECMED S.A.* v. *Mexico*, Award, ICSID Case No. ARB/00/2 (29 May 2003), para. 122. For an

that the investment regime may be encouraging States to harmonize the most traditional kind of constitutional law, namely their own national constitutional laws[863].

As with respect to characterizing the investment regime as a form of global administrative law, calling it a form of "constitutionalization" is contentious in some circles. If investor-State arbitrations are effectively mini-constitutional courts, Gus Van Harten's critique of the *ad hoc* nature of investment arbitration has all the more resonance, for example. Characterizing investment law as a form of constitutionalism is clearly useful to those who aspire to certain reforms, such as establishment of a permanent international investment court. "Constitutional" courts, after all, are permanent bodies, not *ad hoc* panels appointed from time to time as disputes emerge. It is certainly easier to suggest as well that in the selection of the permanent international judges for such a court, consideration be given to appointing persons who regard themselves not as mere agents for the litigating parties but as agents of a wider international community[864]. On the other hand, charac-

---

interesting argument that balancing should be reserved to competing rights that are on the same "axiological plane" and it is therefore improper in the investor-State context, see Orellana, *supra* footnote 703, pp. 720, 774.

[863] See, e.g., M. Tuchnet, "The Inevitable Globalization of Constitutional Law", 49 *Virginia Journal of International Law* 985 (2009) (noting the existence of "top-down" and "bottom-up" pressures, including those associated with transnational dispute settlers charged with resolving property disputes and market processes whereby nations necessarily compete for investment.

[864] See Stone Sweet, *supra* footnote 816 (delineating two models for arbitrators and suggesting that those engaged in proportionality balancing see themselves as agents for the wider community). Sweet prefers the term "judicialization" rather than "constitutionalization" for describing the characteristics that are evolving within

terizing what investor-State arbitrations do as being engaged in "constitutional adjudication" exposes them as law-makers and may only heighten States' fears of according them any more power or status than they already have [865].

But the "constitutionalism" label may have a more radical bite. The most thorough criticism of the investment regime based on its alleged constitutional nature comes from the work of a Canadian scholar, David Schneiderman. In a recent book, *Constitutionalizing Economic Globalization*, Schneiderman argues that investment rules institutionalize, as constitutions do, a particular political project, in this instance neo-liberalism [866]. BITs and FTAs, in his view, force States to recede from the market, restrict its economic functions,

---

investor-State arbitration, namely reliance on precedent, adoption of balancing techniques, the admission of *amicus*, and the desire for appellate supervision. *Ibid*. In other work, however, he has argued that "proportionality-based rights adjudication now constitutes one of the defining features of global constitutionalism". Stone Sweet and Matthews, *supra* footnote 687, p. 75.

[865] This risk is readily acknowledged even by those who advocate constitutionalization. See, e.g., Stone Sweet and Matthews, *supra* footnote 687, pp. 77-78; see also *ibid*., p. 79 (noting that when judges adopt proportionality balancing this "alters the relationship between judicial authority and all other public authority, enhancing the former"); *ibid*., p. 88 ("[B]alancing can never be dissociated from lawmaking; it requires judges to behave as legislators do, or to sit in judgment of a prior act of balancing performed by elected officials"). As some of the attempts by the United States and other States to narrow the scope of arbitration discretion in the investment regime suggest, see *supra* Chap. II, this may be a step too far even for relatively strong State advocates of investment protection and may be even less attractive for those Governments that have deeper doubts about the continued value of the investment regime.

[866] Schneiderman, *supra* footnote 735.

and limit its redistributionist capacity [867]. Unlike forms of liberal constitutions that both empower majoritarian rule while protecting the rights of insular minorities (as through a bill of rights), the investment regime imposes binding constraints that are designed to insulate economic policy from majoritarian politics since they render certain policy options effectively "unconstitutional". Schneiderman describes the object of the regime as "the placing of legal limits on the authority of government, isolating economic from political power, and assigning to investment interests the highest possible protection" as part of a pre-commitment strategy intended to bind future generations [868]. Schneidman's constitutional critique is not only structural. He points out that many of the substantive guarantees in BITs operate in a constitutional fashion and that investor-State jurisprudence, as with respect to the resort to the idea of legitimate expectations, borrows heavily from constitutional doctrines used in Europe and in the United States, as with respect to the latter's regulatory takings and substantive due process doctrines [869].

Schneiderman's critique is principally a "vertical" one. He sees the investment regime as unreasonably constraining "self-government" [870]. But it is also, in part, a horizontal and ideological one as Schneiderman contends that many of the regime's substantive rules, such as its constraint on "indirect takings" and possibly FET, borrow heavily from particular US laws associated with only one nation's approach to balancing the roles of the state vis-à-vis the market [871]. Schneiderman argues that the investment regime elevates some con-

---

[867] See Schneiderman, *supra* footnote 735, p. 2.

[868] *Ibid.*, p. 4.

[869] See, e.g., *ibid.*, p. 107.

[870] *Ibid.*, p. 37.

[871] See *ibid.*, pp. 46-68 (describing the development of the US rule against takings and the parallel development

stitutional values over others such that, for example, it accords the full measure of "citizenship" only to the "global entrepreneur" who is presumed to be acting in the public interest since his actions will benefit consumers through lower prices[872], while it treats as outside its realm the "subaltern . . . who fall outside of 'capitalism's logic' and who have no established agency in the West's culture of consumerism"[873]. When paired with the World Bank's "good governance" approach to the rule of law, the investment regime, in Schneiderman's view, imposes a "neoliberal rule of law" that promises predictability and certainty at the expense of democratic politics[874]. For Schneiderman, the better approach would be to adopt forms of "democratic experimentalism" that encourage "innovation, experimentation, and the capacity to imagine alternative futures for managing the relationship between politics and markets"[875].

Schneiderman's perspective might inform some of the evolutions in the investment regime discussed in prior chapters. As noted, more recent investment treaties and some investor-State decisions, are amenable to his contention that earlier investment treaties and earlier arbitral decisions unduly delimited States' "policy space".

---

of the rule against expropriation in the investment regime, especially indirect takings).

[872] See Schneiderman, *supra* footnote 735, pp. 188-191 (describing the type of people likely to bring foreign investment).

[873] *Ibid.*, p. 186 (contrasting those lacking protection under the investment regime with "the typical market citizen: white, male, English-speaking, and residing in a North Atlantic country").

[874] See *ibid.*, pp. 208-213 (describing the development of "rule of law" as a method for achieving stability and predictability within the investment regime).

[875] See *ibid.*, pp. 8-9.

At the same time, Schneiderman's critique cuts deeper. He is concerned with the regime's constitutionalization of "market citizenship"[876], along with its potential to inspire universally applicable ("neo-liberal") rules of law[877]. This critique is difficult to reconcile with the existing investment regime, at least so long as it retains recognizable features such as investor-State dispute settlement. If these critiques prove convincing to the regime's stakeholders, the regime's days — along with some of the related "investment regulation" now being conducted by international financial institutions — may be numbered.

(10) Humanity's law?

Ruti Teitel and Robert Howse have recently argued that there is yet another way to describe the contemporary evolution of international adjudicative mechanisms[878]. Their more optimistic perspective on the future of such regimes, including investor-State dispute settlement, answers some of the regime's critics.

Teitel and Howse see signs across divergent international adjudicators — from those adjudicating war crimes to those judging investment and trade disputes — of a turn to what they call "humanity's law". They define this as an emerging commitment by these disparate adjudicators to legality itself. They see signs in each of these adjudicative forums of a commitment to interpreting the law in ways that are sensitive to pro-

---

[876] See Schneiderman, *supra* footnote 735, pp. 187-191 (describing "market citizenship" and its prominent place in the investment regime).

[877] See *ibid.*, pp. 206-213 (describing the rule of law's development in the investment regime).

[878] R. Teitel and R. Howse, "Cross-Judging: Tribunalization in a Fragmented but Interconnected Global Order", 41 *New York University Journal of International Law and Politics* 959 (2009).

tecting humanity such that human rights concerns are increasingly amalgamated to the law of war, trade, and investment. For Teitel and Howse, this is suggested by investor-State arbitral outcomes that, as some by the ICTY and the WTO Appellate Body, reflect a more "humanity-oriented balance of rights and obligations"[879]. Teitel and Howse speculate that this is occurring not because international adjudicators are somehow "above" politics but precisely because they are aware that they cannot entirely ignore the politics (and the legitimacy) of their own decisions[880]. They suggest, for instance, that the more humanity-centred investor-State arbitral outcomes they describe stem from a growing awareness that adherence to the traditional "Washington Consensus" is increasingly politically untenable[881].

Whether or not one agrees with their formulation of "humanity's law", the Teitel-Howse thesis would seem to follow from predictions that the post-World War II turn to international law to protect human rights would have eventually fateful and even revolutionary consequences on virtually every aspect of formerly State-centric international law.

Although Teitel and Howse discuss a number of international judicial bodies, they put the international investment regime at the heart of the developments that they describe. Their analysis of the trend toward "humanity's law" is consistent with the progressive narratives inspired by the proliferation of international courts, along with the optimistic literature on the impact of transjudicial networks and the "progressive" nature of cross-judicial communications[882]. Theirs is a

---

[879] Schneiderman, *supra* footnote 735, p. 981.
[880] *Ibid.*
[881] *Ibid.*, p. 979.
[882] See, e.g., A. Slaughter, "Judicial Globalization", 40 *Virginia Journal of International Law* 1103 (2000), pp. 1112-1115.

hopeful account of how many broader developments in international law raised in this section interact in a positive way. In their account, judicialization will lessen over time the risks of fragmentation that is prompted by the growing involvement of non-State actors and the proliferation of international courts. Humanity's law, in their eyes, will help answer some of the critics of economic globalization, including Schneiderman's concerns with constitutionalism. They even suggest that hopes for a more human rights sensitive international investment regime lie precisely in the professional identity of the international adjudicators involved who, over time, will increasingly see themselves as agents of the international community and not narrow dispute settlers. Theirs is an elegant way of connecting the ten points of intersection discussed here into a virtuous circle of progress.

The harshest critics of the investment regime would dispute such optimism. While it is tempting to find support for the Teitel-Howse thesis in investor-State decisions that "balance" investor rights with State regulatory concerns, such as some of those recently issued in the Argentina cases discussed in Chapter IV, it is less evident that such rulings evince a common understanding that accords priority to human rights.

Howse and Teitel's humanity-centred reading of the developments in investment law and elsewhere de-emphasizes the different traditions from which these adjudicators emerge. Some investor-State arbitrators accustomed to adjudicating commercial disputes among private parties may have little in common with those trained in public international law. Howse and Teitel's account does not address what that divide may produce when decisions are produced among them on the basis of consensus. It is also important to consider the prospect that investor-State awards are likely to continue to be based on the issues raised by the parties to these disputes and that, even when NGO *amicus* briefs raise human rights concerns, these may not form the basis of decision unless either the investor or the respondent State relies on them[883]. Thus far, concrete evidence for Howse and Teitel's version of "humanity's law" remains elusive. Even those investor-State arbitrations that have addressed human rights concerns have done so obliquely.

The developments that Howse and Teitel describe might be seen from a different perspective. While it is true that the turn to proportionality that appears in some recent investment arbitral awards may respond to heightened sensitivity to the host State's sovereign right to regulate, we need to recall that this is not a reliable rationale for protecting the rights of all human beings (including investors) from the State. Indeed, when one examines the changes that Howse and Teitel highlight within the investment regime that in their view evince "humanity's law", it is striking how many of these respond to concerns voiced by the leading Governments that established the investment regime, such as the United States, and are reflected in the changes in the US Model BIT of 2004 and the defensive arguments that the United States has made in the 18 NAFTA claims brought against it.

Neither the changes to the US Model BIT nor the

---

[883] As noted, this means that there may be tensions between the issues that NGOs urge such tribunals to consider, through their *amicus* briefs, and those raised by the parties. Compare *Glamis* Quechan Submission, *supra* footnote 830 (arguing for indigenous people's control over traditional property) with *Glamis Gold Ltd.* v. *United States*, Counter-Memorial of the Respondent, UNCITRAL Arbitration Rules (19 September 2006), pp. 7-11 (stating that property and mineral rights in the United States are ultimately under the control of the federal Government and are regulated by federal legislation).

arguments raised in US briefs filed in NAFTA cases suggest genuine concerns with human rights or even the constitutional rights of US nationals. As discussed in Chapter I, the changes to the US Model BIT narrow the rights of investors (sometimes by attempting to make these extend no further than US law) and increase the regulatory space for Governments. The interpretative space that has been opened was not intended to be used to advance the progressive cause of human rights. Such a rationale would certainly have surprised the Bush Administration officials responsible for making them. That Administration was not known for its sensitivity to international human rights and certainly not for encouraging supranational scrutiny of US laws on this basis; it would be strange indeed if it made an exception only with respect to BITs. The changes to US (and in all likelihood) other BITs discussed in Chapter II appear to have been prompted by more pedestrian concerns, including principally States' desire to avoid losing investor claims.

Nor is it likely that even those States that have accepted more supranational scrutiny with respect to human rights (and are, for example, parties to the European Convention on Human Rights) have made changes in their BITs in deference to the human rights revolution. While other States have, through participation in the American and European Convention on Human Rights, accepted binding human rights adjudication, this has occurred among like-minded States or regions. Human rights enforcement at the global level and between the radically different States that often find themselves joined by an investment treaty is spotty or non-existent. Indeed, even NGOs that support more human-rights-sensitive BITs, such as the IISD, report that such provisions do not appear in BITs between developing States. It would be surprising if even activist investor-State arbitrators could create binding human rights enforcement among the disparate States that are parties to the investment regime. Of course, there is scant evidence that those who now serve as investor-State arbitrators share the progressive human rights agenda that may exist among, for example, the judges of *ad hoc* war crimes tribunals or regional human rights courts. And without such a common agenda, it is possible that the "progressive" developments evident in the investment regime may be used precisely to give Governments exactly what they seek, namely, greater discretion to use their regulatory powers, irrespective of whether that regulatory space is used to advance human rights or whether it is used principally to violate the rights of foreign investors. If this turns out to be the case, "humanity's law" may eventually turn out to be just old "sovereignty law" under more attractive labelling.

* * *

This monograph is an attempt to understand the nature of the evolving international investment regime viewed against the broader questions many other international regimes are facing. Like those other regimes, the investment regime is complex. On occasion it may promote harmonization *and* fragmentation, reflect the views of States *and* non-State actors, be both a tool of liberalization/economic globalization *and* of "humanity", enforce *both* treaty and non-treaty sources of law, and serve, at different times or for different audiences, as a tool for hegemony, for review of national administrative actions, and for "constitutionalization". These are not necessarily dichotomous descriptions — though some might portray them as such — and they are assuredly not unique to the international investment regime.

BIBLIOGRAPHY

A. Awards and Opinions

Accordance with International Law of the Unilateral Declaration of Independence in Respect of Kosovo, Advisory Opinion, *ICJ Reports 2010* (22 July 2010).

ADF Group Inc. v. *United States*, Award, NAFTA Chap. 11 Arbitral Tribunal (9 January 2003).

Aguas del Tunari, S.A. v. *Republic of Bolivia*, Decision on Respondent's Objections to Jurisdiction, ICSID Case No. ARB/02/3 (21 October 2005).

American Mfg. & Trading, Inc. v. *Zaire*, Award, ICSID Case No. ARB/93/1 (12 February 1997).

Amoco Int'l Finance Corp. v. *Iran*, Award, *Iran-United States Claims Tribunal Reports* 189 (14 July 1987).

Argentinien-Anleihen: StaatsnotstandberechtigtnichtzurZahlungsverweigerungge-genüberprivatenGläbigern (F.R.G.), Bundesverfassungsgericht [Federal Constitutional Court of Germany], No. 75/2007 (5 July 2007).

Asakura v. *City of Seattle*, United States Supreme Court, 265 *United States Reports* 332 (1924).

Asian Agricultural Products Ltd. v. *Republic of Sri Lanka*, Final Award, ICSID Case No. ARB/87/3 (27 June 1990).

Azurix Corp. v. *Argentine Republic*, Award, ISCID Case No. ARB/01/12 (14 July 2006).

Banco Nacional de Cuba v. *Chase Manhattan Bank*, United States 2nd Circuit Court of Appeals, 658 *Federal Reporter, Second Series* 875 (1981).

Barcelona Traction, Light and Power Co. (Belgium v. *Spain)*, Judgment, *ICJ Reports 1970* 1 (1970).

BG Group PLC v. *Argentina*, Award, UNCITRAL Arbitration Rules (24 December 2007).

Brazil: Measures Affecting Import of Retreaded Tyres, Report of the Appellate Body, World Trade Organization Case No. WT/DS332/AB/R (3 December 2007).

Certain Norwegian Loans (France v. *Norway)*, Judgment, *ICJ Reports 1957* 6 (6 July 1957).

Certain Norwegian Loans (France v. *Norway)*, dissenting opinion of Judge Guerro, *ICJ Reports 1957* 69 (6 July 1957).

CME Czech Republic B.V. v. *Czech Republic*, Partial Award,

UNCITRAL Arbitration Rules, 9 *ICSID Reports* 121 (13 September 2001).

CME Czech Republic B.V. v. *Czech Republic*, Final Award, UNCITRAL Arbitration Rules (14 March 2003).

CMS Gas Transmission Co. v. *Argentina*, Decision on Annulment, ICSID Case No. ARB/01/8 (25 September 2007).

CMS Gas Transmission Co. v. *Argentina*, Award, ICSID Case No. ARB/01/8, 44 *International Legal Materials* 1205 (12 May 2005).

Continental Casualty Co. v. *Argentine Republic*, Award, ICSID Case No. ARB/03/9 (5 September 2008).

Council of Canadians v. *Canada*, Ontario Superior Court of Justice, Court File No. 01-CV-208141 (8 July 2005).

Desert Line Projects LLC v. *Republic of Yemen*, Award, ICSID Case No. ARB/05/17 (6 February 2008).

Elettronica Sicula S.p.A. (United States v. *Italy)*, Judgment, *ICJ Reports 1989* 15 (20 July 1989).

Enron Creditors Recovery Corp. Ponderosa Assets, L.P. v. *Argentine Republic*, Decision on the Application for Annulment of the Argentine Republic, ICSID Case No. ARB/01/3 (30 July 2010).

Enron Corp. v. *Argentina*, Award, ICSID Case No. ARB/01/3 (22 May 2007).

Emilio Agustin Maffezini v. *Kingdom of Spain*, Decision on Jurisdiction, ICSID Case No. ARB/97/7 (25 January 2000).

Feldman v. *Mexico*, Award, ICSID Case No. ARB(AF)/99/1, 42 *International Legal Materials* 625 (16 December 2002).

Fraport v. *Philippines*, Dissenting Opinion, ICSID Case No. ARB/03/25 (16 August 2007).

Funnekotter v. *Zimbabwe*, Award, ICSID Case No. ARB/05/6 (15 April 2009).

GAMI Investments, Inc. v. *Mexico*, Final Award, UNCITRAL Arbitration Rules (15 November 2004).

Glamis Gold Ltd. v. *United States*, Counter-Memorial of the Respondent, UNCITRAL Arbitration Rules (19 September 2006).

Glamis Gold Ltd. v. *United States*, Quechan Indian Nation Application for Leave to File a Non-Party Submission, UNCITRAL Arbitration Rules (16 October 2006).

Glamis Gold Ltd. v. *United States*, Award, UNCITRAL Arbitration Rules (8 June 2009).

Inceysa Vallisoletana v. *El Salvador*, Award, ICSID Case No. ARB/03/26 (2 August 2006).

Interhandel (Switzerland v. *United States)*, Dissenting

Opinion of Sir Hersch Lauterpacht, *ICJ Reports 1959* 95 (21 March 1959).

International Thunderbird Gaming Corp. v. *Mexico*, Award, UNCITRAL Arbitration Rules (26 January 2006).

Kadi v. *Council & Commission*, Judgment, Grand Chamber of the European Court of Justice, Case No. C-402/05 (2008).

Lauder v. *Czech Republic*, Final Award, UNCITRAL Arbitration Rules, 9 *ICSID Reports* 66 (3 September 2001).

Legal Consequences for States of the Continued Presence of South Africa in Namibia (South West Africa) notwithstanding Security Council Resolution 276, Advisory Opinion, *ICJ Reports 1971* 16 (21 June 1971).

LG&E Energy Corp. v. *Argentina*, Decision on Liability, ICSID Case No. ARB/02/1 (3 October 2006).

Limited Liability Company AMTO v. *Ukraine*, Award, Stockholm Chamber of Commerce Arbitration No. 080/2005 (26 March 2008).

Loewen Group, Inc. v. *United States*, ICSID Case No. ARB(AF)/98/3, 42 *International Legal Materials* 811 (26 June 2003).

Malaysian Historical Salvors, SDN, BHD v. *Malaysia*, Decision on Application for Annulment, ICSID Case No. ARB/05/10 (16 April 2009).

MCI Power v. *Ecuador*, Award, ICSID Case No. ARB/03/6 (31 July 2007).

Metalclad Corp. v. *Mexico*, Award, ICSID Case No. ARB (AF)/97/1 (8 August 2001).

Methanex Corp. v. *United States*, Decision on Amici Curiae, UNCITRAL Arbitration Rules (15 January 2001)

Methanex Corp. v. *United States*, Second Opinion of Professor Sir Robert Jennings, QC, NAFTA Chap. 11 Arbitral Tribunal (5 November 2002).

Methanex Corp. v. *United States*, Final Award, UNCITRAL Arbitration Rules, 44 *International Legal Materials* 1345 (3 August 2005).

Mondev International Ltd. v. *United States*, Award, ICSID Case No. ARB(AF)/99/2 (11 October 2002).

MTD Equity SDN BHD & MTD Chile S.A. v. *Chile*, Decision on the Application for Annulment, ICSID Case No. ARB/01/7 (21 March 2007).

National Grid P.L.C. v. *Argentine Republic*, UNCITRAL Award (3 November 2008).

Noble Ventures, Inc. v. *Romania*, Award, ICSID Case No. ARB/01/11 (12 October 2005).

Occidental v. *Ecuador*, Award, UNCITRAL Arbitration Rules, 12 *ICSID Reporter* 59 (1 July 2004).

Öneryildiz v. *Turkey*, Grand Chamber of the European Court of Human Rights, App. No. 48939/99 (30 November 2004).

The Paquete Habana, United States Supreme Court, 175 *United States Reports* 677 (1900).

Patuha Power Ltd. (Bermuda) v. *PT (Persero) Perusahaan Listruik Negara (Indonesia)*, Final Award, 14 *Mealey's International Arbitration Report* (1999).

Penn Central v. *City of New York*, United States Supreme Court, 438 *United States Reports* 104 (1978).

Phoenix Action, Ltd. v. *Czech Republic*, Award, ICSID Case No. ARB/06/5 (15 April 2009).

Plama Consortium Ltd. v. *Republic of Bulgaria*, Award, ICSID Case No. ARB/03/24 (27 August 2008).

Pope & Talbot v. *Canada*, Award on Merits of Phase Two, NAFTA Chap. 11 Arbitral Tribunal (10 April 2001).

Pope & Talbot v. *Canada*, Damages Award, NAFTA Chap. 11 Arbitral Tribunal (21 October 2002).

PSEG Global Inc. v. *Republic of Turkey*, Award, ICSID Case No. ARB/02/5 (19 January 2007).

Reference re Secession of Quebec, Supreme Court of Canada, 2 *Supreme Court Reports* 217 (1998).

Saba Fakes v. *Republic of Turkey*, Award, ICSID Case No. ARB/07/20 (14 July 2010).

Saipem S.p.A. v. *Bangladesh*, Decision on Jurisdiction, ICSID Case No. ARB/05/07 (21 March 2007).

S.D. Myers, Inc. v. *Canada*, Separate Opinion of Schwartz, UNCITRAL Arbitration Rules (12 November 2000).

S.D. Myers, Inc. v. *Canada*, Partial Award on the Merits, UNCITRAL Arbitration Rules (13 November 2000).

Saluka Investment BV v. *Czech Republic*, Partial Award, UNCITRAL Arbitration Rules (17 March 2006).

SEDCO, Inc. v. *National Iranian Oil Company and the Islamic Republic of Iran*, Interlocutory Award, Iran-United States Claims Tribunal, 10 *Iran-United States Claims Reports* 180 (1986).

Sempra Energy International v. *Argentina*, Award, ICSID Case No. ARB/02/16 (28 September 2007).

Sempra Energy International v. *Argentina*, Decision on the Argentine Republic's Request for a Continued Stay of Enforcement of the Award, ICSID Case No. ARB/02/16 (5 March 2009).

Sempra Energy International v. *Argentina*, Decision on the

Argentine's Republic's Application for Annulment of the Award, ICSID Case No. ARB/02/16 (29 June 2010).

Siemens AG v. *Argentina*, Award, ICSID Case No. ARB/02/8 (6 February 2007).

Southern Pacific Properties (Middle East) Ltd. v. *Egypt*, Award and Dissenting Opinion, ICSID Case No. ARB/84/3, 3 *ICSID Reports* 189 (20 May 1992).

Case of the S.S. "Wimbledon" (United Kingdom, France, Italy, Japan, Germany), Permanent Court of International Justice, 1923 (Ser. A), No. 1 (28 June 1923).

Tecnica Medioambietales, TECMED S.A. v. *Mexico*, Award, ICSID Case No. ARB/00/2 (29 May 2003).

Texaco Overseas Petroleum Company/California Asiatic Oil Company and the Government of the Libyan Arab Republic, Award, 17 *International Legal Materials* 1 (1978).

United Mexican States v. *Metalclad Corp.*, British Columbia Supreme Court, 2001 *British Columbia Supreme Court Reports* 664 (2001).

United Parcel Service of America, Inc. v. *Canada*, Decision of the Tribunal on Petitions for Intervention and Participation as Amici Curiae, UNCITRAL Arbitration Rules (17 October 2001).

United Parcel Service of America, Inc. v. *Canada*, Award, UNCITRAL Arbitration Rules (24 May 2007).

United States (Chattin) v. *United Mexican States*, General Claims Commission, 4 *Reports of International Arbitration Awards* 282 (23 July 1927)

United States (Neer) v. *United Mexican States*, General Claims Commission, 4 *Reports of International Arbitration Awards* 60 (15 October 1926).

United States — Measures Affecting the Cross-Border Supply of Gambling and Betting Services, Report of the Appellate Body, World Trade Organization Case No. WT/DS285/AB/R (7 April 2005).

Velásquez Rodríguez v. *Honduras*, Inter-American Court of Human Rights (Ser. C) No. 4 (29 July 1988).

Vivendi Universal S.A. v. *Argentina*, Award, ICSID Case No. ARB/97/3 (21 November 2001).

Waste Management, Inc. v. *Mexico*, Award, ICSID Case No. ARB(AF)/00/3 (30 April 2004).

Wena Hotels v. *Egypt*, Award, ICSID Case No. ARB/98/4 (8 December 2000).

World Duty Free Company v. *Kenya*, Award, ICSID Case No. ARB/00/17 (4 October 2006).

B. Articles and Book Chapters

van Aaken, A., and J. Kurtz, "Emergency Measures and International Investment Law: How Far Can States Go?", in K. P. Sauvant (ed.), *Yearbook on International Investment Law and Policy 2009-2010* (Oxford, Oxford University Press, forthcoming 2010).

van Aaken, A., and J. Kurtz, "The Global Financial Crisis: Will State Emergency Measures Trigger International Investment Disputes?", *Columbia FDI Perspectives*, No. 3 (2009), available at <http://www.vcc.columbia.edu/content/global-financial-crisis-will-state-emergency-measures-trigger-international-investment-dispu>.

Abbott, K., and D. Snidal, "The Concept of Legalization", in J. Goldstein *et al.* (eds.), *Legalization and World Politics* (Boston, MIT Press, 2001).

Acconci, P., "Most-Favoured-Nation Treatment", in P. Muchlinski *et al.* (eds.), *The Oxford Handbook of International Investment Law* (Oxford, Oxford University Press, 2008).

Aguirre Luzi, R., and B. Love, "Individual Nationality in Investment Treaty Arbitration: The Tension between Customary International Law and *Lex Specialis*", in A. K. Bjorklund *et al.* (eds.), *Investment Treaty Law: Current Issues III: Remedies in International Investment Law & Emerging Jurisprudence in International Investment Law* (London, British Institute of International and Comparative Law, 2009).

Alexandrov, S. A., "On the Perceived Inconsistency in Investor-State Jurisprudence", in K. P. Sauvant *et al.* (eds.), *The Evolving International Investment Regime: Expectations, Realities, Options* (Oxford University Press, forthcoming 2010).

Allen, T., "Compensation for Property under the European Convention on Human Rights", 28 *Michigan Journal of International Law* 287 (2007).

Allot, P., "The Concept of International Law", 10 *European Journal of International Law* 31 (1999).

Alvarez, J. E., "The Rise of Emerging Market Multinationals: Legal Challenges Ahead", in W. Mascheck *et al.* (eds.), *Thinking Outward: Global Players in Emerging Markets* (forthcoming).

—, "The Once and Future Investment Regime", in M. Arsanjani *et al.* (eds.), *Looking to the Future: Essays on International Law in Honor of W. Michael Reisman* (The Hague, Martinus Nijhoff Publishers, forthcoming 2010).

—, "Are Corporations 'Subjects' of International Law", *Santa Clara Journal of International Law* (forthcoming 2010).

—, "A BIT on Custom", 42 *New York University Journal of International Law and Politics* 17 (2009).

—, "Contemporary Foreign Investment Law: An 'Empire of Law' or the 'Law of Empire'?", 60 *Alabama Law Review* 943 (2009).

—, "Contemporary International Law: An 'Empire of Law' or the 'Law of Empire'?", 24 *American University International Law Review* 811 (2009).

—, "The Evolving Foreign Investment Regime", *American Society of International Law: IL.post* (29 February 2008), available at <http://www.asil.org/ilpost/president/pres 080229.html>.

—, "The NAFTA's Investment Chapter and Mexico", in R. Dolzer *et al.* (eds.), *Foreign Investment: Its Significance in Relation to the Fight against Poverty, Economic Growth and Legal Culture* (Singapore, Konrad-Adenauer-Siftung, 2006).

—, "Foreword: The Ripples of NAFTA", in T. Weiler (ed.), *NAFTA Investment Law and Arbitration: Past Issues, Current Practice, Future Prospects* (Ardsley Park, Transnational Publishers, 2004).

—, "Hegemonic International Law Revisited", 97 *American Journal of International Law* 873 (2003).

—, "Do Liberal States Behave Better?: A Critique of Slaughter's Liberal Theory", 12 *European Journal of International Law* 183 (2001).

—, "Critical Theory and the North American Free Trade Agreement's Chapter Eleven", 28 *University of Miami Inter-American Law Review* 303 (1997).

Alvarez, J., and T. Brink, "Revisiting the Necessity Defense in the Argentina Cases", *Yearbook on International Law & Policy 2010-2011* (2011), also available on Investment Claims Database (Oxford), see <http://www.investment-claims.com/subscriber_article?script=yes&id=/ic/Journal%20Articles/law-iic-journal052&recno=20&searchType=browse>.

Alvarez, J. E., and K. Khamsi, "The Argentine Crisis and Foreign Investors", in K. P. Sauvant (ed.), *Yearbook on International Investment Law & Policy 2008-2009* (New York, Oxford University Press, 2009).

Atik, J., "Repenser NAFTA Chapter 11: A Catalogue of Legitimacy Critiques", 3 *Asper Review of International Business and Trade Law* 215 (2003).

Aykut, D., and D. Ratha, "South-South FDI Flows: How Big Are They?", 13 *Transnational Corporations* 149 (2003).

Banifatemi, Y., "The Emerging Jurisprudence on the Most-Favoured-Nation Treatment in Investment Arbitration", in A. K. Bjorklund *et al.* (eds.), *Investment Treaty Law: Current Issues III: Remedies in International Investment Law & Emerging Jurisprudence in International Investment Law* (London, British Institute of International and Comparative Law, 2009).

Bekker, P. H. F., "The Use of Non-Domestic Courts for Obtaining Domestic Relief: Jurisdictional Conflicts between NAFTA Tribunals and U.S. Courts", 11 *International Law Students Association Journal of International & Comparative Law* 331 (2005).

Bello, J. H., "The WTO Dispute Settlement Understanding: Less Is More", 90 *American Journal of International Law* 416 (1996).

Binder, C., *et al.*, *International Investment Law for the 21st Century: Essays in Honor of Christoph Schreuer* (New York, Oxford University Press, 2009).

Bjorklund, A., "Investment Treaty Arbitral Decisions as Jurisprudence Constante", in C. Picker *et al.* (eds.), *International Economic Law: The State and Future of the Discipline* (Portland, Oregon, Hart Publishing, 2008).

—, "Private Rights and Public International Law: Why Competition among International Courts Is Not Working", 59 *Hastings Law Journal* 241 (2007).

Bottini, G., "Protection of Essential Interests in the BIT Era", in T. J. Grierson Weiler (ed.), *Investment Treaty Arbitration and Public Law* (Huntington, New York, Juris Publishing, 2008).

Bond, Michael J., "The Americanization of Carlos Calvo", 22 *Mealey's International Arbitration Report* 1 (2007).

Borgen, C., "Transnational Tribunals and the Transmission of Norms", 39 *George Washington International Law Review* 685 (2007).

Braun, T. R., "Globalization: The Driving Force in International Investment Law", in A. Kaushal *et al.* (eds.), *The Backlash against Investment Arbitration* (Netherlands, Kluwer Law International, 2010).

Bridgeman, N. L., and D. B. Hunter, "Narrowing the Accountability Gap: Toward a Foreign Investor Accountability Mechanism", 20 *Georgetown International Environmental Law Review* 187 (2008).

Brower, C. N., "NAFTA's Investment Chapter: Dynamic

Laboratory, Failed Experiments, and Lessons for the FTAA", 97 *Proceedings of the Annual Meeting of the American Society of International Law* 251 (2003).

—, "Investor-State Disputes under NAFTA: The Empire Strikes Back", 40 *Columbia Journal of Transnational Law* 41 (2001).

Brower, C. N., and J. K. Sharpe, "The Creeping Codification of Transnational Commercial Law: An Arbitrator's Perspective", 45 *Virginia Journal of International Law* 199 (2004).

Brown, C., "The Protection of Legitimate Expectations as a General Principle of Law: Some Preliminary Thoughts", 6:1 *Transnational Dispute Management* (2009).

Burke-White, W. W., "The Argentine Financial Crisis: State Liability under BITs and the Legitimacy of the ICSID System", 3:1 *Asian Journal of WTO & International Health Law and Policy* 199 (2008).

Burke-White, W. W., and A. von Staden, "Investment Protection in Extraordinary Times: The Interpretation and Application of Non-Precluded Measures Provisions in Bilateral Investment Treaties", 48 *Virginia Journal of International Law* 307 (2008).

Büthe, T., and H. V. Milner, "Bilateral Investment Treaties and Foreign Direct Investment: A Political Analysis", in L. Sachs and K. P. Sauvant, *The Effect of Treaties on Foreign Direct Investment* (New York, Oxford University Press, 2009).

Caron, D. D., "Towards a Political Theory of International Courts and Tribunals", 24 *Berkeley Journal of International Law* 401 (2006).

Catá Backer, L., "Multilateral Corporations as Objects and Sources of Transnational Regulation", 14 *International Law Students Association Journal of International and Comparative Law* 499 (2008).

—, "Economic Globalization and the Rise of Efficient Systems of Global Private Law-Making: Wal-Mart as Global Legislator", 39 *Connecticut Law Review* 1739 (2007).

Chalamish, E., "The Future of Bilateral Investment Treaties: A De Facto Multilateral Agreement", 34 *Brooklyn Journal of International Law* 304 (2009).

Chander, A., "Globalization and Distrust", 114 *Yale Law Journal* 1193 (2005).

Charney, J., "The Impact on the International Legal System of the Growth of International Courts and Tribunals", 31

New York University Journal of International Law and Politics 697 (1999).

Cheng, T. H., "Precedent and Control in Investment Treaty Arbitration", 30 *Fordham International Law Journal* 1014 (2007).

Chimni, B. S., "The Past, Present and Future of International Law: A Critical Third World Approach", 8 *Michigan Journal of International Law* 499 (2007).

—, "A Just World under Law: A View from the South", 22 *American University International Law Review* 199 (2007).

—, "International Institutions Today: An Imperial Global State in the Making", 15 *European Journal of International Law* 1 (2004).

Choudhury, B., "Recapturing Public Power: Is Investment Arbitration's Engagement of the Public Interest Contributing to the Democratic Deficit?", 41 *Vanderbilt Journal of Transnational Law* 775 (2008).

Christain, T., "Quel remède à l'éclatement de la jurisprudence CIRDI sur les investissements en Argentine? La decision du Comité ad hoc dans l'affaire *CMS c. Argentine*", 111 *Revue générale de droit international public* 879 (2007).

Chua, A., "The Privatization-Nationalization Cycle: The Link between Markets and Ethnicity in Developing Countries", 95 *Columbia Law Review* 223 (1995).

Clarkson, S., "Hijacking the Canadian Constitution: NAFTA's Investor-State Dispute Arbitration", in A. S. Alexandroff (ed.), *Investor Protection in the NAFTA and Beyond: Private Interest and Public Purpose* (Toronto, Ontario, C. D. Howe Institute, 2006).

Coe, J. J., "Transparency in the Resolution of Investor-State Disputes — Adoption, Adaptation, and NAFTA Leadership", 54 *University of Kansas Law Review* 1339 (2006).

Commission, J. P., "An Analysis of a Developing Jurisprudence in International Investment Law — What Investment Treaty Tribunals Are Saying and Doing", 6:1 *Transnational Dispute Management* (2009).

Congyan, C., "China-US BIT Negotiations and the Future of Investment Treaty Regime: A Grand Bilateral Bargain with Multilateral Implications", 12 *Journal of International Economic Law* 457 (2009).

Davies, K., "While Global FDI Falls, China's Outward FDI Doubles", *Columbia FDI Perspectives* No. 5 (2009).

Davis, K. E., "What Can the Rule of Law Variable Tell Us

about Rule of Law Reforms?", 26 *Michigan Journal of International Law* 141 (2004).

Davis, K. E., and M. B. Kruse, "Taking the Measure of Law: The Case of the Doing Business Project", 32 *Law & Social Inquiry* 1095 (2007).

Davis, M., "China's New Nonprofit Regulations: Season of Instability", *Asia Catalyst: Economic & Social Rights in Asia* (14 June 2010), available at <http://asiacatalyst.org/blog/2010/06/chinas-new-nonprofit-regulations-season-of-instability.html#more>.

Denza, E., and S. Brooks, "Investment Protection Treaties: United Kingdom Experience", 36 *International & Comparative Law Quarterly* 908 (1987).

Dhir, A. A., "Of Takeover, Foreign Investment and Human Rights: Unpacking the Noranda-Minmetals Conundrum", 22 *Banking & Finance Law Review* 77 (2006).

—, "Realigning the Corporate Building Blocks: Shareholder Proposals as a Vehicle for Achieving Corporate Social and Human Rights Accountability", 43 *American Business Law Journal* 365 (2006).

Douglas, Z., "Nothing if Not Critical for Investment Treaty Arbitration: *Occidental*, *Eureko* and *Methanex*", 22 *Arbitration International* 27 (2006).

—, "The Hybrid Foundations of Investment Treaty Arbitration", 74 *British Year Book of International Law* 151 (2003).

Dunoff, J. L., "Constitutional Conceits: The WTO's 'Constitution' and the Discipline of International Law", 17 *European Journal of International Law* 647 (2006).

Elkins, Z., *et al.*, "Competing for Capital: The Diffusion of Bilateral Investment Treaties: 1960-2000", 60 *International Organizations* 811 (2006).

Emmerson, A., "Conceptualizing Security Exceptions: Legal Doctrine or Political Excuse?", 11 *Journal of International Economic Law* 135 (2008).

Endicott, M., "Remedies in Investor-State Arbitration: Restitution, Specific Performance and Declaratory Awards", in P. Kahn and T. Wälde (eds.), *New Aspects of International Investment Law* (Leiden, Martinus Nijhoff, 2007).

Falsafi, A., "The International Minimum Standard of Treatment of Foreign Investors' Property: A Contingent Standard", 30 *Suffolk Transnational Law Review* 317 (2007).

Fauchald, O. K., "The Legal Reasoning of ICSID Tribunals

— An Empirical Analysis", 19 *European Journal International Law* 301 (2008).

Fidler, D. P., "The Return of the Standard of Civilization", 2 *Chicago Journal of International Law* 137 (2001).

—, "A Kinder, Gentler System of Capitulations? International Law, Structural Adjustment Policies, and the Standard of Liberal, Globalization Civilization", 35 *Texas International Law Journal* 387 (2000).

Fiss, O. M., "Foreword: The Forms of Justice", 93 *Harvard Law Review* 1 (1979).

Forcese, C., "Does the Sky Fall? NAFTA Chapter 11 Dispute Settlement and Democratic Accountability", 14 *Michigan State Journal of International Law* 315 (2006).

"The Forum Panel Discussion: Precedent in Investment Arbitration", in A. K. Bjorklund *et al.* (eds.), *Investment Treaty Law: Current Issues III: Remedies in International Investment Law & Emerging Jurisprudence in International Investment Law* (London, British Institute of International and Comparative Law, 2009).

Franck, S. D., "International Investment Arbitration: Winning, Losing and Why", *Columbia FDI Perspectives*, No. 7 (2009), available at <http://www.vcc.columbia.edu/content/fdi-perspectives>.

—, "Development and Outcomes of Investment Arbitration Awards", 50 *Harvard International Law Journal* 435 (2009).

—, "Empirically Evaluating Claims about Investment Treaty Arbitration", 86 *North Carolina Law Review* 1 (2008).

—, "Foreign Direct Investment, Investment Treaty Arbitration, and the Rule of Law", 19 *Pacific McGeorge Global Business & Development Law Journal* 337 (2007).

—, "The Role of International Arbitrators", 12 *International Law Students Association Journal of International & Comparative Law* 499 (2006).

—, "The Legitimacy Crisis in Investment Treaty Arbitration: Privatizing International Law through Inconsistent Decisions", 73 *Fordham Law Review* 1521 (2005).

—, "The Nature and Enforcement of Investor Rights under Investment Treaties: Do Investment Treaties Have a Bright Future?", 12 *University of California Davis Journal of International Law & Policy* 52 (2005).

—, "On Proportionality of Countermeasures in International Law", 102 *American Journal of International Law* 715 (2008).

Friedman, W., "General Course in Public International Law", *Recueil des cours*, Vol. 127 (The Hague, Leiden, 1969).

Fry, J. D., "International Human Rights Law in Investment Arbitration: Evidence of International Law's Unity", 18 *Duke Journal of Comparative & International Law* 77 (2007).

Gagné, G., and J. Morin, "The Evolving American Policy on Investment Protection: Evidence from Recent FTAs and the 2004 Model BIT", 9 *Journal of International Economic Law* 357 (2006).

Gal-Or, N., "The Investor and Civil Society as Twin Global Citizens: Proposing a New Interpretation in the Legitimacy Debate", 32 *Suffolk Transnational Law Review* 271 (2009).

Gantz, D. A., "An Appellate Mechanism for Review of Arbitral Decisions in Investor-State Disputes: Prospects and Challenges", 39 *Vanderbilt Journal of Transnational Law* 39 (2006).

—, "International Decision: *Pope & Talbot, Inc.* v. *Canada*", 97 *American Journal of International Law* 937 (2003).

Gathii, J. T., "Foreign and Other Economic Rights upon Conquest and under Occupation: Iraq in Comparative and Historical Context", 25 *University of Pennsylvania Journal of International Economic Law* 491 (2004).

Giegerich, T., "The Is and the Ought of International Constitutionalism: How Far Have We Come on Habermas's Road to a 'Well-Considered Constitutionalization of International Law'?", 10 *German Law Journal* 31 (2009).

Ginsburg, T., "International Substitutes for Domestic Institutions: Bilateral Investment Treaties and Governance", 25 *International Review of Law and Economics* 107 (2005).

Goldsmith, J. L., and E. A. Posner, "Understanding the Resemblance between Modern and Traditional Customary International Law", 40 *Virginia Journal of International Law* 639 (2004).

Goldstein, D. M., "Neoliberal Violence and 'Self-Help' Security in Bolivia", 25 *Critique of Anthropology* 389 (2005).

Goldstein, J., *et al.*, "Introduction: Legalization and World Politics", 54 *International Organizations* 385 (2000).

Goodman, R., and D. Jinks, "International Law and State Socialization: Conceptual, Empirical, and Normative Challenges", 54 *Duke Law Journal* 983 (2005).

Goodman, R., and D. Jinks, "How to Influence States: Socialization and International Human Rights Law", 54 *Duke Law Journal* 621 (2004).

Gottwald, E. J., "Leveling the Playing Field: Is it Time for a

Legal Assistance Center for Developing Nations in Investment Treaty Arbitration?", 22 *American University Law Review* 237 (2007).

Grigsby, W. E., "The Mixed Courts of Egypt", 12 *Law Quarterly Review* 252 (1896).

Guzman, A. T., "Explaining the Popularity of Bilateral Investment Treaties", in L. Sachs and K. P. Sauvant, *The Effect of Treaties on Foreign Direct Investment* (New York, Oxford University Press, 2009).

—, "The Cost of Credibility: Explaining Resistance to Interstate Dispute Settlement Mechanisms", 31 *Journal of Legal Studies* 303 (2002).

—, "Why LDCs Sign Treaties That Hurt Them: Explaining the Popularity of Bilateral Investment Treaties", 38 *Virginia Journal of International Law* 639 (1998).

Guzman, A. T., and T. L. Meyer, "International Common Law: The Soft Law of International Tribunals", 9 *Chicago Journal of International Law* 515 (2009).

van Harten, G., "A Case for an International Investment Court", *Society for International Economic Law*, Working Paper No. 22/08 (2008), available at <http://papers.ssrn.com/sol3/papers.cfm?abstract_id=1153424>.

van Harten, G., and M. Loughlin, "Investment Treaty Arbitration as a Species of Global Administrative Law", 17 *European Journal of International Law* 121 (2006).

Henkin, L., "That 'S' Word: Sovereignty and Globalization and Human Rights, et cetera", 68 *Fordham Law Review* 1 (1999).

Jackson, J. H., "The WTO Dispute Settlement Understanding — Misunderstandings on the Nature of Legal Obligations", 91 *American Journal of International Law* 60 (1997).

Jackson, J. H., and A. F. Lowenfeld, "Helms-Burton, the U.S., and the WTO", *American Society of International Law Insights* (March 1997), available at <http://www.asil.org/insight7.cfm>.

Kalderimis, D., "IMF Conditionality as Investment Regulation: A Theoretical Analysis", 13 *Social & Legal Studies* 104 (2004).

Kantor, M., "New Amendments to ICSID Arbitration Rules", 2006:1 *Stockholm International Arbitration Review* 213 (2006).

Katz Cogan, J., "Competition and Control in International Adjudication", 48 *Virginia Journal of International Law* 411 (2007).

Kelly, J. P., "The Twilight of Customary International Law", 40 *Virginia Journal of International Law* 449 (2000).

Kennedy, D., "The 'Rule of Law' Political Choices, and Development Common Sense", in D. M. Trubek and A. Santos (eds.), *The New Law and Economic Development* (New York, Cambridge University Press, 2006).

Kentin, E., "Economic Crisis and Investment Arbitration: The Argentina Cases", in P. Kahn and T. Wälde, (eds.), *New Aspects of International Investment Law* (Leiden, Martinus Nijhoff, 2007).

Keohane, R. O., *et al.*, "Legalized Dispute Settlement: Interstate and Transnational", 54 *International Organizations* 457 (2000).

Kingsbury, B., "Sovereignty and Inequality", 9 *European Journal of International Law* 599 (1998).

Kingsbury, B., and S. Schill, "Investor-State Arbitration as Governance: Fair and Equitable Treatment, Proportionality and the Emerging Global Administrative Law", in *El nuevo derecho administrativo global en América Latina: desafíos para las inversiones extranjeras, la regulación nacional y el financiamiento para el desarrollo* (Buenos Aires, Ediciones RAP S.A., 2009).

Kingsbury, B., *et al.*, "The Emergence of Global Administrative Law", 68 *Law and Contemporary Problems* 15 (2005).

Kinnear, M., "The Fair and Equitable Treatment Standard", in A. K. Bjorklund *et al.* (eds.), *Investment Treaty Law: Current Issues III: Remedies in International Investment Law & Emerging Jurisprudence in International Investment Law* (London, British Institute of International and Comparative Law, 2009).

Kovacs, C., "Sovereign Wealth Funds: Much Ado about Some Money", *Columbia FDI Perspectives*, No. 14 (2009), available at <http://www.vcc.columbia.edu/content/sovereign-wealth-funds-much-ado-about-some-money>.

Kriebaum, U., "Privatizing Human Rights", in A. Reinisch and U. Kriebaum (eds.), *The Law of International Relations: Liber Amicorum HanspeterNeuhold* (Utrecht, Eleven International Publishing, 2007).

—, "Privatizing Human Rights — The Interface between International Investment Protection and Human Rights", 3 *Transnational Dispute Management* 165 (2006).

Krisch, N., "International Law in Times of Hegemony: Unequal Power and the Shaping of the International Legal Order", 16 *European Journal of International Law* 369 (2005).

Krislov, S., "Do Free Markets Create Free Societies?", 33 *Syracuse Journal of International Law & Comparative Politics* 155 (2005).

Kurtz, J., "The Use and Abuse of WTO Law in Investor-State Arbitration: Competition and Its Discontents", 20 *European Journal of International Law* 749 (2009).

Kuruk, P., "Renegotiating Transnational Investment Agreements: Lessons for Developing Countries from the Ghana-Valco Experience", 13 *Michigan Journal of International Law* 43 (1991).

Latter, A. M., "The Government of the Foreigners in China", 19 *Law Quarterly Review* 316 (1903).

Lévesque, C., "Influences on the Canadian FIPA Model and the U.S. Model BIT: NAFTA Chapter 11 and Beyond", 44 *Annuaire canadien de droit international* 249 (2006).

Legum, B., "Lessons Learned from the NAFTA: The New Generation of U.S. Investment Treaty Arbitration Provisions", 19 *ICSID Review* 344 (2004).

—, "The Innovation of Investor-State Arbitration under NAFTA", 43 *Harvard International Law Journal* 531 (2002).

Liberti, L., "Investissements et droits de l'homme", in P. Kahn and T. Wälde (eds.), *New Aspects of International Investment Law* (Leiden, Martinus Nijhoff, 2007).

Lillich, R. B., and B. H. Weston, "Lump Sum Agreements: Their Continuing Contribution to the Law of International Claims", 82 *American Journal of International Law* 69 (1988).

Macdonald, R. St. J., "The Margin of Appreciation", in R. St. J. Macdonald (ed.), *The European System for the Protection of Human Rights* (Netherlands, Kluwer, 1993).

Magraw, D., and R. H. Karpatkin, "Separate Comments on the U.S.-Morocco Free Trade Agreement" (n.p.: Center for International Environmental Law, 2004), available at <http://www.ciel.org/Publications/TEPAC_Comments_Morocco.pdf>.

Mann, H., "The Emperor's Clothes Come Off: A Comment on *Republic of Ghana* v. *Telekom Malaysia Berhard*, and the Problem of Arbitrator Conflict of Interest", 2:1 *Transnational Dispute Management* (2005).

—, "International Investment Agreements: Building the New Colonialism?", 97 *Proceedings of the Annual Meeting of the American Society of International Law* 247 (2003).

Marks, S., "Empire's Law", 10 *Indiana Journal Global Studies* 449 (2003).

—, "Big Brother is Bleeping Us — With the Message that Ideology Doesn't Matter", 12 *European Journal of International Law* 109 (2001).

Mattei, U., "A Theory of Imperial Law: A Study on U.S. Hegemony and the Latin Resistance", 10 *Indiana Journal of Global Legal Studies* 383 (2003).

Mavroidis, P. C., "Remedies in the WTO Legal System: Between a Rock and a Hard Place", 11:4 *European Journal of International Law* 763 (2000).

McCorquodale, R., "An Inclusive International Legal System", 17 *Leiden Journal of International Law* 477 (2004).

McGinnis, J. O., "The Comparative Disadvantage of Customary International Law", 30 *Harvard Journal of Law and Public Policy* 7 (2006).

McIlroy, J., "Canada's New foreign Investment Protection and Promotion Agreement Two Steps Forward, One Step Back?", 5 *Journal of World Investment & Trade* 621 (2004).

McLachlan, C., "Investment Treaties and General International Law", in A. K. Bjorklund *et al.* (eds.), *Investment Treaty Law: Current Issues III: Remedies in International Investment Law & Emerging Jurisprudence in International Investment Law* (London, British Institute of International and Comparative Law, 2009).

—, "Investment Treaties and General International Law", 57 *International & Comparative Law Quarterly* 361 (2008).

—, "The Principle of Systemic Integration and Article 31 (3) *(c)* of the Vienna Convention", 54 *International & Comparative Law Quarterly* 279 (2005).

McRae, D., "The WTO Appellate Body: A Model for an ICSID Appeals Facility?", 1 *Journal of International Dispute Settlement* 1 (2010), available at <http://jids.oxfordjournals.org/content/early/2010/07/01/jnlids.idq003.full>.

von Mehren, R. B., and P. N. Kourides, "International Arbitration between States and Foreign Private Parties: The Libyan Nationalization Cases", 75 *American Journal of International Law* 476 (1981).

Merolla, J., *et al.*, "Globalization, Globalización, Globalisation: Public Opinion and NAFTA", 11 *Law & Business Review of the Americas* 573 (2005).

Meyers, D. S., "In Defense of the International Treaty Arbitration System", 31 *Houston Journal of International Law* 47 (2008).

Monaghan, H. P., "Article III and Supranational Judicial Review", 107 *Columbia Law Review* 833 (2007).

Montt, S., "What International Investment Law and Latin American Can and Should Demand from Each Other: Updating the Bello/Calvo Doctrine in the BIT Generation", 3 *Res Publica Argentina* 75 (2007), available at <http://www.iilj.org/GAL/documents/SantiagoMontt. GAL.pdf>.

Moravcsik, A., "The Origins of Human Rights Regimes: Democratic Delegation in Postwar Europe", 54 *International Organizations* 253 (2000).

—, "Taking Preferences Seriously: A Liberal Theory of International Politics", 51 *International Organizations* 513 (1997).

—, "Explaining International Human Rights Regimes: Liberal Theory & Western Europe", 1 *European Journal of International Relations* 157 (1995).

Movesian, M. L., "International Commercial Arbitration and International Courts", 18 *Duke Journal of Comparative & International Law* 423 (2008).

Muchlinski, P., "Policy Issues", in P. Muchlinski *et al.* (eds.), *The Oxford Handbook of International Investment Law* (Oxford, Oxford University Press, 2008).

—, "'Caveat Investor'? The Relevance of the Conduct of the Investor under the Fair and Equitable Treatment Standard", 55 *International & Comparative Law Quarterly* 527 (2006).

Newcombe, A., "Sustainable Development and Investment Treaty Law", 8 *Journal of World Investment & Trade* 357 (2007).

Norton, P. M., "A Law of the Future or a Law of the Past? Modern Tribunals and the International Law of Expropriation", 85 *American Journal of International Law* 474 (1991).

Olivares, G., "The Essence of Economic Globalization: The Legal Dimension", 36:1 *Revue belge de droit international* (2003).

Orellana, M., "Science, Risk, and Uncertainty: Public Health Measures and Investment Disciplines," in P. Kahn and T. Wälde (eds.), *New Aspects of International Investment Law* (Leiden, Martinus Nijhoff, 2007).

Orrego-Vicuña, F., "Softening Necessity", in M. Arsanjani *et al.* (eds.), *Looking to the Future: Essays on International Law in Honor of W. Michael Reisman* (forthcoming in 2010).

Ortíz, R., "The Bilateral Investment Treaties and the Cases at ICSID: The Argentine Experience at the Beginning of the XXI Century", *Foro Ciudadano de Participación por la Justicia y los Derechos Humanos*, Working Paper No. 2 (2006), available at <http://www.foco.org.ar/documentos/ Documentos%20de%20trabajo/La_Argentina__los_BITs_y_ el_CIADI.pdf> (English translation on file with author).

Paulsson, J., "Awards — And Awards", in A. K. Bjorklund *et al.* (eds.), *Investment Treaty Law: Current Issues III: Remedies in International Investment Law & Emerging Jurisprudence in International Investment Law* (London, British Institute of International and Comparative Law, 2009).

—, "Arbitration without Privity", 10 *ICSID Review* 232 (1995).

Perkams, M., "Piercing the Corporate Veil in International Investment Agreements", in A. Reinisch and C. Knahr (eds.), *International Investment Law in Context* (Utrecht, Netherlands, Eleven International Publishing, 2007).

Perry, A., "An Ideal Legal System for Attracting Foreign Direct Investment?: Some Theory and Reality", 125 *American University International Law Review* 1627 (2000).

Petersmann, E. U., "Theories of Justice, Human Rights, and the Constitution of International Markets", 37 *Loyola of Los Angeles Law Review* 407 (2003).

Peterson, L. E., "International Investment Law and Media Disputes: A Complement to WTO Law", *Columbia FDI Perspectives* No. 17 (2010), available at <http://www. vcc.columbia.edu/content/fdi-perspectives>.

—, "Human Rights and Bilateral Investment Treaties: Mapping the Role of Human Rights within Investor-State Arbitration" (Montreal, Quebec, International Centre for Human Rights & Democratic Development, 2009), available at <http://www.dd-rd.ca/site/_PDF/publications/ globalization/HIRA-volume3-ENG.pdf>.

—, "South Africa's Bilateral Investment Treaties: Implications for Development and Human Rights", Dialogue on Globalization, Occasional Papers Series, No. 26 (2006), available at <http://library.fes.de/pdf-files/iez/global/04137-20080708.pdf>.

Peterson, L. E., and K. R. Grey, "International Human Rights in Bilateral Investment Treaties and in Investment Treaty Arbitration", *International Institute for Sustainable*

Development (2003), available at <http://www.iisd.org/pdf/2003/investment_int_human_rights_bits.pdf>.

Plotkin, M. E., and D. N. Fagan, "The Revised National Security Review Process for FDI in the US", *Columbia FDI Perspectives* No. 2 (2009), available at <http://www.vcc.columbia.edu/content/fdi-perspectives>.

Posner, E. A., "International Law and the Disaggregated State", 32 *Florida State University Law Review* 797 (2005).

Posner, E. A., and J. Yoo, "A Theory of International Adjudication", University of Chicago Law School, Olin Working Paper No. 206 (2004).

Poulsen, L. S., "The Importance of BITs for Foreign Direct Investment and Political Risk Insurance: Revisiting the Evidence", in K. P. Sauvant (ed.), *Yearbook on International Investment Law and Policy 2009-2010* (Oxford, Oxford University Press, forthcoming 2010).

Price, D. M., "Keep International Protections", *Washington Times* (14 May 2009).

—, "NAFTA Chapter 11 Investor-State Dispute Settlement: Frankenstein or Safety Valve?", 26 *Canada US Law Journal* 107 (2001).

Putnam, R., "Diplomacy and Domestic Politics: The Logic of Two-Level Games", 42 *International Organizations* 427 (1988).

Reed, L., and J. Sutcliffe, "The 'Americanization' of International Arbitration?", 16:4 *Mealey's International Arbitration Reporter* 11 (2001).

Reisman, W. M., and R. D. Sloane, "Indirect Expropriation and Its Valuation in the BIT Generation", 74 *British Year Book of International Law* 115 (2004).

Roberts, A., "Power and Persuasion in Investment Treaty Arbitration: The Dual Role of States", 104 *American Journal of International Law* 179 (2010).

Rodrik, D., "Growth Strategies", in P. Aghion and S. N. Durlauf (eds.), *Handbook of Economic Growth* (Amsterdam: Elsevier, 2005), available at <http://econ2.econ.iastate.edu/classes/econ502/tesfatsion/GrowthStrategies.DRodrik.GrowthHB2005.pdf>.

Rogers, C. A., "The Ethics of International Arbitrators", in L. W. Newman and R. D. Hill (eds.), *The Leading Arbitrators' Guide to International Arbitration* (Huntington, New York, Juris Publishing, 2nd ed., 2008).

Ruggie, J. G., "Taking Embedded Liberalism Global: The Corporate Connection", in J. G. Ruggie, *Embedding*

Global Markets: An Enduring Challenge (Burlington, Vermont, Ashgate, 2008).

Sachs, L., and K. P. Sauvant, "BITs, DTTs, and FDI Flows: An Overview", in L. Sachs and K. P. Sauvant, *The Effect of Treaties on Foreign Direct Investment* (New York, Oxford University Press, 2009).

Salacuse, J. W., "The Treatification of International Investment Law: A Victory of Form over Life? A Crossroads Crossed?", 3 *Transnational Dispute Management Issue* 3 (2006).

Sassen, S., "De-Nationalized State Agendas and Privatized Norm-Making", in K. Ladeur (ed.), *Public Governance in the Age of Globalization* (Burlington, Vermont, Ashgate Publishing, 2004).

Sauvant, K. P., "Driving and Countervailing Forces: A Rebalancing of National FDI Policies", in K. P. Sauvant (ed.), *Yearbook on International Investment Law & Policy 2008-2009* (New York, Oxford University Press, 2009).

—, "The FDI Recession Has Begun", *Columbia FDI Perspectives* No. 1 (2008), available at <http://www.vcc.columbia.edu/pubs/documents/KPSPerspective-FDIrecessionhasbegun_001.pdf>.

—, "The Rise of International Investment, Investment Agreements and Investment Disputes", in K. P. Sauvant (ed.), *Appeals Mechanism in International Investment Disputes* (New York, Oxford University Press, 2008).

—, "A Backlash against Foreign Investment?", in *World Investment Prospects to 2010: Boom or Backlash?* (London, Economist Intelligence Unit, 2006), available at <http://www.vcc.columbia.edu/pubs/documents/WIP_to_2010_Backlash_KPS.pdf>.

—, "New Sources of FDI: The BRICs — Outward FDI from Brazil, Russia, India, and China", 6 *Journal of World Investment & Trade* 639 (2005).

Sauvant, K. P., and J. E. Alvarez, "International Investment Law in Transition", in K. P. Sauvant *et al.* (eds.), *The Evolving International Investment Regime: Expectations, Realities, Options* (Oxford University Press, forthcoming 2010).

Sauvé, P., "Multilateral Rules on Investment: Is Forward Movement Possible?", 9 *Journal of International Economic Law* 325 (2009).

Schill, S. W., "Enabling Private Ordering — Function, Scope and Effect of Umbrella Clauses in International Investment Treaties", Institute for International Law & Justice Working Paper (2008/9), available at <http://www.iilj.org/publications/documents/2008-9.Schill.pdf>.

—, "Tearing Down the Great Wall: The New Generation Investment Treaties of the People's Republic of China", 15 *Cardozo Journal of International & Comparative Law* 73 (2007).

Schlemmmer, E. C., "Investment, Investor, Nationality, and Shareholders", in P. Muchlinski *et al.* (eds.), *The Oxford Handbook of International Investment Law* (Oxford, Oxford University Press, 2008).

Schwartz, A., and R. E. Scott, "Contract Theory and the Limits of Contract Law", 113 *Yale Law Journal* 541 (2003).

Schwarzenberger, G., "The ABS-Shawcross Draft Convention on Investments Abroad: A Critical Commentary", 9 *Journal of Public Law* 147 (1960).

Schwebel, S. M., "The United States 2004 Model Bilateral Investment Treaty: An Exercise in the Regressive Development of International Law", 3:2 *Transnat'l Dispute Management* (2006).

—, "The Influence of Bilateral Investment Treaties on Customary International Law", 98 *American Society of International Law* 27 (2004).

Simi, T. B., and A. Kaushik, "The Banana War at the GATT/WTO", 2008:1 *Trade Law Brief: Making Trade Law Simple* (2008), available at <http://www.cuts-citee.org/pdf/TLB08-01.pdf>.

Simma, B., and T. Kill, "Harmonizing Investment Protection and International Human Rights: First Steps Towards a Methodology", in C. Binder *et al.* (eds.), *International Investment Law for the 21st Century: Essays in Honor of Christoph Schreuer* (New York, Oxford University Press, 2009).

Simma, B., and D. Pulkowski, "Of Planets and the Universe: Self-Contained Regimes in International Law", 17 *European Journal of International Law* 483 (2006).

Simmons, B., *et al.*, "Introduction: The International Diffusion of Liberalism", 60 *International Organizations* 781 (2006).

Sinclair, A. C., "The Umbrella Clause Debate", in A. K. Bjorklund *et al.* (eds.), *Investment Treaty Law: Current Issues III: Remedies in International Investment Law & Emerging Jurisprudence in International Investment Law* (London, British Institute of International and Comparative Law, 2009).

Slaughter, A., "Breaking Out: The Proliferation of Actors in the International System", in Y. Dezalay and B. G. Garth (eds.), *Global Prescriptions* (Ann Arbor, Michigan, University of Michigan Press, 2002).

—, "Judicial Globalization", 40 *Virginia Journal of International Law* 1103 (2000).

—, "International Law in a World of Liberal States", 6 *European Journal of International Law* 503 (1995).

Smith, J. M., "The Politics of Dispute Settlement Design: Explaining Legalism in Regional Trade Pacts", 54 *International Organizations* 137 (2000).

Sornarajah, M., "The Neo-Liberal Agenda in Investment," in W. Shah *et al.* (eds.), *Redefining Sovereignty in International Economic Law* (Portland, Oregon, Hart Publishing, 2008).

Spiermann, O., "Applicable Law", in P. Muchlinski *et al.* (eds.), *The Oxford Handbook of International Investment Law* (Oxford, Oxford University Press, 2008).

—, "Individual Rights, State Interests and the Power to Waive ICSID Jurisdiction under Bilateral Investment Treaties", 20 *Arbitration International* 179 (2004).

Spiro, P., "Accounting for NGOs", 3 *Chicago Journal of International Law* 161 (2002).

Stiglitz, J., "Foreword", in K. Polanyi, *The Great Transformation* (Boston, Massachusetts, Beacon Press, 2001 ed., 1944).

Stone Sweet, A., "Investor-State Arbitration: Proportionality's New Frontier", 4 *Law & Ethics of Human Rights* 47 (2010).

—, "Judicialization and the Construction of Governance", 32 *Comparative Political Studies* 147 (1999).

Stone Sweet, A., and J. Matthews, "Proportionality Balancing and Constitutionalism", 47 *Columbia Journal of Transnational Law* 73 (2008).

Sykes, A. O., "The Least Restrictive Means", 70 *University of Chicago Law Review* 403 (2003).

Symposium Issue: "Proliferation of International Tribunals: Piecing Together the Puzzle", 31 *New York University Journal of International Law and Politics* 679 (1999).

Sunkel, O., "Big Business and 'Dependencia'", 50 *Foreign Affairs* 517 (1972).

Teitel, R., "Humanity's Law: Rule of Law for the New Global Politics", 35 *Cornell Journal of International Law* 355 (2001).

Teitel, R., and R. Howse, "Cross-Judging: Tribunalization in a Fragmented but Interconnected Global Order", 41 *New York University Journal of International Law and Politics* 959 (2009).

Tomuschat, C., "The European Court of Human Rights and Investment Protection", in C. Binder *et al.* (eds.), *International Investment Law for the 21st Century: Essays in Honor of Christoph Schreuer* (New York, Oxford University Press, 2009).

—, "Court of Justice: Case T-306/01, Ahmed Ali Yusuf and Al Barakaat International Foundation v. Council and Commission; Case T-315/01, Yassin Abdullah Kadi v. Council and Commission", 43 *Common Market Law Review* 537 (2006).

Trofimov, Y., "In Africa, China's Expansion Begins to Stir Resentment", *Wall Street Journal* (2 February 2007).

Tushnet, M., "The Inevitable Globalization of Constitutional Law", 49 *Virginia Journal of International Law* 985 (2009).

von Walter, A., "The Investor's Expectations in International Investment Arbitration", in A. Reinisch and C. Knahr (eds.), *International Investment Law in Context* (Utrecht, Netherlands, Eleven International Publishing, 2007).

Vandevelde, K. J., "A Brief History of International Investment Agreements", in L. Sachs and K. P. Sauvant, *The Effect of Treaties on Foreign Direct Investment: Bilateral Investment Treaties, Double Taxation Treaties, and Investment Flows* (Oxford, Oxford University Press, 2009).

—, "A Comparison of the 2004 and 1994 U.S. Model BITs: Rebalancing Investor and Host Country Interests", in K. P. Sauvant (ed.), *Yearbook on International Investment Law & Policy 2008-2009* (New York, Oxford University Press, 2009).

—, "Investment Liberalization and Economic Development: The Role of Bilateral Investment Treaties", 36 *Columbia Journal of Transnational Law* 501 (1998).

—, "Of Politics and Markets: The Shifting Ideology of the BITs", 11 *International Tax & Business Lawyer* 159 (1993).

—, "The BIT Program: A Fifteen-Year Appraisal", 86 *ASIL Proceedings* 532 (1992).

Veenstra-Kjos, H. E., "Counter-claims by Host States in Investment Dispute Arbitration 'without Privity'", in P. Kahn and T. Wälde (eds.), *New Aspects of International Investment Law* (Leiden, Martinus Nijhoff, 2007).

Vernon, R., "The Multilateral Enterprise: Power Versus Sovereignty", 49 *Foreign Affairs* 736 (1971).

Wälde, T. W., "Improving the Mechanisms for Treaty Negotiation and Investment Disputes: Competition and Choice as the Path to Quality and Legitimacy", in K. P. Sauvant (ed.), *Yearbook on International Investment Law & Policy 2008-2009* (New York, Oxford University Press, 2009).

—, "Introduction: International Investment Law Emerging from the Dynamics of Direct Investor-State Arbitration," in P. Kahn and T. Wälde (eds.), *New Aspects of International Investment Law* (Leiden, Martinus Nijhoff, 2007).

—, "The Specific Nature of Investment Arbitration", in P. Kahn and T. Wälde (eds.), *New Aspects of International Investment Law* (Leiden, Martinus Nijhoff, 2007).

—, "Alternatives for Obtaining Greater Consistency in Investment Arbitration: An Appellate Institution after the WTO, Authoritative Treaty Arbitration or Mandatory Consolidation?", 2:2 *Transnational Dispute Management* 71 (2005).

—, "Remedies and Compensation in International Investment Law", 2:5 *Transnational Dispute Management* (2005).

Wälde, T. W., and B. Sabahi, "Compensation, Damages, and Valuation", in P. Muchlinski *et al.* (eds.), *The Oxford Handbook of International Investment Law* (Oxford, Oxford University Press, 2008).

Waldron, J., "The Rule of International Law", 30 *Harvard Journal of Law & Public Policy* 15 (2006).

Weiler, T., "A First Look at the Interim Measures Award in *S.D. Myers, Inc.* v. *Canada*: It Is Possible to Balance Legitimate Environmental Concerns with Investment Protection", 24 *Hastings International and Comparative Law Review* 173 (2001).

Yackee, J. W., "Pacta Sunt Servanda and State Promises to Foreign Investors before Bilateral Investment Treaties: Myth and Reality", 32 *Fordham International Law Journal* 1550 (2009).

—, "Bilateral Investment Treaties, Credible Commitment, and the Rule of (International) Law: Do BITs Promote Foreign Direct Investment?", 42 *Law & Society Review* 805 (2008).

Zaring, D., "Rulemaking and Adjudication in International Law", 46 *Columbia Journal of Transnational Law* 563 (2008).

C. Press Releases, News Articles and Blogs

Alford, R., "International Arbitrators vs. International Judges", *Opinio Juris* (5 October 2007), available at <http://opinio-juris.org/2007/10/05/international-arbitrators-vs-international-judges/>.

—, "The Inferior Quality of ECJ Decisions", *Opinio Juris* (31 October 2007), available at <http://opiniojuris.org/2007/10/31/the-inferior-quality-of-ecj-decisions/>.

Antonovics, N., "Vivendi Wins Decade-Long Argentina Legal Battle", *Reuters* (21 August 2007), available at <http://www.reuters.com/article/idUSL2181989720070821>.

Beattie, A., "Concern Grows over Global Trade Regulation", *Financial Times* (12 March 2008).

Burke-White, W. W., and A. von Staden, "Investment Protection in Extraordinary Times: A Reply to Professor Franck", *Opinio Juris* (30 January 2008), available at <http://opinio-juris.org/2008/01/30/investment-protection-in-extraordinary-times-a-reply-to-professor-franck/>.

Elliott, J., "Riding the Elephant", *Fortune* (17 December 2007), available at <http://ridingtheelephant.wordpress.com/2007/12/17/tata-hits-image-problems-in-the-us/>.

Gardiner, J. L., *et al.*, "Ecuador Moves to Denounce and Leave the ICSID Convention, Attempts to Curtail Investor-State Arbitration Rights", *Skadden, Arps, Slate, Meagher & Flom LLP* (17 June 2009), available at <http://www.skadden.com/content/Publications/Publications1810_0.pdf>.

—, "Ecuador Attempts to Withdraw Consent to ICSID Jurisdiction for Natural Resource Disputes", 16:1 *Latin American Law & Business Report* (2008), available at <http://www.skadden.com/content/Publications/Publications1377_0.pdf>.

—, "New ICSID Annulment Decision Exposes Possible Gap in United States Investment Treaty Protection", *Skadden, Arps, Slate, Meagher & Flom LLP* (19 July 2010), available at <http://www.skadden.com/Index.cfm?contentID=51&itemID=2159>.

Giridharadas, A., "Lobbying in U.S., Indian Firms Present an American Face", *New York Times* (4 September 2007), available at <http://www.nytimes.com/2007/09/04/business/worldbusiness/04outsource.html>.

ICSID, "ICSID News Release: Bolivia Submits a Notice under Article 71 of the ICSID Convention" (16 May 2007), available at <http://icsid.worldbank.org/ICSID/StaticFiles/Announcement3.html>.

IMF, "Argentina — Letter of Intent, Memorandum of Economic Policies, Technical Memorandum of Understanding" (30 August 2001), available at <http://www.imf.org/external/np/loi/2001/arg/02/index.htm>.

Lobdell, K. A., "USTR Initiates 2009 and 2010 GSP Reviews", *Drinker, Biddle & Reath LLP* (2010), available at <http://www.drinkerbiddle.com/People/detailpub.aspx?id=806andMainAuthors=806>.

O'Grady, M., "Free Markets, Free People", *Wall Street Journal* (9 January 2004).

Peterson, L. E., "Analysis: Arbitrators Diverge as to whether Mexican Tax Is Performance Requirement, and a Legit Counter-measure", *Investment Arbitration Reporter* (6 April 2009).

—, "Round-up: Where Things Stand with Argentina and Its Many Investment Treaty Arbitrations", *Investment Arbitration Reporter* (17 December 2008).

Reed, L., "The Consequences of Market Regulation", *Kluwer Arbitration Blog* (11 March 2010), available at <http://kluwerarbitrationblog.com/blog/2010/03/11/the-consequences-of-market-intervention-by-lucy-reed-and-phillip-riblett/>.

United Nations Conference on Trade and Development ("UNCTAD"), "The Entry into Force of Bilateral Investment Treaties (BITs)", *International Investment Agreements Monitor*, No. 3, UNCTAD Doc. No. UNCTAD/WEB/ITE/IIA/2006/9 (2006).

Vis-Dunbar, D., "NGOs Claim the Philippine-Japan Free Trade Agreement Is Unconstitutional", *Investment Treaty News* (8 June 2009).

—, "Norway Shelves Its Draft Model Bilateral Investment Treaty", *Investment Treaty News* (8 June 2009).

D. Books

Aghion, P., and S. N. Durlauf (eds.), *Handbook of Economic Growth* (Amsterdam, Elsevier, 2005).

Alexandroff, A. S. (ed.), *Investor Protection in the NAFTA and Beyond: Private Interest and Public Purpose* (Toronto, Ontario, C. D. Howe Institute, 2006).

Alvarez, J. E., *International Organizations as Law-Makers* (New York, Oxford University Press, 2005).

Anderson, S., and S. Grusky, *Challenging Corporate Investor Rule: How the World Bank's Investment Court, Free Trade Agreements, and Bilateral Investment Treaties Have Unleashed a New Era of Corporate Power and What to Do about It* (n.p.: Institute for Policy Studies, 2007), available at <http://www.ips-dc.org/reports/challenging_corporate_investor_rule>.

Anghie, A., *Imperialism, Sovereignty, and the Making of International Law* (Cambridge, Cambridge University Press, 2005).

Arsanjani, M., *et al.* (eds.), *Looking to the Future: Essays on International Law in Honor of W. Michael Reisman* (The Hague, Martinus Nijlhoff Publishers, forthcoming 2010).

Binder, C., *et al.* (eds.), *International Investment Law for the 21st Century: Essays in Honor of Christoph Schreuer* (New York, Oxford University Press, 2009).

Bishop, R. D., *et al.*, *Foreign Investment Disputes: Cases, Materials, and Commentary* (The Hague, Kluwer Law International, 2005).

Bjorklund, A. K., *et al.* (eds.), *Investment Treaty Law: Current Issues III: Remedies in International Investment Law & Emerging Jurisprudence in International Investment Law* (London, British Institute of International & Comparative Law, 2009).

Cass, D. Z., *The Constitutionalization of the World Trade Organization* (New York, Oxford University Press, 2005).

Chayes, A., and A. Chayes, *The New Sovereignty: Compliance with International Regulatory Agreements* (Cambridge, Harvard University Press, 1995).

Choate, P., *Agents of Influence* (New York, Knopf, 1990).

Crawford, J., *The International Law Commission's Articles on State Responsibility: Introduction, Text and Commentaries* (Cambridge, Cambridge University Press, 2002).

Dezalay, Y., and B. G. Garth (eds.), *Global Prescriptions* (Ann Arbor, Michigan, University of Michigan Press, 2002).

Dolzer, R., *et al.* (eds.), *Foreign Investment: Its Significance in Relation to the Fight against Poverty, Economic Growth and Legal Culture* (Singapore, Konrad-Adenauer-Siftung, 2006).

Dolzer, R., and C. Schreuer, *Principles of International Investment Law* (Oxford, Oxford University Press, 2008).

Douglas, Z., *The International Law of Investment Claims* (Cambridge, Cambridge University Press, 2009).

Dunoff, J., *et al.*, *International Law: Norms, Actors, Process* (New York, Aspen Publishers, 2006).

Emberland, M., *The Human Rights of Companies* (Oxford, Oxford University Press, 2006).

Fletcher, G. P., *Tort Liability for Human Rights Abuses* (Portland, Oregon, Hart Publishing, 2008).

Friedman, B., *The Will of the People: How Public Opinion Has Influenced the Supreme Court and Shaped the Meaning of the Constitution* (New York, Farrar, Straus and Giroux, 2009).

Friedman, T., *The Lexus and the Olive Tree* (New York, Anchor Publishing, 1st ed., 2000).

Fukuyama, F., *The End of History and the Last Man* (New York, Free Press, 1992).

Glickman, N. J., and D. P. Woodward, *The New Competitors* (New York, Basic Books, 1989).

Goldstein, J., *et al.* (eds.), *Legalization and World Politics* (Boston, MIT Press, 2001).

Graham, E. M., and P. R. Krugman, *Foreign Direct Investment in the United States* (Washington, DC, Institute for International Economics, 1995).

Grieder, W., *One World, Ready or Not: The Manic Logic of Global Capitalism* (New York, Touchstone, 1997).

Grierson Weiler, T. J. (ed.), *Investment Treaty Arbitration and Public Law* (Huntington, New York, Juris Publishing, 2008).

Gruber, L., *Ruling the World* (Princeton, Princeton University Press, 2000).

Hardt, M., and A. Negri, *Empire* (Cambridge, Harvard University Press, 2000).

van Harten G., *Investment Treaty Arbitration and Public Law* (Oxford, Oxford University Press, 2007).

Hathaway, J., *The Rights of Refugees under International Law* (New York, Cambridge University Press, 2005).

Held, D., *et al.*, *Global Transformations: Politics, Economics and Culture* (Stanford, Stanford University Press, 1999).

Jessup, P. C., *Transnational Law* (New Haven, Connecticut, Yale University Press, 1956).

Kahn, P., and T. Wälde (eds.), *New Aspects of International Investment Law* (Leiden, Martinus Nijhoff, 2007).

Kaushal, A., *et al.* (eds.), *The Backlash against Investment Arbitration* (Netherlands, Kluwer Law International, 2010).

Keohane, R., *After Hegemony: Cooperation and Discord in the World Political Economy* (Princeton, Princeton University Press, 1984).

Ladeur, K. (ed.), *Public Governance in the Age of Globalization* (Burlington, Vermont, Ashgate Publishing, 2004).

Lowenfeld, A. F., *International Economic Law* (Oxford, Oxford University Press, 2002).

Macdonald, R. St. J. (ed.), *The European System for the Protection of Human Rights* (Netherlands, Kluwer, 1993).

Mann, H., *et al.*, *Model International Agreement on Investment for Sustainable Development: Negotiator's Handbook* (International Institute for Sustainable Development, 2nd ed., 2006), available at <http://www.iisd.org/pdf/2005/investment_model_int_handbook.pdf>.

Mascheck, W., *et al.* (eds.), *Thinking Outward: Global Players in Emerging Markets* (forthcoming).

McLachlan, C., *et al.*, *International Investment Arbitration: Substantive Principles* (Oxford, Oxford University Press, 2007).

Mead, W. R., *God and Gold: Britain, America, and the Making of the Modern World* (New York, Vintage Books, 2007).

Moran, T. H. H., *Foreign Direct Investment and Development* (Washington, DC, Institute for International Economics, 1999).

Muchlinski, P., *et al.* (eds.), *The Oxford Handbook of International Investment Law* (Oxford, Oxford University Press, 2008).

Newcombe, A., and L. Paradell, *Law and Practice of Investment Treaties* (The Hague, Kluwer Law International, 2009).

Newman, L. W., and R. D. Hill (eds.), *The Leading Arbitrators' Guide to International Arbitration* (Huntington, New York, Juris Publishing, 2nd ed., 2008).

El Nuevo derecho administrativo global en América Latina: desafíos para las inversions extranjeras, la regulación nacional y el financiamiento para el desarrollo (Buenos Aires, Ediciones RAP S.A., 2009).

Paulsson, J., *Denial of Justice in International Law* (New York, Cambridge University Press, 2005).

Picker, C., *et al.* (eds.), *International Economic Law: The State and Future of the Discipline* (Portland, Oregon, Hart Publishing, 2008).

Polanyi, K., *The Great Transformation* (Boston, Massachusetts, Beacon Press, 2001 ed., 1944).

Rawls, J., *A Theory of Justice* (Cambridge, Harvard University Press, 1971).

Reinisch, A., and C. Knahr (eds.), *International Investment Law in Context* (Utrecht, Netherlands, Eleven International Publishing, 2007).

Ruggie, J. G., *Embedding Global Markets: An Enduring Challenge* (Burlington, Vermont, Ashgate, 2008).

Sachs, L. E., and K. P. Sauvant (eds.), *The Effect of Treaties on Foreign Direct Investment: Bilateral Investment Treaties, Double Taxation Treaties, and Investment Flows* (Oxford, Oxford University Press, 2009).

Sauvant, K. P. (ed.), *Yearbook on International Investment Law & Policy 2008-2009* (New York, Oxford University Press, 2009).

—, *Appeals Mechanism in International Investment Disputes* (New York, Oxford University Press, 2008).

Sauvant, K. P., *et al.* (eds.), *The Evolving International Investment Regime: Expectations, Realities, Options* (Oxford University Press, forthcoming 2010).

Schill, S. W., *The Multilateralization of International Investment Law* (New York, Cambridge University Press, 2009).

Schneiderman, D., *Constitutionalizing Economic Globalization: Investment Rules and Democracy's Promise* (Cambridge, Cambridge University Press, 2008).

Shah, W., *et al.* (eds.), *Redefining Sovereignty in International Economic Law* (Portland, Oregon, Hart Publishing, 2008).

Schwarzenberger, G., *International Law as Applied by International Courts and Tribunals* (London, Stevens, 3rd ed., 1957).

Shapiro, M., *Courts: A Comparative and Political Analysis* (Chicago, University of Chicago Press, 1981).

Shaw, M., *International Law* (Cambridge, Cambridge University Press, 2003).

Slaughter, A., *A New World Order* (Princeton, Princeton University Press, 2004).

Sornarajah, M., *The International Law on Foreign Investment* (Cambridge, Cambridge University Press, 3rd ed., 2010).

Sen, A., *Development as Freedom* (New York, Anchor, 2000).

Servan-Schreiber, J. J., *The American Challenge* (New York, Atheneum, 1968).

Steiner, H. J., and P. Alston, *International Human Rights in Context: Law, Politics, Morals* (Oxford, Oxford University Press, 2nd ed., 2000).

Stiglitz, J. E., *Globalization and Its Discontents* (New York, W. W. Norton and Co., 2002).

Subedi, S., *International Investment Law: Reconciling Policy and Principle* (Portland, Hart Publishing, 2008).

Tolchin, M., and S. J. Tolchin, *Selling Our Security: The Erosion of America's Assets* (New York, Knopf, 1992).

Tudor, I., *The Fair and Equitable Treatment Standard in the International Law of Foreign Investment* (New York, Oxford University Press, 2008).

Vandevelde, K. J., *United States Investment Treaties: Policy and Practice* (Boston, Kluwer Law and Taxation, 1992).

Vernon, R., *Sovereignty at Bay: The Multinational Spread of US Enterprises* (New York, Basic Books, 1971).

Waibel, M., *et al.* (eds.), *The Backlash against Investment Arbitration: Perceptions and Reality* (Netherlands, Kluwer Law International, 2010).

Weiler, T. (ed.), *NAFTA Investment Law and Arbitration: Past Issues, Current Practice, Future Prospects* (Ardsley Park, Transnational Publishers, 2004).

Zamora, S., and R. A. Brand, 1 *Basic Documents of International Economic Law* (Chicago, Commerce Clearing House International, 1990).

E. Treaties

Accord entre le Gouvernement de la République française et le Gouvernement de la République du Guatemala sur l'encouragement et la protection réciproques des investissements, signed on 27 May 1998, entered into force on 28 October 2001, available at <http://www.unctad.org/sections/dite/iia/docs/bits/france_guatemala_fr.pdf>.

Acuerdo entre El Gobierno de la República de Venezúela y El Gobierno de la República Argentina para la Promoción y Protección Recíprocas de Inversiones, signed on 16 November 1993, entered into force on 1 July 1995, available at <http://www.unctad.org/sections/dite/iia/docs/bits/argentina_venezuela_sp.pdf>.

Agreement between the Government of Australia and the Government of the Argentine Republic on the Promotion and Protection of Investments, 1997 *Australian Treaty Series*, No. 4, signed on 23 August 1995, entered into force on 11 January 1997, available at <http://www.unctad.org/sections/dite/iia/docs/bits/argentina_australia.pdf>.

Agreement between the Government of Canada and the Republic of Poland for the Promotion and Reciprocal Protection of Investments, signed on 6 April 1990, entered into force on 14 November 1991, available at <http://www.unctad.org/sections/dite/iia/docs/bits/canada_poland.pdf>.

Agreement between the Government of the Kingdom of Cambodia and the Government of the Republic of Cuba concerning the Promotion and Protection of Investments, signed on 28 May 2001, available at <http://www.unctad.org/sections/dite/iia/docs/bits/cuba_cambodia.pdf>.

Agreement between Japan and the Republic of Peru for the Liberation, Promotion, and Protection of Investment, signed on 21 November 2008, entered into force on 10 December 2009.

Agreement between the Government of the Republic of the Philippines and the Government of the People's Republic of Bangladesh for the Promotion and Reciprocal Protection of Investment, signed on 8 September 1997, entered into force on 1 August 1998, available at <http://www.unctad.org/sections/dite/iia/docs/bits/bangladesh_philippines.pdf>.

Agreement on Trade Related Investment Measures, signed on 15 April 1994, entered into force on 1 January 1995.

Agreement on Trade-Related Aspects of Intellectual Property Rights, 1869 *United Nations Treaty Series* 299, signed on 15 April 1994, entered into force on 1 January 1995.

American Convention on Human Rights, 1144 *United Nations Treaty Series* 123, signed on 22 November 1969, entered into force on 18 July 1978.

Bilateral Investment Treaty, Mexico-People's Republic of China, reportedly signed in Beijing on 11 July 2008 (on file with *Transnational Dispute Management*).

Charter of the United Nations, 1 *United Nations Treaty Series* 16, signed on 26 June 1945, entered into force on 24 October 1945.

Comprehensive Economic Cooperation Agreement between the Republic of India and the Republic of Singapore, signed on 29 June 2005, entered into force on 1 August 2005.

Convention on the Elimination of All Forms of Discrimination against Women, 1249 *United Nations Treaty Series* 13, 19 *International Legal Materials* 33, signed on 18 December 1979, entered into force 3 September 1981.

Convention on the Settlement of Investment Disputes between States and Nationals of Other States, Washington, 575 *United Nations Treaty Series* 259, signed on 18 March 1965, entered into force on 14 October 1966, available at <http://icsid.worldbank.org/ICSID/StaticFiles/basicdoc/CRR_English-final.pdf>.

Convention Establishing the Multilateral Investment Guarantee Agency, 1508 *United Nations Treaty Series* 100, signed on 10 November 1985, entered into force on 12 April 1988.

Energy Charter Treaty, 2080 *United Nations Treaty Series* 95, signed on 17 December 1994, entered into force on 16 April 1998, available at <http://www.encharter.org/fileadmin/user_upload/document/EN.pdf>.

European Convention on Human Rights, 213 *United Nations Treaty Series* 222, signed on 4 November 1950, entered into force on 3 September 1953.

Free Trade Agreement between the Government of New Zealand and the People's Republic of China, signed 7 April 2008, entered into force 1 October, 2008, available at <http://www.chinafta.govt.nz/1-The-agreement/2-Text-of-the-agreement/0-downloads/NZ-ChinaFTA-Agreement-text.pdf>.

General Agreement on Tariffs and Trade, 55 *United Nations Treaty Series* 187, signed on 30 October 1947, entered into force 1 January 1948.

General Agreement on Trade in Services, 1869 *United Nations Treaty Series* 183, signed on 15 April 1994, entered into force on 1 January 1995.

International Covenant on Civil and Political Rights, 999 *United Nations Treaty Series* 171, signed on 16 December 1966, entered into force on 23 March 1976.

International Covenant on Economic, Social, and Cultural Rights, 999 *United Nations Treaty Series* 3, signed on 16 December 1966, entered into force on 3 January 1976, reprinted in 6 *International Legal Materials* 360.

Model Treaty on Extradition, General Assembly res. A/RES/45/116 (XLV) (1990).

North American Free Trade Agreement, 32 *International Legal Materials* 612, signed on 17 December 1992, entered into force on 1 January 1994.

Peru-United States Free Trade Agreement, signed 12 April 2006, entered into force 1 February 2009, available at <http://www.ustr.gov/trade-agreements/free-trade-agreements/peru-tpa/final-text>.

Treaty between the United States of America and the Argentine Republic concerning the Reciprocal Encouragement and Protection of Investment, signed on 14 November 1991, entered into force on 20 October 1994, available at <http://www.unctad.org/sections/dite/iia/docs/bits/argentina_us.pdf>.

Treaty between the United States of America and Grenada concerning the Reciprocal Encouragement and Protection of Investment, signed on 2 May 1986, entered into force on 3 March 1989, <http://www.state.gov/documents/organization/43562.pdf>.

Understanding on the Rules and Procedures Governing the Settlement of Disputes, 1869 *United Nations Treaty Series* 401, 33 *International Legal Materials* 1226, in Marrakesh Agreement Establishing the World Trade Organization, Annex 2, signed on 15 April 1994, entered into force on 1 January 1995.

United Nations Convention on the Recognition and Enforcement of Foreign Arbitral Awards, 330 *United Nations Treaty Series* 38, signed on 10 June 1958, entered into force on 7 June 1959.

United States-Morocco Free Trade Agreement, Chapter Ten, signed on 15 June 2004, entered into force 1 January 2006, available at <http://www.moroccousafta.com/ftafulltext.htm>.

Vienna Convention on the Law of Treaties, 1155 *United Nations Treaty Series* 331, signed on 23 May 1969, entered into force on 27 January 1980.

F. Model Treaties and Model Laws

Foreign Affairs and International Trade Canada, "Foreign Investment Promotion and Protection Agreement Model" (2003), available at <http://ita.law.uvic.ca/documents/Canadian2004-FIPA-model-en.pdf>.

Norway Model BIT, available at <http://ita.law.uvic.ca/documents/NorwayModel2007.doc>.

UNCITRAL Model Law on International Commercial Arbitration, UN Sales No. E.08.V.4 (Vienna, United Nations, 2008), available at <http://www.uncitral.org/pdf/english/texts/arbitration/ml-arb/07-86998_Ebook.pdf> (adopted by UN General Assembly resolution A/RES/61/33 on 18 December 2006).

"US Model BIT of 1984", in S. Zamora and R. A. Brand (eds.), 1 *Basic Documents of International Economic Law* 655 (Chicago, Illinois, Custom Clearing House International, 1990).

US Department of State and US Trade Representative, "2004 U.S. Model BIT", available at <http://www.state.gov/documents/organization/117601.pdf>.

G. General Assembly Resolutions

Charter of Economic Rights and Duties of States, General Assembly res. 3281 (XXIX), 29 *General Assembly Official Records*, Supp. No. 31, p. 50, UN doc. A/9631 (1974).

Declaration of Permanent Sovereignty over Natural Resources, General Assembly res. 3171 (XXVIII), 28 *General Assembly Official Records*, Supp. No. 30, p. 52, UN doc. A/9030 (1973).

General Assembly res. 46/86, 46 *General Assembly Official Records* 39, UN doc. A/Res/46/86 (1991).

General Assembly res. 48/180, 48 *General Assembly Official Records* 159, UN doc. A/Res/48/180 (1993).

Universal Declaration on Human Rights, General Assembly res. 217A (III), UN doc. A/777 (1948).

H. Miscellaneous

Aktion Finanzplatz Schweiz, International Conference on Illegitimate Debts, Berne, 3-4 October 2007, *Argentina 1976-2007: The Paradigmatic Case of an Extraordinarily Legitimate Debt*, available at <http://www.aktionfinanzplatz.ch/pdf/kampagnen/illegitime/Keene_handout_en.pdf>.

Anderson, S., and S. Grusky, "Challenging Corporate Investor Rule", *Institute for Policy Studies and Food and Water Watch* (2007), available at <http://www.ips-dc.org/getfile.php?id=146>.

"Bill Moyers Reports: Trading Democracy", *NOW* (1 February 2002), available at <http://www.pbs.org/now/transcript/transcript_tdfull.html>.

Bottari, M., and L. Wallach, *NAFTA's Threat to Sovereignty and Democracy: The Record of NAFTA Chapter 11 Investor-State Cases 1994-2005* (Public Citizen, 2005), available at <http://www.citizen.org/documents/Chapter%2011%20Report%20Final.pdf>.

Braun, T. R., "Globalization-Fueled Innovation: The Investor as Subject of International Law" (copy on file with author).

Brower II, C. H., "Legitimacy and Inconsistency: Is Investment Treaty Arbitration Broken?", Third Annual Investment Treaty Arbitration Conference: Interpretation in Investment Arbitration, Washington, DC (30 April 2009) (copy on file with author).

Brower, C. H., "Balancing the Rule of Law and National Interests", *Symposium on Preventing and Managing Conflict in Energy and Other Natural Resource Investment Relations: Columbia University School of Law* (13 May 2009).

Center for International Environmental Law's (CIEL) comments on the report filed by the US Government's Trade and Environment Policy Advisory Committee ("TEPAC") on the United States-Morocco Free Trade Agreement, 6 April 2004, available at <http://ustraderep.gov/ assets/Trade_Agreements/Bilateral/Morocco_FTA/Reports /asset_upload_file892_3119.pdf>.

The Economist Intelligence Unit, "Evaluating a Potential US-China Bilateral Investment Treaty: Background, Context, and Implications" (30 March 2010), available at <http://www.uscc.gov/researchpapers/2010/EIU_Report _on_US-China_BIT—FINAL_14_April_2010.pdf>.

Hickenlooper Amendment to the Foreign Assistance Act of 1964, 22 *United States Code Annotated* § 2370 (e) (2), as amended by Public Law 89-171 § 301 (d) (2) (6 September 1965).

International Finance Corporation, "Stabilization Clauses and Human Rights" (27 May 2009), available at <http:// www.ifc.org/ifcext/sustainability.nsf/Content/Publications_ LOE_Stabilization>.

International Institute for Sustainable Development ("IISD"), "Revising the UNCITRAL Arbitration Rules to Address Investor-State Arbitrations" (2007), available at <http:// www.iisd.org/pdf/2008/investment_revising_uncitral_arbi-tration_dec.pdf>.

IISD Working Paper on Transparency, draft distributed at the Barcelona Conference on 6 July 2010 (forthcoming).

IMF Independent Evaluation Office, "Report on the Evaluation of the Role of the IMF in Argentina: 1991-2001" (2004), available at <http://www.imf.org/External/ NP/ieo/2004/arg/eng/index.htm>.

International Law Association, Committee on the Formation of Customary (General) International Law, "Statement of Principles Applicable to the Formation of General Customary International Law" (2000), available at <http:// www.ila-hq.org/download.cfm/docid/A709CDEB-92D6-4CFA-A61C4CA30217F376>.

International Law Commission, "Draft Articles on Responsi-bility of States for Internationally Wrongful Acts", 2:2 *Yearbook of the International Law Commission* 1 (2001), available at <http://untreaty.un.org/ilc/texts/instruments/ english/commentaries/9_6_2001.pdf>.

International Law Commission, *Fragmentation of Interna-tional Law: Difficulties arising from the Diversification and Expansion of International Law*, UN doc. A/CN.4/ L.702 (18 July 2006).

ICSID Administrative Council, *Rules Governing the*

Additional Facility for the Administration of Proceedings by the Secretariat of the International Centre for Settlement of Investment Disputes (Washington, DC: ICSID, 2006), available at <http://icsid.worldbank.org/ICSID/ICSID/AdditionalFacilityRules.jsp>.

The ICSID Caseload — Statistics, Issue No. 2010-2, available at <http://icsid.worldbank.org/ICSID/FrontServlet?requestType=ICSIDDocRH&actionVal=CaseLoadStatistics>.

Mann, H., *International Investment Agreements, Business and Human Rights: Key Issues and Opportunities* (International Institute for Sustainable Development, 2008), available at <http://www.iisd.org/pdf/2008/iia_business_human_rights.pdf>.

NAFTA Claims, available at <http://www.naftalaw.org/>.

"Notes of Interpretation of Certain Chapter 11 Provisions", *NAFTA Free Trade Commission* (31 July 2001), available at <http://www.international.gc.ca/trade-agreements-accords-commerciaux/disp-diff/nafta-interpr.aspx?lang=en>.

Office of the High Commissioner of Human Rights, *Human Rights, Trade and Investment*, UN doc. E/CN.4/Sub.2/2003/9 (2003).

Organisation for Economic Co-operation and Development ("OECD"), Directorate for Financial and Enterprise Affairs, *OECD Guidelines for Multinational Enterprises* (OECD, 2008), available at <http://www.oecd.org/dataoecd/56/36/1922428.pdf>.

OECD, "Improving the System of Investor-State Dispute Settlement: An Overview", Working Papers on International Investment No. 2006/1 (2006), available at <http://www.oecd.org/dataoecd/3/59/36052284.pdf>.

OECD, "Novel Features in OECD Countries' Recent Investment Agreements: An Overview" (2005), available at <http://www.oecd.org/dataoecd/42/9/35823420.pdf>.

OECD, Directorate for Financial and Enterprise Affairs, *OECD Code of Liberalization of Capital Movements* (OECD, 2010), available at <http://www.oecd.org/dataoecd/10/62/39664826.pdf >.

OECD Secretariat, *Novel Features in OECD Countries' Recent Investment Agreements: An Overview* (Paris, OECD, 2005), available at <http://www.oecd.org/dataoecd/42/9/35823420.pdf>.

Organization for International Investment, "Summary of Bills Affecting Foreign Investment in the United States" (1993) (copy on file with author).

Overseas Private Investment Corporation's ("OPIC") legislative charter, 22 *United States Code Annotated* §§ 2191-2200b (2010).

"Public Statement on the International Investment Regime" (31 August 2010), available at <http://www.osgoode.yorku.ca/public_statement/>.

"UNCITRAL Revised Rules Adopted", *United Nations Information Service* (29 June 2010), available at <http://www.unis.unvienna.org/unis/pressrels/2010/unisl139.html>.

United Nations ECOSOC, "Draft Code of Conduct on Transnational Corporations", in S. Zamora and R. A. Brand, 1 *Basic Documents of International Economic Law* (Chicago, Commerce Clearing House International, 1990).

US Government Accountability Office, "Sovereign Wealth Funds: Laws Limiting Foreign Investment Affect Certain U.S. Assets and Agencies Have Various Enforcement Processes", Doc. No. GAO-09-608 (2009), available at <http://www.gao.gov/new.items/d09608.pdf>.

US House of Representatives, Committee on Ways & Means, Subcommittee on Trade, "Hearing on Investment Protections in U.S. Trade and Investment Agreements", Serial No. 111-120 (14 May 2009), available at <http://www.gpo.gov/fdsys/pkg/CHRG-111hhrg11153473/pdf/CHRG-111hhrg11153473.pdf>.

US Department of State Letter of Submittal to US Senate, for Treaty with Argentina concerning the Reciprocal Encouragement and Protection of Investment, *Treaty Documents* No. 103-2 (19 January 1993).

US Department of State, NAFTA Investor-State Arbitrations, available at <http://www.state.gov/s/l/c3439.htm>.

US Senate, Committee on Foreign Relations, "Report on the International Covenant on Civil and Political Rights", *Senate Executive Reports*, No. 102-23 (1992), reprinted in 31 *International Legal Materials* 645 (1992).

US Department of State, Advisory Committee on International Economic Policy, "Report of the Subcommittee on Investment of the Advisory Committee on International Economic Policy Regarding the Model Bilateral Investment Treaty" (30 September 2009), available at <http://www.state.gov/e/eeb/rls/othr/2009/131098.htm>.

US Trade Promotion Act of 2002, Public Law No. 107-210 § 2102 (b) (3) (G) (iv) (codified as 19 USC § 3802 (2004)).

United Nations Conference on Trade and Development ("UNCTAD"), "De-Mystifying the 2004 United States Model BIT", Draft (25 February 2008).

UNCTAD, "Consultation Report on the Feasibility of an

Advisory Facility on International Investment Law and Investor-State Disputes for Latin American Countries" (2009) (copy on file with author).

UNCTAD, "Latest Developments in Investor-State Dispute Settlement", *International Investment Arbitration Monitor*, No. 1, Doc. No. UNCTAD/WEB/ITE/IIA/2008/3 (2008) available at <http://www.unctad.org/en/docs/iteiia20083 _en.pdf>.

UNCTAD, "Recent Developments in Investor-State Dispute Settlement", *International Investment Arbitration Monitor*, No. 2, Doc. No. UNCTAD/WEB/ITE/IIT/2005/1 (2005), available at <http://www.unctad.org/en/docs/webiteiit 20051_en.pdf>.

UNCTAD, "Latest Developments in Investor-State Dispute Settlement", *International Investment Arbitration Monitor*, No. 4, Doc. No. UNCTAD/WEB/ITE/IIT/2005/2 (2005), available at <http://www.unctad.org/en/docs/webiteiit 20051_en.pdf>.

UNCTAD Work Programme on International Investment Agreements, Policies and Capacity-building Branch, Division on Investment and Enterprise, "Consultations Report on the Feasibility of an Advisory Facility on International Investment Law and Investor-State Disputes for Latin American Countries", non-paper (2009) (copy on file with author).

UNCTAD, Trade and Development Board, Investment, Enterprise and Development Commission, "Report of the Multi-year Expert Meeting on Investment for Development on Its First Session" (2009), available at <http://www.unctad.org/en/docs/ciimem3d3_en.pdf>.

Vale Columbia Center on Sustainable International Investment, "Chinese Multinationals Make Steady Progress", Press Release, 22 October 2008, available at <http://www.vcc.columbia.edu/files/vale/documents/RankingofCh ineseMultinationals-Final_2008.pdf>.

World Development Report 2005: A Better Investment Climate for Everyone (New York, World Bank and Oxford University Press, 2004), available at <http://siteresources. worldbank.org/INTWDR2005/Resources/complete_report. pdf>.

ABOUT THE AUTHOR

Biographical Note

José Enrique Alvarez, born Punta Brava, Cuba, in 1955.

Herbert and Rose Rubin Professor of Law, New York University School of Law (fall 2009 to present); formerly Hamilton Fish Professor of International Law and Diplomacy and Director, Center on Global Legal Problems, Columbia Law School; Professor of Law, University of Michigan Law School, and Assistant Professor of Law, George Washington University School of Law.

Adjunct Professor of Law, Georgetown Law School; Attorney-Adviser, Office of the Legal Adviser, US Department of State (1983-1989).

Attorney, Shea & Gardner, Washington, DC (1982-1983). Law clerk in the Chambers of the Honorable Judge Thomas Gibbs Gee, US Court of Appeals for the Fifth Circuit (1981-1982).

Special Adviser on Public International Law for the Office of the Prosecutor, International Criminal Court (from May 2010); Member, Advisory Committee on Public International Law, US Department of State (1994-2008; 2009-present); President, American Society of International Law (2006-2008); Vice President, American Society of International Law (2002-2004); Member of the editorial boards of *American Journal of International Law* (1997-2007), *Global Governance* (1994-1996), *Journal of International Criminal Justice* (2003-2007); Member, American Law Institute (since 1999); Adviser, American Law Institute's Project on Principles of Trade Law (2002-2006); Member, Council on Foreign Relations (since 1994); Board, Center on Reproductive Rights (since 2009); Member, Curatorium, Xiamen Academy of International Law (since 2009); Member, Global Agenda Council on International Legal System, World Economic Forum (since 2008).

Harvard Law School, J.D., *Cum Laude*, 1981; Magdalen College, Oxford University, B.A., Jurisprudence, First Class Honours, 1979; Harvard College, Harvard University, B.A., *Summa Cum Laude*, Social Studies, 1977.

Principal Publications

Books

International Organizations as Law-Makers, Oxford, Oxford University Press, 2005, paperback edition, 2006.

The Evolving International Investment Regime: Expectations, Realities, Options (with Karl P. Sauvant, Kamil Gérald Ahmed and Gabriela del P. Vizcanio), New York, Oxford University Press, forthcoming 2011.

Selected Lectures

"Are Corporations 'Subjects of International Law'?", *Santa Clara Journal of International Law*, forthcoming 2011.

"The Evolving BIT", in Ian A. Laird and Todd Weiler (eds.), *Investment Treaty Arbitration and International Law* 1 (2010).

"Three Responses to 'Proliferating' Tribunals", 41 *New York University Journal of International Law and Politics* 991 (2009).

"Contemporary International Law: An 'Empire of Law' or the 'Law of Empire'?", 24 *American University International Law Review* 811 (2009); also published in Spanish in 4 *Bajo Palabra, Revista de Filosofía* (2009).

"Contemporary Foreign Investment Law: An 'Empire of Law' or the 'Law of Empire'?", 60 *Alabama Law Review* 943 (2009).

"Speech: The Internationalization of U.S. Law", 47 *Columbia Journal of Transnational Law* 537 (2009).

"The Future of Our Society" and "Fifty Ways International Law Hurts Our Lives", *American Society of International Law, Proceedings of the 102nd Annual Meeting* 499 (2008), and <http://www.asil.org/ilpost/president/pres070406.html>

"Governing the World: International Organizations as Law-makers", 31 *Suffolk Transnational Law Review* 591 (2008).

"Institutionalized Legalization and the Asia-Pacific Region", 5 *New Zealand Journal of Public and International Law* 9 (2007).

"Torturing the Law", 37 *Case Western Journal of International Law* 175 (2006).

"The New Treaty Makers", XXV *Boston College International and Comparative Law Review* 213 (2002).

"How *Not* to Link: Institutional Conundrums of an Expanded Trade Regime", VII *Widener Law Symposium Journal* 1 (2001).

"Critical Theory and the North American Free Trade Agreement's Chapter Eleven", 28 *Inter-American Law Review* 303 (1996-1997).

Selected Articles and Book Chapters

"Revisiting the Necessity Defense in the Argentina Cases" (with Tegan Brink), *Yearbook of International Investment Law and Policy 2010-2011* (2011), also available of Investment Claims Database (Oxford), see <http://www.investmentclaims.com/subscriber_article?script=yest&id=ic/Journal%20Articles/law-iic-journal052&recno=20&searchType=browse>.

"The Argentine Crisis and Foreign Investors: A Glimpse into the Heart of the Investment Regime" (with Kathryn Khamsi), *Yearbook on International Investment Law and Policy* 379 (2008-2009).

"The Once and Future Foreign Investment Regime", in Mahnoush Arsanjani, Jacob Katz Cogan, Robert D. Sloane and Siegfried Wiessner (eds.), *Looking to the Future: Essays on International Law in Honor of W. Michael Reisman* (The Netherlands, Martinus Nijhoff, 2010).

"A BIT on Custom", 42 *New York University Journal of International Law and Politics* 17 (2009).

"Implications for the Future of International Investment Law", in Karl P. Sauvant (ed.), *Appeals Mechanism in International Investment Disputes* 29 (New York, Oxford University Press, 2008).

"Alternatives to International Criminal Justice", in A. Cassese (ed.), *The Oxford Companion to International Criminal Justice* 25 (Oxford, Oxford University Press, 2009).

"Legal Perspectives", in T. Weiss and S. Daws (eds.), *The Oxford Handbook on International Organizations* 82 (Oxford, Oxford University Press, 2007).

"The NAFTA's Investment Chapter and Mexico", in R. Dolzer, M. Herdegen and B. Vogel (eds.), *Foreign Investment Its Significance in Relation to the Fight against Poverty, Economic Growth, and Legal Culture* 241 (Singapore, Konrad Adenauer Stiftung, 2006) (also published in German).

"The Dark Side of the UN's War on Terrorism", in András Sajó (ed.), *Abuse: The Dark Side of Fundamental Rights* 163 (Utrecht, Eleven International Publishing, 2006).

"International Organizations: Then and Now", 100 *American Journal of International Law* 324 (2006).

"Trying Hussein: Between Hubris and Hegemony", 2 *Journal of International Criminal Justice* 319 (2004).

"Foreword: The Ripples of NAFTA", in Todd Weiler (ed.), *NAFTA Investment Law and Arbitration: Past Issues, Current Practice, Future Prospects* xxi (Ardsley, Transnational Publishers, 2004).

"Legal Unilateralism", in Margaret Crahan, John Goering and Thomas G. Weiss (eds.), *Wars on Terrorism and Iraq: Human Rights, Unilateralism, and U.S. Foreign Policy* (New York and London, Routledge, 2004).

"Hegemonic International Law Revisited", 97 *American Journal of International Law* 873 (2003).

"The Security Council's War on Terrorism: Problems and Policy Options", in Erika de Wet and André Nollkaemper (eds.), *Review of the Security Council by Member States* 119 (Antwerp, Intersentia, 2003).

"The New Dispute Settlers: (Half) Truths and Consequences", 38 *Texas International Law Journal* 1 (2003).

"Foreword" and "The WTO as Linkage Machine", 96 *American Journal of International Law* 1 and 146 (2002).

"Do Liberal States Behave Better?: A Critique of Slaughter's Liberal Theory", 12 *European Journal of International Law* 183 (2001).

"Consitutional Interpretation in International Organizations", in Jean-Marc Coicaud and Veijo Heiskanen (eds.), *The Legitimacy of International Organizations* 104 (New York, UN University Press, 2001).

"Multilateralism and Its Discontents", 11 *European Journal of International Law* 393 (2000).

"Crimes of States/Crimes of Hate: Lessons from Rwanda", 24 *Yale Journal of International Law* 365 (1999).

"Rush to Closure: Lessons of the Tadic Judgment", 96 *Michigan Law Review* 2031 (1998).

"Foreword: Why Nations Behave", 19 *Michigan Journal of International Law* 303 (1998).

"Nuremberg Revisited: The Tadic Case", 7 *European Journal of International Law* 245 (1996).

"Judging the Security Council", 90 *American Journal of International Law* 1 (1996).

"Legal Issues" (chapters in annual editions of *A Global Agenda: Issues before the General Assembly of the United Nations* (New York, UN Association, 1990-1995).

"The Once and Future Security Council", 18 *Washington Quarterly* 5 (1995).

"Financial Responsibility of Members", in O. Schachter and

C. Joyner (eds.), *The United Nations and the International Legal Order* 1091 (Cambridge, Cambridge University Press, 1995); revised for paperback edition (1997).

"Positivism Regained, Nihilism Postponed", Review Essay of Danilenko, *Law-Making in the International Community*, 15 *Michigan Journal of International Law* 747 (1994).

"Burdens of Proof", Review Essay of *Fact-Finding before International Tribunals*, 14 *Michigan Journal of International Law* 399 (1993).

"The Quest for Legitimacy", Review Essay of Thomas M. Franck's *The Power of Legitimacy among Nations*, 24 *New York University Journal of International Law and Politics* 199 (1991).

"Legal Remedies and the UN à la Carte Problem", 12 *Michigan Journal of International Law* 229 (1991).

"Promoting the 'Rule of Law' in Latin America: Problems and Prospects", 25 *George Washington Journal of International Law and Economics* 281 (1991); also published in Spanish, as "El Estado de Derecho en Latinoamérica: Problemas y Perspectivas", in T. Buergenthal and A. Cançado Trindade (eds.), *Estudios Especializados de Derechos Humanos* (1996).

"Political Protectionism and U.S. International Investment Obligations: The Hazards of Exon-Florio", 30 *Virginia Journal of International Law* 1 (1989).

Printed in July 2011
by Triangle Bleu,
59600 Maubeuge (France)

Setting : R. Mirland,
59870 Warlaing (France)